Teach Yourself VISUALLY™ Mac OS® X v.10.3 Panther™

From
maranGraphics®
&

Wiley Publishing, Inc.

Teach Yourself VISUALLY™ Mac OS® v.10.3 Panther™

Published by
Wiley Publishing, Inc.
909 Third Avenue
New York, NY 10022

Published simultaneously in Canada

Library of Congress Control Number: 2003114448

ISBN: 0-7645-4393-8

Manufactured in the United States of America

10 9 8 7 6 5 4 3 2

1K/RX/RR/QT/MG

Trademark Acknowledgments

Important Numbers

For U.S. corporate orders, please call maranGraphics at 800-469-6616 or fax 905-890-9434.

For general information on our other products and services or to obtain technical support, please contact our Customer Care Department within the U.S. at 800-762-2974, outside the U.S. at 317-572-3993 or fax 317-572-4002.

Permissions

U.S. Corporate Sales
Contact maranGraphics at (800) 469-6616 or fax (905) 890-9434.

U.S. Trade Sales
Contact Wiley at (800) 762-2974 or fax (317) 572-4002.

Some comments from our readers...

"I have to praise you and your company on the fine products you turn out. I have twelve of the *Teach Yourself VISUALLY* and *Simplified* books in my house. They were instrumental in helping me pass a difficult computer course. Thank you for creating books that are easy to follow."

–Gordon Justin (Brielle, NJ)

"I commend your efforts and your success. I teach in an outreach program for the Dr. Eugene Clark Library in Lockhart, TX. Your *Teach Yourself VISUALLY* books are incredible and I use them in my computer classes. All my students love them!"

–Michele Schalin (Lockhart, TX)

"Thank you so much for helping people like me learn about computers. The Maran family is just what the doctor ordered. Thank you, thank you, thank you."

–Carol Moten (New Kensington, PA)

"I would like to take this time to compliment maranGraphics on creating such great books. Thank you for making it clear. Keep up the good work."

–Kirk Santoro (Burbank, CA)

"I write to extend my thanks and appreciation for your books. They are clear, easy to follow, and straight to the point. Keep up the good work!"

–Seward Kollie (Dakar, Senegal)

"What fantastic teaching books you have produced! Congratulations to you and your staff. You deserve the Nobel prize in Education in the Software category. Thanks for helping me to understand computers."

–Bruno Tonon (Melbourne, Australia)

"Over time, I have bought a number of your 'Read Less-Learn More' books. For me, they are THE way to learn anything easily."

–José A. Mazón (Cuba, NY)

"I was introduced to maranGraphics about four years ago and YOU ARE THE GREATEST THING THAT EVER HAPPENED TO INTRODUCTORY COMPUTER BOOKS!"

–Glenn Nettleton (Huntsville, AL)

"Compliments To The Chef!! Your books are extraordinary! Or, simply put, Extra-Ordinary, meaning way above the rest! THANK YOU THANK YOU THANK YOU! for creating these."

–Christine J. Manfrin (Castle Rock, CO)

"I'm a grandma who was pushed by an 11-year-old grandson to join the computer age. I found myself hopelessly confused and frustrated until I discovered the Visual series. I'm no expert by any means now, but I'm a lot further along than I would have been otherwise. Thank you!"

–Carol Louthain (Logansport, IN)

"Thank you, thank you, thank you...for making it so easy for me to break into this high-tech world. I now own four of your books. I recommend them to anyone who is a beginner like myself. Now... if you could just do one for programming VCR's, it would make my day!"

–Gay O'Donnell (Calgary, Alberta, Canada)

"You're marvelous! I am greatly in your debt."

–Patrick Baird (Lacey, WA)

maranGraphics is a family-run business located near Toronto, Canada.

At **maranGraphics**, we believe in producing great computer books—one book at a time.

Each maranGraphics book uses the award-winning communication process that we have been developing over the last 25 years. Using this process, we organize screen shots, text and illustrations in a way that makes it easy for you to learn new concepts and tasks.

We spend hours deciding the best way to perform each task, so you don't have to! Our clear, easy-to-follow screen shots and instructions walk you through each task from beginning to end.

Our detailed illustrations go hand-in-hand with the text to help reinforce the information. Each illustration is a labor of love—some take up to a week to draw!

We want to thank you for purchasing what we feel are the best computer books money can buy. We hope you enjoy using this book as much as we enjoyed creating it!

Sincerely,

The Maran Family

Please visit us on the Web at:
www.maran.com

CREDITS

Authors:
Ruth Maran
Kelleigh Johnson

Copy Editing & Screen Captures:
Roderick Anatalio

Project Manager:
Judy Maran

Editing and Screen Captures:
Raquel Scott
Adam Giles

Layout Designer:
Steven Schaerer

Illustrator & Screen Artist:
Russ Marini

Illustrator, Screen Artist & Assistant Layout Designer:
Richard Hung

Indexer:
Raquel Scott

Wiley Vice President and Executive Group Publisher:
Richard Swadley

Wiley Vice President and Publisher:
Barry Pruett

Wiley Editorial Support:
Jody Lefevere
Sandy Rodrigues
Lindsay Sandman

Post Production:
Robert Maran

ACKNOWLEDGMENTS

Thanks to the dedicated staff of maranGraphics, including Roderick Anatalio, Adam Giles, Richard Hung, Kelleigh Johnson, Wanda Lawrie, Jill Maran, Judy Maran, Robert Maran, Ruth Maran, Russ Marini, Steven Schaerer, Raquel Scott and Roxanne Van Damme.

Finally, to Richard Maran who originated the easy-to-use graphic format of this guide. Thank you for your inspiration and guidance.

TABLE OF CONTENTS

Chapter 1

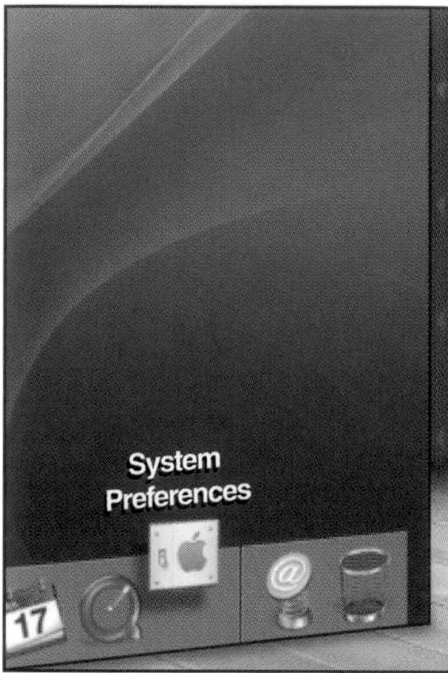

MAC OS X BASICS

Chapter 2

VIEW FILES

Chapter 3

WORK WITH FILES

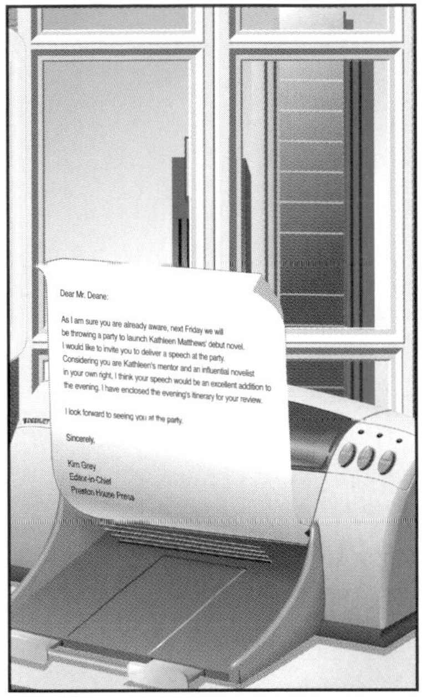

Chapter 4

CUSTOMIZE YOUR COMPUTER

TABLE OF CONTENTS

Chapter 5 USING MAC OS X APPLICATIONS

Chapter 6 PLAY MUSIC USING iTUNES

Chapter 7 MANAGE PHOTOS USING iPHOTO

Chapter 8

CREATE MOVIES USING iMOVIE

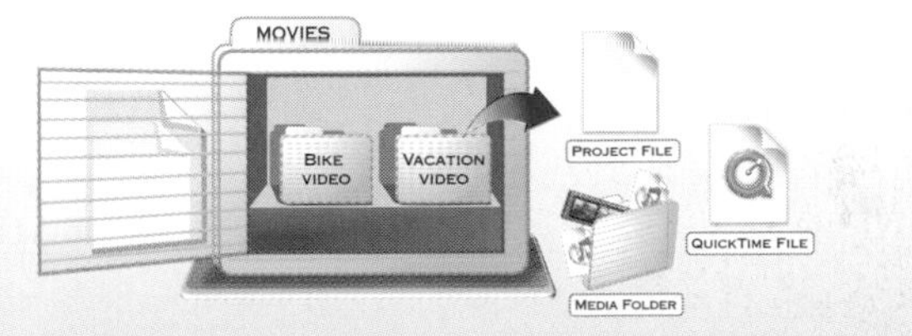

Chapter 9

SHARE YOUR COMPUTER

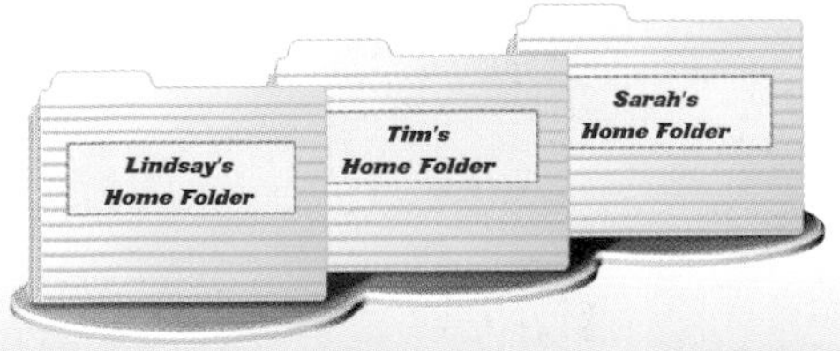

Chapter 10 WORK ON A NETWORK

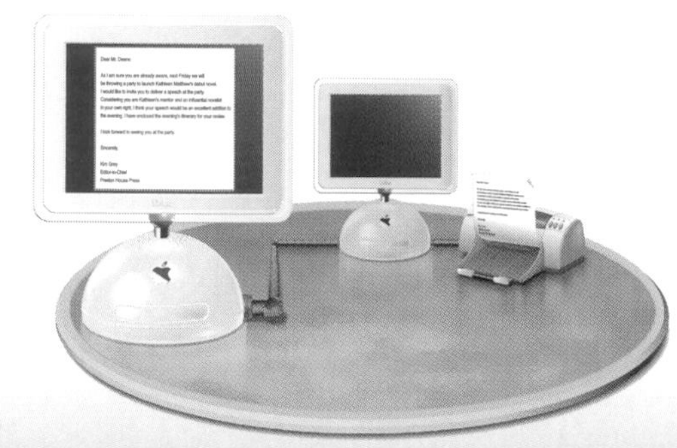

Chapter 11 BROWSE THE WEB USING SAFARI

Chapter 12 SEARCH THE INTERNET USING SHERLOCK

Chapter 13 EXCHANGE E-MAIL USING MAIL

Chapter 14 EXCHANGE INSTANT MESSAGES USING iCHAT

INTRODUCTION TO MAC OS X

Mac OS® X v. 10.3 Panther Edition controls the overall activity of your computer and ensures that all parts of your computer work together smoothly and efficiently.

Work with Files

Mac OS allows you to effectively manage the files stored on your computer. You can open, rename, duplicate, move, delete, print, fax and search for files. You can also copy files to a recordable CD or DVD.

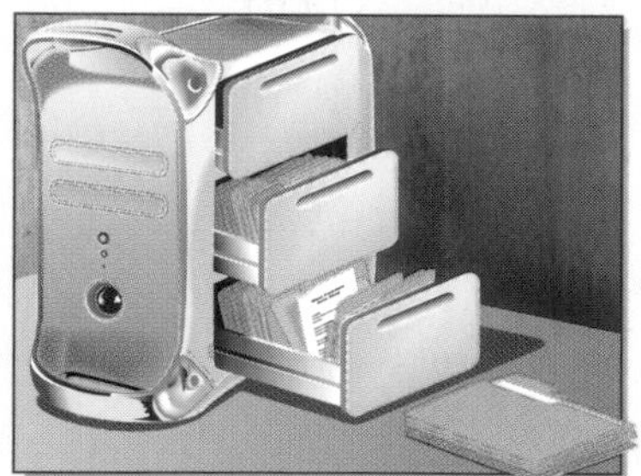

Customize Mac OS

You can customize Mac OS to suit your preferences. You can change the picture used to decorate your desktop, change the way your mouse works, add fonts and turn on speech recognition to use spoken commands to perform tasks on your computer. Mac OS also allows you to change the screen saver that appears when you do not use your computer for a period of time.

Use Mac OS Applications

Mac OS offers many applications you can use to perform tasks on your computer. You can use TextEdit to create documents, Address Book to store information for people you frequently contact and Font Book to view and manage fonts on your computer. You can also use an on-screen calculator, play QuickTime movies and use an electronic calendar to keep track of your appointments.

Play and Organize Music

Mac OS allows you to play music CDs and listen to radio stations that broadcast on the Internet. You can also create playlists that contain your favorite songs, create your own music CDs and copy songs from your computer to a portable MP3 player.

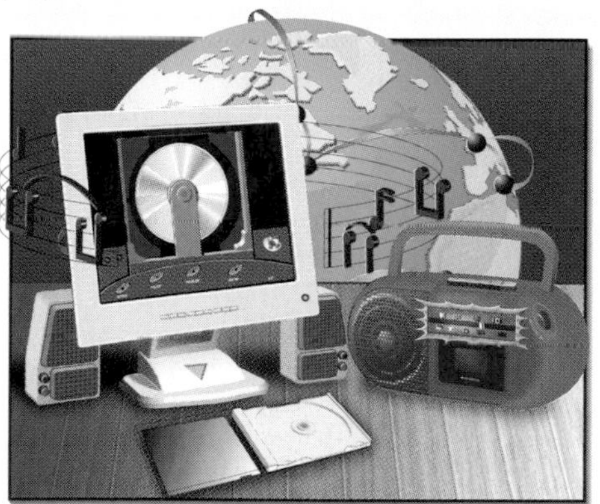

Manage Photos and Create Movies

You can use iPhoto to copy photos from a digital camera to your computer so you can view, organize and edit the photos. You can use iMovie to transfer video from a digital video camera to your computer so you can organize and edit the video before sharing it with friends and family.

Share Your Computer

If you share your computer with other people, you can create a separate user account for each person to keep the personal files and settings for each person separate. You can also share files with other users, delete a user account you no longer need and quickly switch between users without having to quit your applications and log out.

Access the Internet

Mac OS offers several applications you can use to access the Internet. Safari™ allows you to browse through information on the Web. You can use Sherlock to search the Internet for information of interest, including stock information and movies playing in your area. You can use Mail to exchange electronic mail and iChat to exchange instant messages with friends and family over the Internet.

USING THE DOCK

You can use the Dock to quickly access frequently used applications.

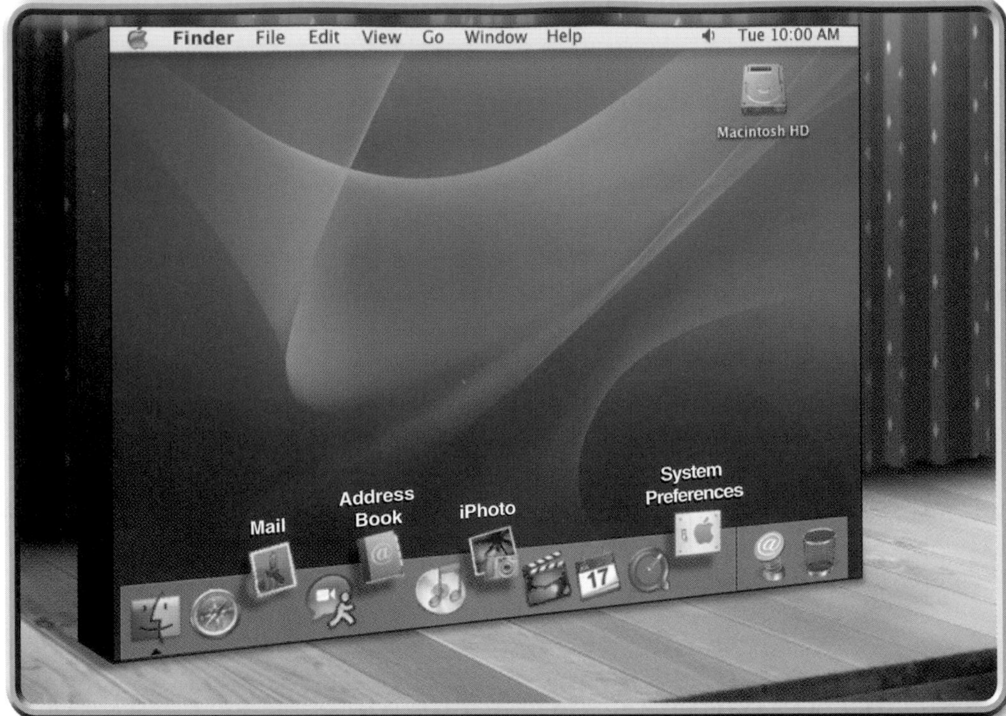

The Dock automatically displays icons for several applications, such as Mail, Address Book, iPhoto and System Preferences.

USING THE DOCK

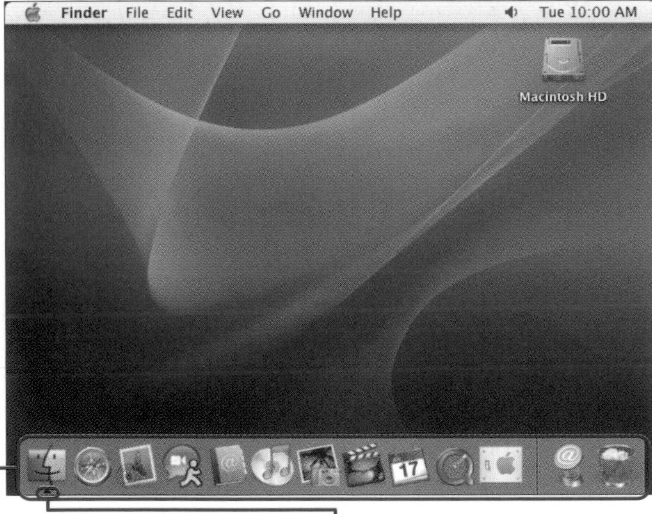

■ By default, the Dock appears at the bottom of your screen and displays the icons for several applications.

■ A triangle (▲) appears below the icon for each application that is currently open.

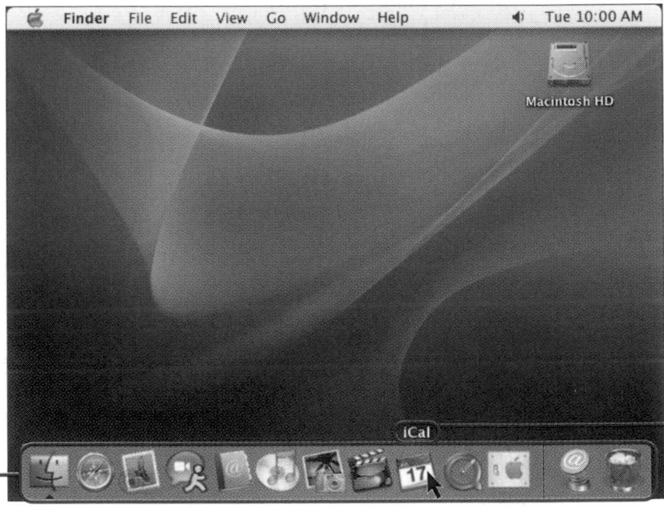

IDENTIFY A DOCK ICON

1 To identify an icon in the Dock, position the mouse over the icon.

■ The name of the icon appears above the Dock.

Will other icons appear in the Dock as I work?

When you open an application that does not appear in the Dock by default, an icon for the application appears to the left of the line in the Dock. The icon for the application will disappear when you quit the application.

When you minimize a window, an icon for the window appears to the right of the line in the Dock. To minimize a window, see page 14.

Can I use the Dock to quickly quit an application?

Yes. Press and hold down the control key as you click the icon for the application you want to quit. On the menu that appears, click **Quit** to quit the application.

OPEN AN APPLICATION

1 To open an application displayed in the Dock, click the icon for the application.

■ When you open an application, the application's icon bounces while the application opens.

■ The application appears on your screen.

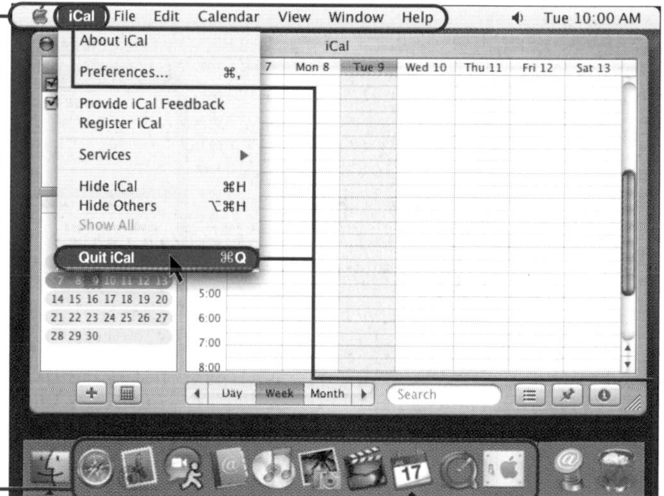

QUIT AN APPLICATION

1 When you finish working with an application, click the icon for the application in the Dock.

■ This area displays the menu bar for the application you selected.

2 Click the name of the application in the menu bar.

3 Click **Quit** to quit the application.

Note: You cannot quit the Finder application.

SCROLL THROUGH A WINDOW

You can use a scroll bar to browse through the information in a window. Scrolling is useful when a window is not large enough to display all the information it contains.

SCROLL THROUGH A WINDOW

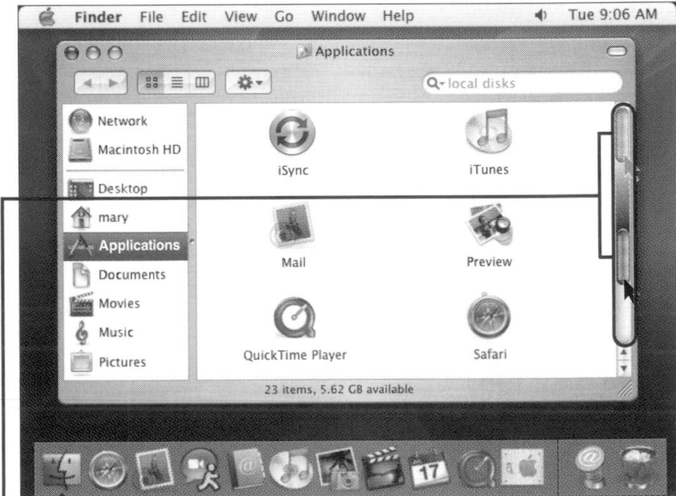

SCROLL UP OR DOWN

1 Click ▲ or ▼ to scroll up or down through the information in a window.

Note: If all the information in a window is displayed, you cannot scroll through the window.

SCROLL TO ANY POSITION

1 Position the mouse ↖ over the scroller on a scroll bar.

2 Drag the scroller along the scroll bar until the information you want to view appears.

■ The location of the scroller indicates which part of the window you are viewing. For example, when the scroller is halfway down the scroll bar, you are viewing information from the middle of the window.

CLOSE A WINDOW

When you finish working with a window, you can close the window to remove it from your screen.

CLOSE A WINDOW

1 Click ● in the window you want to close.

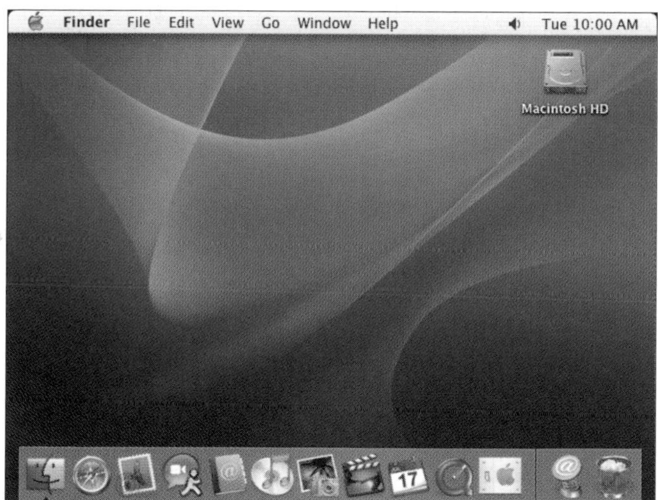

■ The window disappears from your screen.

Note: To close all windows in the same application at once, such as all your open word processing files, press and hold down the option *key as you click* ● *in one of the application's windows.*

USING THE SIDEBAR

Finder windows display a Sidebar that allows you to quickly access commonly used disks and folders on your computer.

You can hide the Sidebar at any time to reduce clutter in a window and display more of the window's contents. You can also add a file or folder you frequently access to the Sidebar. The item you add will appear in the Sidebar of all your Finder windows.

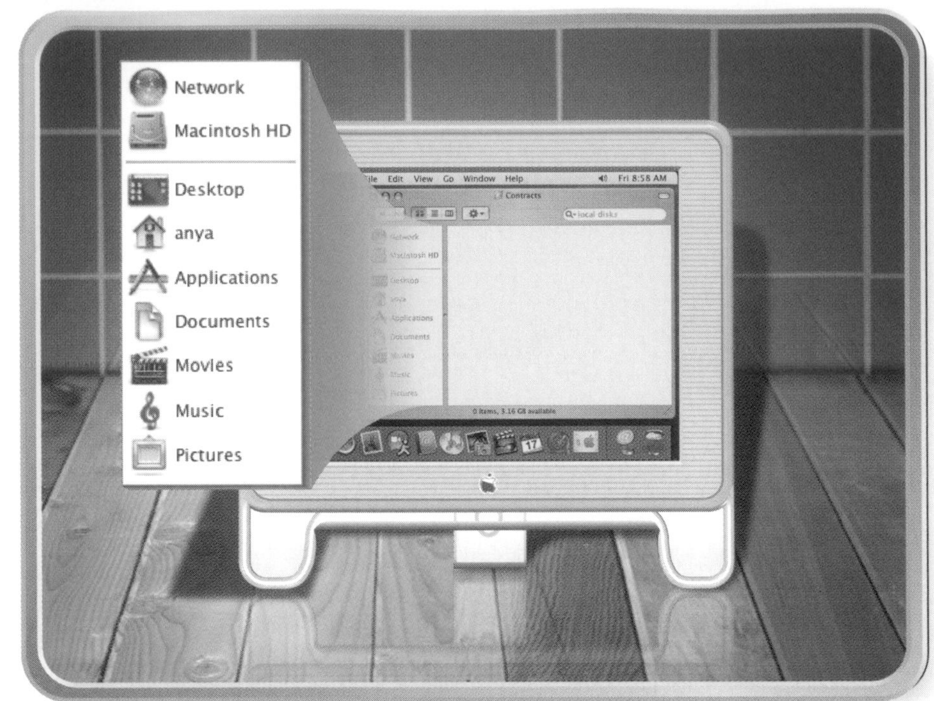

USING THE SIDEBAR

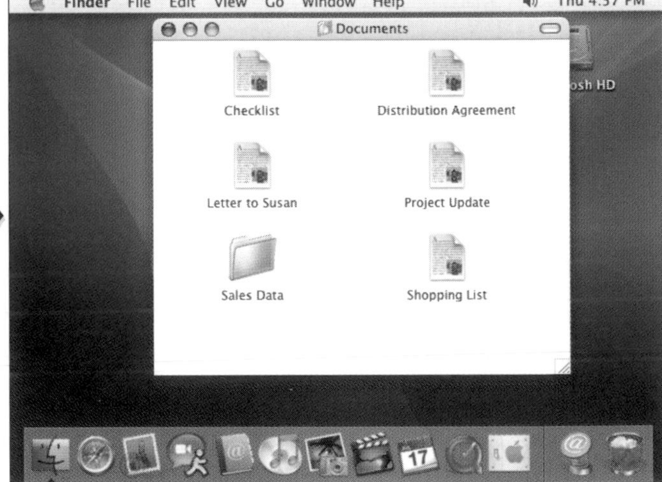

1 To display the contents of a Sidebar location in a window, click the location in the Sidebar.

■ The contents of the location appear in the window.

HIDE THE SIDEBAR

1 To hide the Sidebar in a Finder window, click ⬭ in the window.

Note: If the ⬭ button is not available in a window, you cannot hide the Sidebar.

■ The Sidebar disappears from the window.

Note: The tool area at the top of the window also disappears.

■ To once again display the Sidebar and tool area in the window, click ⬭ again.

What locations are available in the Sidebar?

Location:	Displays Contents of:
Network	The Network window. See page 230.
Macintosh HD	Your hard disk. See page 24.
Desktop	Your desktop.
Your User Name	Your home folder. See page 22.
Applications	The Applications folder.
Documents	Your Documents folder.
Movies	Your Movies folder.
Music	Your Music folder.
Pictures	Your Pictures folder.

How can I remove a location I no longer need from the Sidebar?

If the Sidebar displays items you do not frequently use, you can remove the items to reduce the clutter in the Sidebar. To remove an item from the Sidebar, position the mouse over the item you want to remove and then drag the item out of the Sidebar. The item disappears in a puff of smoke. Removing an item from the sidebar does not remove the file or folder from your computer.

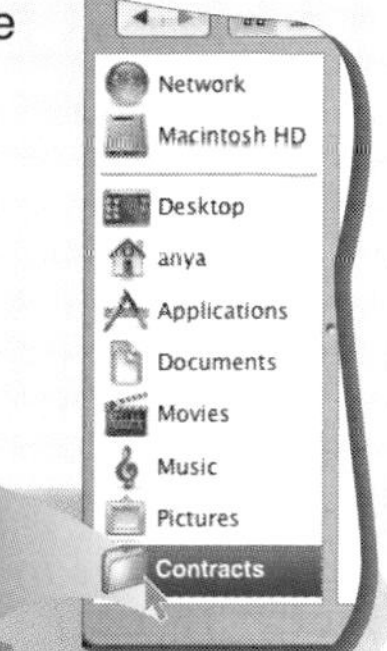

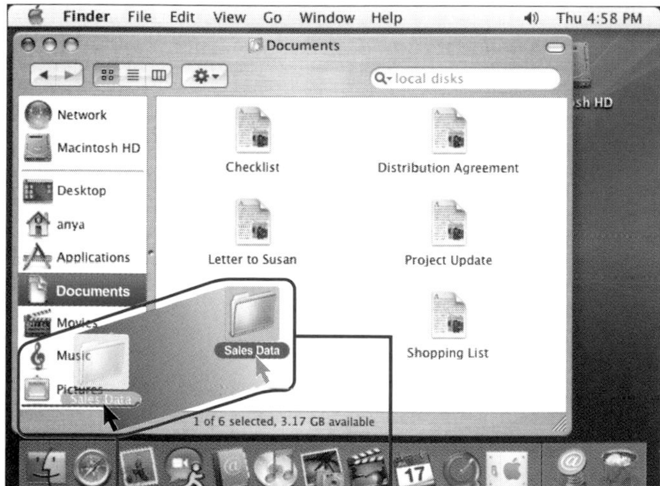

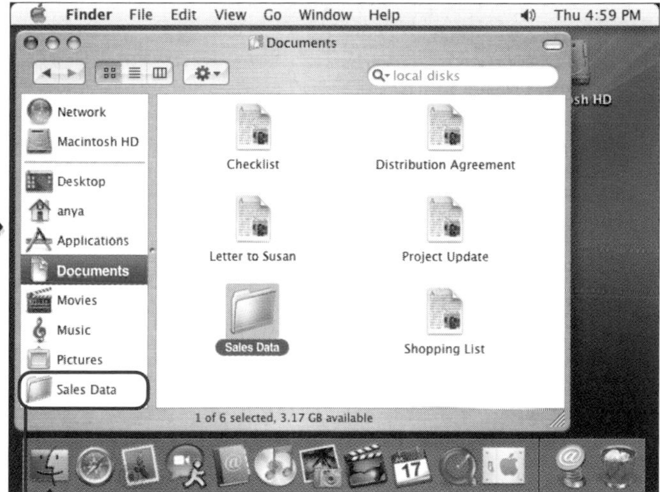

ADD AN ITEM TO THE SIDEBAR

1 To add a file or folder you frequently access to the Sidebar that appears in Finder windows, open a Finder window on your desktop.

2 Position the mouse over the file or folder you want to add to the Sidebar.

3 Drag the file or folder to the bottom of the Sidebar.

Note: A blue line indicates where the item will appear.

■ The name of the file or folder appears at the bottom of the Sidebar. You can now click the item in the Sidebar to display the contents of the item.

Note: A file or folder you add to the Sidebar will be available in the Sidebar of every Finder window you open.

SWITCH BETWEEN WINDOWS

If you have more than one window open on your screen, you can easily switch between windows.

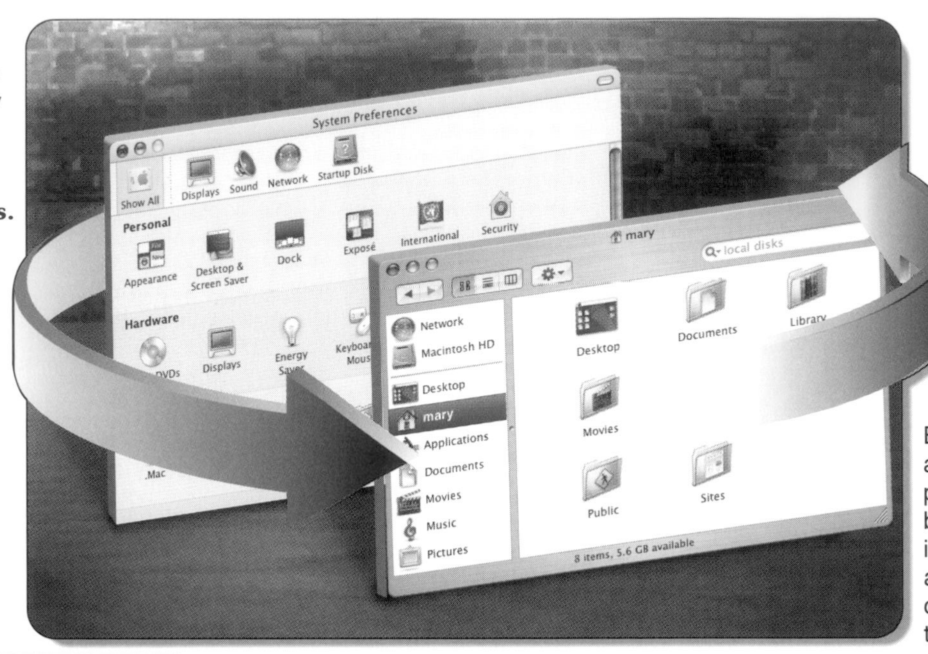

Each window is like a separate piece of paper. Switching between windows is like placing a different piece of paper at the top of the pile.

SWITCH BETWEEN WINDOWS

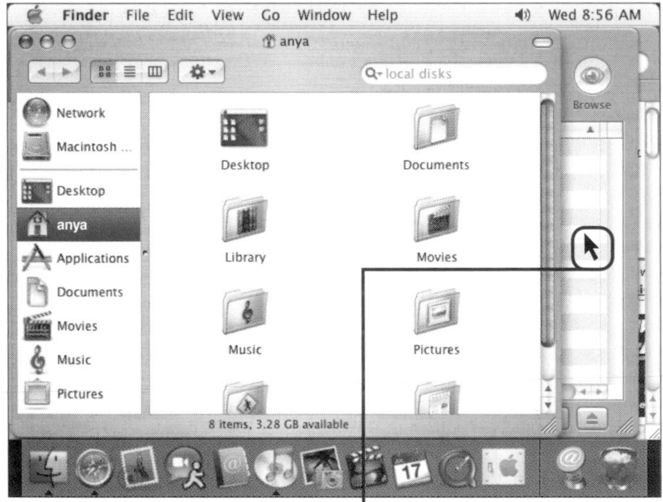

■ You can work in only one window at a time. The active window appears in front of all other windows.

1 Click inside a window you want to make the active window.

■ The window becomes active and appears in front of all other windows. You can now clearly view the contents of the window.

■ This area displays the menu bar for the active window.

Note: The menu bar changes, depending on the active window. Make sure the window you want to work with is the active window before using the menu bar to perform a task.

Can I quickly clear all open windows from my screen so I can access the desktop?

Yes. Mac OS allows you to instantly remove all the windows from your screen. Press the F11 key to hide all your open windows so you can view and work with items on the desktop. To once again display all open windows on the desktop, press the F11 key again.

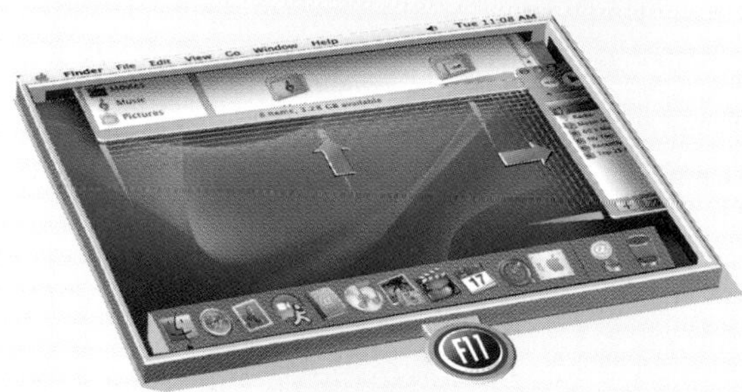

Is there another way I can make an application window the active window?

If an icon for the application you want to work with appears in the Dock, you can click the icon in the Dock to make the application window the active window. The application window will move in front of all other open windows.

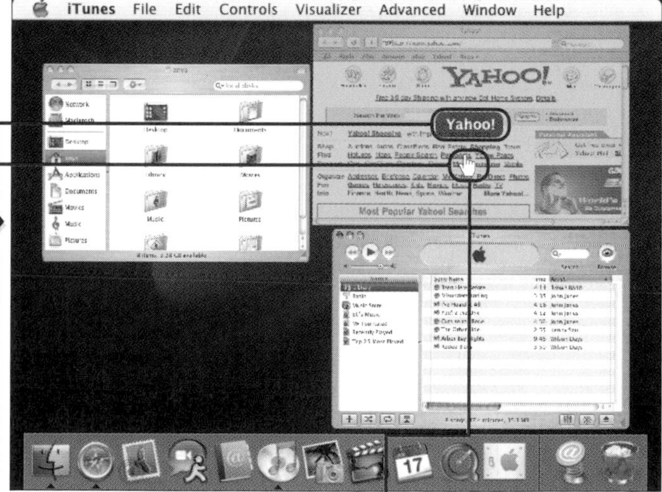

QUICKLY VIEW ALL OPEN WINDOWS

■ If you cannot click inside the window you want to make the active window, you can have Mac OS arrange the open windows for you.

1 Press the F9 key to reduce the size of all the open windows and arrange them on your screen.

■ Each open window is displayed on your desktop so you can view all the windows at once.

2 Move the mouse over a window of interest.

■ The name of the window appears in the center of the window.

3 To make a window the active window, click the window.

■ All your open windows return to normal size and the active window appears in front of all other windows.

MOVE A WINDOW

If a window covers items on your screen, you can move the window to a different location on the screen.

You may also want to move windows so you can view the contents of several windows at once.

MOVE A WINDOW

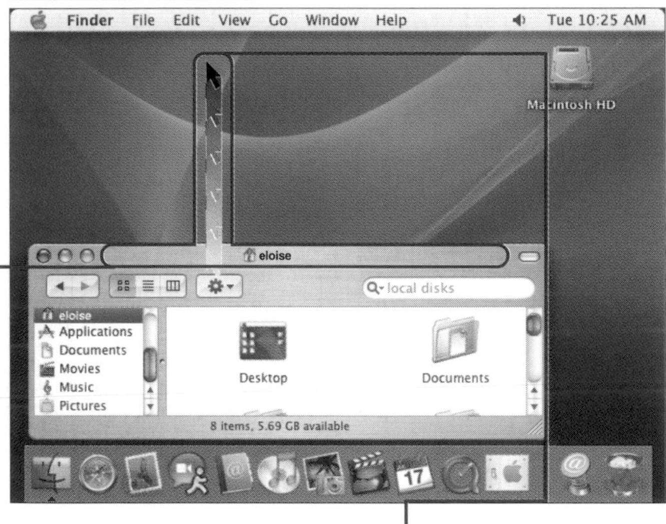

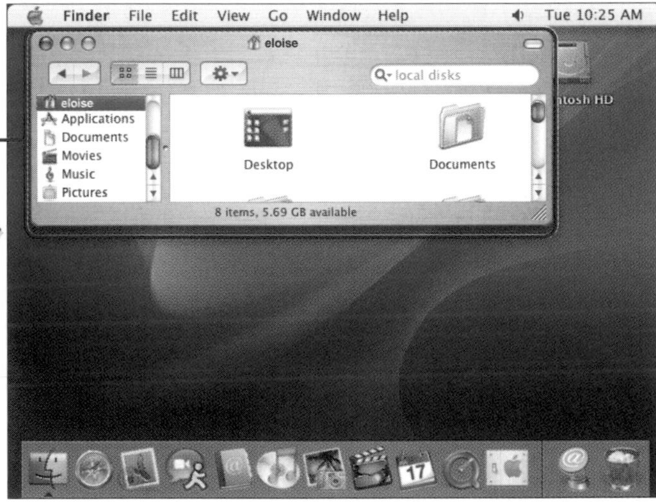

1 Position the mouse over the title bar of the window you want to move.

2 Drag the mouse to where you want to place the window.

■ The window moves to the new location.

RESIZE A WINDOW

You can easily change the size of a window displayed on your screen.

Increasing the size of a window allows you to view more information in the window. Decreasing the size of a window allows you to view items covered by the window.

RESIZE A WINDOW

1 Position the mouse over the resize icon at the bottom right corner of the window you want to resize.

2 Drag the mouse until the window displays the size you want.

■ The window displays the new size.

ZOOM A WINDOW

1 To quickly increase or decrease the size of a window to better display its contents, click the zoom button.

■ To return the window to its previous size, click the zoom button again.

MINIMIZE A WINDOW

If you are not using a window, you can minimize the window to temporarily remove it from your screen. You can redisplay the window at any time.

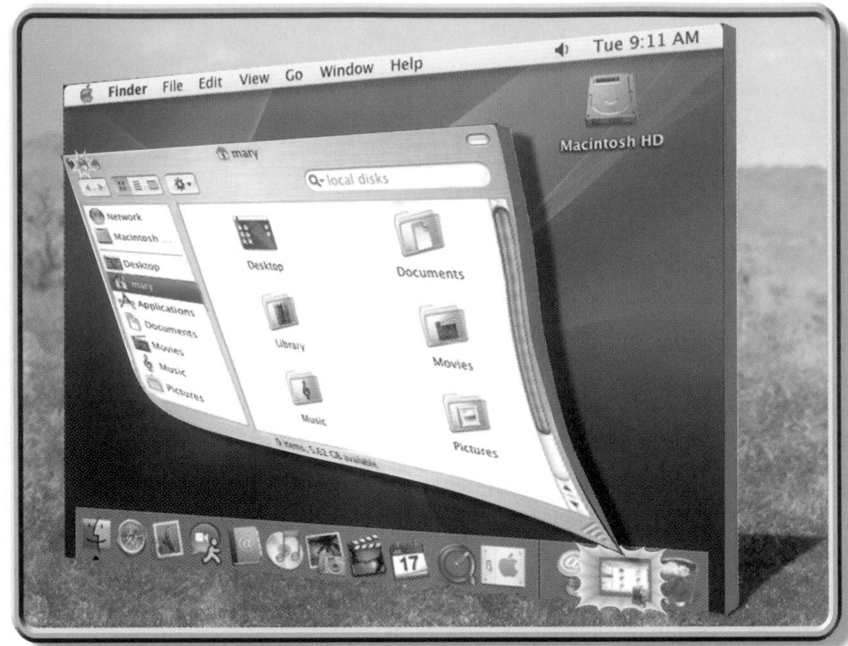

Minimizing a window allows you to temporarily put the window aside so you can work on other tasks.

MINIMIZE A WINDOW

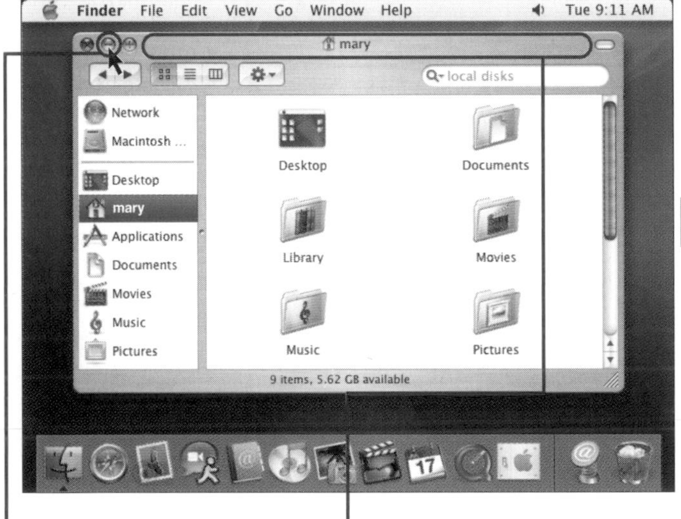

1 Click ◯ in the window you want to minimize.

■ You can also double-click the title bar of a window to minimize the window.

■ The window reduces to an icon in the Dock.

■ To redisplay the window, click its icon in the Dock.

Note: To minimize all windows in the same application at once, such as all your open word processing files, press and hold down the **option** *key as you click* ◯ *in one of the application's windows.*

FORCE AN APPLICATION TO QUIT

If an application is no longer responding, you can force the application to quit without having to shut down your computer.

When you force an application to quit, you will lose any information you did not save in the application.

Forcing an application to quit should not affect other open applications.

FORCE AN APPLICATION TO QUIT

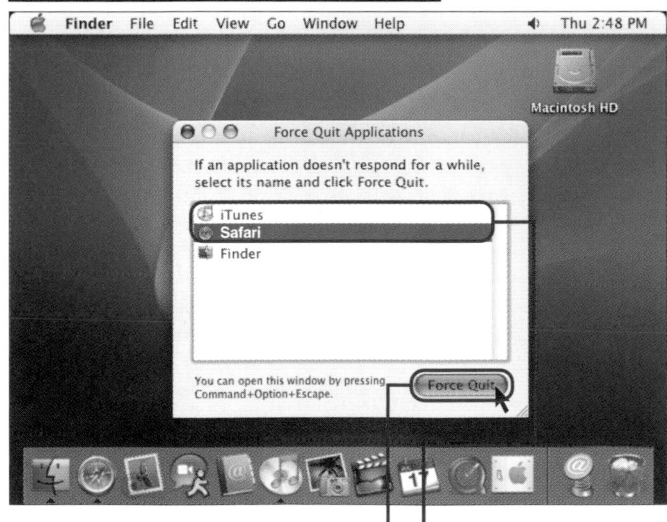

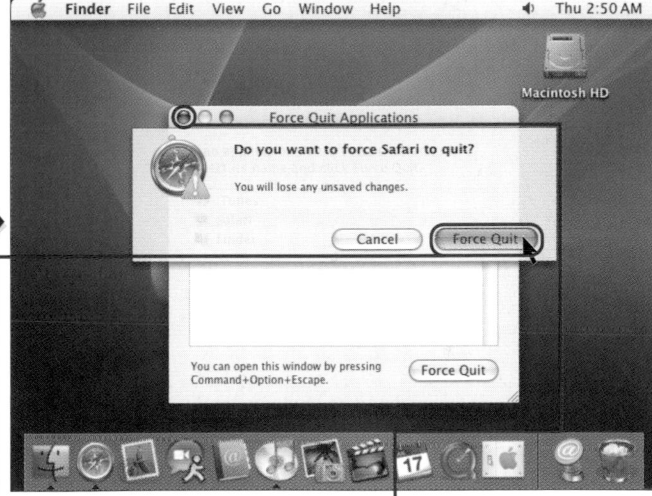

1 To force an application to quit, press and hold down the option and ⌘ keys as you press the esc key.

■ The Force Quit Applications window appears, listing the applications that are currently open.

2 Click the application you want to quit.

3 Click **Force Quit**.

■ A dialog sheet appears, confirming that you want to quit the application.

4 Click **Force Quit** to quit the application.

5 Click ● to close the Force Quit Applications window.

Note: You can try starting the application again. If you continue to have problems, try re-installing the application or contact the application's manufacturer for help.

RESTART YOUR COMPUTER

If your computer is not operating properly, you can restart the computer to try to fix the problem.

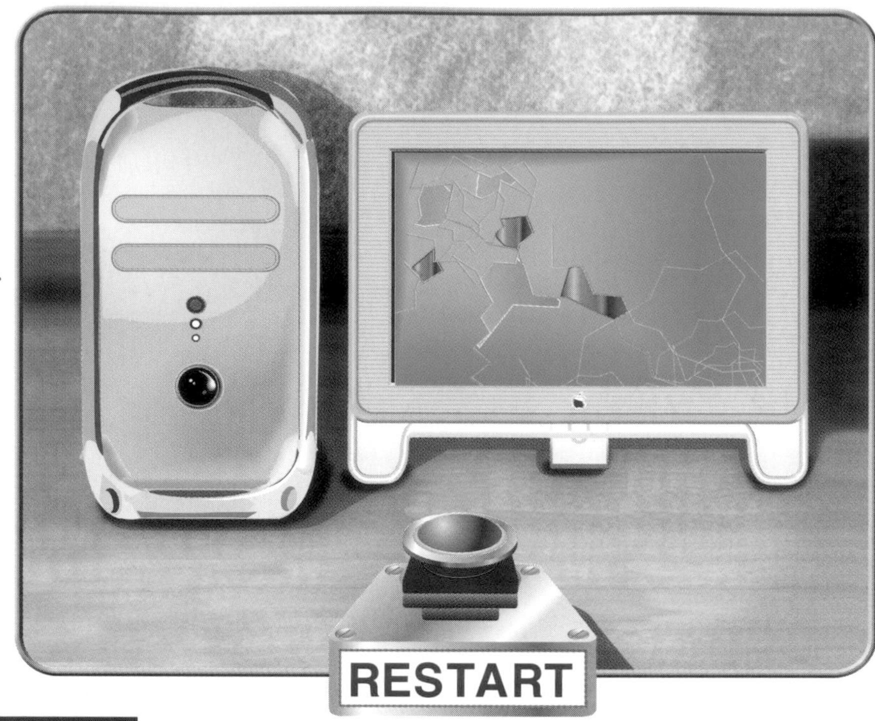

Restarting your computer shuts down the computer and then immediately starts it again.

RESTART YOUR COMPUTER

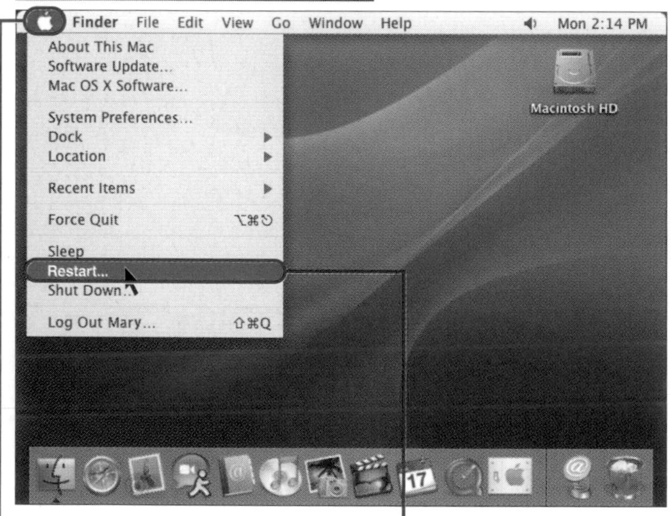

■ Before restarting your computer, make sure you close any files and applications you have open.

1 Click to display the Apple menu.

2 Click **Restart**.

■ A dialog box appears, confirming that you want to restart your computer.

3 Click **Restart** to restart your computer.

*Note: If you do not perform step **3** within 120 seconds, your computer will restart automatically.*

SHUT DOWN YOUR COMPUTER

When you finish using your computer, you should shut down the computer to turn it off.

If you turn off the power to your computer without first shutting down the computer, you could lose data.

SHUT DOWN YOUR COMPUTER

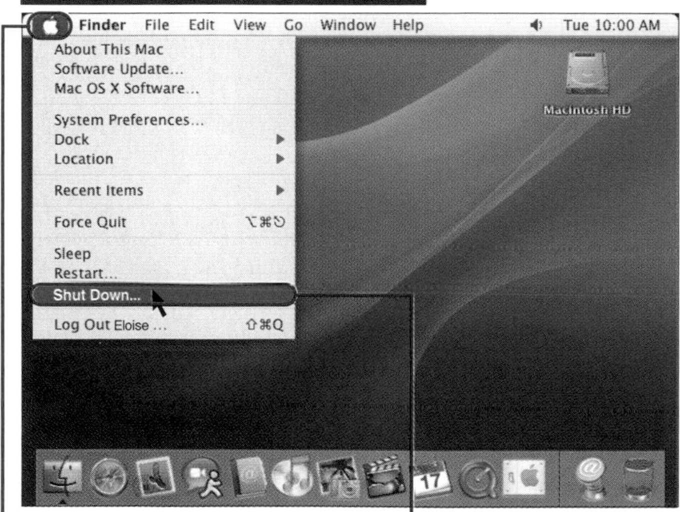

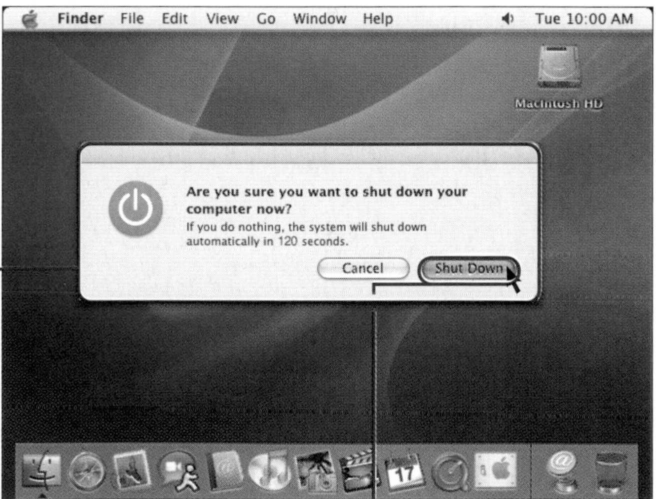

■ Before shutting down your computer, make sure you close any files and applications you have open.

1 Click to display the Apple menu.

2 Click **Shut Down**.

■ A dialog box appears, confirming that you want to shut down your computer.

3 Click **Shut Down** to shut down your computer.

Note: If you do not perform step ***3*** *within 120 seconds, your computer will shut down automatically.*

If you do not know how to perform a task on your computer, you can use the Help Viewer to find information on the task.

GETTING HELP

1 Click **Help**.

2 Click the Help command.

Note: The name of the Help command depends on the active application.

■ The Help window appears.

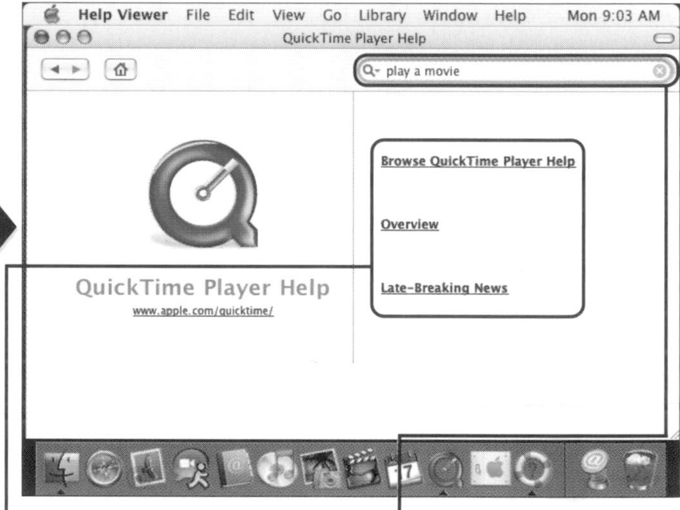

■ This area may display links to information about the active application. You can click a link to browse through the available information.

3 To search for specific help information about a Mac OS topic, click this area and type a word or phrase that describes the topic of interest.

4 To start the search, press the return key.

Why does a blue, underlined phrase appear at the bottom of some help topics?

Some help topics display a blue, underlined phrase that you can click to obtain additional help.

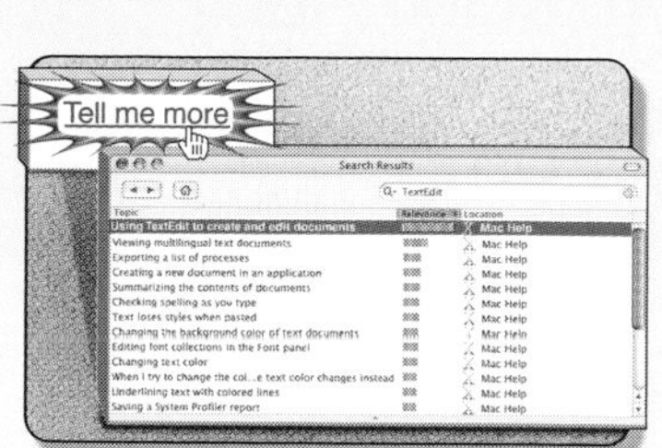

Tell me more

Displays a list of related help topics. You can double-click a help topic of interest to display the help topic.

Open *application or feature* for me

Opens a specific application or feature that allows you to perform the task discussed in the help topic.

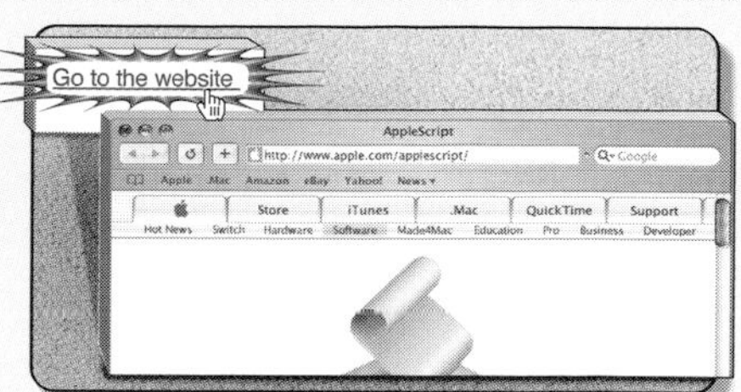

Go to the website

Displays a Web site in your Web browser so you can find the latest information available for the help topic.

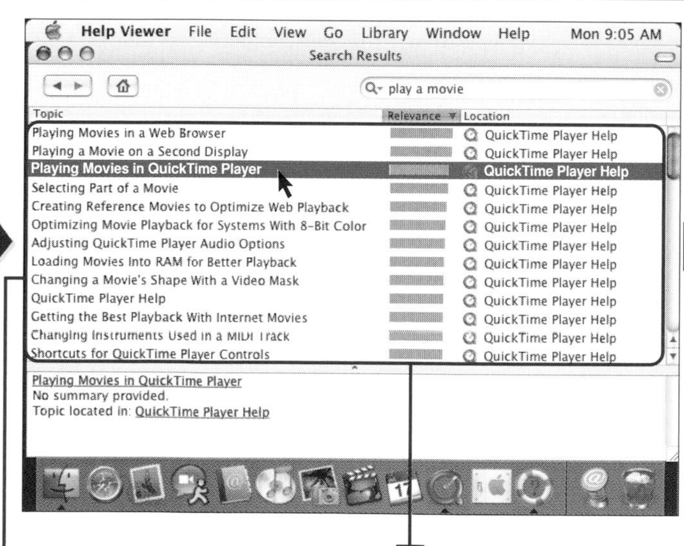

■ This area lists help topics related to the word or phrase you entered. A bar beside each help topic indicates the relevance of the topic to the word or phrase you entered.

5 Double-click a help topic of interest.

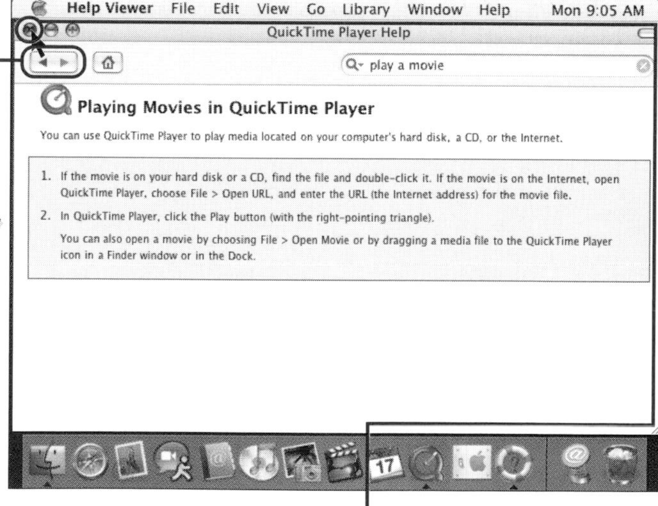

■ The information for the help topic you selected appears.

■ You can click ◄ or ► to move backward or forward through the help pages you have viewed.

Note: The ► button is available only after you use the ◄ button to return to a help page.

6 When you finish reviewing help information, click ● to close the Help window.

CHAPTER 2

View Files

Read this chapter to learn how to view the files and folders stored on your computer as well as the contents of a CD or DVD.

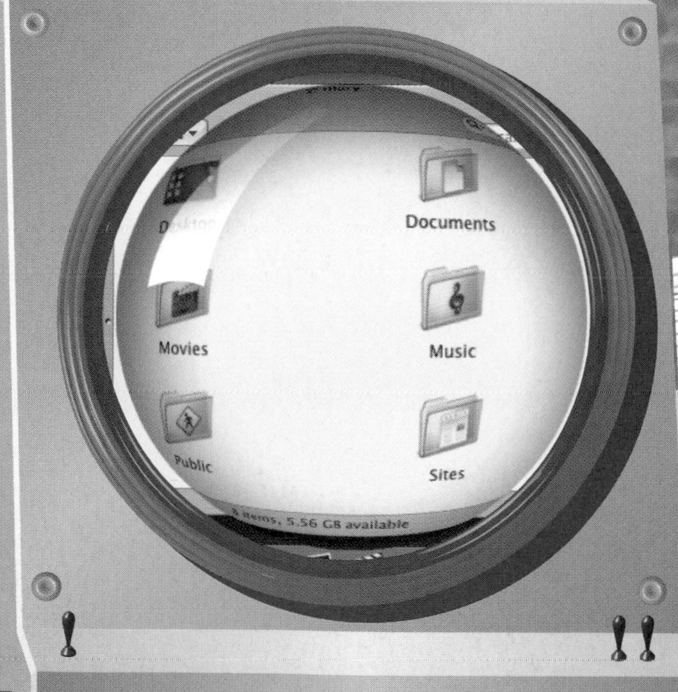

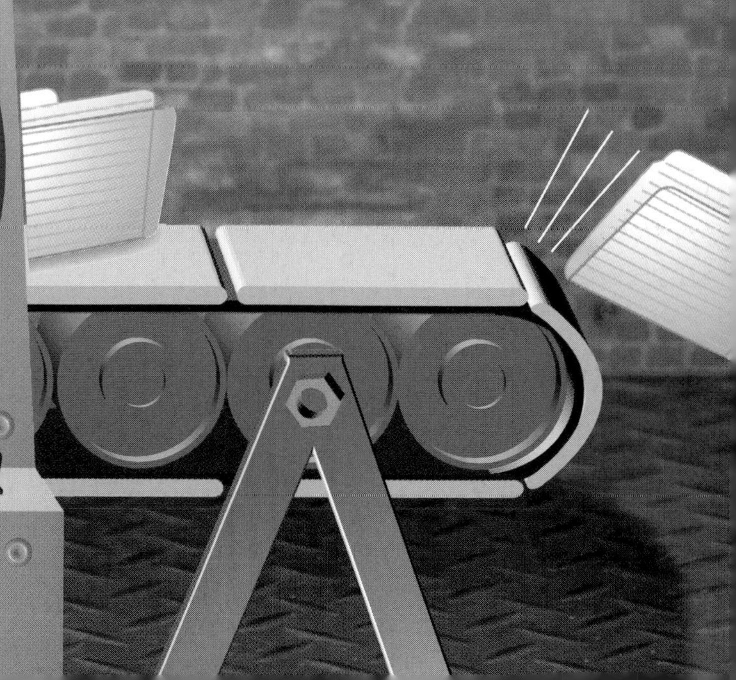

VIEW PERSONAL FOLDERS AND APPLICATIONS

You can view the personal folders and applications stored on your computer.

The home folder stores your personal folders, which provide a convenient place for you to store and manage your files.

The Applications folder stores the applications available on your computer. Mac OS comes with many applications that you can use.

VIEW PERSONAL FOLDERS

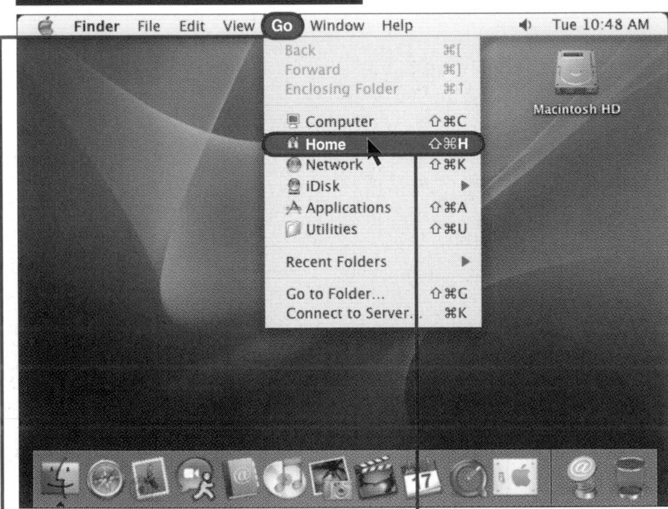

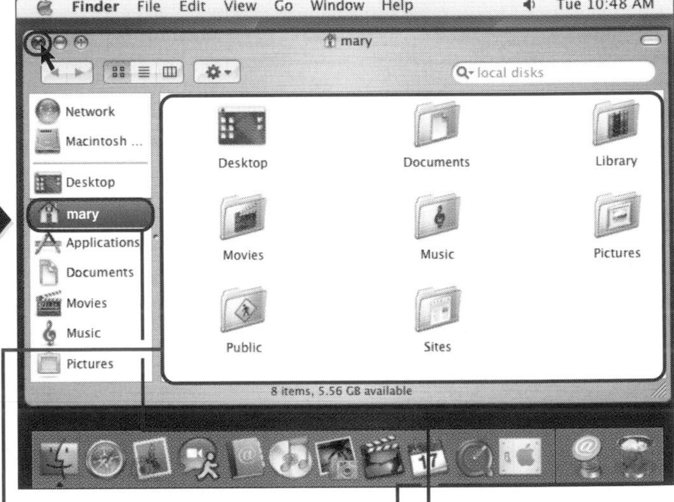

1 Click **Go**.

Note: If Go is not available, click a blank area on your desktop to display the Finder menu bar.

2 Click **Home** to view your personal folders.

■ A window appears, displaying your personal folders.

■ To display the contents of a personal folder, double-click the folder.

■ You can also click your name in any open window to view your personal folders.

3 When you finish viewing your personal folders, click ● to close the window.

What personal folders does Mac OS include?

Desktop Stores the items displayed on the desktop. 	**Movies, Music and Pictures** Provide convenient places to store your movies, music and pictures. 
Documents Provides a convenient place to store files you create. 	**Public** Stores files you want to share with every user on your computer. For more information on the Public folder, see page 223. 
Library Stores items such as fonts and sounds for your user account. 	**Sites** Stores Web pages you created that you want to make available on the Internet. 

VIEW APPLICATIONS

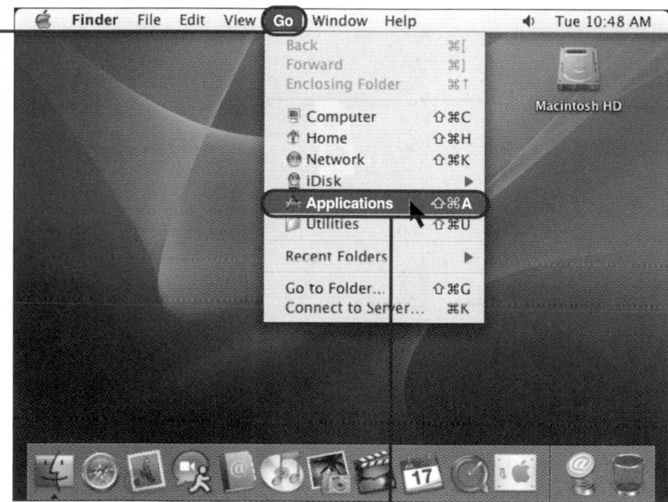

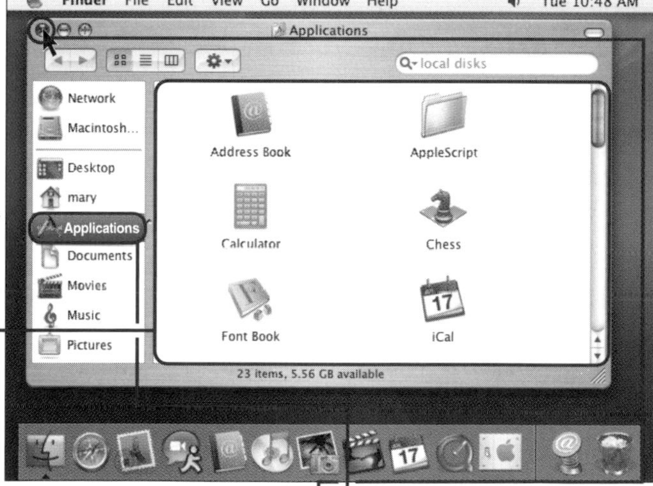

1 Click **Go**.

Note: If Go is not available, click a blank area on your desktop to display the Finder menu bar.

2 Click **Applications** to view the applications available on your computer.

■ The Applications window appears, displaying the applications available on your computer.

■ To start an application, double-click the application.

■ You can also click **Applications** in any open window to view the applications available on your computer.

3 When you finish viewing the applications available on your computer, click ● to close the Applications window.

VIEW THE CONTENTS OF YOUR COMPUTER

You can browse through the disks, folders and files on your computer.

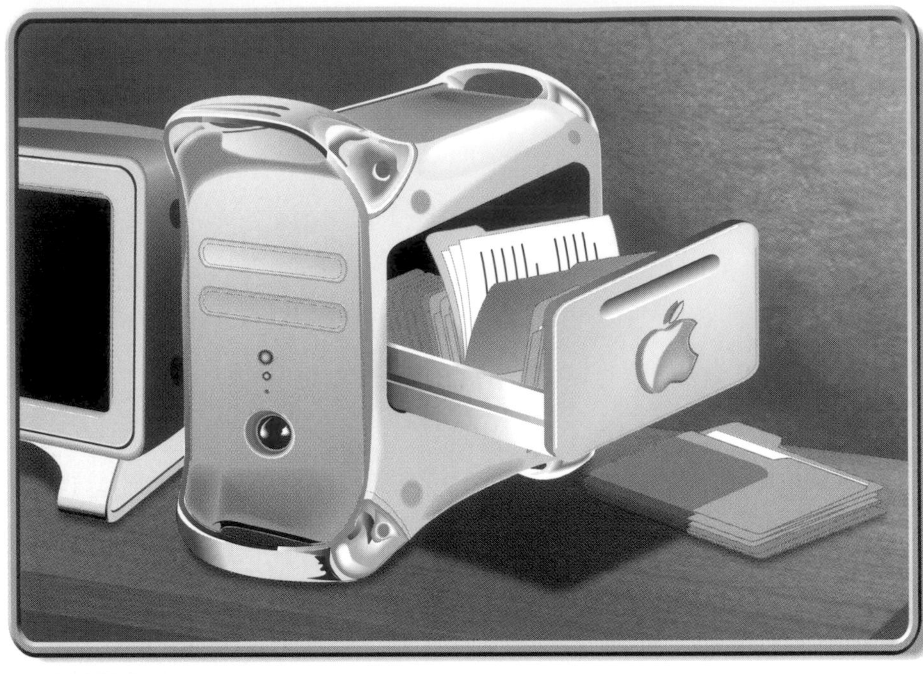

Mac OS uses folders to organize the information stored on your computer.

VIEW THE CONTENTS OF YOUR COMPUTER

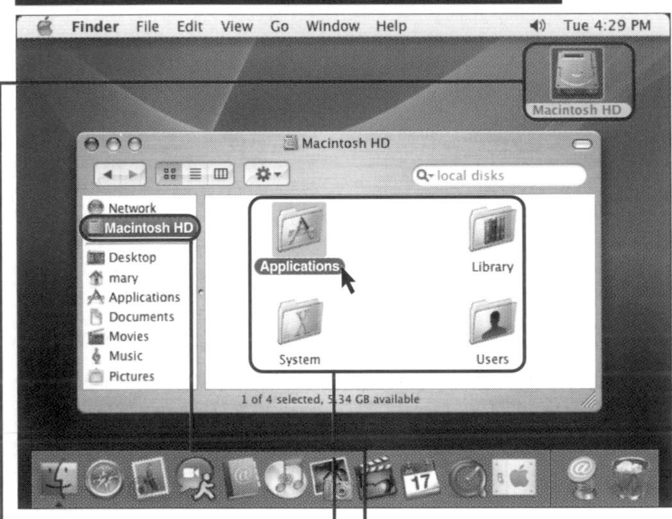

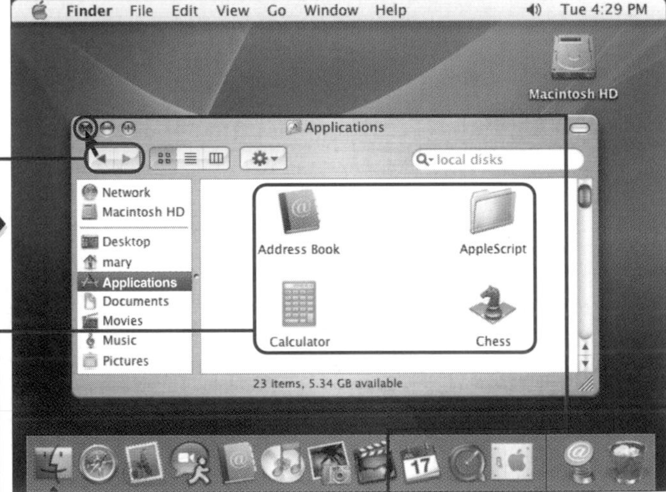

VIEW THE CONTENTS OF YOUR HARD DISK

1 Double-click your hard disk icon on the desktop to view the contents of your hard disk.

■ A window appears, displaying the contents of your hard disk.

■ You can also click the name of your hard disk in any open window to display the contents of the hard disk.

2 To display the contents of a folder, double-click the folder.

■ The contents of the folder you selected appear.

■ To display the contents of another folder, double-click the folder.

■ You can click ◄ or ► to move backward or forward through the windows you have viewed.

Note: The ► button is available only after you click the ◄ button.

3 When you finish viewing the contents of your hard disk, click ● to close the window.

What folders does Mac OS automatically include on my hard disk?

Applications Stores the applications available on your computer, such as Safari and TextEdit.	**Library** Stores system items available to every user account on your computer, such as desktop pictures, fonts and screen savers.	**System** Stores a Library folder that contains the files Mac OS requires to run.	**Users** Stores a home folder for each user account on your computer. For more information on the Users folder, see page 222.

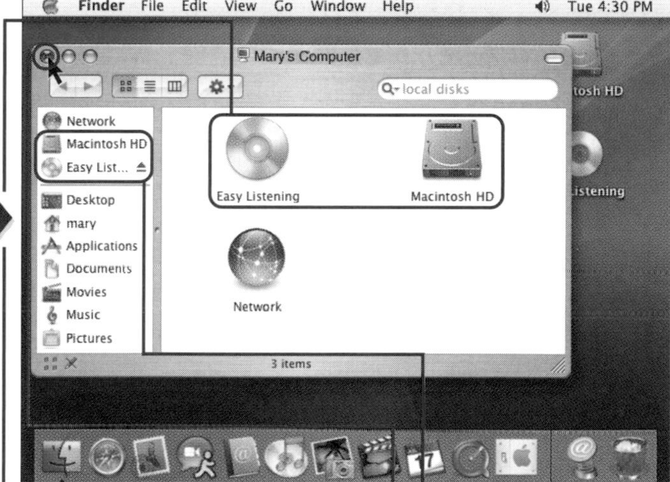

VIEW THE CONTENTS OF YOUR COMPUTER

1 Click **Go**.

Note: If Go is not available, click a blank area on your desktop to display the Finder menu bar.

2 Click **Computer** to view the disks available on your computer.

Note: The desktop also displays the disks available on your computer.

■ The Computer window appears, displaying an icon for each disk available on your computer, including your hard disk and any CD or DVD inserted into a drive on your computer.

■ To display the contents of a disk, double-click the disk.

■ You can also click a disk in this area in any open window to display the contents of the disk.

3 When you finish viewing the contents of your computer, click ● to close the window.

VIEW THE CONTENTS OF A DISC

You can view the contents of a CD, DVD or other type of disc. When you finish working with a disc, you can eject the disc from your computer.

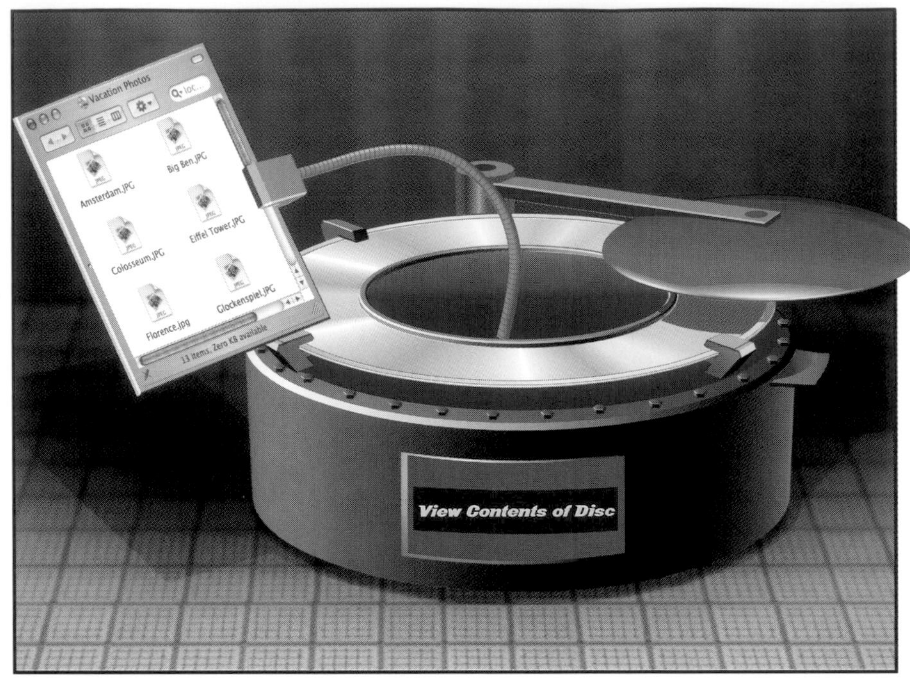

The drive(s) available on your computer determine what types of discs you can view. For example, in addition to viewing the contents of CDs or DVDs, you may also be able to view the contents of Jaz or Zip disks.

VIEW THE CONTENTS OF A DISC

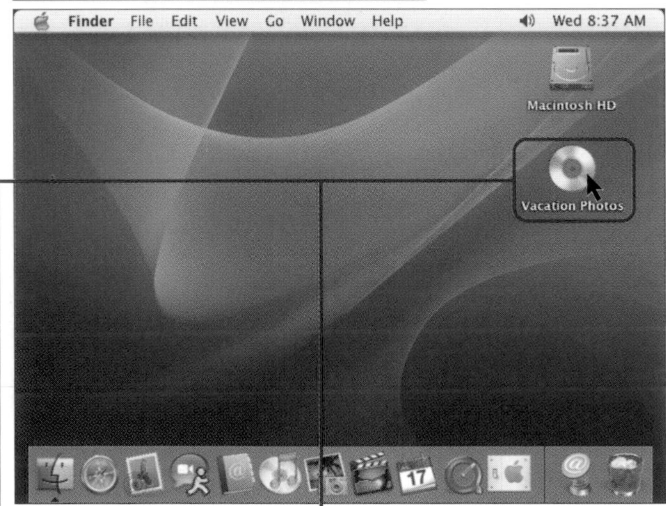

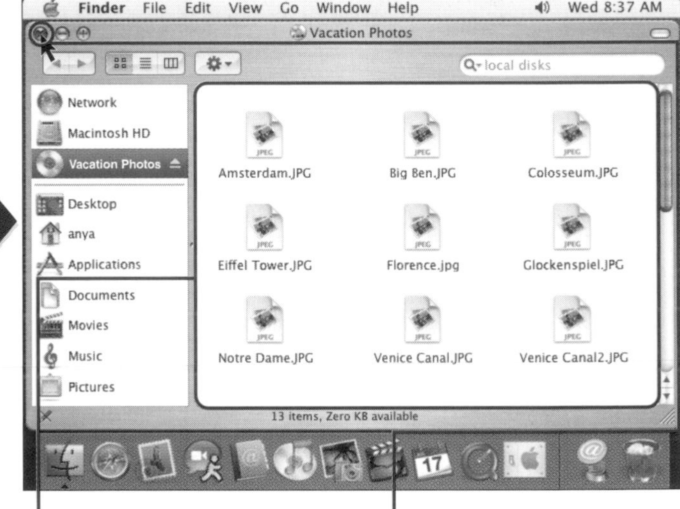

1 Insert a CD, DVD or other type of disc into your computer's drive.

■ An icon for the disc appears on your desktop.

Note: If the disc contains photos or music, iPhoto or iTunes may open. For information on iPhoto, see pages 164 to 183. For information on iTunes, see pages 144 to 161.

2 Double-click the disc's icon to view the contents of the disc.

■ A window appears, displaying the contents of the disc.

3 When you finish viewing the contents of the disc, click ● to close the window.

Why did my computer's drive eject my disc?

Your computer's drive may eject a disc if there is a problem with the disc. For example, you may need to clean the disc or the disc may be unreadable due to scratches.

Why did a dialog box appear when I tried to eject a disc?

A dialog box may appear if one or more files on the disc are open when you try to eject the disc. To close the dialog box, click **OK**. Close the files that are open and quit any applications that may be using files on the disc. Then try to eject the disc again.

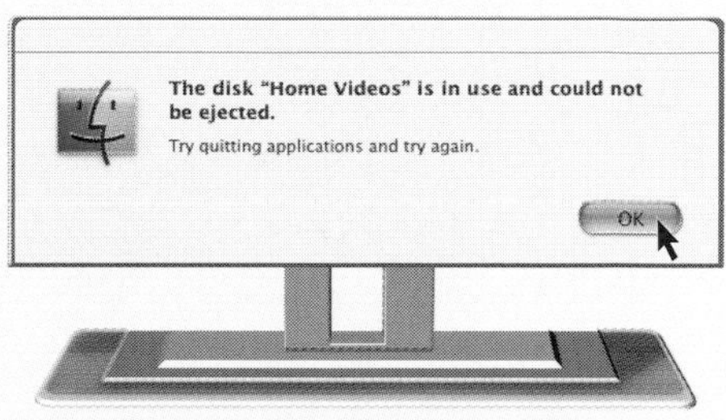

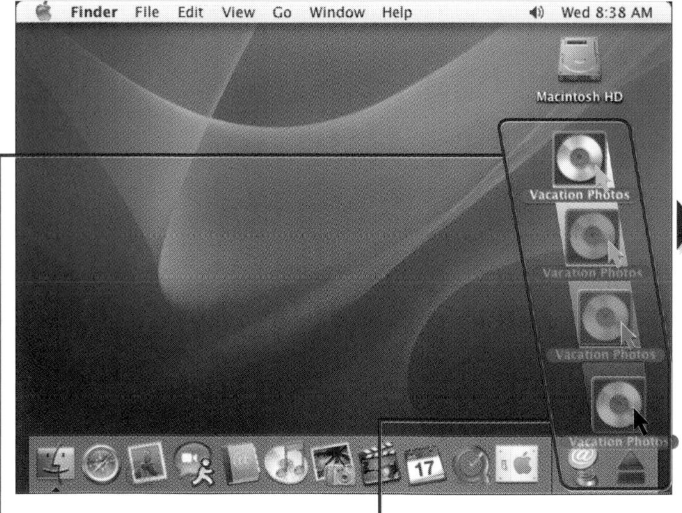

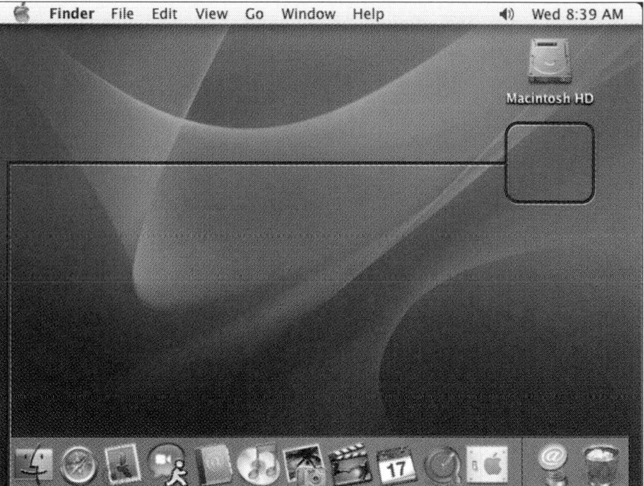

EJECT A DISC

1 To eject a disc, position the mouse over the disc's icon on your desktop.

2 Drag the disc's icon to the Trash icon (changes to).

■ The disc's icon disappears from your desktop and the disc is physically ejected from the drive.

Note: If your keyboard has an Eject key, you can also press the Eject key to eject the disc.

CHANGE THE VIEW OF ITEMS IN A WINDOW

You can change the view of items in a window. The view you select determines the way files and folders will appear in the window.

CHANGE THE VIEW OF ITEMS IN A WINDOW

1 Click a button to specify the way you want to view items in the window.

- Icons
- List
- Columns

ICONS

■ The Icons view displays items as icons.

■ By default, the name of each item appears below each icon.

Can I sort items displayed in the List view?

Yes. You can sort items by name, date last modified, size or kind. Click the heading for the column you want to use to sort the items. To sort the items in the reverse order, you can click the heading again.

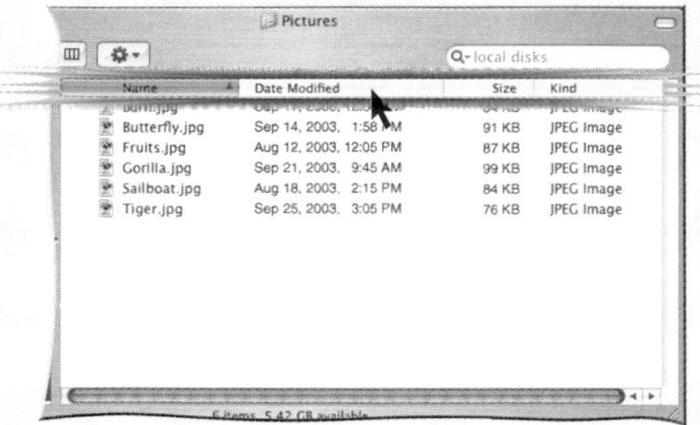

How do I change the width of a column in the List view?

To change the width of a column in the List view, position the mouse ↖ over the right edge of the column heading (↖ changes to ↔) and then drag the column edge until the column displays the width you want.

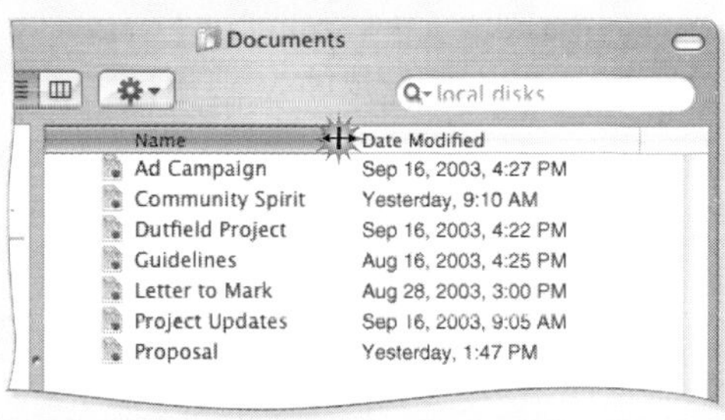

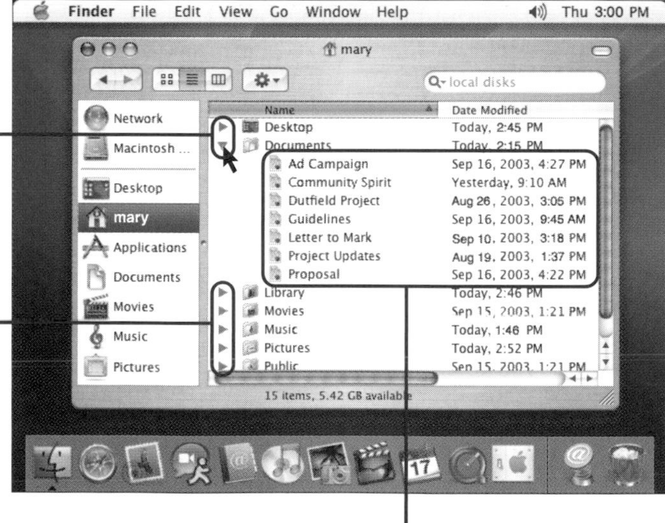

LIST

■ The List view displays items as small icons arranged in a list. This view displays information about each item, including the name, date last modified, size and kind of item.

1 To display the contents of a folder, click ▶ beside the folder (▶ changes to ▼).

■ The contents of the folder appear.

Note: To once again hide the contents of a folder, click ▼ beside the folder.

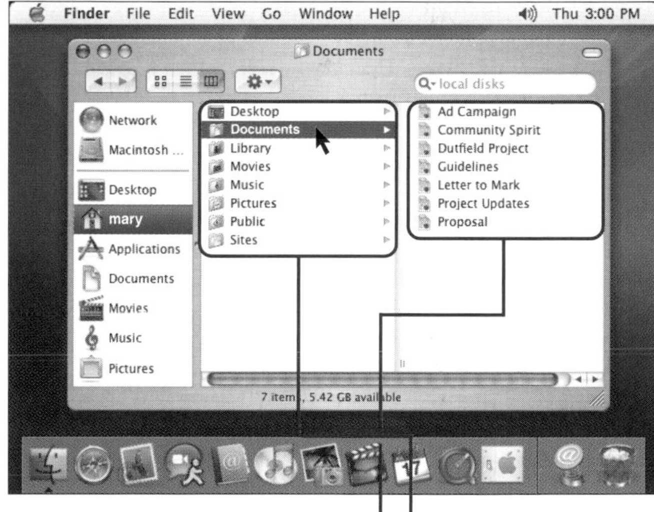

COLUMNS

■ The Columns view shows the location of the current folder in relation to the disks, folders and files on your computer.

Note: Each column shows the contents of the item selected in the previous column.

1 To display the contents of a folder, click the folder.

■ The contents of the folder appear in the next column.

ARRANGE ICONS IN A WINDOW

You can arrange the icons displayed in a window to help you find files and folders more quickly.

You can arrange icons in a window by name, size, kind, date the items were last changed or created or by label color. For information on labeling files, see page 53.

ARRANGE ICONS IN A WINDOW

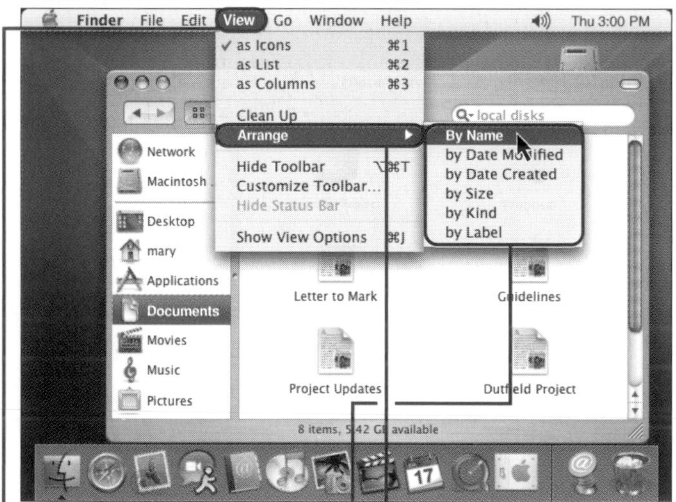

1 Click a blank area in the window that contains the icons you want to arrange.

Note: To arrange the icons on your desktop, click a blank area on the desktop.

2 Click **View**.

3 Position the mouse over **Arrange**.

4 Click the way you want to arrange the icons in the window.

Note: The Arrange command is available only when files are displayed as icons. To change the view of files, see page 28.

■ The icons are arranged in the window. In this example, the icons are arranged by name.

CLEAN UP A WINDOW

You can clean up a window by neatly arranging the files and folders in the window.

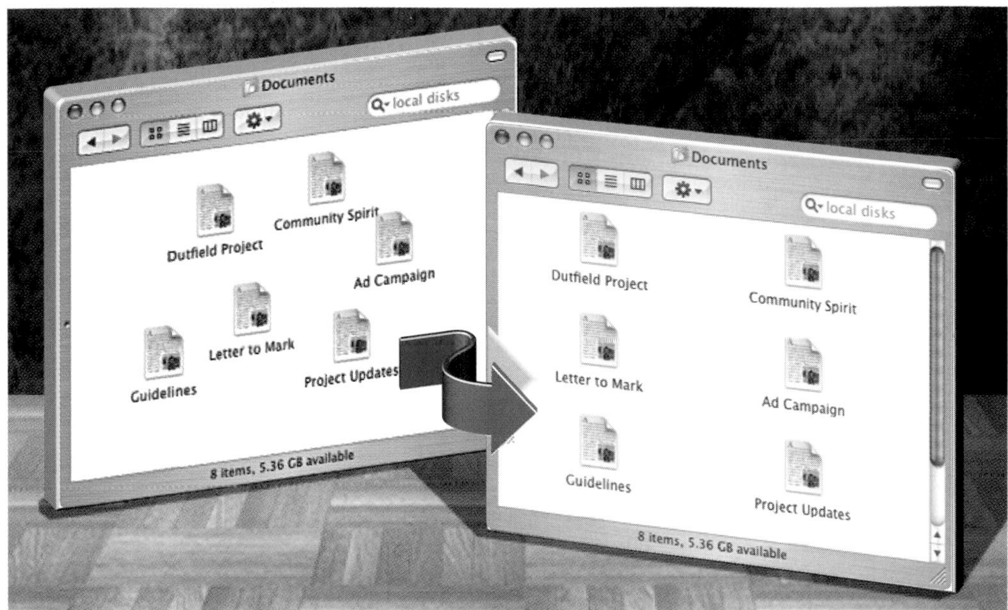

CLEAN UP A WINDOW

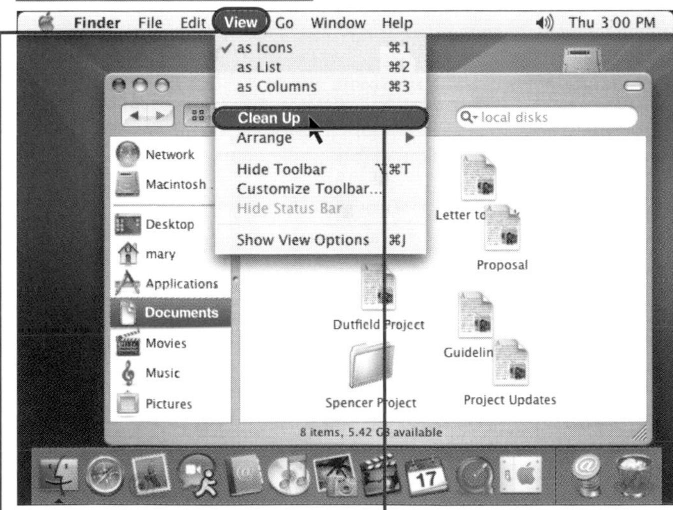

1 Click a blank area in the window you want to clean up.

Note: To clean up the icons on your desktop, click a blank area on the desktop.

2 Click **View**.

3 Click **Clean Up**.

Note: The Clean Up command is available only when files are displayed as icons. To change the view of files, see page 28.

■ The icons move to the nearest empty positions in the window's invisible grid.

DISPLAY FILE INFORMATION

You can display information about a file, such as the file size and date you last modified the file.

You can display information about folders, disks, applications and aliases the same way you display information about files.

DISPLAY FILE INFORMATION

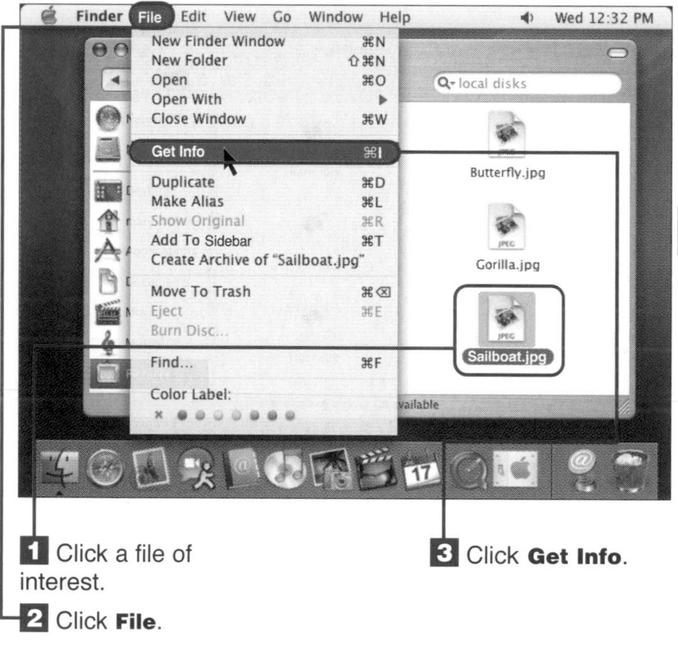

1 Click a file of interest.

2 Click **File**.

3 Click **Get Info**.

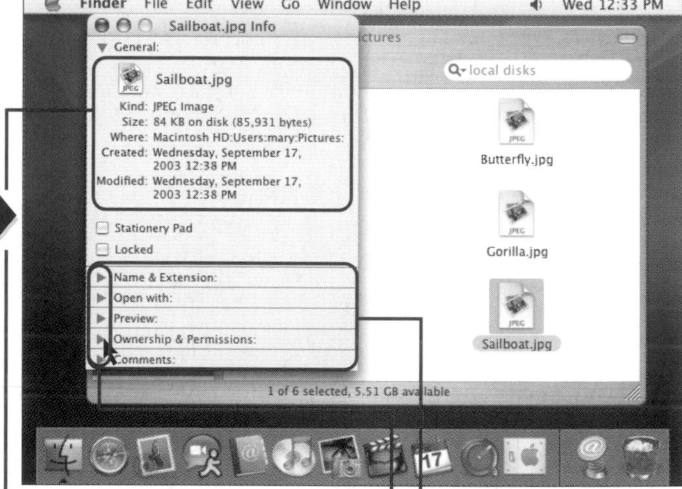

■ The Info window appears, displaying general information about the file, including the name, kind, size, location and dates the file was created and last modified.

■ This area displays additional categories of information you can display for the file.

4 To display the information in a category, click ▶ beside the category of interest (▶ changes to ▼).

What additional categories of information can I display for a file?

Name & Extension

Allows you to view and change the **file name** and **extension** of a file, such as **Report.rtf**.

Open with

Allows you to view and change the application that opens a file.

Preview

Allows you to preview some types of files, such as pictures, movies and sounds. If a preview is unavailable, a larger version of the file's icon appears.

Ownership & Permissions

Allows you to specify who owns a file and who you want to be able to access the file. This is useful if you share your computer with other people or are connected to a network.

Comments

Allows you to enter and view comments about a file.

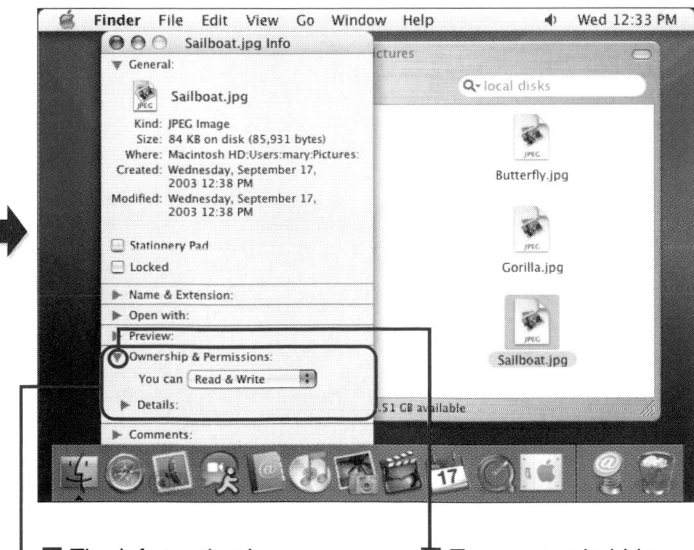

■ The information in the category appears. In this example, information about the file's ownership and permissions appears.

■ To once again hide the information in the category, click ▼.

5 When you finish reviewing information about the file, click ● to close the Info window.

■ You can repeat steps **1** to **5** to display information about another file.

File Factory
OFFICE
Sales

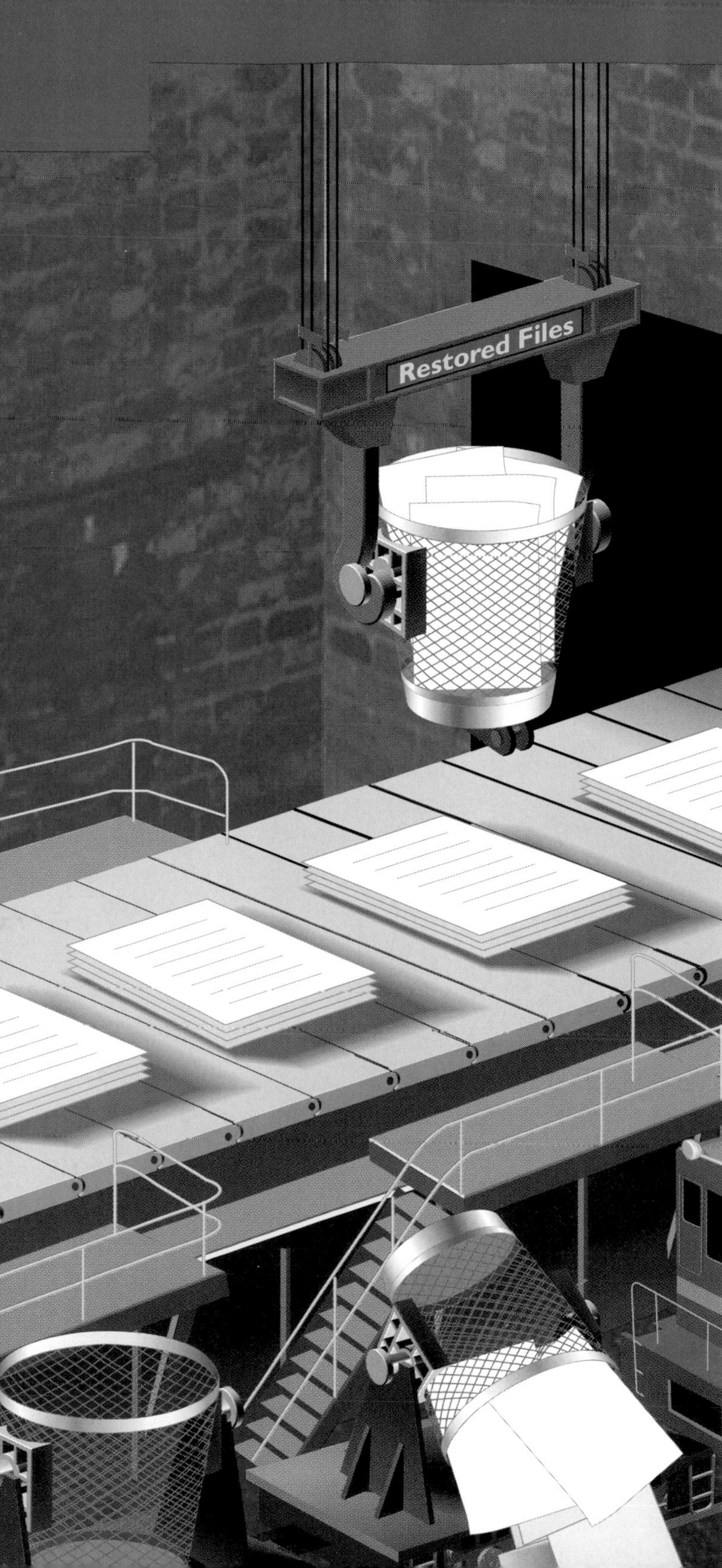

CHAPTER 3

Work With Files

This chapter teaches you how to efficiently manage your files. Learn how to print files, search for files, copy files to a CD or DVD, fax files from your computer and more.

SELECT FILES

Before working with files, you often need to select the files you want to work with. Selected files appear highlighted on your screen.

You can select folders the same way you select files. Selecting a folder selects all the files in the folder.

SELECT FILES

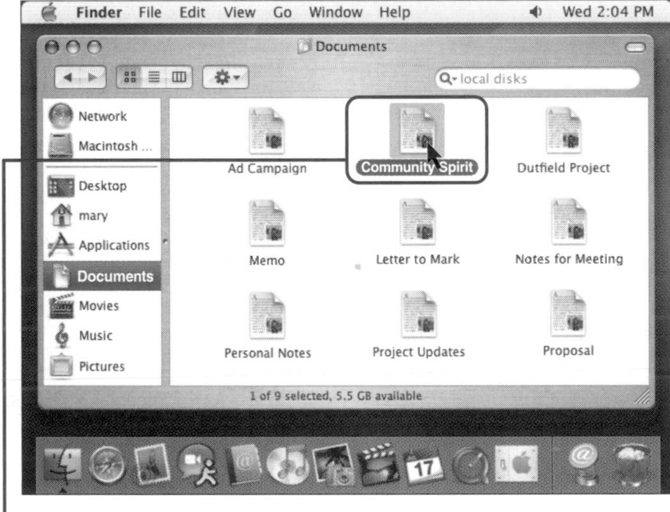

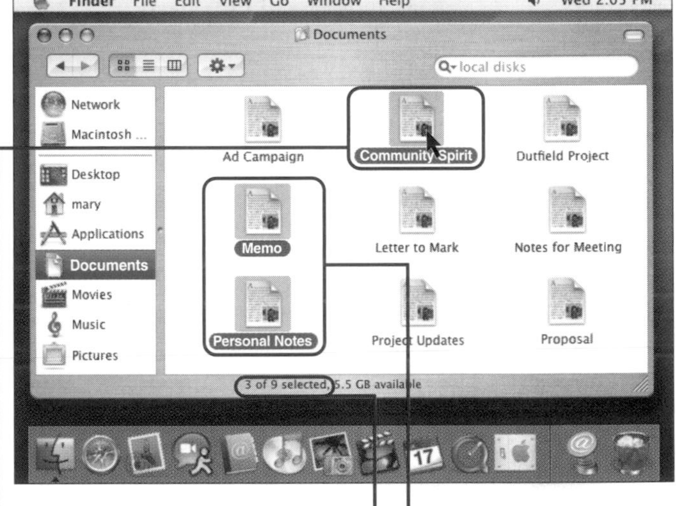

SELECT ONE FILE

1 Click the icon for the file you want to select.

■ The file is highlighted.

SELECT RANDOM FILES

1 Click the icon for a file you want to select.

2 Press and hold down the ⌘ key as you click the icon for each additional file you want to select.

■ This area displays the number of files you selected.

How can I select all the files in a window?

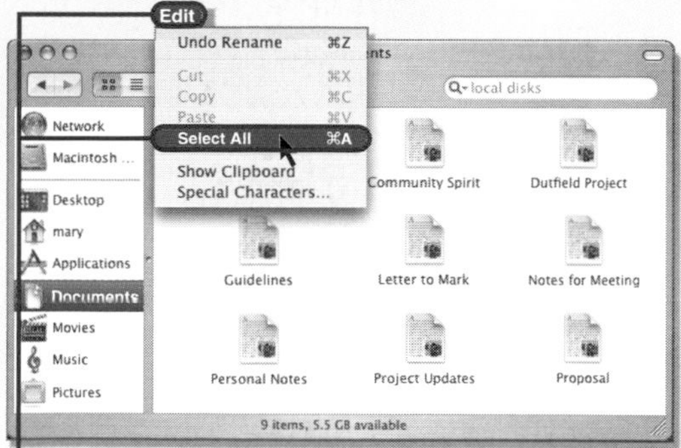

1 Click a blank area in the window that contains the files you want to select.

2 Click **Edit**.

3 Click **Select All** to select all the files in the window.

How do I deselect files?

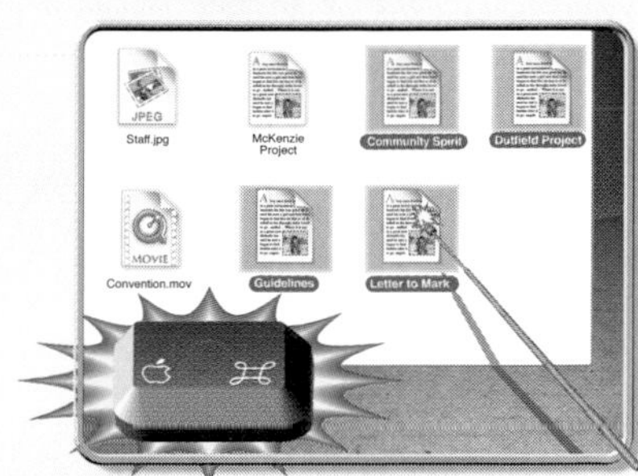

To deselect all the files in a window, click a blank area in the window.

To deselect one or more files from a group of selected files, press and hold down the ⌘ key as you click the icon for each file you want to deselect.

Note: You can deselect folders the same way you deselect files.

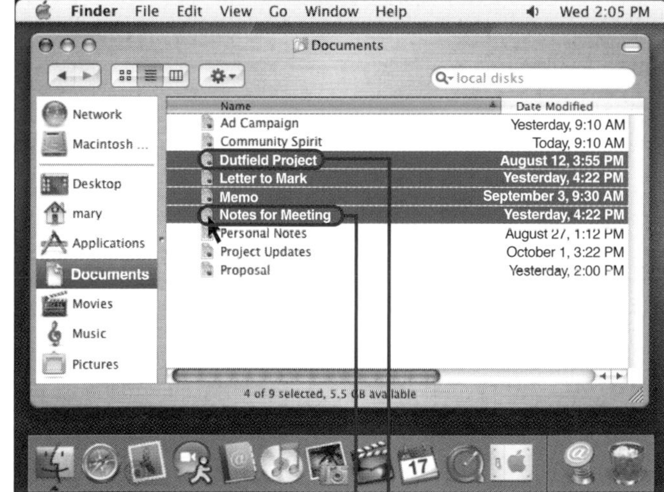

SELECT A GROUP OF FILES

1 Position the mouse slightly above and to the left of the first file you want to select.

2 Drag the mouse diagonally across the files you want to select.

■ While you drag the mouse, a box appears around the files that will be selected.

SELECT A GROUP OF FILES IN LIST OR COLUMNS VIEW

■ You can use this method to select a group of files in the List or Columns view. To change the view of files, see page 28.

1 Click the icon for the first file you want to select.

2 Press and hold down the shift key as you click the icon for the last file you want to select.

OPEN A FILE

You can open a file to display its contents on your screen. Opening a file allows you to review and make changes to the file.

You can open a folder the same way you open a file.

OPEN A FILE

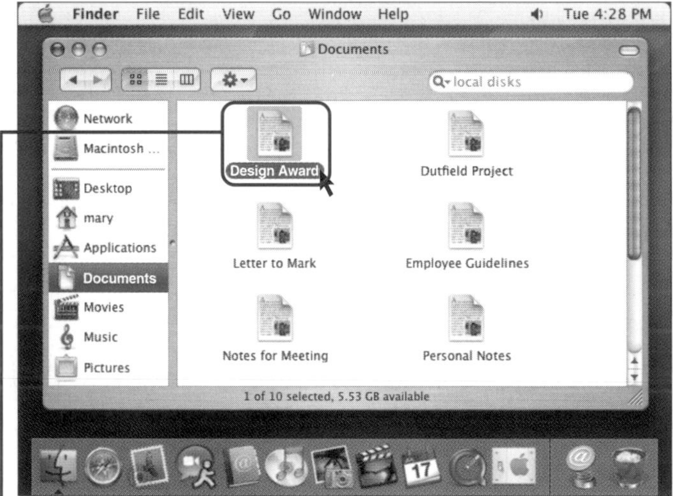

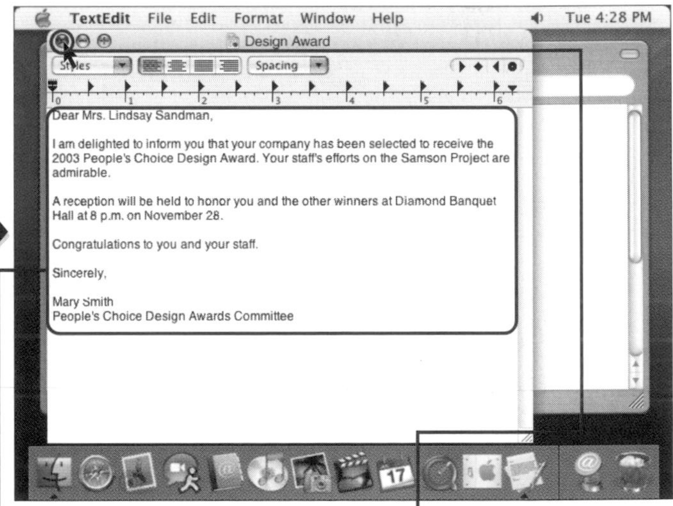

1 Double-click the icon for the file you want to open.

■ The file opens. You can review and make changes to the file.

Note: If you opened a picture, the picture opens in the Preview application. The Preview application allows you to only review the picture. For information on the Preview application, see page 112.

2 When you finish working with the file, click ● to close the file.

OPEN A RECENTLY USED FILE

Mac OS keeps track of the files you have recently used. You can quickly open any of these files.

Mac OS also keeps track of applications you have recently used. You can open a recently used application at any time.

OPEN A RECENTLY USED FILE

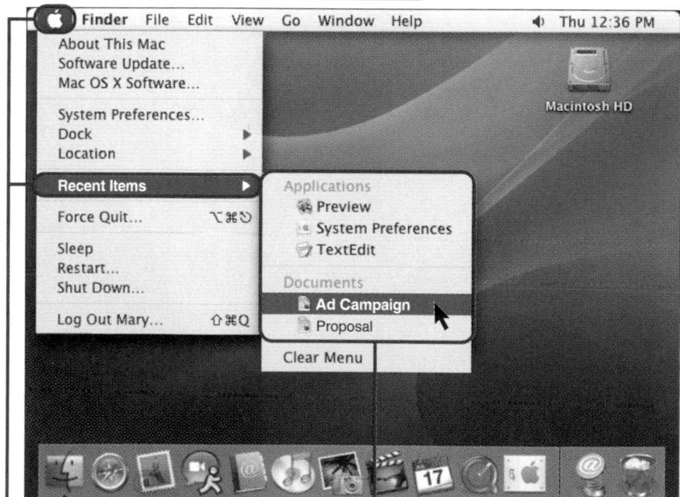

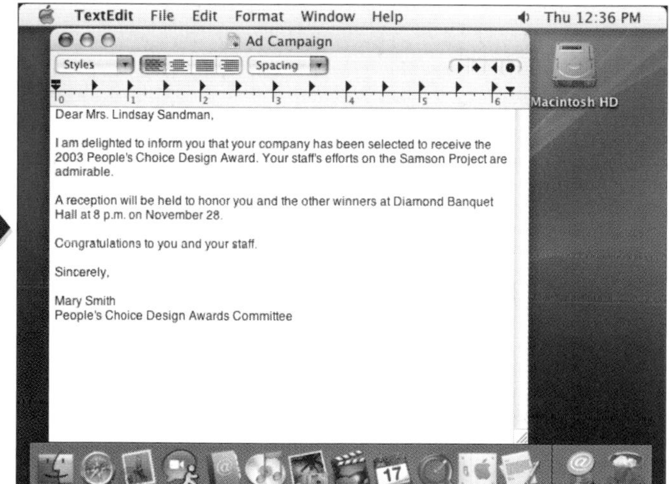

1 Click to display the Apple menu.

2 Position the mouse over **Recent Items**.

■ A list of files and applications you have recently used appears.

3 Click the file you want to open.

Note: You can click an application to open the application.

■ The file you selected opens.

*Note: To clear the list of files and applications you have recently used, perform steps **1** to **3**, selecting **Clear Menu** in step **3**. Clearing the list of recently used files and applications will not delete the items from your computer.*

RENAME A FILE

You can rename a file to better describe the contents of the file. Renaming a file can help you more quickly locate the file in the future.

You can rename folders the same way you rename files. You should not rename folders that Mac OS or your applications require to operate.

RENAME A FILE

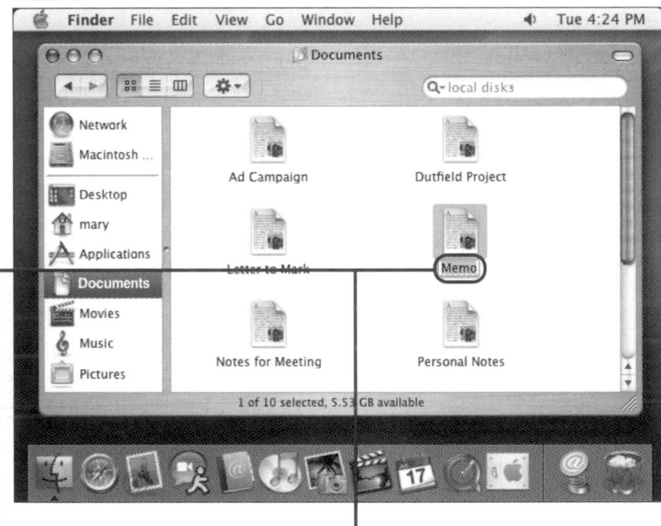

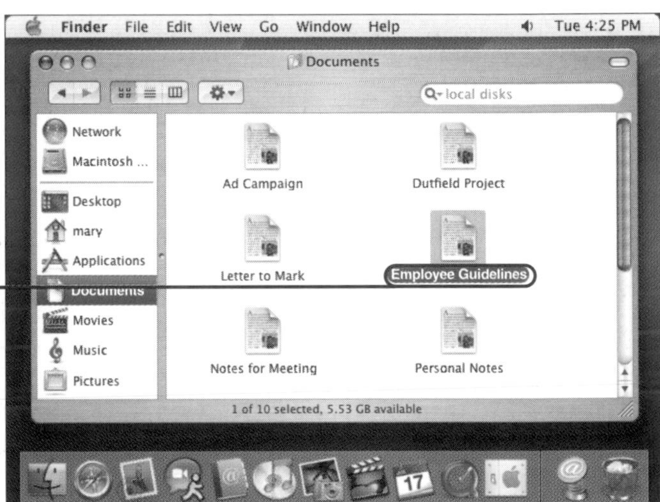

1 Click the name of the file you want to rename.

■ After a moment, a box appears around the file name and the file name is selected.

Note: If a box does not appear around the file name, press the return *key.*

2 Type a new name for the file and then press the return key.

Note: A file name cannot contain a colon (:) or begin with a period (.). Each file in the same location must have a unique name.

■ If you change your mind while typing a new file name, you can press the esc key to return to the original file name.

DUPLICATE A FILE

You can quickly create a duplicate of a file.

Creating a duplicate of a file is useful if you plan to make major changes to a file, but you want to keep a copy of the original file. Creating a duplicate gives you two copies of a file—the original file and a file that you can change.

You can duplicate a folder the same way you duplicate a file. When you duplicate a folder, all the files in the folder are also duplicated.

DUPLICATE A FILE

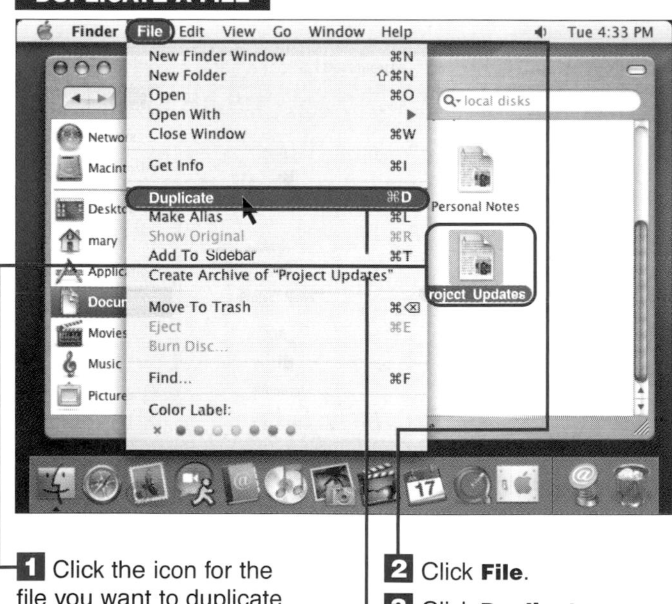

1 Click the icon for the file you want to duplicate.

2 Click **File**.

3 Click **Duplicate**.

■ A duplicate of the file appears. The word "copy" appears in the name of the duplicate file.

Note: To move the duplicate file to another location on your computer, see page 46. To rename the duplicate file, see page 40.

CREATE A FOLDER

You can create a new folder to help you organize the files stored on your computer.

Creating a new folder is useful when you want to keep related files together, such as the files for a particular project.

After you create a new folder, you can move files and other folders to the new folder. To move files and folders, see page 46.

CREATE A FOLDER

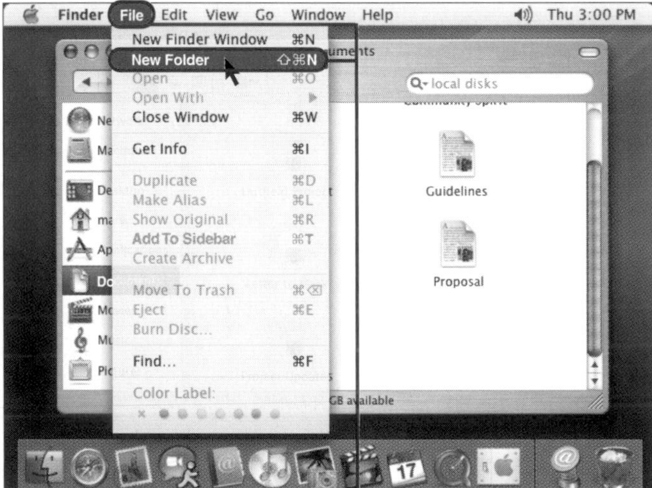

1 Click anywhere in the window for the folder you want to contain a new folder.

■ To create a new folder on your desktop, click a blank area on the desktop.

2 Click **File**.

3 Click **New Folder**.

■ The new folder appears, displaying a temporary name.

4 Type a name for the new folder and then press the return key.

*Note: If you cannot type a name, press the return key and then perform step **4**.*

■ A folder name cannot contain a colon (:) or begin with a period (.). Each folder in the same location must have a unique name.

DELETE A FILE

You can delete a file you no longer need. The Trash stores all the files you delete.

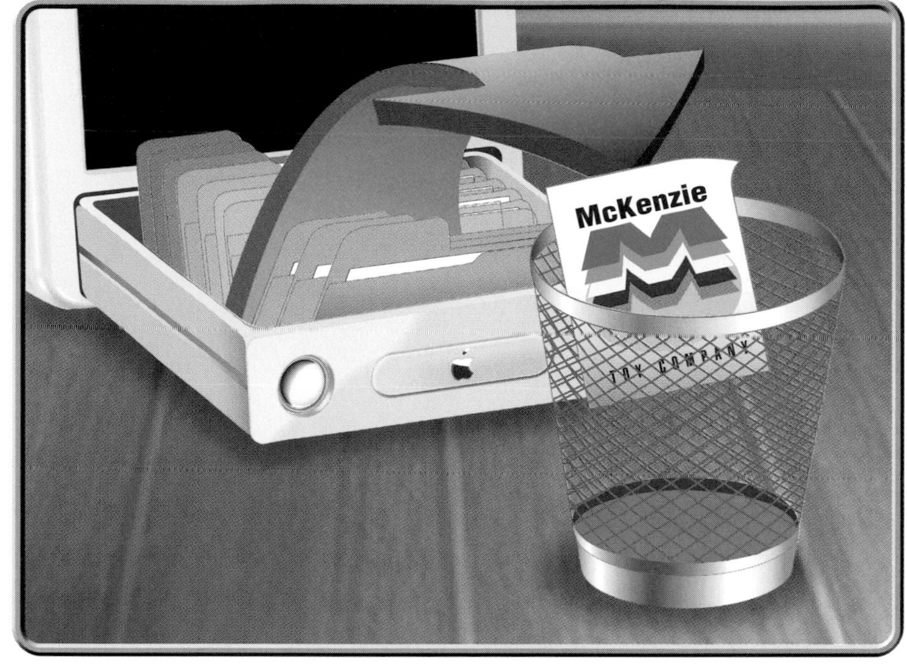

You can delete a folder the same way you delete a file. When you delete a folder, all the files in the folder are also deleted.

DELETE A FILE

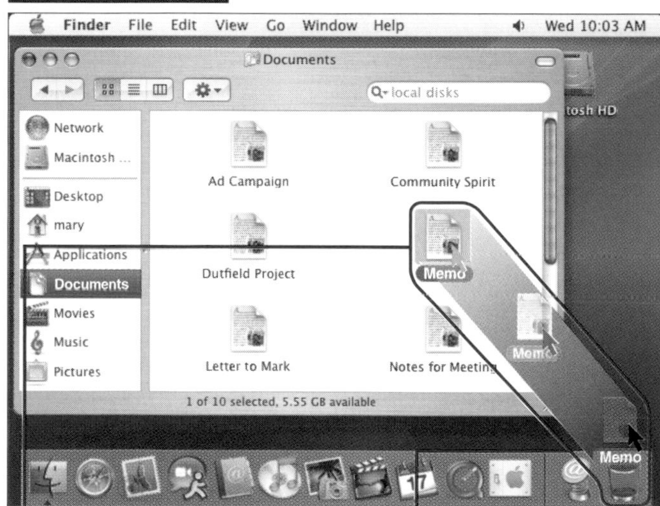

1 Position the mouse over the file you want to delete.

■ To delete more than one file, select all the files you want to delete. To select multiple files, see page 36.

2 Drag the file to the Trash icon.

Note: To delete a file, you can also click the icon for the file and then press and hold down the ⌘ key as you press the delete key.

■ The file disappears.

■ Mac OS places the file in the Trash in case you later want to restore the file. To restore a file from the Trash, see page 44.

■ Files you delete remain in the Trash until you empty the Trash. To empty the Trash, see page 45.

RESTORE A DELETED FILE

The Trash stores all the files you have deleted. If you regret deleting a file, you can restore the file from the Trash.

After deleting files, you can empty the Trash to create more free space on your computer. When you empty the Trash, the files in the Trash are removed from your computer and cannot be restored.

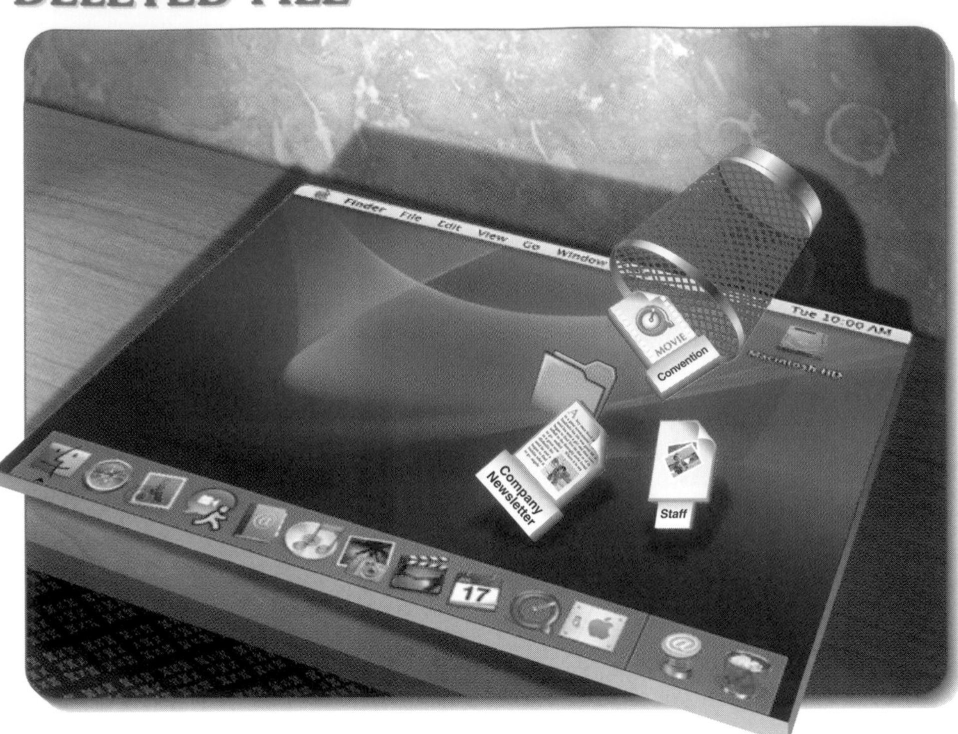

RESTORE A DELETED FILE

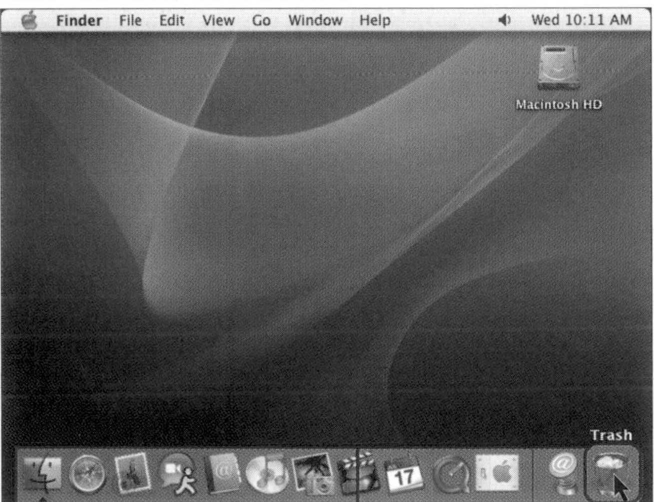

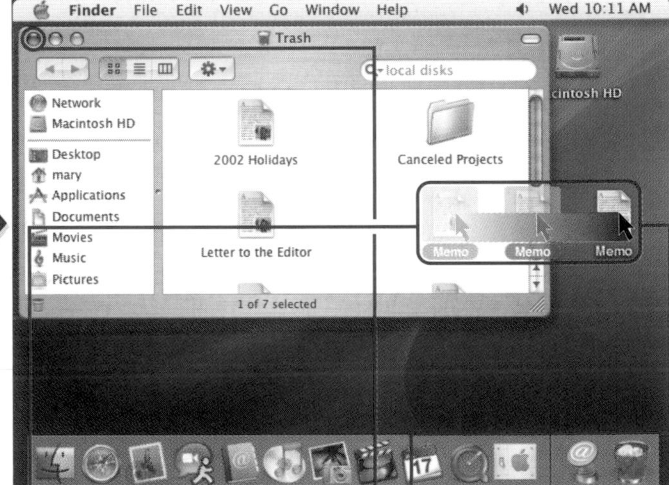

■ The appearance of the Trash icon indicates whether or not the Trash contains deleted files.

Contains deleted files.

Does not contain deleted files.

1 Click the Trash icon.

■ The Trash window appears, displaying all the files you have deleted.

2 Position the mouse over the file you want to restore.

■ To restore more than one file, select all the files you want to restore. To select multiple files, see page 36.

3 Drag the file to the desktop or to a folder.

■ The file will disappear from the Trash window and move to the location you specified.

4 Click to close the Trash window.

How can I ensure that no one will be able to retrieve data from files I have deleted after I empty the Trash?

Even after you delete files from the Trash, it may still be possible for an experienced user to access the data that was stored in the files. Mac OS allows you to securely delete files from the Trash. When you choose to securely empty the Trash, your computer writes random data over the deleted files to make it more difficult for other people to retrieve the original data.

■ To securely empty the Trash, perform steps **1** to **4** on page 45, except select **Secure Empty Trash** in step **3**.

EMPTY THE TRASH

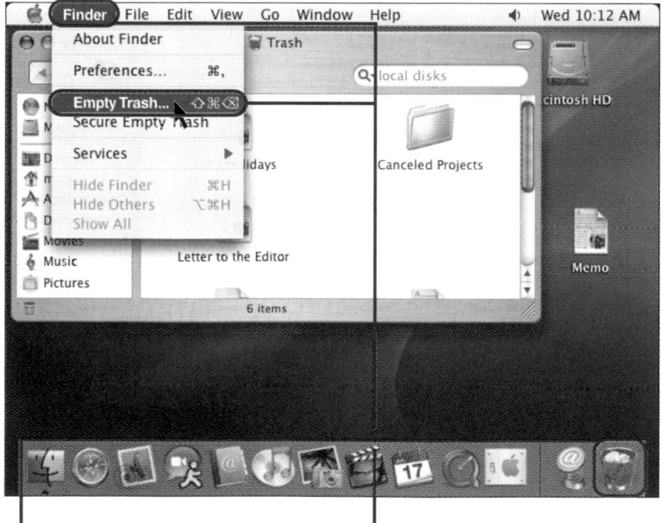

1 Click the Trash icon.

■ The Trash window appears, displaying all the files you have deleted.

2 Click **Finder**.

3 Click **Empty Trash**.

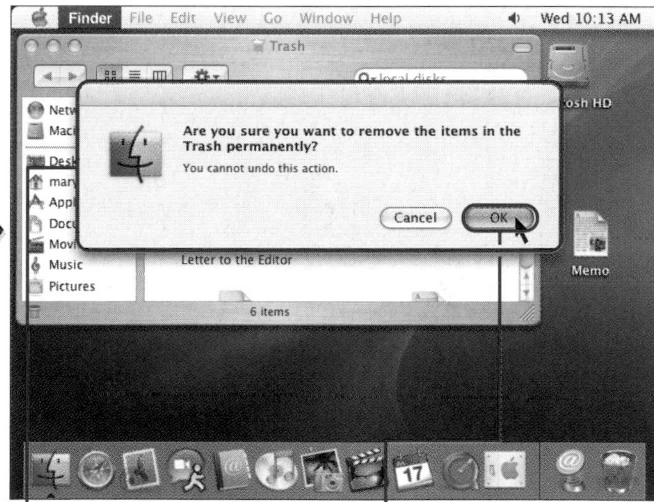

■ A warning dialog box appears, confirming that you want to permanently remove all the files in the Trash.

4 Click **OK** to permanently remove all the files in the Trash and close the Trash window.

MOVE OR COPY A FILE

You can move or copy a file to a new location on your computer.

You can move or copy a folder the same way you move or copy a file. When you move or copy a folder, all the files in the folder are also moved or copied.

You can move or copy a file to the desktop, a folder or another disk.

MOVE A FILE

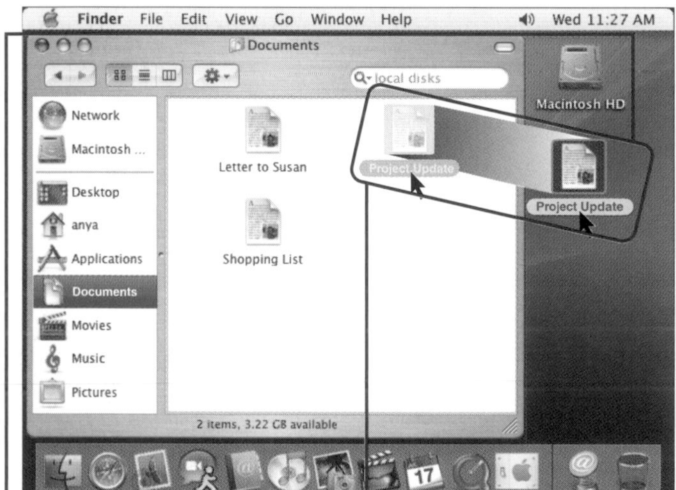

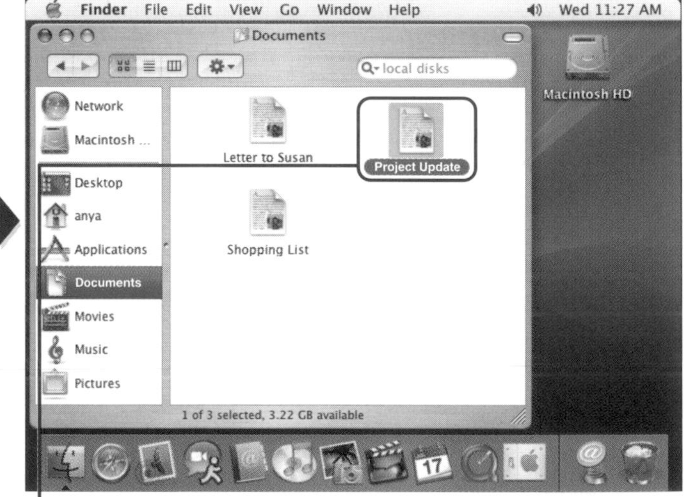

■ Before moving a file, make sure you can clearly see the location where you want to move the file.

1 Position the mouse over the file you want to move.

■ To move more than one file at once, select all the files you want to move. Then position the mouse over one of the files. To select multiple files, see page 36.

2 Drag the file to a new location.

■ The file moves to the new location.

■ The file disappears from its original location.

Can I quickly move or copy a file to a commonly used folder?

Yes. Mac OS displays a list of commonly used disks and folders, such as Documents and Pictures, in the Sidebar of every open Finder window. You can use the methods described below to move or copy a file to one of these commonly used disks or folders. A blue highlight appears around the name of the folder the file will be moved or copied to. For more information on the Sidebar, see page 8.

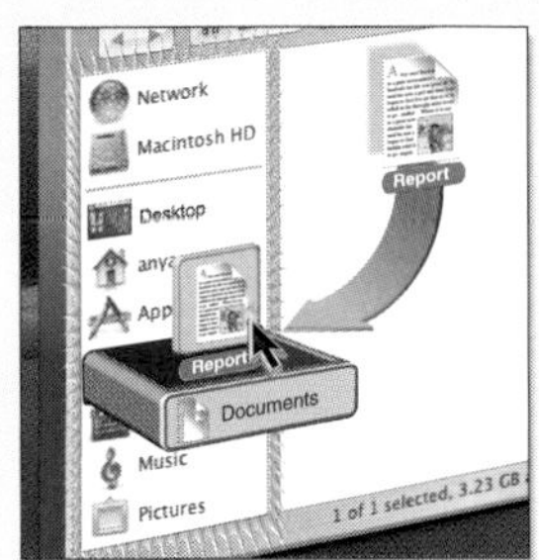

When I drag a file to another disk, why does Mac OS copy rather than move the file?

When you drag a file to another disk, Mac OS creates a copy of the file on the other disk. To move a file to another disk instead of copying the file, press and hold down the ⌘ key as you drag the file.

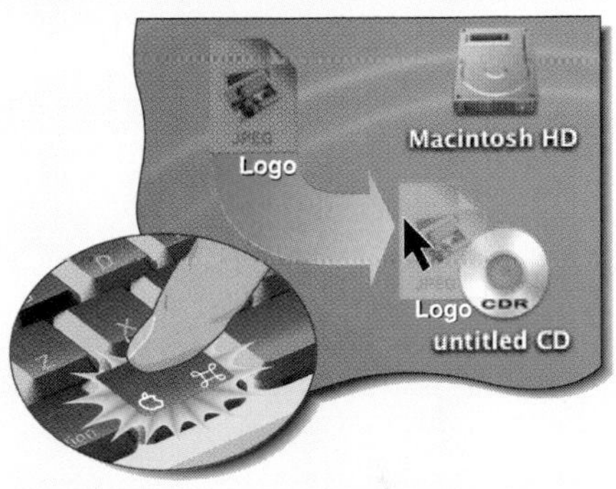

COPY A FILE

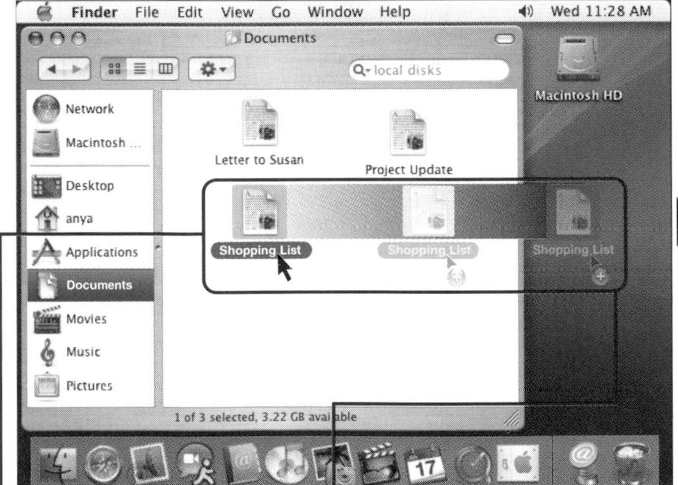

■ Before copying a file, make sure you can clearly see the location where you want to copy the file.

1 Position the mouse over the file you want to copy.

■ To copy more than one file at once, select all the files you want to copy. Then position the mouse over one of the files. To select multiple files, see page 36.

2 Press and hold down the option key as you drag the file to a new location.

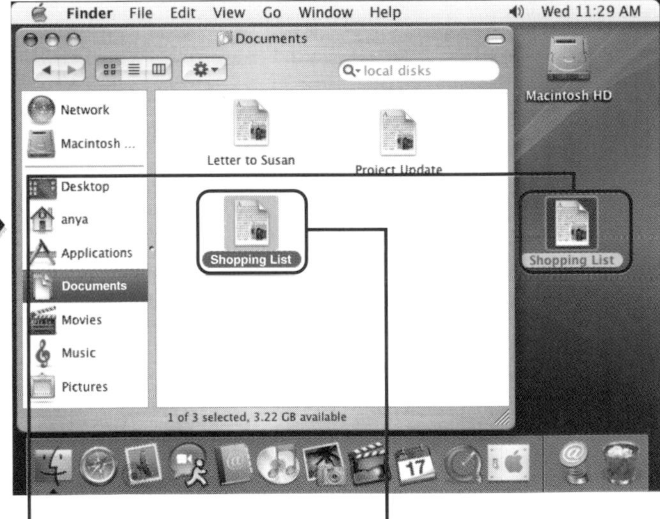

■ A copy of the file appears in the new location.

■ The original file remains in the original location.

CREATE AN ALIAS

You can create an alias for a file you frequently use to provide a quick way of opening the file.

An alias points to an original file. If you delete the original file, the alias will no longer work.

CREATE AN ALIAS

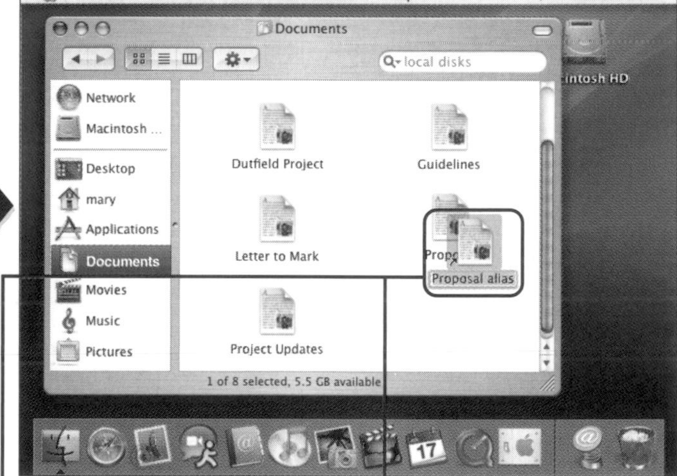

1 Click the icon for the file you want to create an alias for.

2 Click **File**.

3 Click **Make Alias**.

■ The alias appears, displaying a temporary name.

4 To use the temporary name, press the return key.

Note: To use a different name, type the new name and then press the return *key.*

■ You can tell the difference between the alias and the original file because the alias displays an arrow (↗).

Can I create an alias to a folder or application on my computer?

You can create an alias for a folder or an application the same way you create an alias for a file. Creating an alias for a folder gives you quick access to all the files in the folder. Creating an alias for an application allows you to quickly start the application.

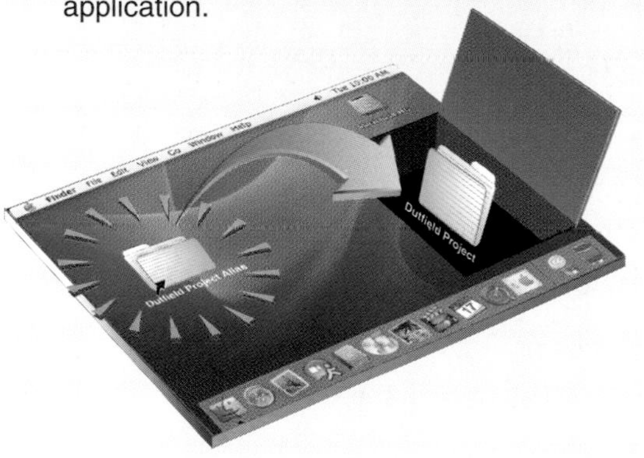

How do I rename or delete an alias?

You can rename or delete an alias the same way you would rename or delete any file. Renaming or deleting an alias will not affect the original file. To rename a file, see page 40. To delete a file, see page 43.

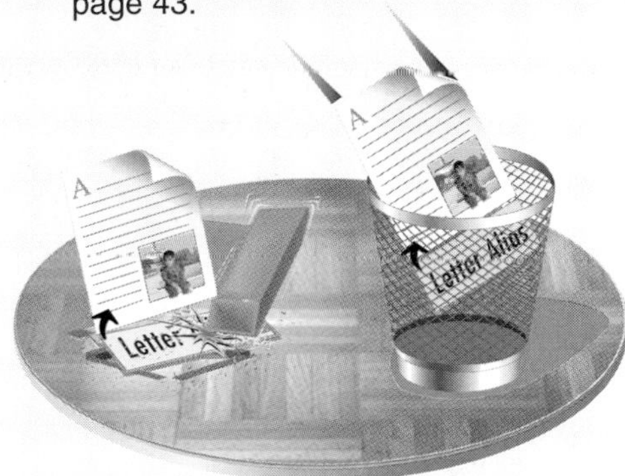

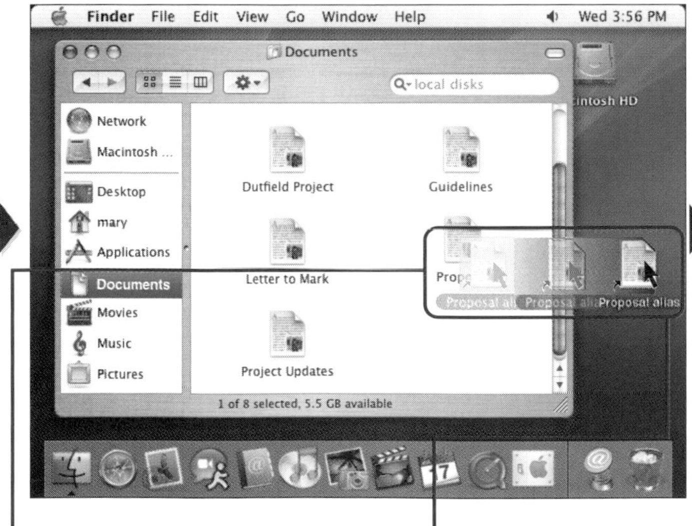

5 To move the alias to the desktop or to another location on your computer, position the mouse over the alias.

6 Drag the alias to the desktop or to another location.

■ The alias appears in the new location.

■ You can double-click the alias to open the original file at any time.

SEARCH FOR FILES

If you cannot remember the exact name or location of a file you want to work with, you can have Mac OS search for the file on your computer.

You can search for a file by file name and content. You should provide as much search information as possible to help narrow your search.

SEARCH FOR FILES

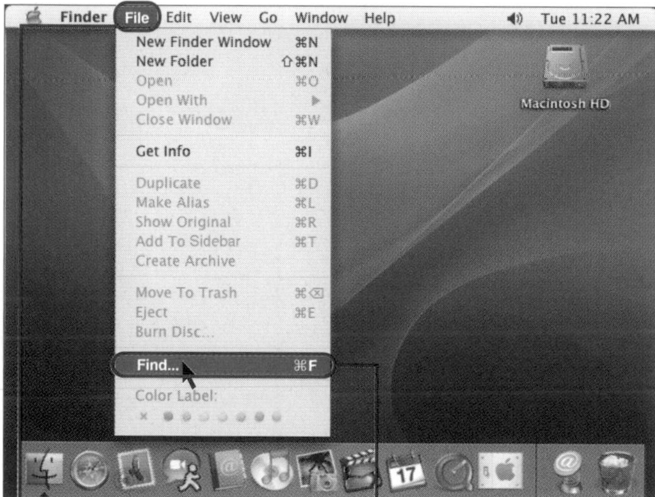

1 Click **File**.

Note: If File is not available, click a blank area on your desktop to display the Finder menu bar.

2 Click **Find** to search for a file on your computer.

■ The Find dialog box appears.

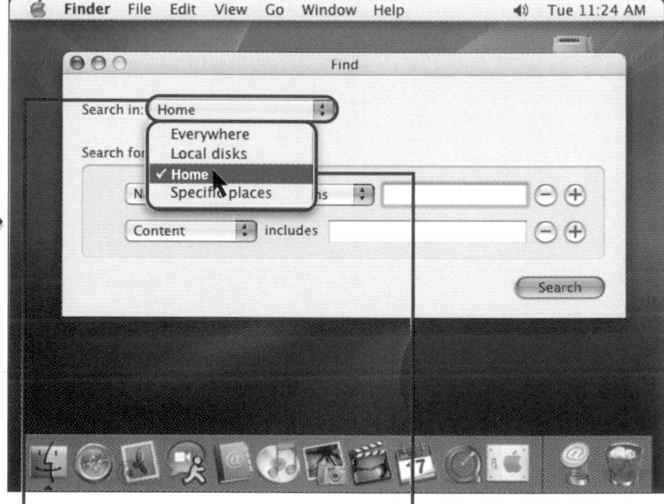

3 To specify the location you want to search, click this area.

4 Click the location you want to search.

What locations can I search for files?

Mac OS lets you search four different locations for your files.

Everywhere searches the disks on your computer and all available network disks.

Local disks searches the disks on your computer.

Home searches your home folder, which stores your personal files.

Specific places allows you to specify the location you want to search.

Can I search for files based on criteria other than file name and content?

Yes. You can click a plus sign (⊕) in the Find dialog box to display an area where you can specify additional search criteria, such as date, file size or extension. Click the criteria in the area that appears to specify the criteria you want to use and then specify the information for the criteria.

Note: To remove a criteria area you do not want to include in your search, click the minus sign (⊖) beside the area.

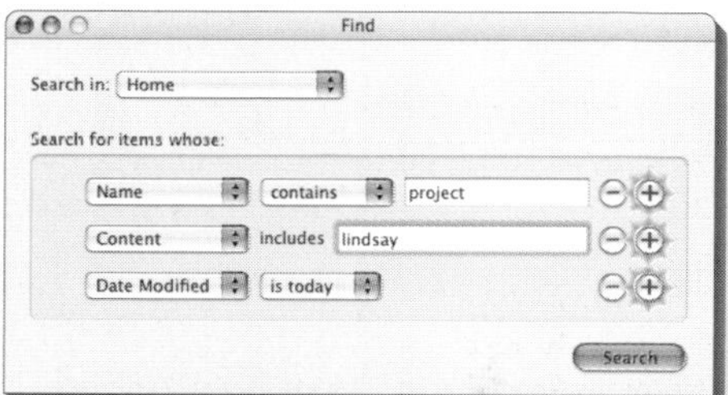

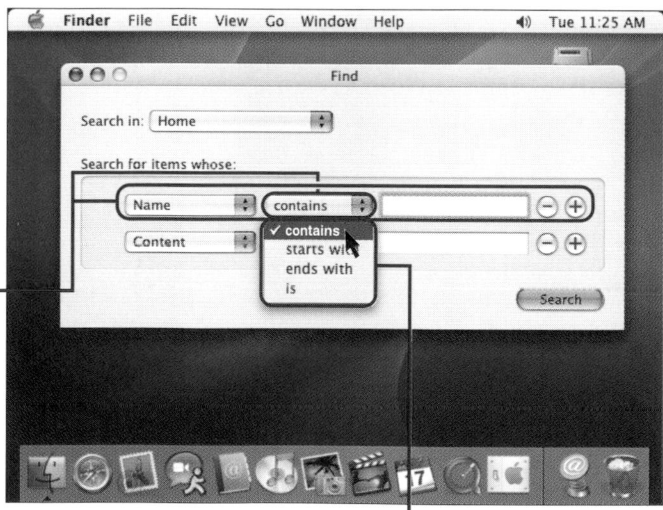

SEARCH BY NAME

■ This area allows you to search by file name.

5 To display a list of options you can use to search by file name, click this area.

6 Click the option you want to use.

Note: You can search for a file name that contains, starts with, ends with or exactly matches text you specify.

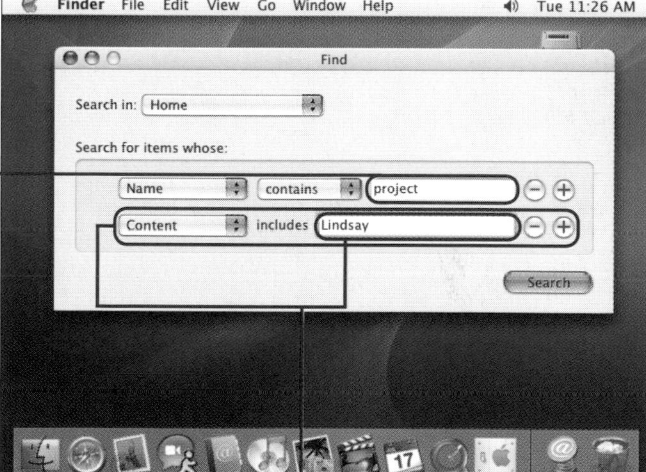

7 Click this area and type all or part of the file name you want to search for.

SEARCH BY CONTENT

■ This area allows you to search by file content.

8 Click this area and type a word or phrase that appears within the file.

CONTINUED

When a search is complete, Mac OS displays all the files that match the information you specified and details about each file, such as the folder where the file is located and the date the file was last modified.

SEARCH FOR FILES (CONTINUED)

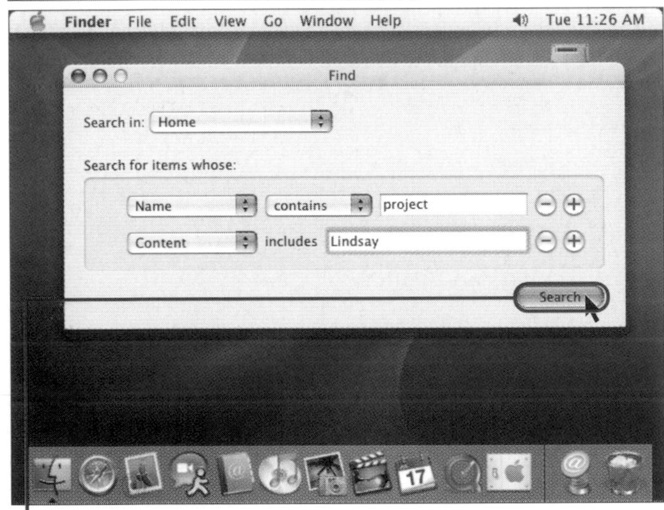

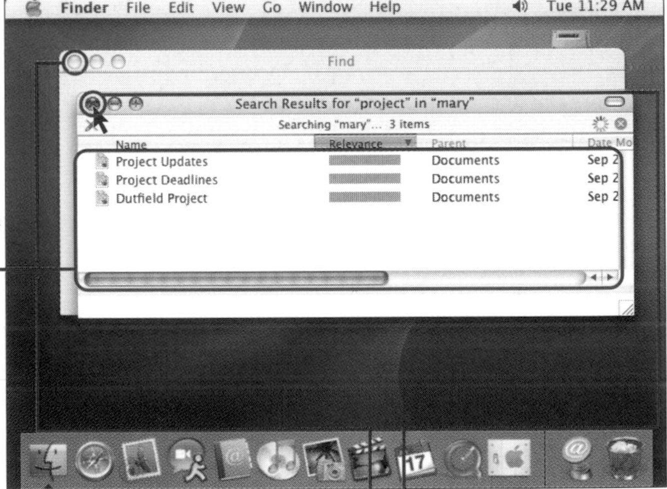

9 To start the search, click **Search**.

■ The Search Results window appears.

■ This area lists the matching files that Mac OS found and information about each file.

■ To open a file, double-click the name of the file.

10 When you finish viewing the results of the search, click ● to close the Search Results window.

11 Click ● to close the Find dialog box.

LABEL A FILE

You can add color labels to your files and folders to color code information on your computer.

You can use color labels to help organize items on your computer. For example, business files and folders may display red color labels while personal files and folders display green color labels.

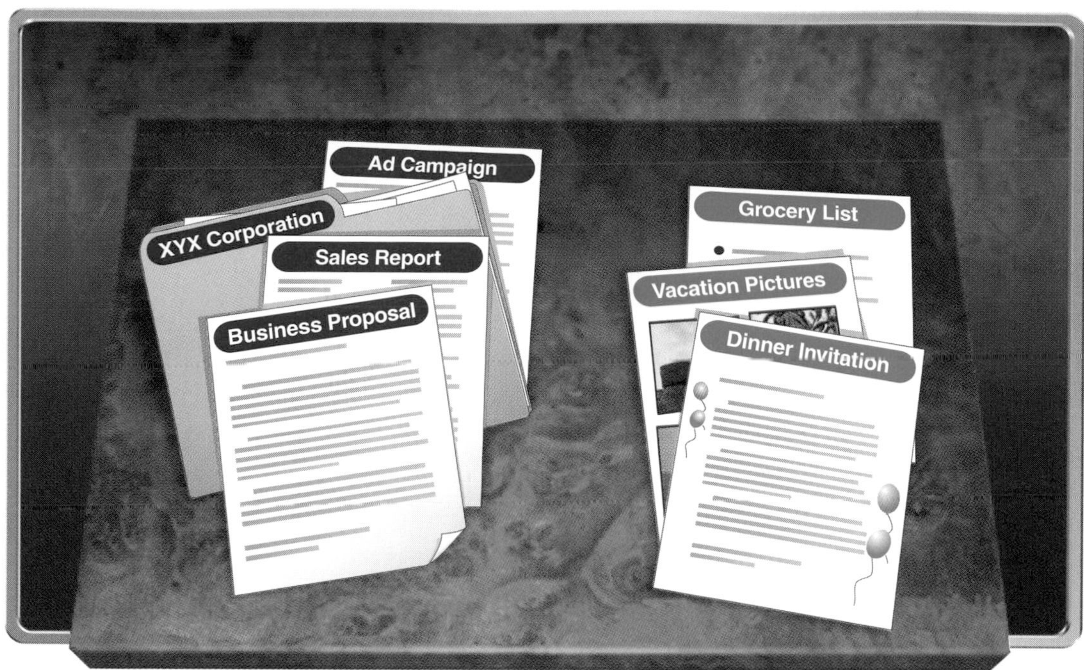

LABEL A FILE

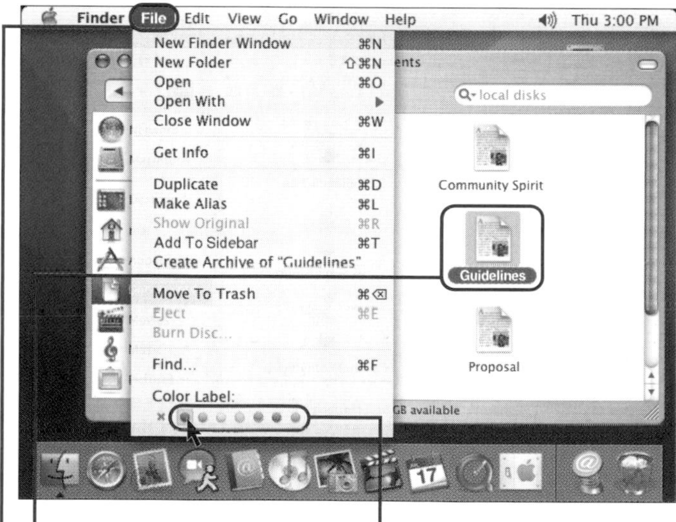

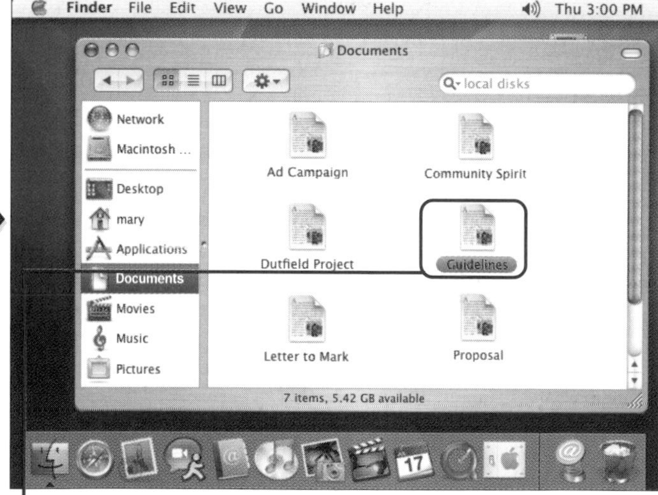

1 Click the icon for the file or folder you want to label.

2 Click **File**.

3 Click the color you want to use to label the file or folder.

■ The file name displays the color label you selected.

Note: To clearly view the color label, click outside the icon for the file or folder.

■ To remove a color label from a file or folder, perform steps **1** to **3**, except select ✖ in step **3**.

PRINT A FILE

You can produce a paper copy of a file stored on your computer.

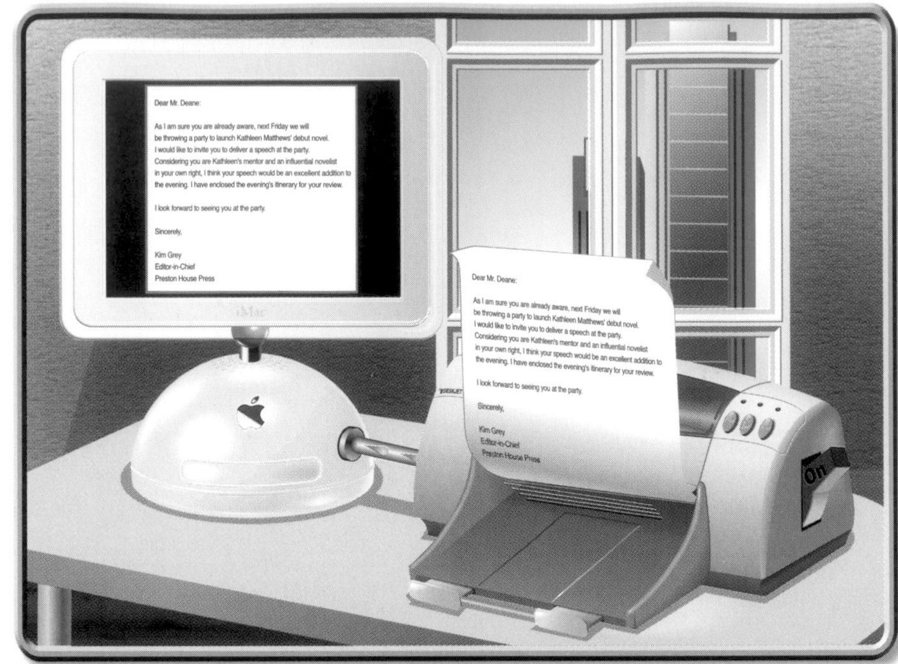

Before printing, make sure your printer is turned on and contains paper.

PRINT A FILE

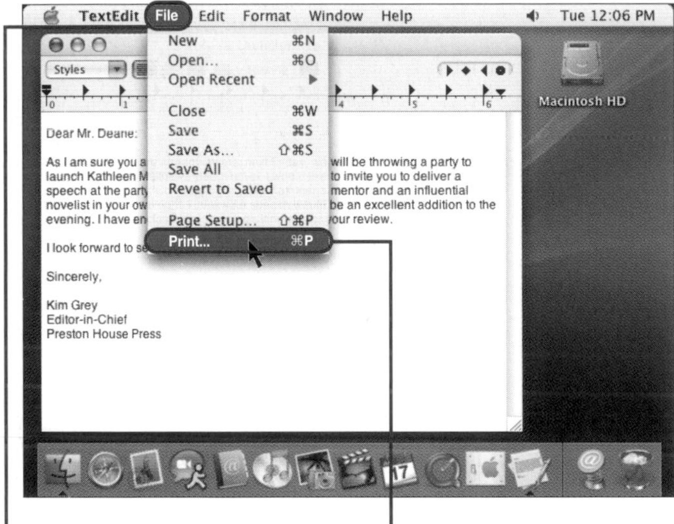

1 Open the file you want to print. To open a file, see page 38.

2 Click **File**.

3 Click **Print** to print the file.

Note: The name of the Print command depends on the active application.

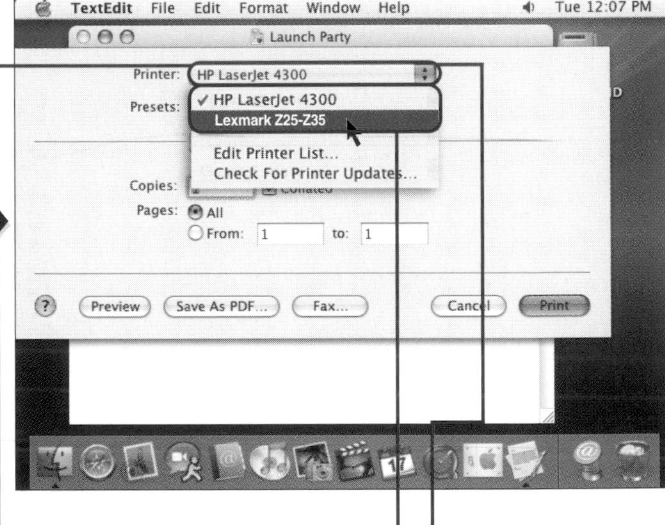

■ A dialog sheet appears.

■ This area displays the printer your computer will use to print the file.

4 To change the printer your computer will use, click this area.

5 Click the printer you want to use to print the file.

Can I preview a file before printing?

Yes. You can preview a file to see how the file will look when printed. To preview a file, perform steps **1** to **3** below. In the dialog sheet that appears, click **Preview**. A window appears, displaying a preview of the file. If the file contains multiple pages, a thumbnail of each page will appear on the side of the window. You can click the thumbnail of a page you want to view. When you finish previewing the file, click to close the window.

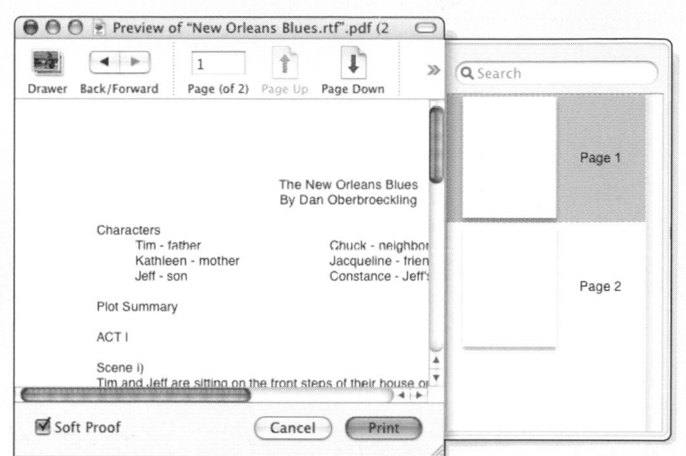

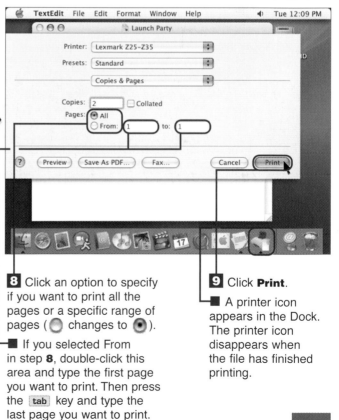

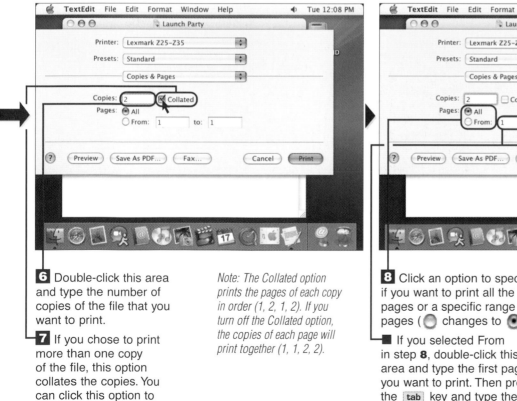

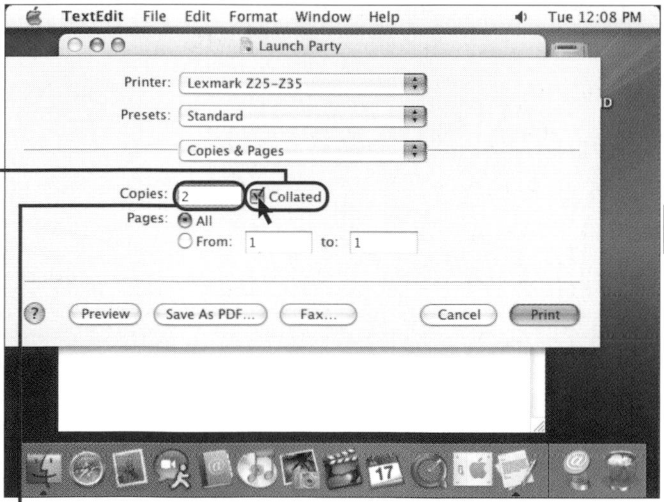

6 Double-click this area and type the number of copies of the file that you want to print.

7 If you chose to print more than one copy of the file, this option collates the copies. You can click this option to turn the option on ( ) or off ( ).

Note: The Collated option prints the pages of each copy in order (1, 2, 1, 2). If you turn off the Collated option, the copies of each page will print together (1, 1, 2, 2).

8 Click an option to specify if you want to print all the pages or a specific range of pages (changes to).

■ If you selected From in step **8**, double-click this area and type the first page you want to print. Then press the tab key and type the last page you want to print.

9 Click **Print**.

■ A printer icon appears in the Dock. The printer icon disappears when the file has finished printing.

MANAGE FILES WAITING TO PRINT

You can view the status of files waiting to print. You can then pause the printing of a file, temporarily stop all files from printing or cancel the printing of a file.

MANAGE FILES WAITING TO PRINT

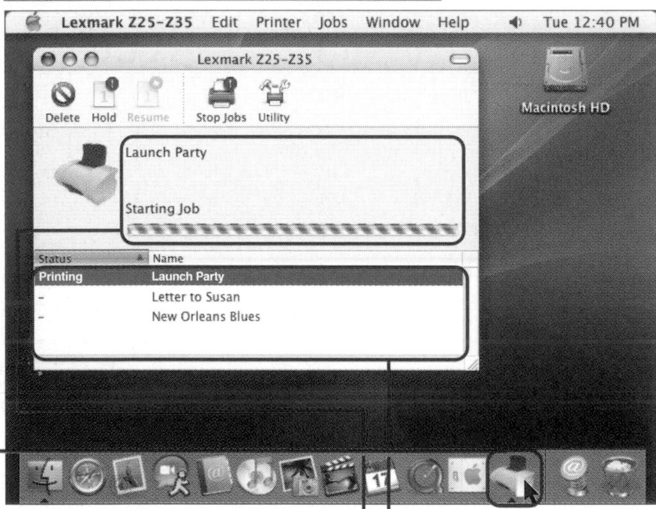

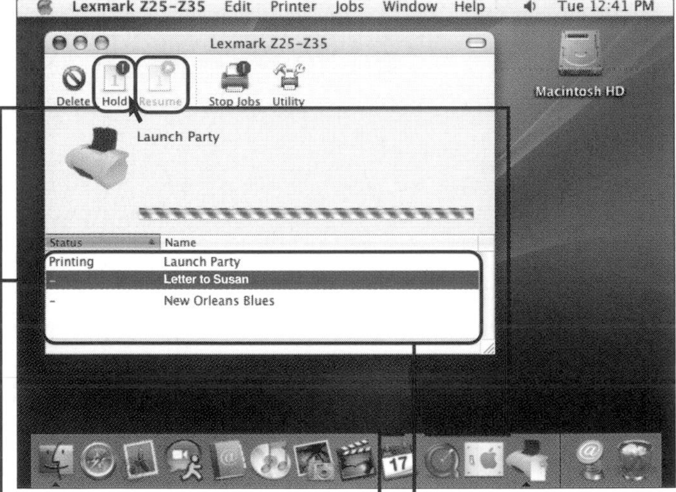

VIEW FILES WAITING TO PRINT

1 Click the printer icon to view the status of the files waiting to print.

Note: If the printer icon is not displayed, the files have finished printing.

■ A window appears, displaying the status and name of each file waiting to print. The file at the top of the list will print first.

■ This area displays the status of the printer.

PAUSE A PRINT JOB

1 Click the name of the file you want to pause.

2 Click **Hold** to pause the print job.

3 When you are ready to resume printing a paused print job, click the name of the file you want to resume printing.

4 Click **Resume** to resume printing the file.

Why would I pause or stop a file from printing?

Pausing the printing of a file is useful when you want to allow more important files to print first.

Temporarily stopping all files from printing is useful when you want to change the toner or add more paper to the printer.

Stopping a file from printing is useful if you accidentally printed the wrong file or want to make last-minute changes to the file.

Can I cancel the printing of several files at once?

Yes. To cancel the printing of several files at once, click the printer icon in the Dock to display the files waiting to print. Press and hold down the ⌘ key as you click the name of each file you no longer want to print. Then click **Delete** to cancel the print jobs.

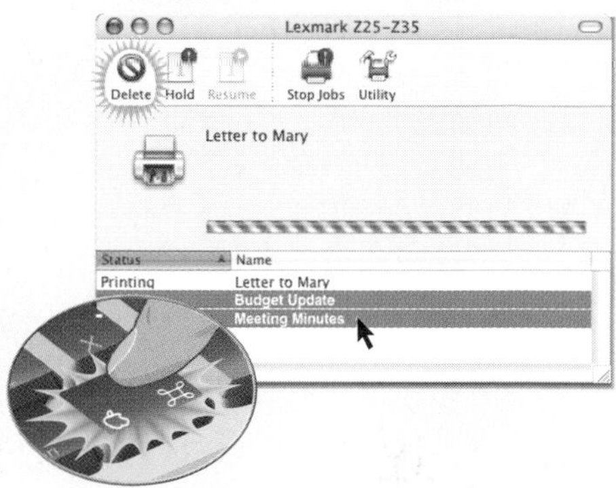

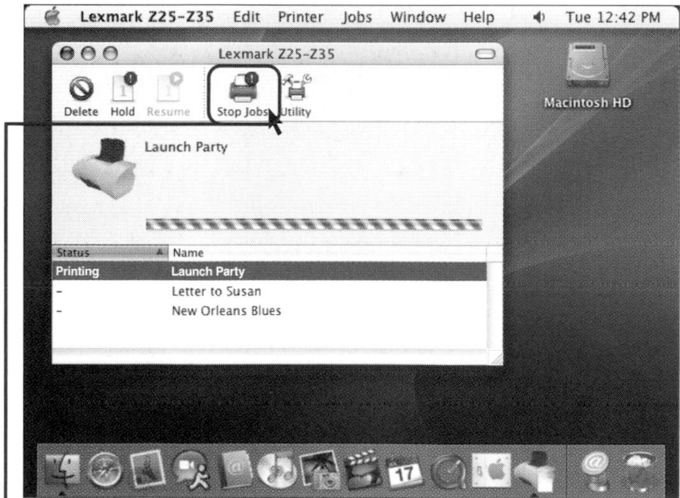

TEMPORARILY STOP ALL PRINT JOBS

1 To temporarily stop the printer from printing, click **Stop Jobs**.

Note: After you click Stop Jobs, the name of the button changes to Start Jobs and the status of the printer changes to "Jobs Stopped."

■ To resume printing, click **Start Jobs**.

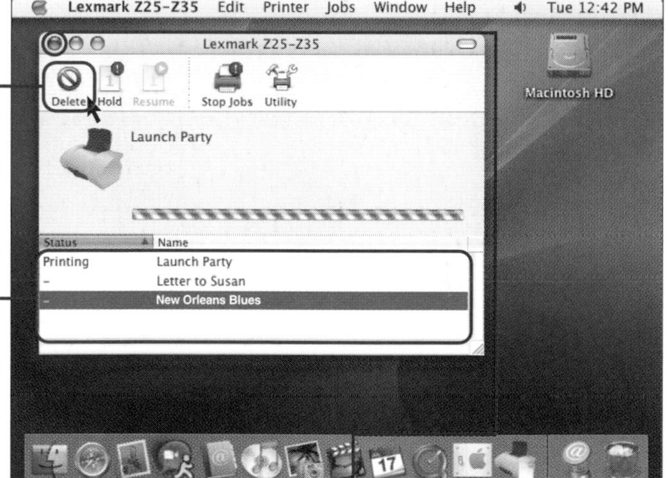

CANCEL A PRINT JOB

1 Click the name of the file you no longer want to print.

2 Click **Delete** to cancel the print job.

■ The file disappears from the window and will no longer print.

CLOSE THE PRINTER WINDOW

1 When you finish managing the files waiting to print, click ● to close the printer window.

COPY FILES TO A CD OR DVD

You can copy files, such as pictures and movies, from your computer to a recordable CD or DVD.

To copy files to a recordable CD, you need a computer with a recordable CD drive. To copy files to a recordable DVD, you need a computer with a recordable DVD drive.

If you want to copy only songs to a recordable CD, see page 158 for information on using iTunes to create a music CD.

COPY FILES TO A CD OR DVD

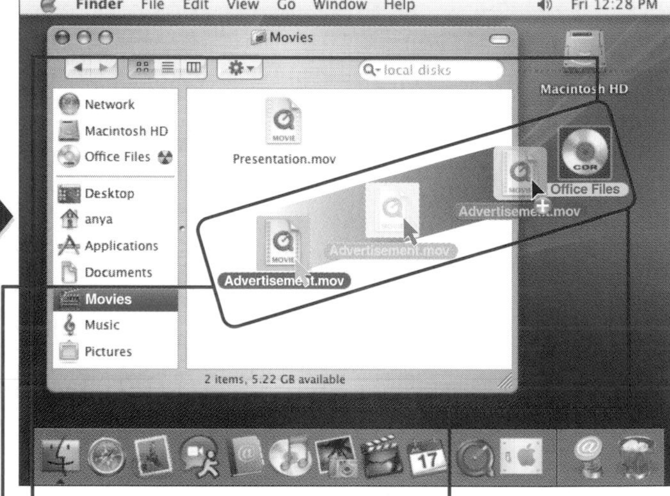

1 Insert a blank, recordable CD or DVD into your computer's recordable CD or DVD drive.

■ A dialog box appears, stating that you inserted a blank CD or DVD.

2 Type a name for the disc.

3 Click **OK** to continue.

■ An icon for the disc appears on the desktop, displaying the name you specified.

4 Position the mouse over a file you want to copy to the disc.

5 Drag the file to the disc's icon on the desktop.

6 Repeat steps **4** and **5** for each file you want to copy to the disc.

What type of disc can I copy files to?

You can copy files to a CD-R (Compact Disc-Recordable) or DVD-R (Digital Versatile Disc-Recordable). You can copy files to a CD-R or DVD-R only once. After you copy files to a CD-R or DVD-R, you cannot erase or change the contents of the disc.

If your computer has a CD-RW drive, you can also copy files to a CD-RW (Compact Disc-ReWritable). You can erase the contents of a CD-RW in order to copy new files to the disc.

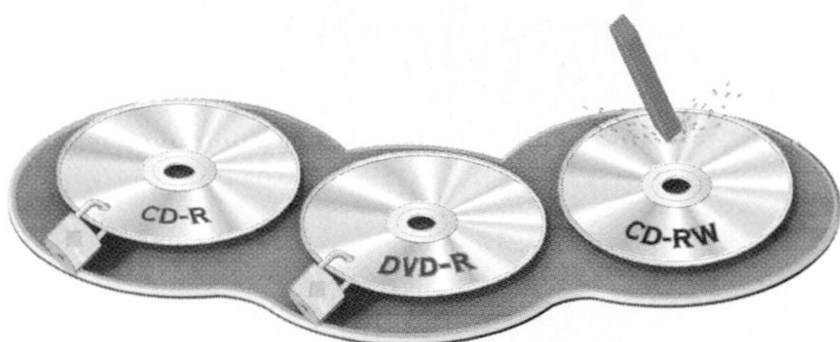

Why would I copy files to a recordable CD or DVD?

You can copy files to a recordable CD or DVD to transfer large amounts of information between computers. You can also copy important files stored on your computer to a CD or DVD in case you accidentally erase the files or your computer fails.

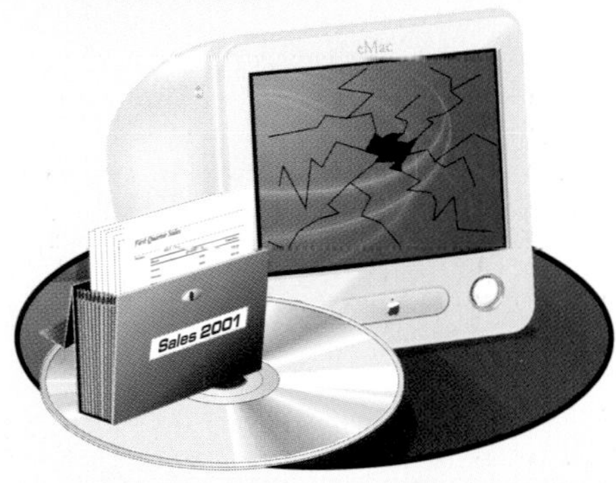

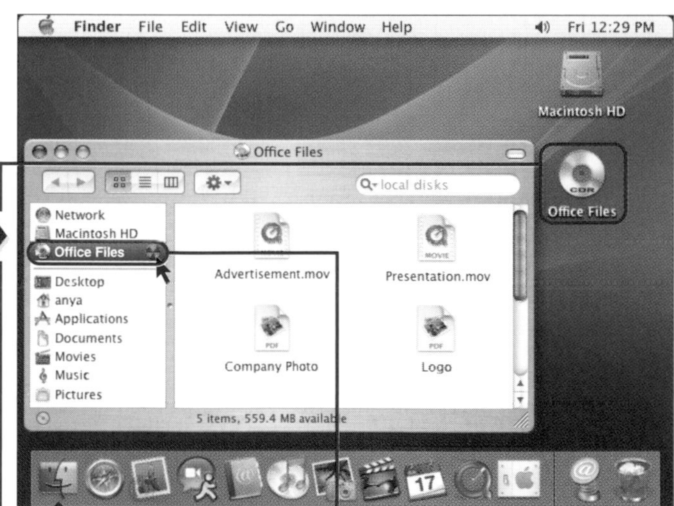

7 To display the files you selected to copy to the disc, double-click the disc's icon.

■ A window appears, displaying the files you selected to copy to the disc.

Note: If the window displays a file you no longer want to copy to the disc, drag the file to the Trash icon in the Dock to no longer copy the file.

■ The name of the disc appears in this area.

8 To copy the files to the disc, click .

■ A dialog box appears, confirming that you want to burn the disc.

9 Click **Burn** to copy the files to the disc.

■ The Burn dialog box is displayed on your screen until the copy is complete.

10 When the copy is complete, you can drag the disc's icon to the Trash icon in the Dock to eject the disc.

ERASE A CD-RW DISC

If a CD-RW (CD-ReWritable) disc contains information, you may need to erase the disc before you can copy new information to the disc.

Before erasing a CD-RW disc, make sure the disc does not contain information you want to keep. Erasing a CD-RW disc will permanently remove all the information from the disc.

ERASE A CD-RW DISC

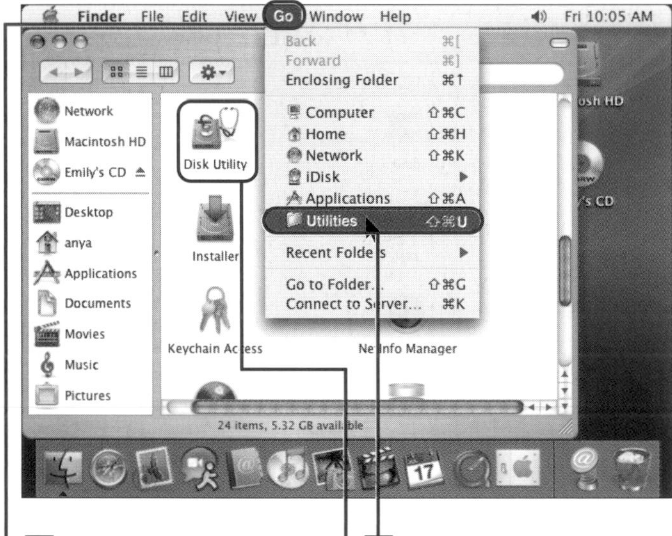

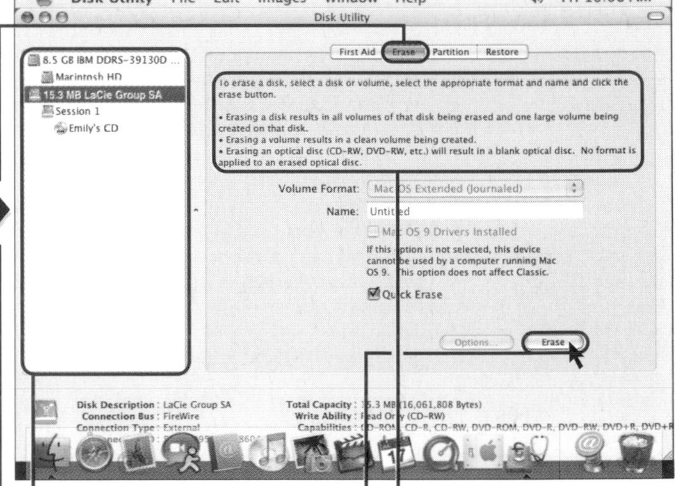

1 Insert the disc you want to erase into your computer's CD drive.

2 Click **Go**.

Note: If Go is not displayed, click a blank area on your desktop to display the Finder menu bar.

3 Click **Utilities** to view the utilities available on your computer.

■ The Utilities window appears.

4 Double-click **Disk Utility** to start Disk Utility.

5 Click the drive containing the disc you want to erase.

6 Click the **Erase** tab.

■ This area displays information about erasing a disk.

7 Click **Erase** to erase the contents of the disc in the drive you selected.

Is there a limit to the number of times I can re-use a CD-RW disc?

Some CD-RW discs may no longer be able to store information after being erased many times. You should check the information that came with your disc to find out how many times you can safely erase and re-use the disc.

Can I erase a DVD-RW disc?

Yes. If your computer has a DVD-RW drive, you can perform the steps below to erase a DVD-RW disc to prepare the disc for storing new information. Before erasing a DVD-RW disc, make sure the disc does not contain information you want to keep.

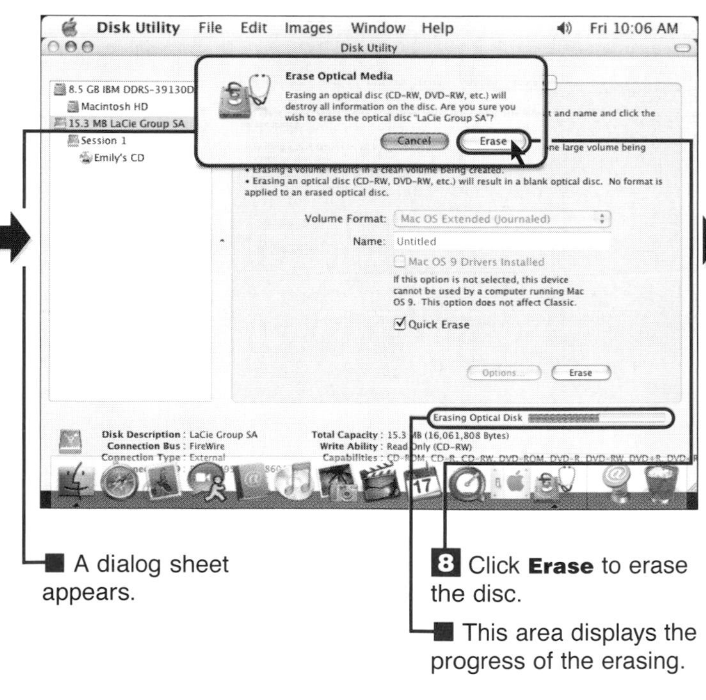

■ A dialog sheet appears.

8 Click **Erase** to erase the disc.

■ This area displays the progress of the erasing.

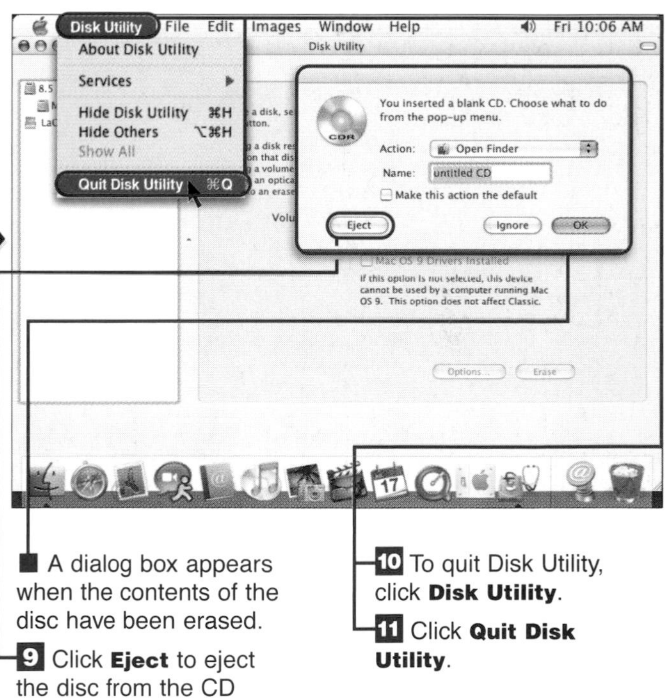

■ A dialog box appears when the contents of the disc have been erased.

9 Click **Eject** to eject the disc from the CD drive.

10 To quit Disk Utility, click **Disk Utility**.

11 Click **Quit Disk Utility**.

SEND A FAX

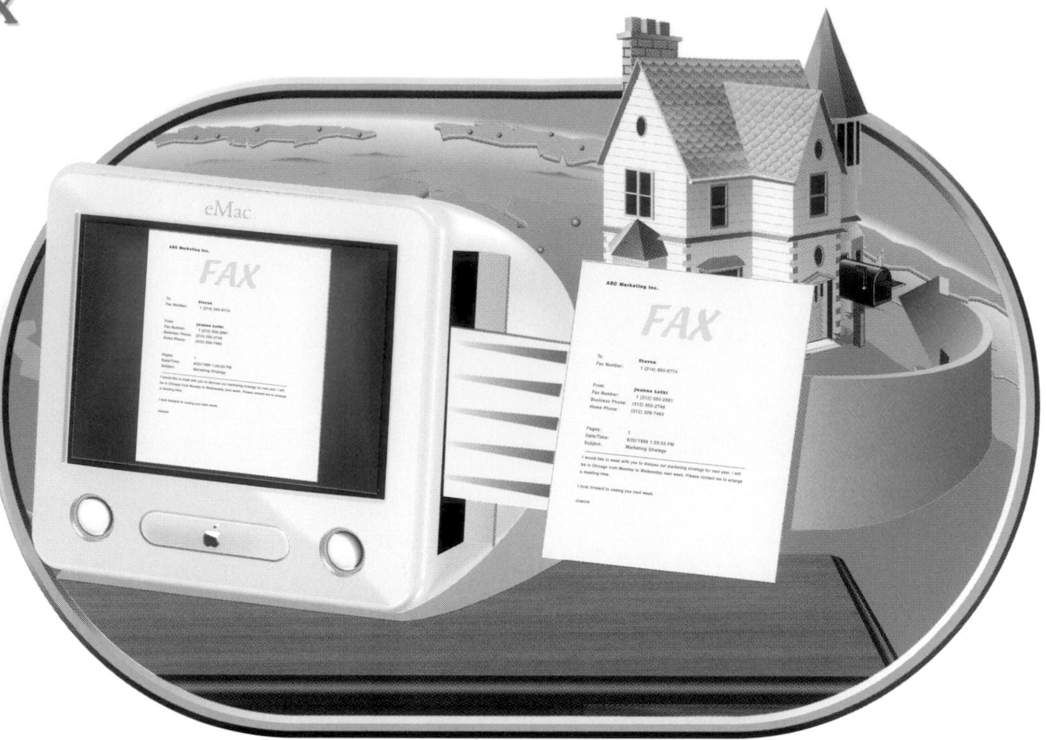

You can send a fax directly from your computer to a person across the city or around the world.

You can send a fax from most applications that allow you to print. For example, you can fax a text document using TextEdit or fax a picture using Preview.

You must have a fax device, such as a fax modem, installed on your computer to send faxes.

SEND A FAX

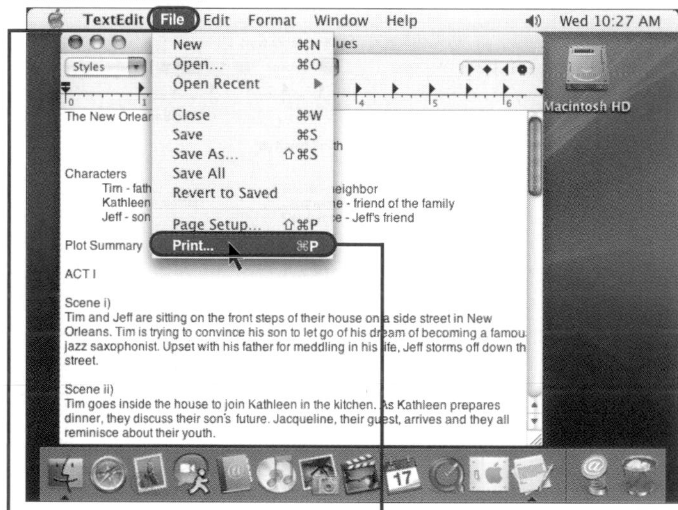

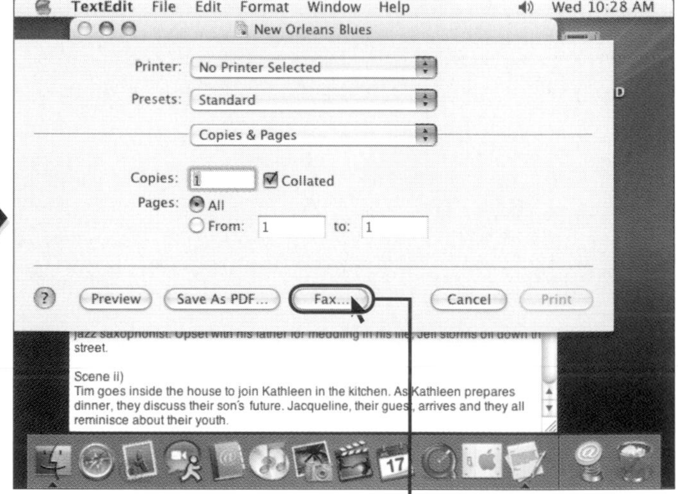

1 Open the file you want to fax. To open a file, see page 38.

2 Click **File**.

3 Click **Print**.

Note: The name of the Print command depends on the active application.

■ A dialog sheet appears.

4 Click **Fax** to fax the file to another person.

Can I view the status of the fax while it is being sent?

A fax machine icon appears in the Dock while Mac OS is sending a fax. The fax machine icon disappears when the fax has been sent. You can click the fax machine icon in the Dock to open a window that displays information about the status of the fax.

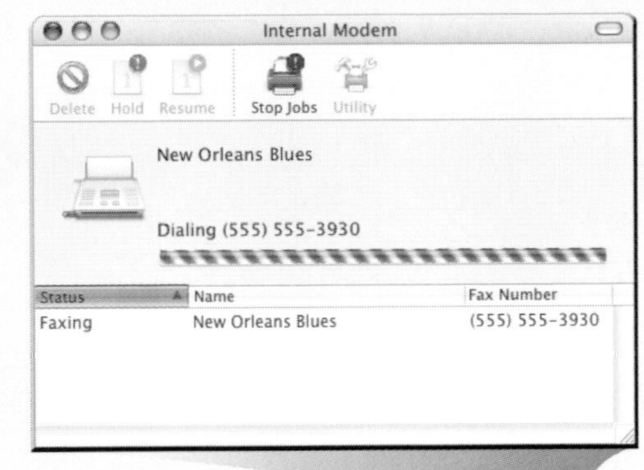

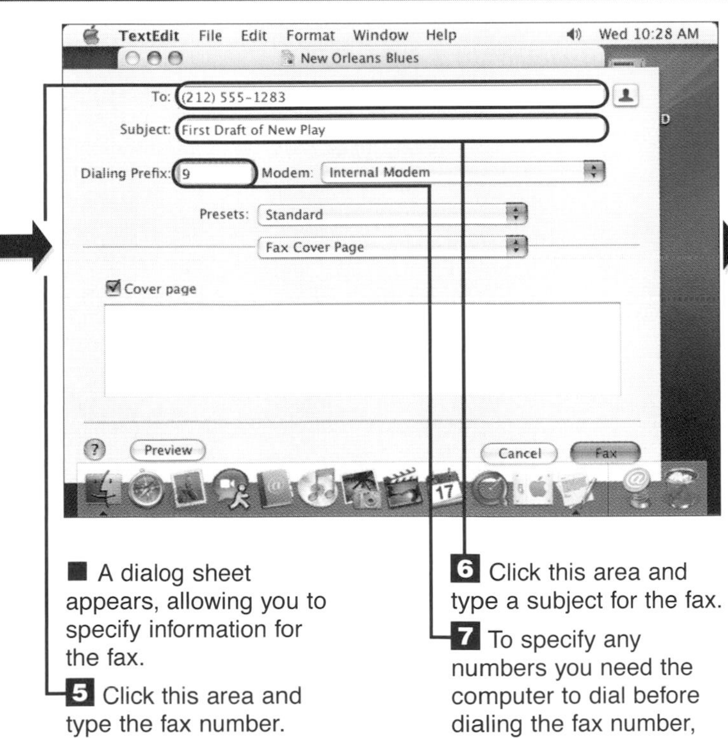

■ A dialog sheet appears, allowing you to specify information for the fax.

5 Click this area and type the fax number.

6 Click this area and type a subject for the fax.

7 To specify any numbers you need the computer to dial before dialing the fax number, click this area and type the numbers.

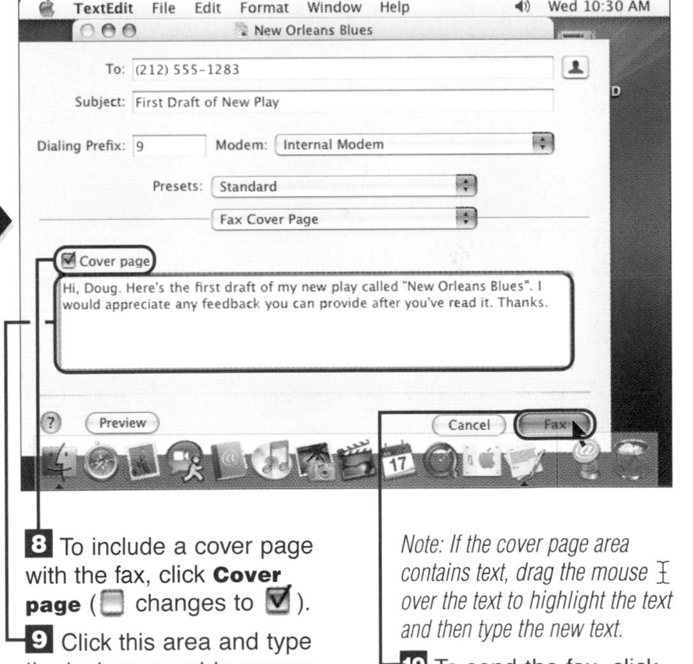

8 To include a cover page with the fax, click **Cover page** (☐ changes to ☑).

9 Click this area and type the text you want to appear on the cover page you include with the fax.

Note: If the cover page area contains text, drag the mouse I over the text to highlight the text and then type the new text.

10 To send the fax, click **Fax**.

SET UP YOUR COMPUTER TO RECEIVE FAXES

Before you can receive faxes on your computer, you must set up your computer to receive faxes.

You must have an administrator account to set up your computer to receive faxes.

You must have a fax device, such as a fax modem, installed on your computer to receive faxes.

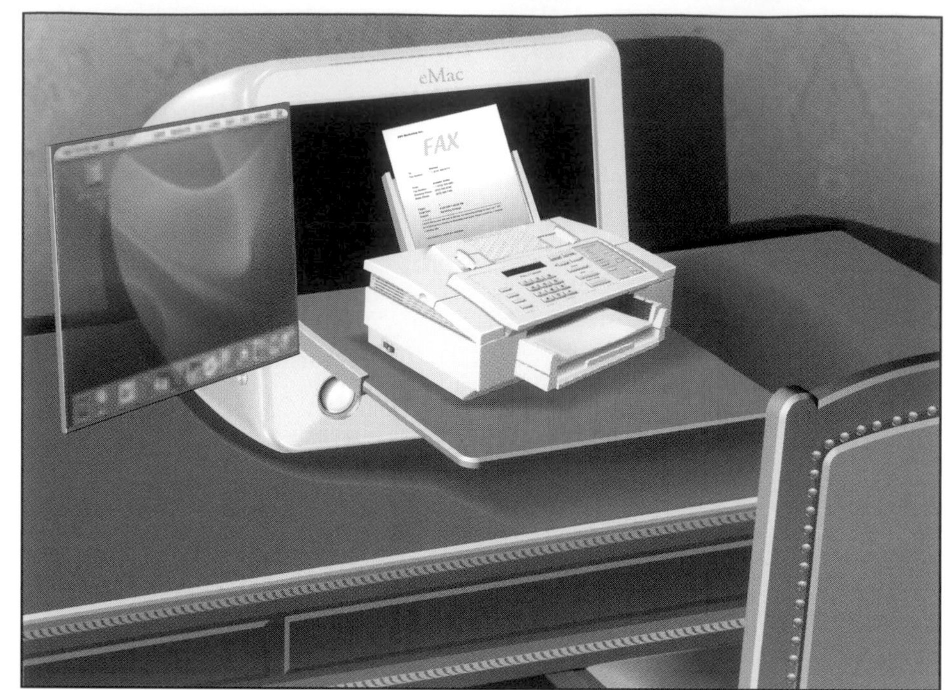

SET UP YOUR COMPUTER TO RECEIVE FAXES

1 Click the System Preferences icon to access your system preferences.

■ The System Preferences window appears.

2 Click **Print & Fax** to change your fax settings.

■ The Print & Fax window appears.

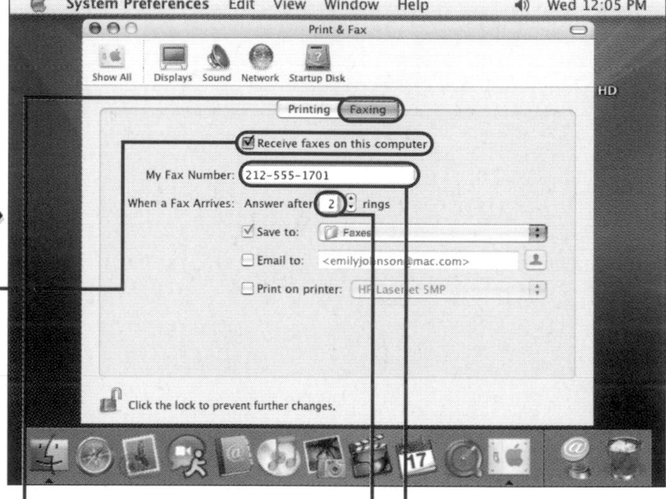

3 Click the **Faxing** tab.

4 Click this option to enable your computer to receive faxes (☐ changes to ☑).

5 Click this area and type your fax number.

6 To change the number of rings before the computer will answer a fax, double-click this area and type a new number.

How can I view and work with faxes I receive?

To display the faxes you have received, you must display the contents of the folder that stores the faxes. By default, faxes you receive are stored in the Shared Faxes folder.

To view the contents of the Shared Faxes folder, display the contents of your Users folder (see page 24). Double-click the Shared folder and then double-click the Faxes folder.

To view a fax you have received, double-click the fax. The Preview window opens, displaying the contents of the fax. For more information on using Preview to view documents, see page 112.

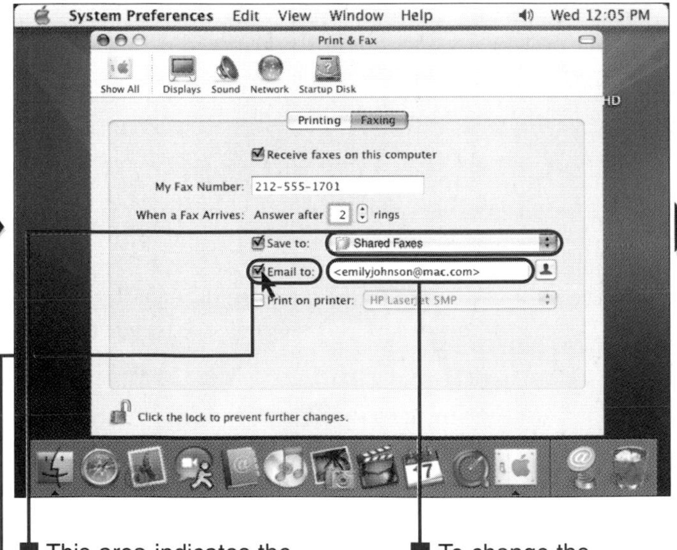

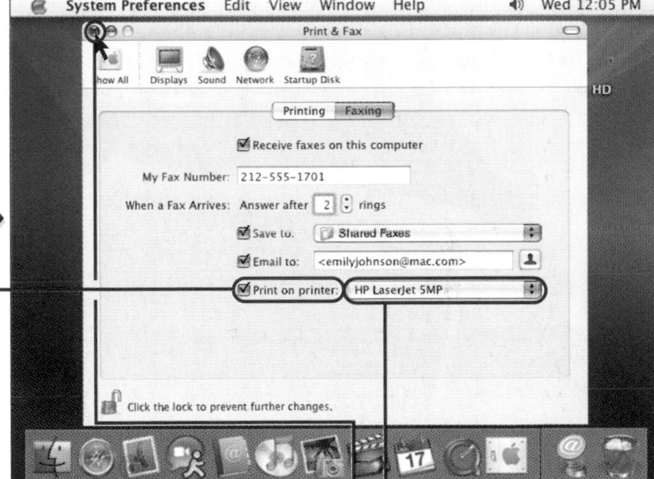

■ This area indicates the folder where faxes you receive will be saved. You can click this area to select a different folder.

7 To have your computer e-mail a copy of each fax you receive, click this option (☐ changes to ☑).

■ To change the e-mail address faxes will be sent to, drag the mouse Ⅰ over the text in this area to highlight the text and then type the new e-mail address.

8 To have your computer print a copy of each fax you receive, click this option (☐ changes to ☑).

■ This area displays the printer faxes will be printed on. You can click this area to select a different printer.

9 To quit System Preferences, click .

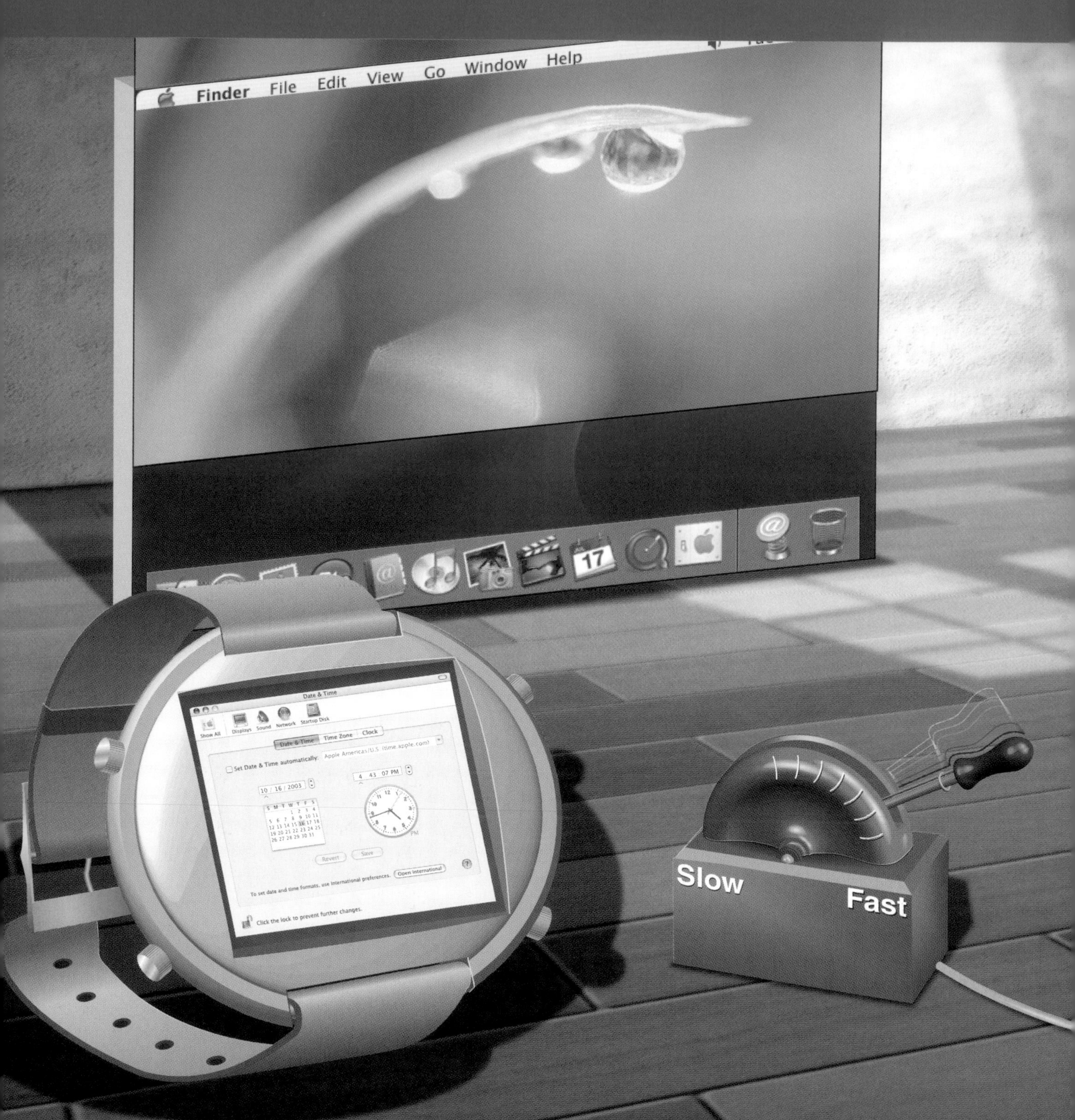
Finder File Edit View Go Window Help
17
Date & Time
Show All
Displays
Sound
Network
Startup Disk
Date & Time
Time Zone
Clock
Set Date & Time automatically:
Revert
Save
Open International
To set date and time formats, use International preferences.
Click the lock to prevent further changes.
Slow
Fast

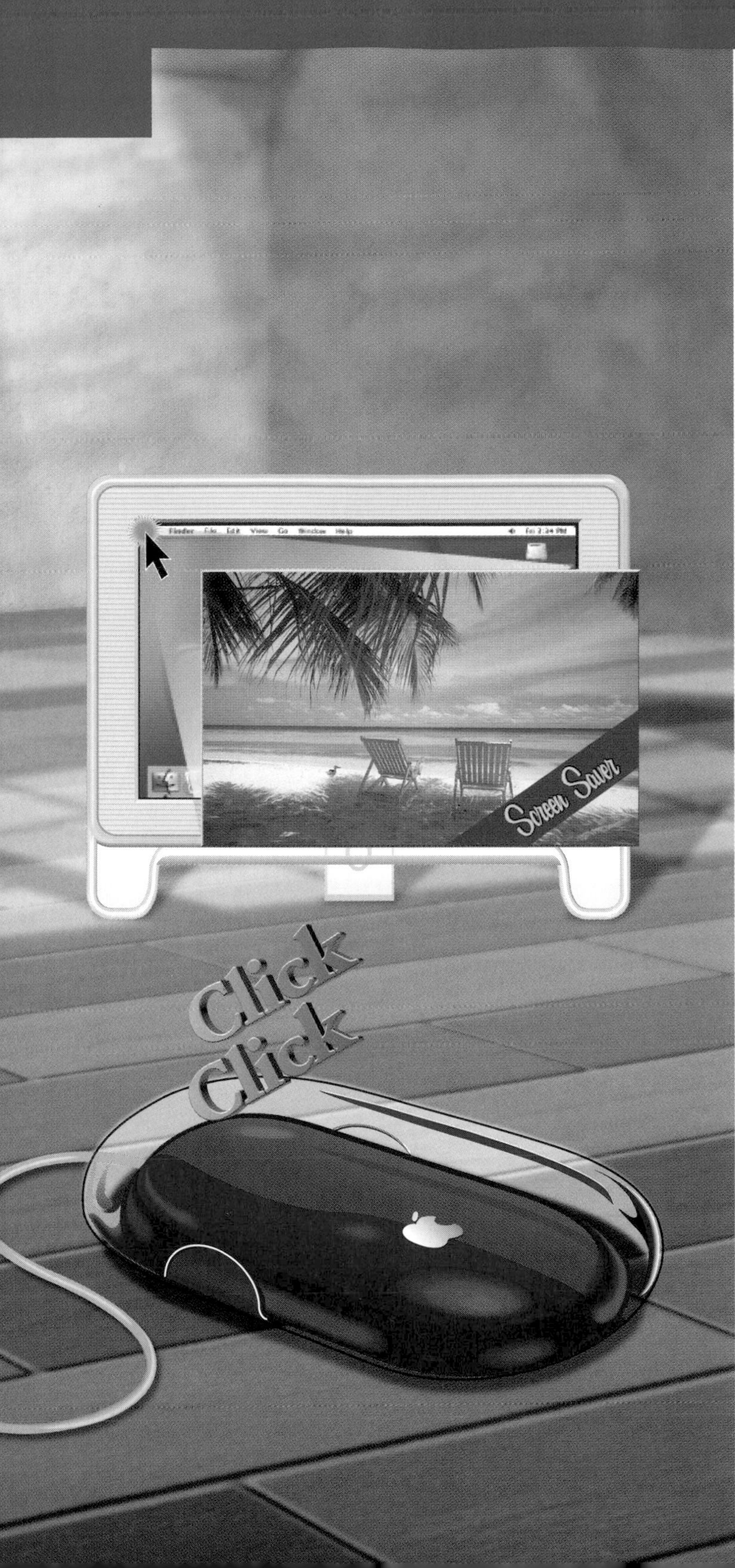

CHAPTER 4

Customize Your Computer

In this chapter, you will learn how to customize your computer by changing the screen saver, desktop picture and mouse settings. You will also learn how to turn on speech recognition so you can use spoken commands to perform tasks on your computer.

ADD OR REMOVE ICONS FROM THE DOCK

You can customize the Dock to include icons for the applications, folders and files you use most often. Adding icons to the Dock gives you quick access to these items at any time.

You can also remove icons for applications, folders and files that you do not frequently use. This helps reduce clutter in the Dock.

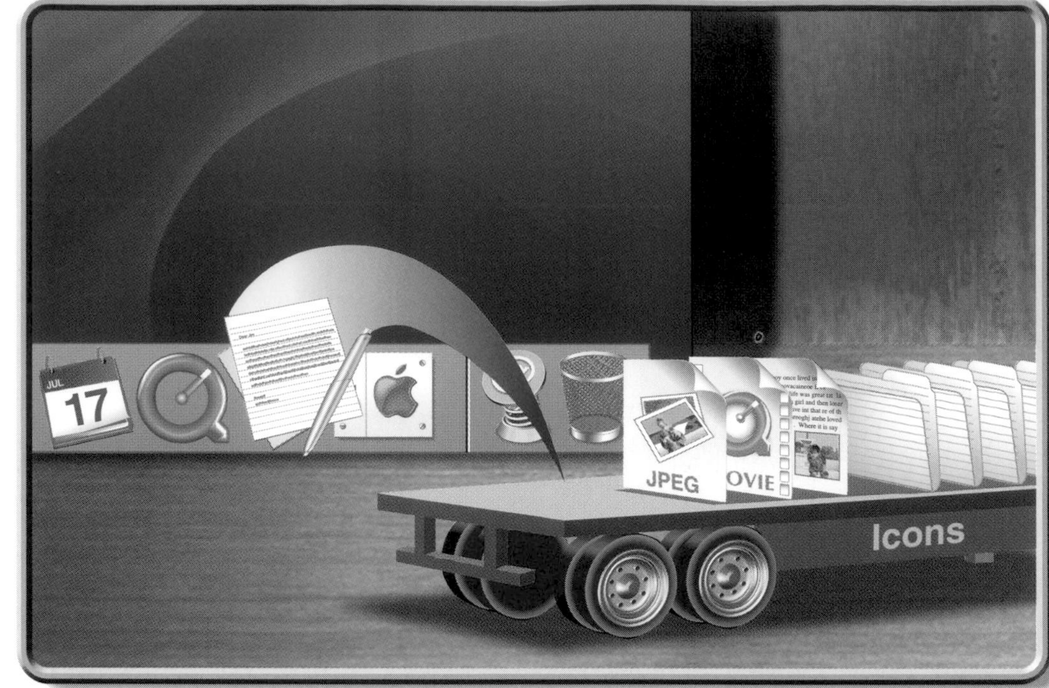

ADD AN ICON TO THE DOCK

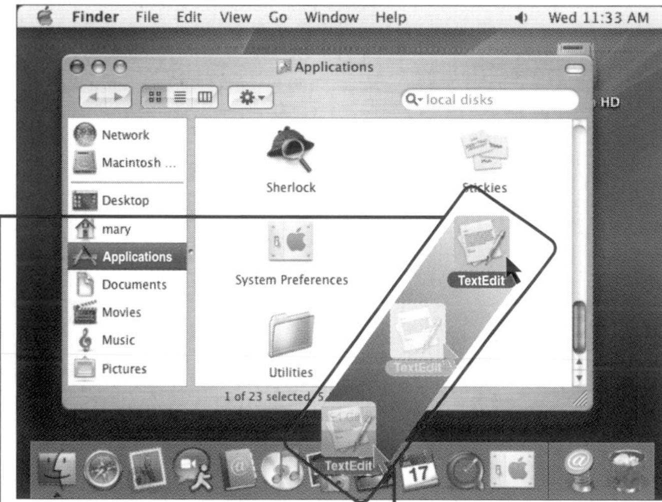

1 Locate the application, folder or file you want to add to the Dock.

2 Position the mouse over the icon for the application, folder or file.

3 Drag the icon to the Dock.

Note: Drag applications to the left of the line in the Dock. Drag folders and files to the right of the line in the Dock.

■ The icon for the application, folder or file appears in the Dock.

Note: Adding an icon to the Dock does not remove the application, folder or file from its original location on your computer.

■ To open an application, folder or file displayed in the Dock, click its icon in the Dock.

Where can I find applications that I can add to the Dock?

You can find most of the applications available on your computer in the Applications folder.

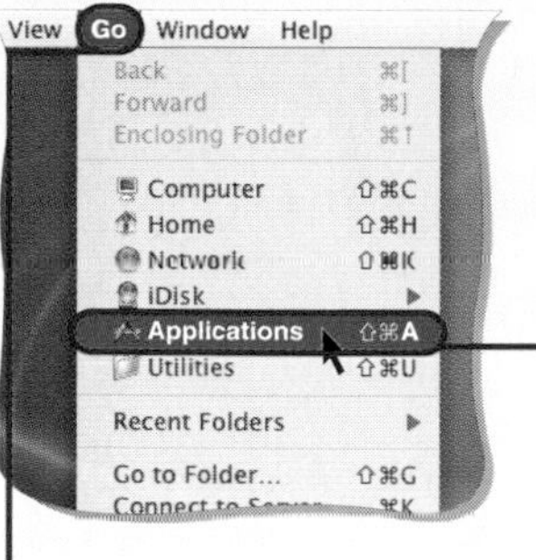

Note: If Go is not available, click a blank area on your desktop to display the Finder menu bar.

2 Click **Applications**.

1 To display the contents of the Applications folder, click **Go**.

How do I move an icon to a different location in the Dock?

To move an icon in the Dock, position the mouse over the icon and then drag the icon to a new location. The other icons in the Dock will move to make room for the icon. You cannot move the Finder or Trash icon. You also cannot move icons across the line in the Dock.

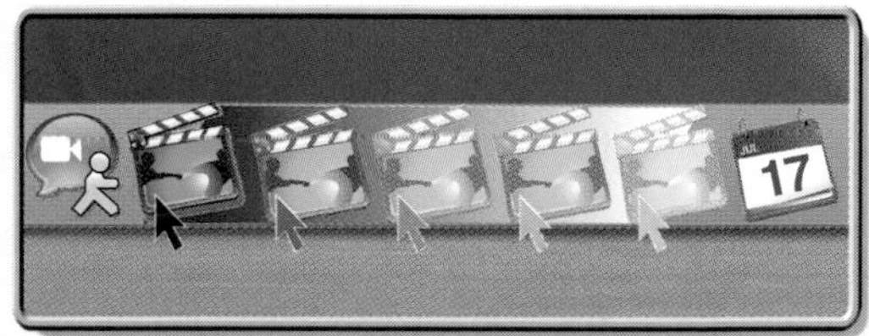

REMOVE AN ICON FROM THE DOCK

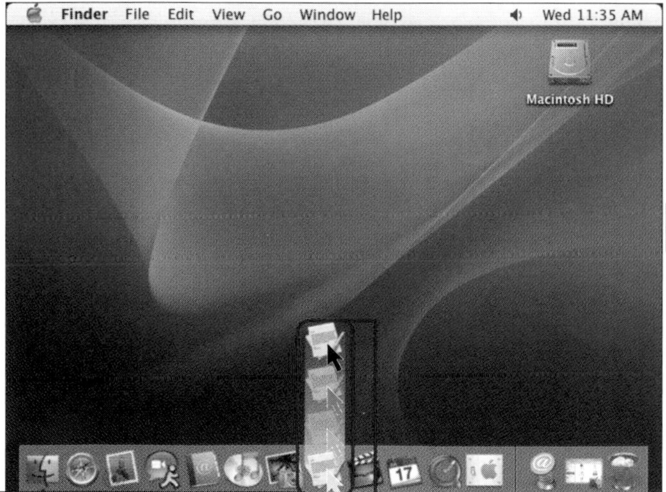

1 Position the mouse over the icon you want to remove from the Dock.

2 Drag the icon out of the Dock.

Note: You cannot remove the Finder ( ) or Trash ( ) icon from the Dock.

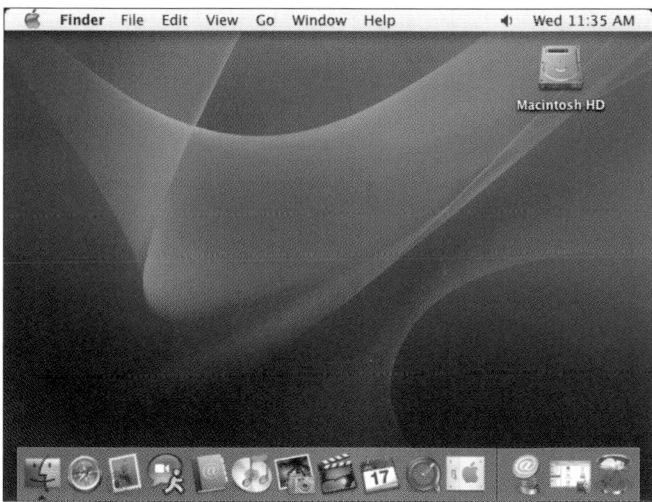

■ The icon disappears from the Dock in a puff of smoke.

■ When you remove the icon for an open application, the icon will not disappear from the Dock until you quit the application.

Note: Removing an icon from the Dock does not remove the application, folder or file from your computer.

CUSTOMIZE THE DOCK

You can change the appearance of the Dock and the way the Dock functions.

For example, you can change the size of the Dock and stop application icons in the Dock from bouncing when you click the icons.

CUSTOMIZE THE DOCK

1 Click the System Preferences icon to access your system preferences.

■ The System Preferences window appears.

2 Click **Dock** to customize the Dock.

■ The Dock window appears.

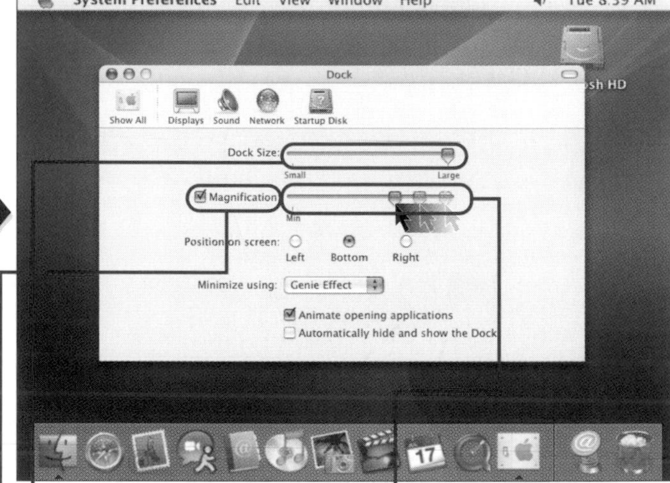

3 To decrease or increase the size of the Dock, drag this slider (▽) left or right.

4 This option magnifies icons in the Dock when you position the mouse ↖ over the icons. You can click the option to turn the option on (☑) or off (☐).

5 To decrease or increase the amount of magnification that will be used, drag this slider (▽) left or right.

Why would I use the Magnification option when customizing the Dock?

If you decrease the size of the Dock, you can use the Magnification option to magnify icons in the Dock when you position the mouse over the icons. This will allow you to clearly view an icon you are about to select in the Dock.

When the Dock is hidden, how do I redisplay the Dock?

To redisplay the Dock, position the mouse over the edge of your screen where the Dock last appeared. When you move the mouse away from the Dock, the Dock will disappear again.

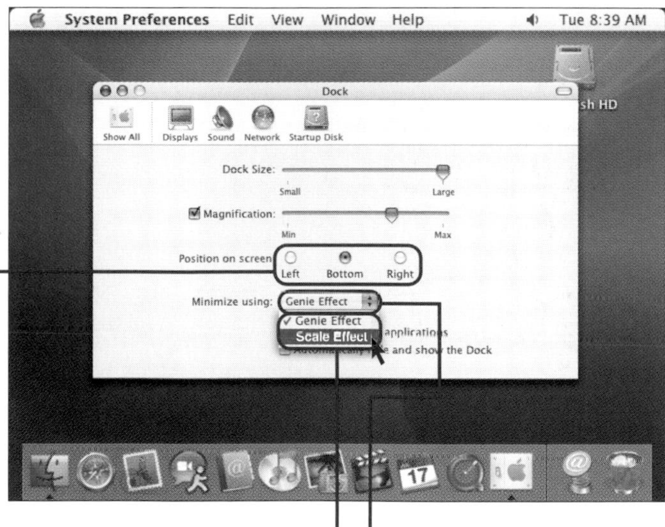

6 Click an option to position the Dock on the left side, bottom or right side of your screen (○ changes to ◉).

7 To specify the way you want windows to minimize to icons in the Dock, click this area to display the available effects.

8 Click the effect you want to use.

Note: To minimize a window to an icon in the Dock, see page 14.

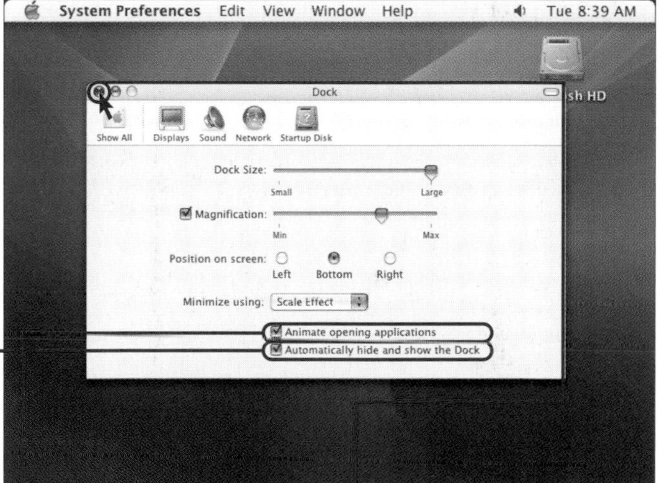

9 This option makes an application's icon in the Dock bounce when you click the icon. You can click the option to turn the option on (☑) or off (☐).

10 This option hides the Dock when you are not using the Dock. You can click the option to turn the option on (☑) or off (☐).

11 To quit System Preferences, click .

CHANGE THE SCREEN SAVER

A screen saver is a picture or pattern that automatically appears on the screen when you do not use your computer for a period of time.

You can use a screen saver to hide your work while you are away from your desk.

By default, a screen saver will appear on your screen when you do not use your computer for 20 minutes.

CHANGE THE SCREEN SAVER

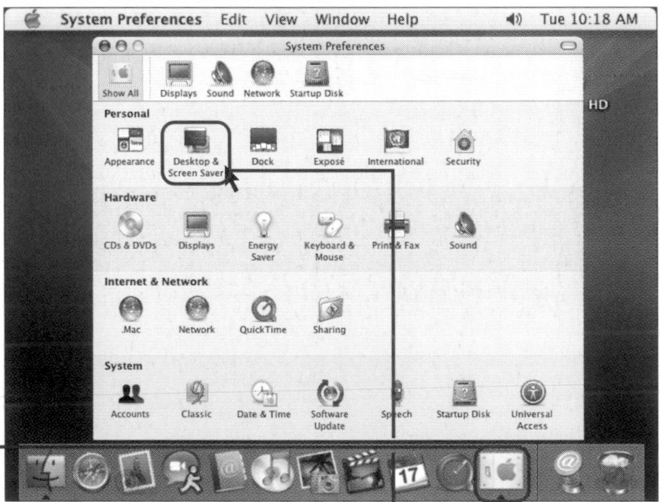

1 Click the System Preferences icon to access your system preferences.

■ The System Preferences window appears.

2 Click **Desktop & Screen Saver** to change your screen saver.

■ The Desktop & Screen Saver window appears.

3 Click the **Screen Saver** tab.

4 Click the screen saver you want to use.

■ This area displays a preview of the screen saver.

5 To specify the number of minutes your computer must be inactive before the screen saver will start, drag this slider (⬟) to the desired number of minutes.

*Note: If you never want the screen saver to start, drag the slider to **Never**.*

What are the .Mac and Pictures Folder screen savers?

The .Mac screen saver allows you to display a slide show published on the Internet by a .Mac member. You can click **Options** to specify the .Mac membership name of the person who published the slide show you want to use.

The Pictures Folder screen saver displays a slide show of the pictures in your Pictures folder. You can click **Choose Folder** to specify a different folder containing pictures you want to use.

Can I use a random screen saver?

Yes. You can have your computer automatically pick a screen saver for you each time the screen saver appears. Perform steps **1** to **3** below and then click **Use random screen saver** (☐ changes to ☑). Then perform step **10**.

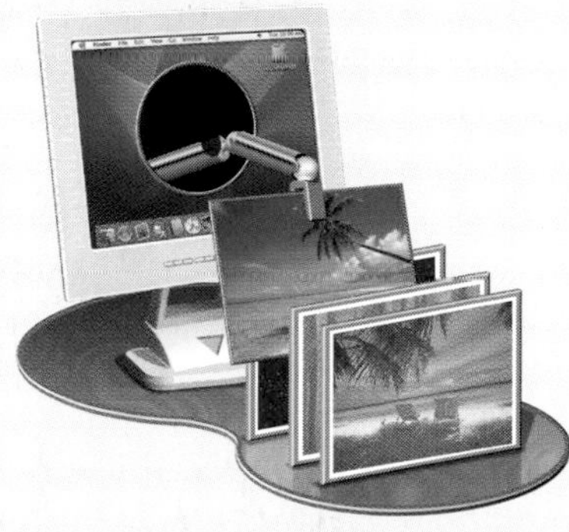

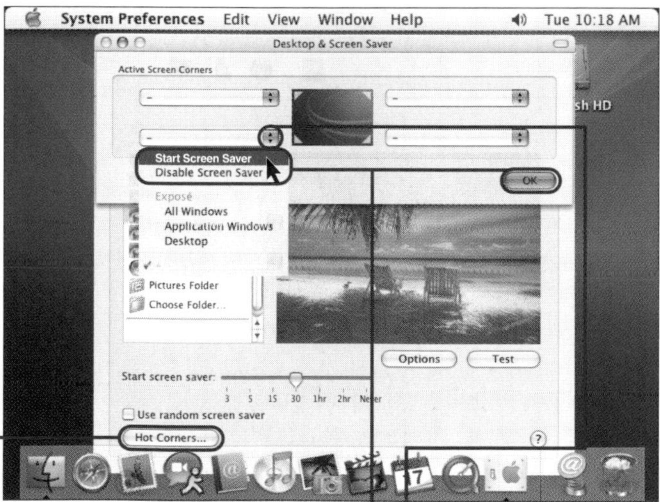

6 To create a hot corner on your screen that will start or turn off the screen saver when you position the mouse over the corner, click **Hot Corners**.

■ A dialog sheet appears.

7 Click beside the corner you want to make a hot corner.

8 Click an option to specify if you want the hot corner to start or disable the screen saver.

9 Click **OK** to save your changes.

10 To quit System Preferences, click ●.

■ The screen saver appears when you do not use your computer for the number of minutes you specified.

■ You can move the mouse or press a key on the keyboard to remove the screen saver from your screen.

CHANGE THE DESKTOP PICTURE

You can change the picture used to decorate your desktop.

Mac OS comes with several collections of pictures that you can choose from, including background images, nature pictures, abstract pictures and solid colors.

You can also use your own pictures on the desktop by selecting a picture from your Pictures folder.

CHANGE THE DESKTOP PICTURE

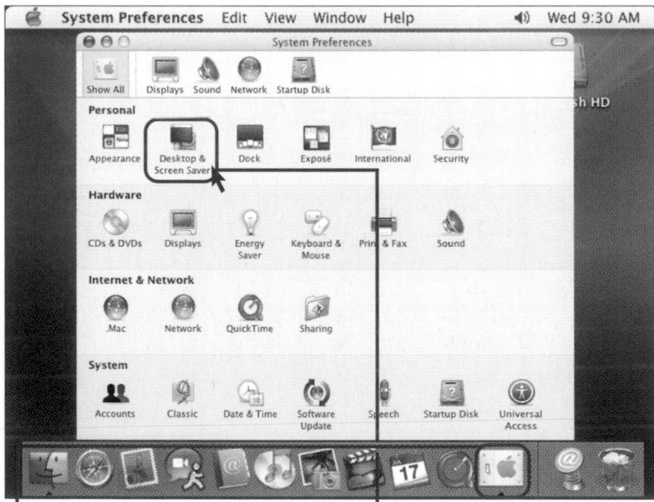

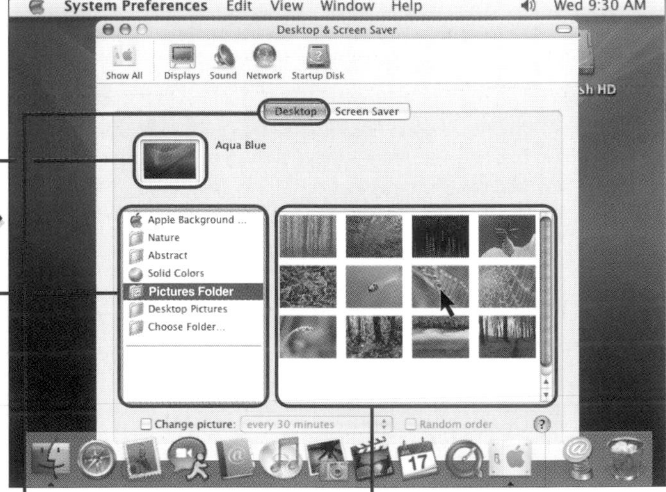

1 Click the System Preferences icon to access your system preferences.

■ The System Preferences window appears.

2 Click **Desktop & Screen Saver** to set up a screen saver.

■ The Desktop & Screen Saver window appears.

3 Click the **Desktop** tab.

■ This area displays the picture currently displayed on your desktop.

4 Click a collection of pictures of interest.

■ This area displays the pictures that are available in the collection you selected.

5 Click the picture you want to display on your desktop.

How can I display a picture from the Pictures Folder collection on my desktop?

Mac OS offers four ways you can display a picture from the Pictures Folder collection on your desktop.

Fill screen Enlarges the picture to cover your entire desktop. The top and bottom edges of the picture may be cut off.	**Stretch to fill screen** Stretches the picture to cover your entire desktop.	**Center** Displays the picture in the middle of your desktop.	**Tile** Repeats the picture until it fills your entire desktop.

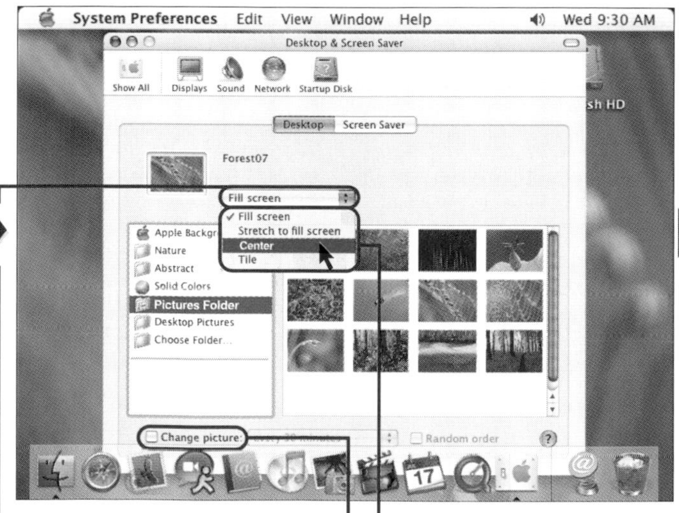

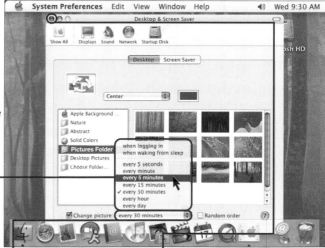

■ The picture you selected appears on your desktop.

6 If you selected a picture from the Pictures Folder collection, click this area to specify how you want to display the picture on your desktop.

7 Click the way you want to display the picture.

8 To have Mac OS automatically change the desktop picture to other pictures in the same collection, click this option (☐ changes to ☑).

9 To specify how often you want to display a new picture, click this area.

10 Click the option you want to use.

11 To quit System Preferences, click ●.

■ To return to the original desktop picture, repeat steps **1** to **11**, selecting **Apple Background Images** in step **4** and **Aqua Blue** in step **5**.

CHANGE THE DISPLAY SETTINGS

You can change the way information appears on your screen.

Resolution

Determines the amount of information displayed on your screen. A higher resolution displays more information on your screen at once.

Colors

Determines the number of colors displayed on your screen.

Refresh Rate

Determines how often the screen is redrawn. A higher refresh rate reduces screen flicker and eyestrain.

CHANGE THE DISPLAY SETTINGS

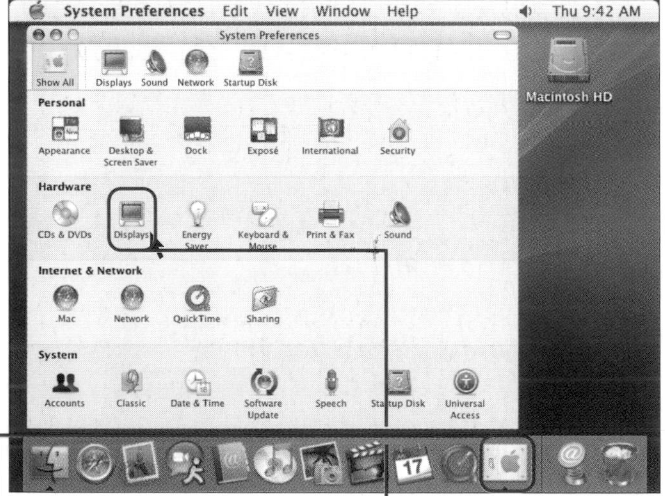

1 Click the System Preferences icon to access your system preferences.

■ The System Preferences window appears.

2 Click **Displays** to change your display settings.

■ A window appears, allowing you to change your display settings.

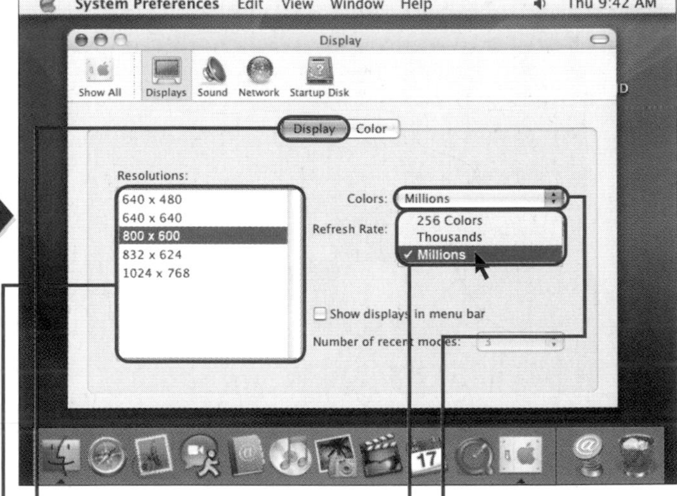

3 Click the **Display** tab.

4 Click the resolution you want to use.

Note: A dialog box may appear. Click ***OK*** *to continue. If a confirmation dialog box appears, click* ***Revert*** *or* ***Confirm*** *to specify if you want to use the new resolution.*

5 To specify the number of colors you want your screen to display, click this area.

6 Click the number of colors you want your screen to display.

Note: The current number of colors displays a check mark (✓).

Why are my display settings different than the display settings shown below?

The available display settings depend on the monitor you are using. For example, you may have combined resolution and refresh rate settings or settings that allow you to change the contrast and brightness of your display. You may also have additional tabs, such as a Color tab that allows you to select a display profile for your monitor.

How do I change the display settings using the icon (▭) in the menu bar?

Click the icon (▭) in the menu bar to display a list of display settings, including resolution, refresh rate and color options. You can select the display setting you want to use. A check mark (✓) appears beside the currently selected display setting.

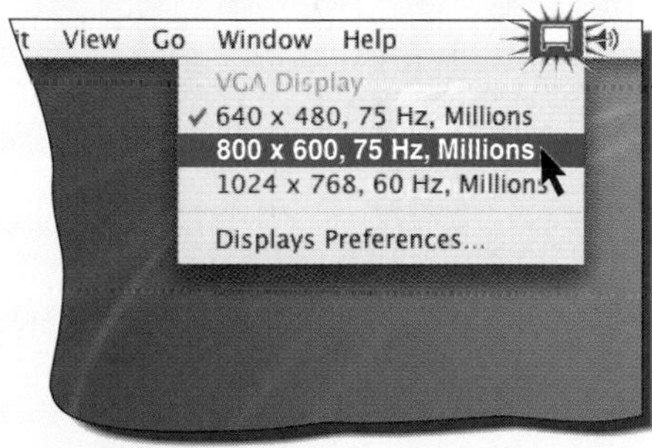

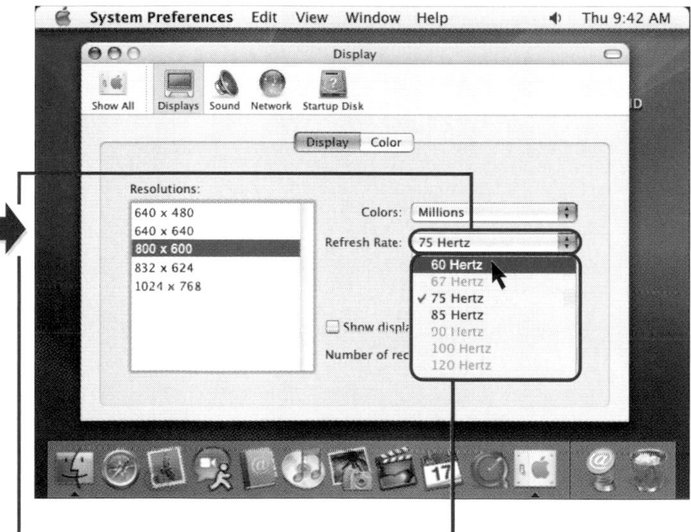

7 To specify the refresh rate you want your screen to use, click this area.

8 Click the refresh rate you want your screen to use.

Note: The current refresh rate displays a check mark (✓).

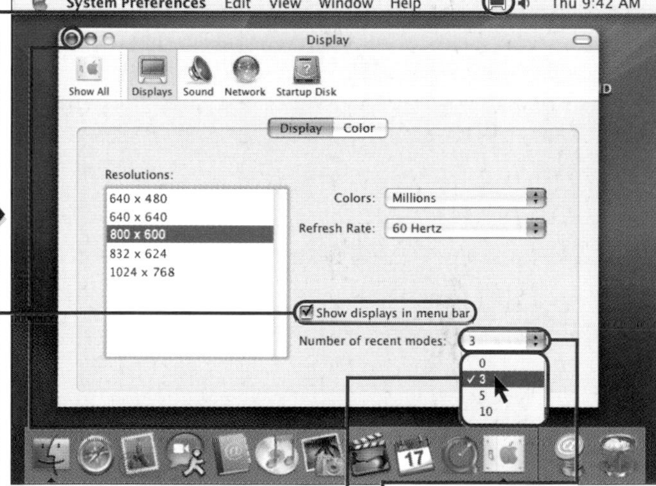

9 To be able to change the display settings using an icon (▭) in the menu bar, click this option (☐ changes to ☑).

■ An icon (▭) appears in the menu bar.

10 To specify the number of display settings you want to choose from using the icon (▭), click this area.

11 Click the number of display settings you want.

12 To quit System Preferences, click ●.

CHANGE THE ENERGY SAVING SETTINGS

You can change the energy saving settings for your computer. These settings allow you to specify how long your computer must be inactive before automatically going to sleep to conserve power.

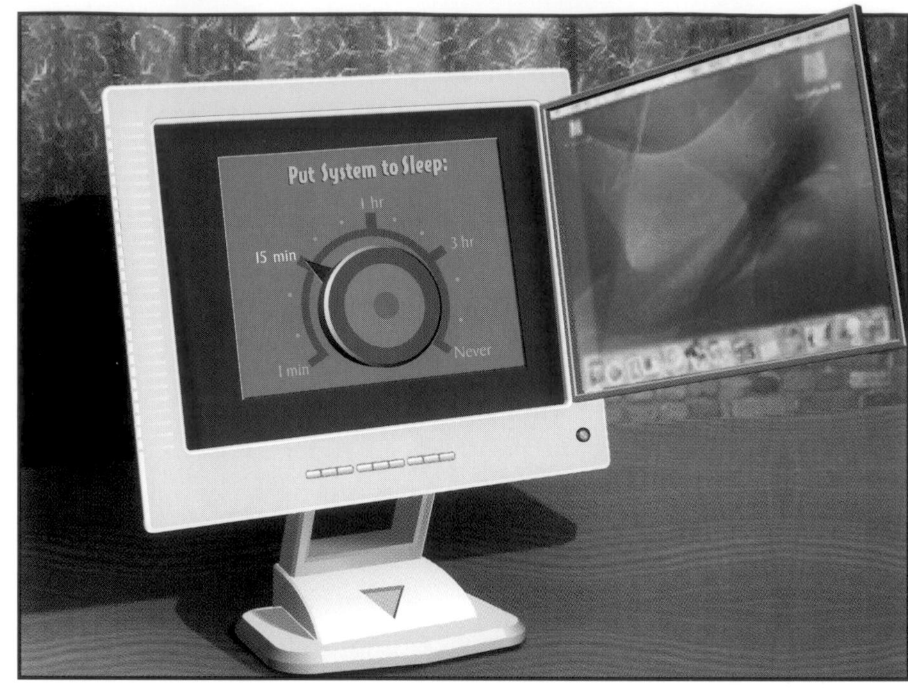

By default, your computer automatically goes to sleep when you do not use the computer for 10 minutes. When your computer goes to sleep, your screen will turn black.

CHANGE THE ENERGY SAVING SETTINGS

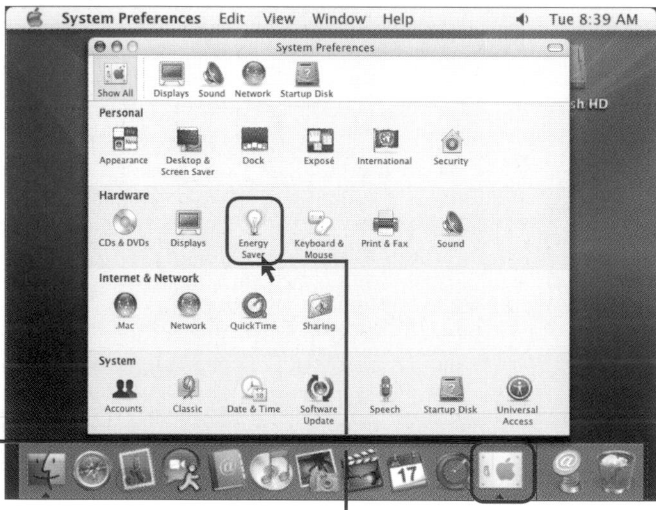

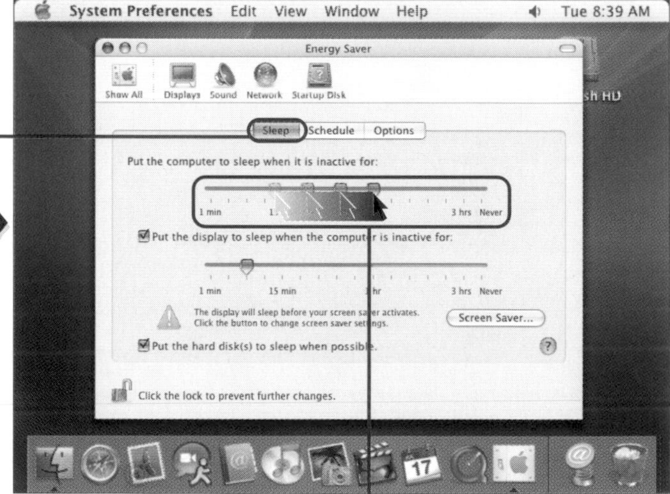

1 Click the System Preferences icon to access your system preferences.

■ The System Preferences window appears.

2 Click **Energy Saver** to change your energy saving settings.

■ The Energy Saver window appears.

3 Click the **Sleep** tab.

4 To change the amount of time your computer must be inactive before automatically going to sleep, drag this slider (▽) to a new position.

*Note: If you never want the computer to automatically go to sleep, drag the slider to **Never**.*

How can I wake a sleeping computer?

To wake a sleeping computer, move the mouse or press a key on your keyboard. When you wake the computer, any open applications and files will appear as you left them. You may have to wait several seconds for the computer to wake.

Why did this warning message appear in the Energy Saver window?

This warning message appears when you specify an amount of time in step **4** or **5** that is shorter than the amount of time your computer must be inactive before the screen saver starts. You may want to change when the screen saver starts so the screen saver will appear before your computer goes to sleep. For information on changing a screen saver, see page 72.

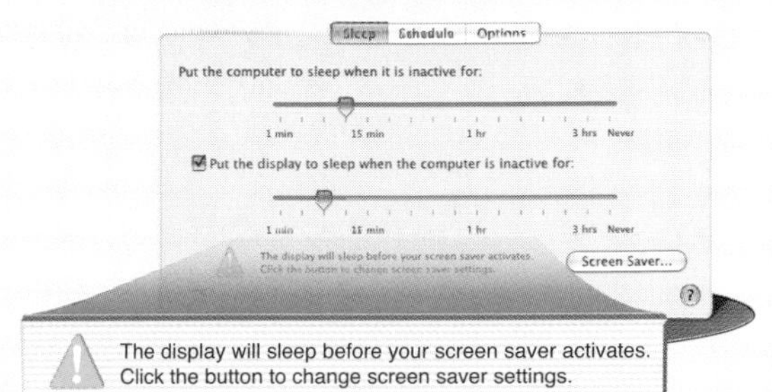

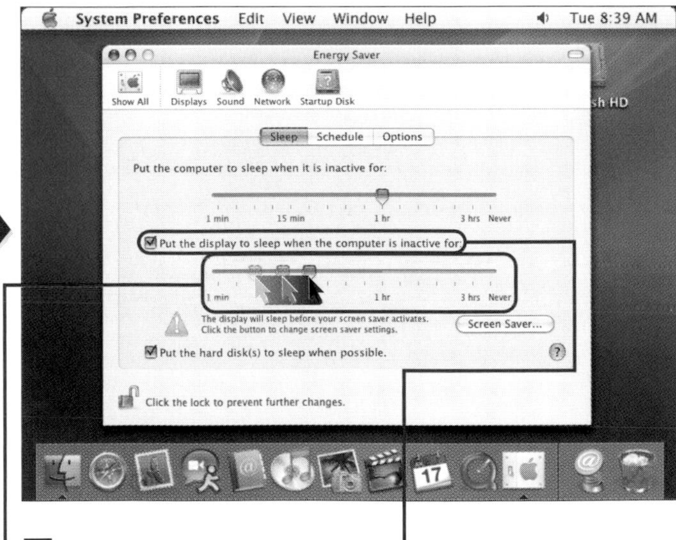

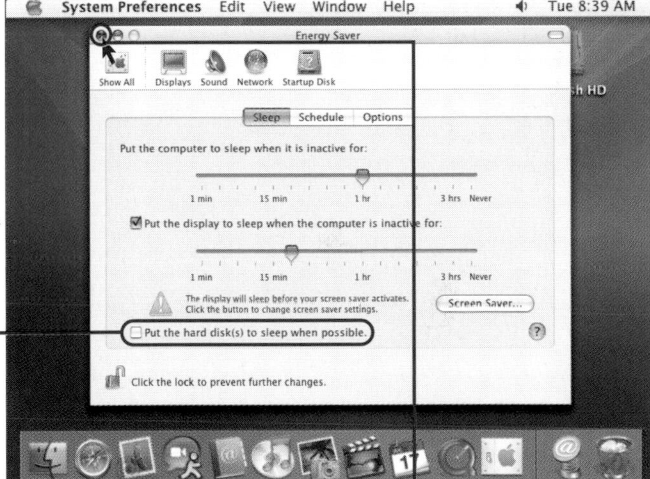

5 To change the amount of time your computer must be inactive before the display goes to sleep, drag this slider (⬇) to a new position.

*Note: You cannot specify a longer amount of time for the display than you specified for the computer in step **4**.*

■ If you do not want the display to go to sleep at a different time than the rest of the computer, click this option (☑ changes to ☐).

6 This option puts your hard disk to sleep whenever possible. You can click the option to turn the option on (☑) or off (☐).

7 To quit System Preferences, click 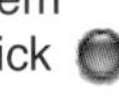.

CHANGE THE SOUND SETTINGS

You can change your computer's sound settings to suit your preferences. For example, you can change the alert sound your computer uses and adjust the volume of sound on the computer.

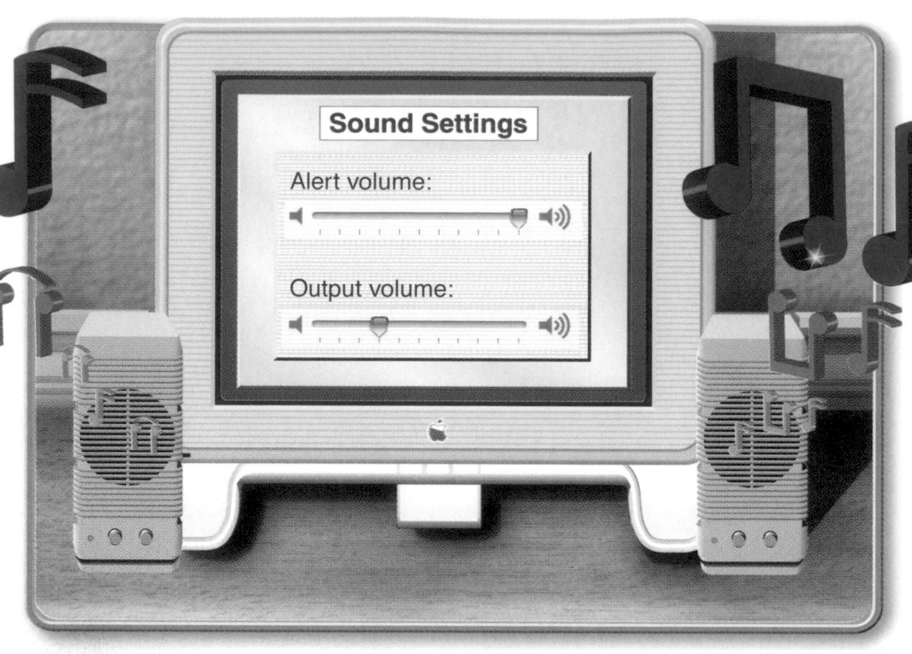

Your computer uses the alert sound to get your attention or notify you of a problem.

CHANGE THE SOUND SETTINGS

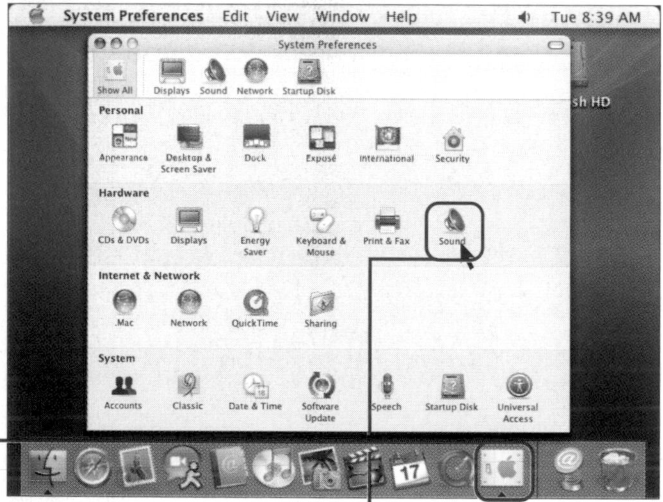

1 Click the System Preferences icon to access your system preferences.

■ The System Preferences window appears.

2 Click **Sound** to change your computer's sound settings.

■ The Sound window appears.

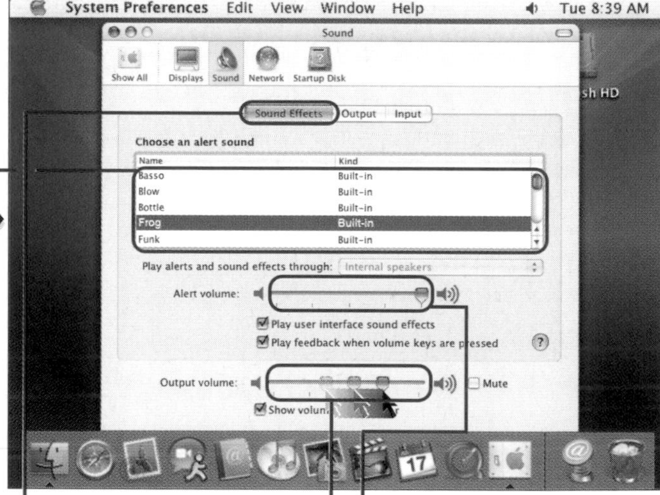

3 Click the **Sound Effects** tab.

4 Click the sound you want to use for alerts. The alert sound you selected plays.

5 To decrease or increase the alert volume, drag this slider (◘) left or right. The current alert sound plays at the new volume.

6 To decrease or increase the computer's volume, drag this slider (◘) left or right. The current alert sound plays at the new volume.

How do I change my computer's volume using the speaker icon (🔊) in the menu bar?

To change your computer's volume, click the speaker icon (🔊) in the menu bar. On the volume control bar that appears, drag the slider (●) up or down to increase or decrease your computer's volume.

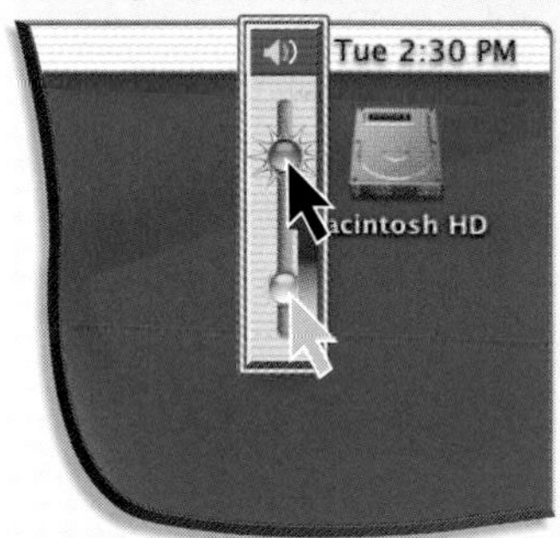

How can I turn off the sound on my computer?

To turn off the sound on your computer, perform steps **1** and **2** below to display the Sound window. Click **Mute** to turn off the sound on your computer (☐ changes to ☑). To once again turn on the sound, click **Mute** again (☑ changes to ☐).

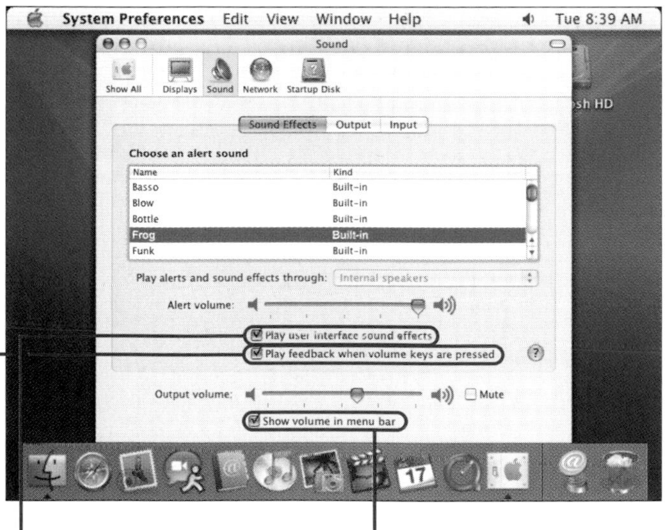

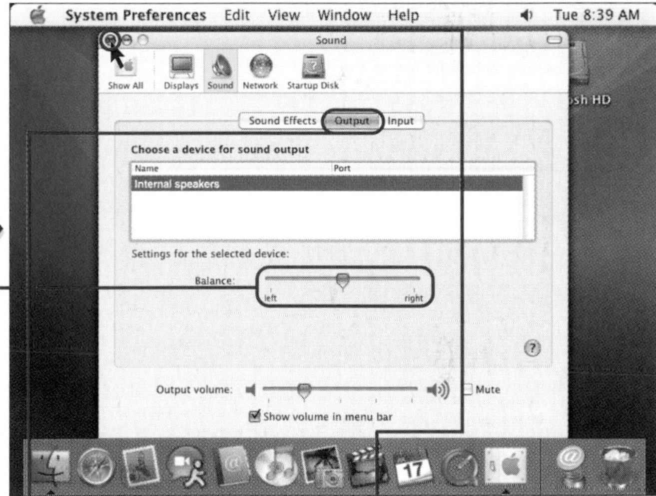

■ This option plays a sound when you perform certain actions on your computer, such as deleting a file.

■ This option plays a sound when you press a volume key on your keyboard.

■ This option allows you to adjust the volume of your computer using a speaker icon (🔊) in the menu bar.

7 You can click an option to turn the option on (☑) or off (☐).

8 Click the **Output** tab.

9 To adjust the balance between your left and right speakers, drag this slider (▽) left or right.

Note: Changing the balance between your speakers increases the volume of one speaker while decreasing the volume of the other speaker.

10 To quit System Preferences, click ● .

CHANGE THE MOUSE SETTINGS

You can change the way your mouse works to make the mouse easier to use.

You can change how fast the mouse pointer moves on your screen and the speed at which you can double-click an item to open the item.

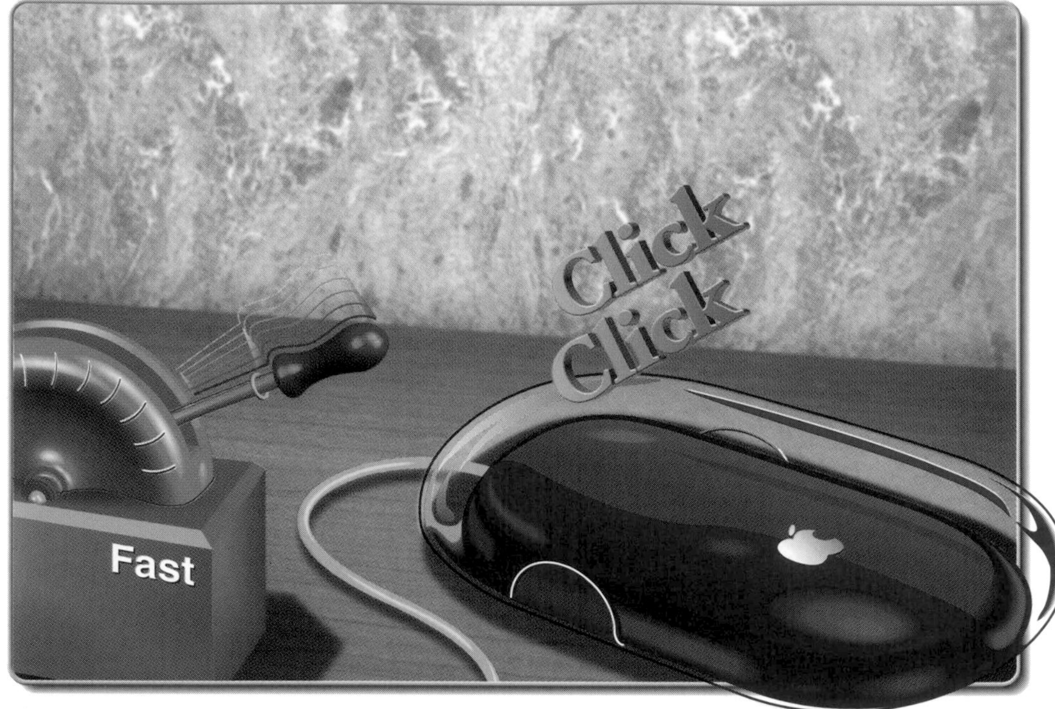

CHANGE THE MOUSE SETTINGS

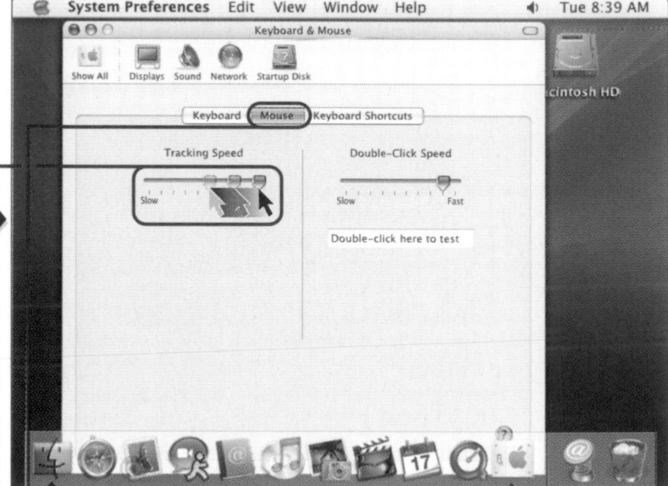

1 Click the System Preferences icon to access your system preferences.

■ The System Preferences window appears.

2 Click **Keyboard & Mouse** to change your mouse settings.

■ The **Keyboard & Mouse** window appears.

3 Click the **Mouse** tab.

4 To change how fast the mouse moves on your screen, drag this slider ( ) to a new position.

Note: If you perform detailed work, you may want to use a slower speed. If you have a large monitor, you may want to use a faster speed.

Should I use a mouse pad?

A mouse pad provides a smooth surface for moving the mouse on your desk. If you use a mechanical mouse with a roller ball, a mouse pad helps reduce the amount of dirt that enters the mouse. If you use an optical mouse, a mouse pad may be necessary when you are working on a highly reflective or transparent surface, such as a glass table. The mouse pad you use with an optical mouse should be a solid color.

Can I make my optical mouse easier to click?

If a ring surrounds the light on the bottom of your optical mouse, you can turn the ring to adjust the click tension and make the mouse easier to click. The **-** setting reduces the click tension, making the mouse easier to click. The **o** setting provides moderate click tension and the **+** setting provides the highest click tension.

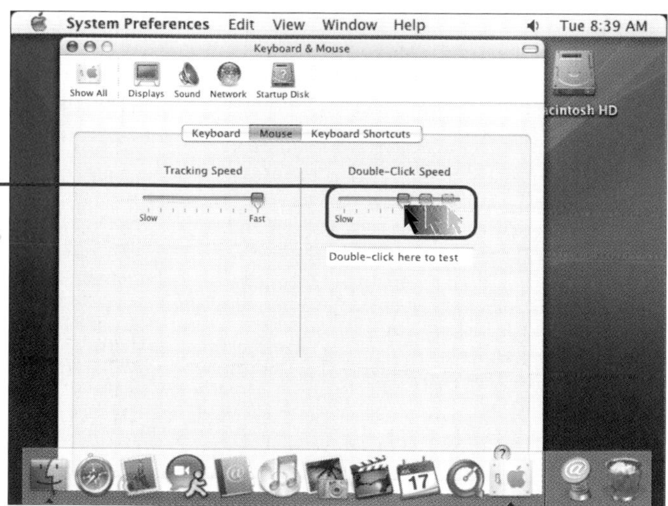

5 To change the amount of time that can pass between two clicks of the mouse button for Mac OS to recognize a double-click, drag this slider (⬡) to a new position.

Note: If you have difficulty using the mouse, you may want to use a slower double-click speed.

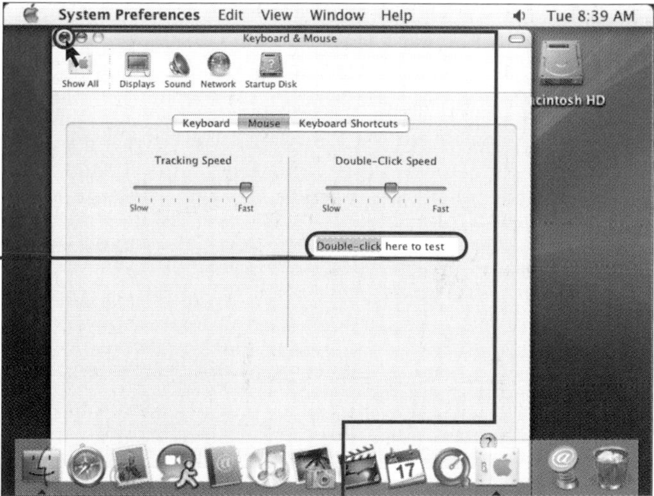

6 To test the new double-click speed, double-click the text in this area.

7 To quit System Preferences, click ●.

CHANGE THE KEYBOARD SETTINGS

You can change the way your keyboard responds to the keys you type.

For example, you can change how fast a character repeats when you hold down a key on your keyboard.

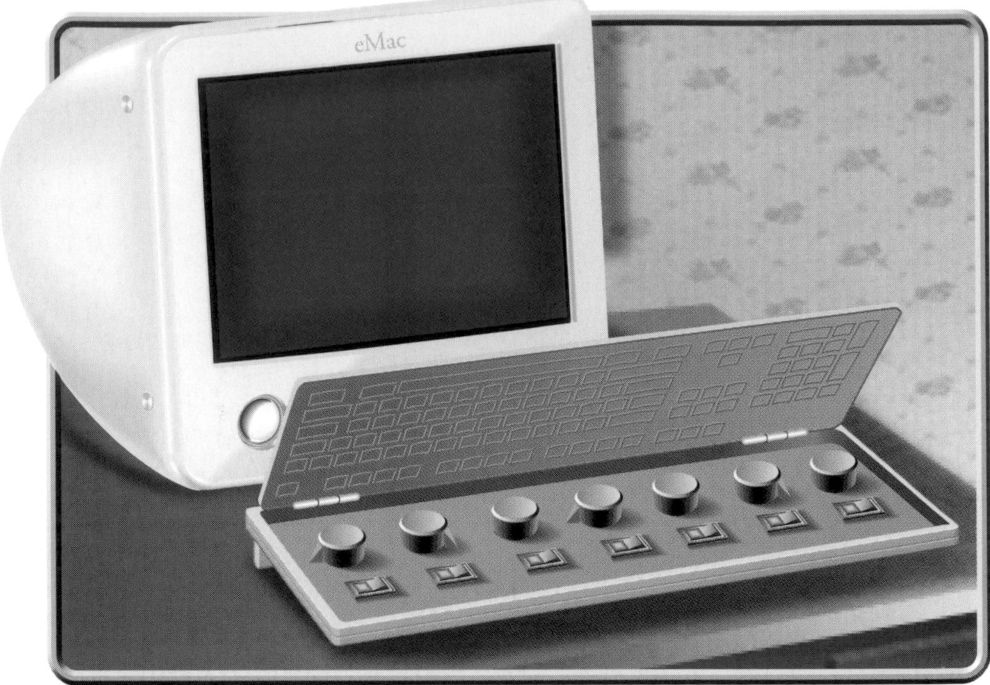

CHANGE THE KEYBOARD SETTINGS

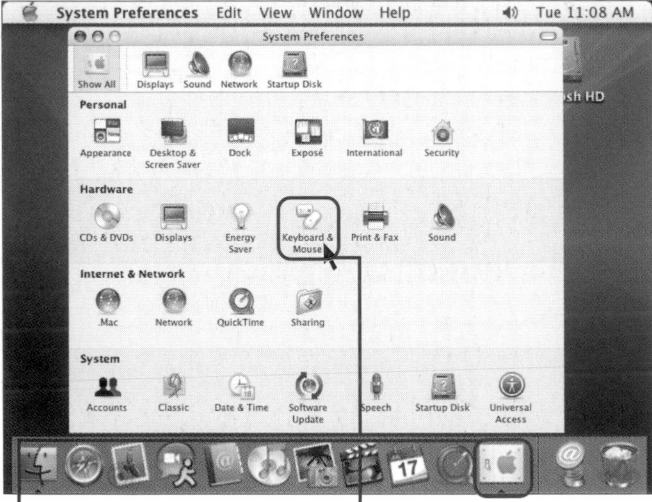

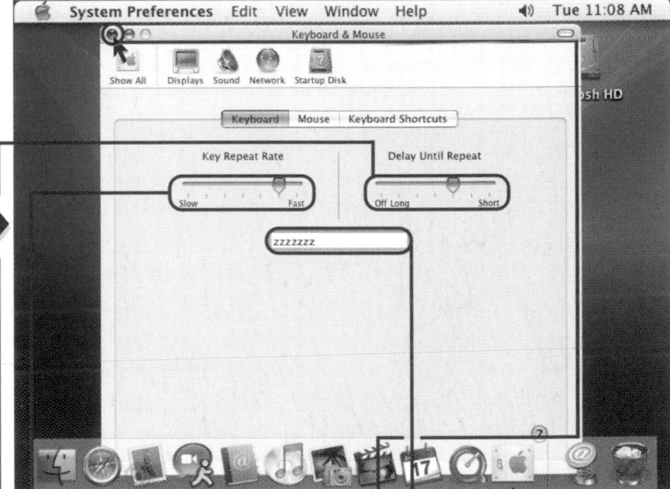

1 Click the **System Preferences** icon to access your system preferences.

■ The System Preferences window appears.

2 Click **Keyboard & Mouse** to change your keyboard settings.

■ The Keyboard & Mouse window appears.

3 To change how quickly characters repeat when you hold down a key, drag this slider ( ) to a new position.

4 To change how long you must hold down a key before the character starts repeating, drag this slider ( ) to a new position.

5 To test the keyboard settings, drag the mouse over the text in this area and then press and hold down a key on your keyboard.

6 To quit System Preferences, click .

ADD FONTS

You can add extra fonts to your computer to give you more choices when creating documents.

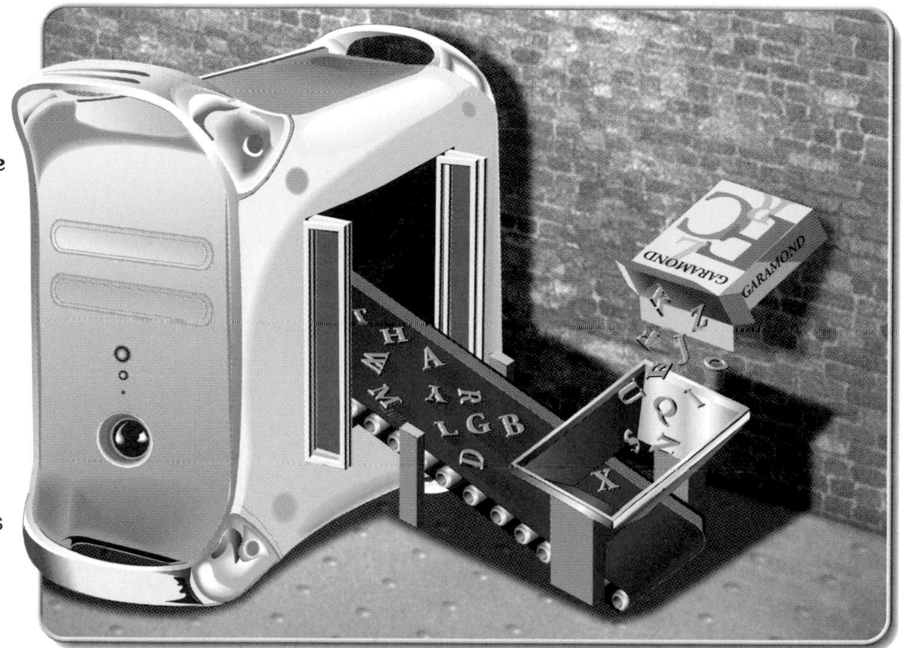

After you add fonts to your computer, you will be able to use the fonts in all your applications.

You can find fonts at Web sites, such as www.fontfiles.com, and at stores that sell computer software. Make sure the fonts you choose are designed for Macintosh computers.

ADD FONTS

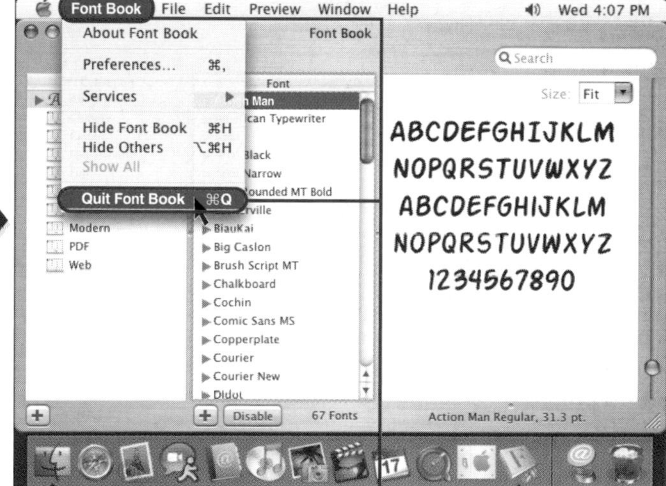

1 Locate the font you want to install on your computer.

2 Double-click the font you want to install.

■ A window appears, displaying the characters for the font.

3 To install the font on your computer, click **Install Font**.

■ The Font Book window appears, displaying the characters for the font you installed.

Note: For more information about using Font Book, see page 138.

4 To close the Font Book window, click **Font Book**.

5 Click **Quit Font Book**.

CHANGE THE DATE OR TIME

You can change the date or time set in your computer. You can have your computer's clock automatically synchronize with a time server on the Internet or change the date or time yourself.

Your computer must be connected to the Internet to synchronize its clock with a time server on the Internet. To connect to the Internet, see page 236.

CHANGE THE DATE OR TIME

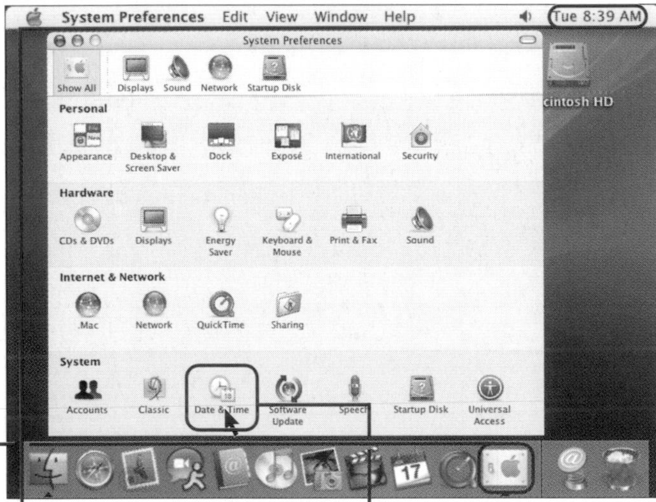

■ By default, the clock appears in the menu bar, displaying the current day and time.

1 To change the date or time, click the System Preferences icon to access your system preferences.

■ The System Preferences window appears.

2 Click **Date & Time** to change the date or time set in your computer.

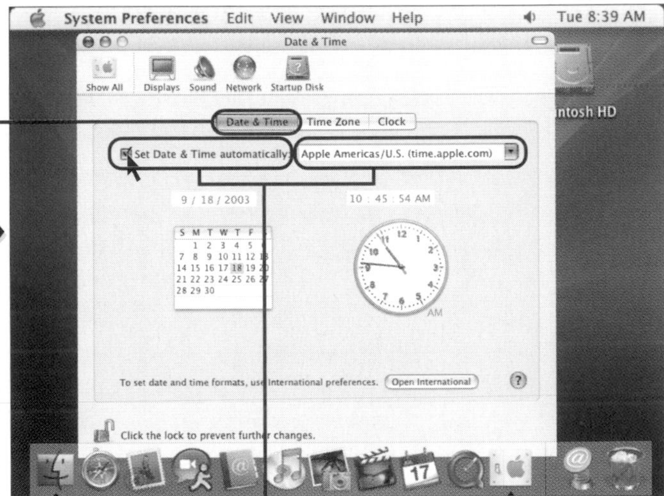

■ The Date & Time window appears.

3 Click the **Date & Time** tab.

SYNCHRONIZE WITH INTERNET TIME SERVER

4 This option automatically synchronizes your computer's clock with a time server on the Internet. You can click the option to turn the option on (☑) or off (☐).

■ This area displays the address of the time server on the Internet that your computer will use.

How can I quickly display the current date?

To display the current date, click the clock in the menu bar. A menu appears, displaying the current date set in your computer. To close the menu, click outside the menu.

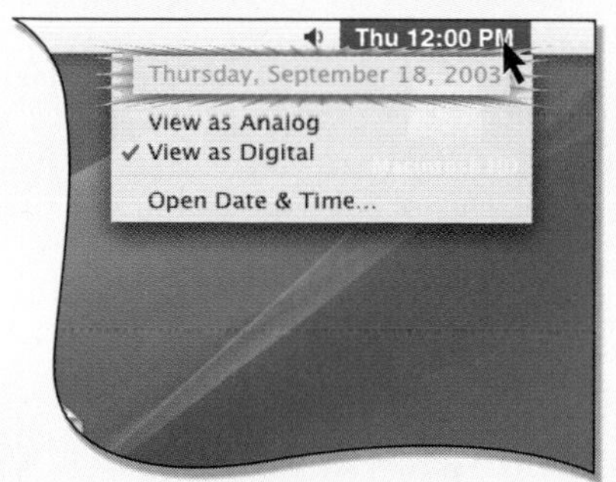

Can I use the analog clock on the Date & Time tab to change the time?

Yes. To change the time, position the mouse over the hour, minute or second hand on the analog clock and then drag the hand to the new location.

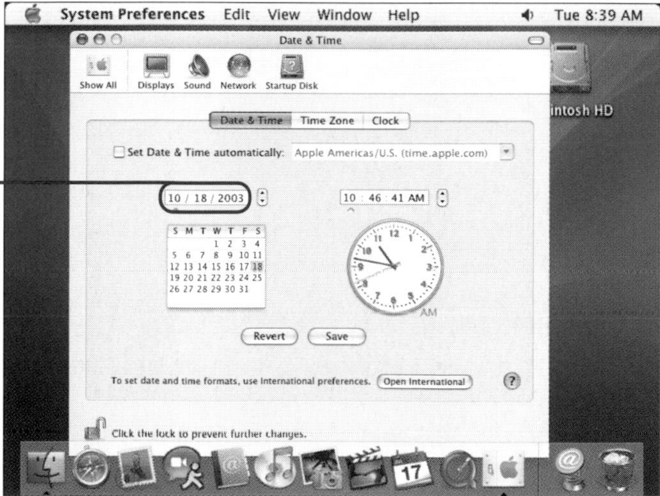

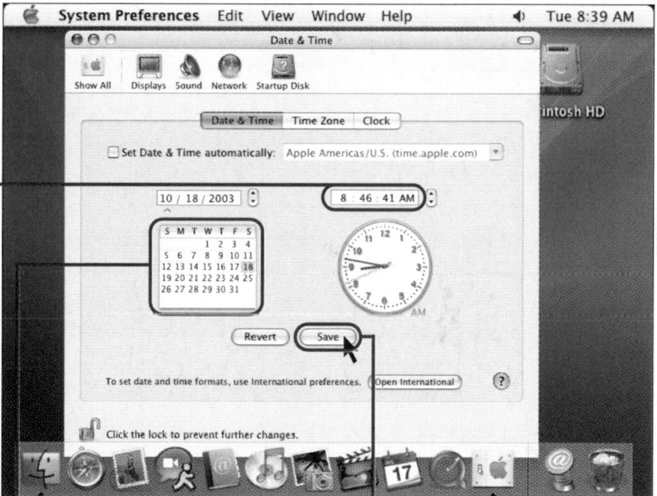

CHANGE THE DATE OR TIME

5 This area displays the current date. To change the date, double-click the part of the date you want to change and type the correct information.

*Note: You cannot change the date or time if your computer's clock automatically synchronizes with a time server on the Internet. To stop using a time server, see step **4**.*

■ This area displays the days in the current month. The current day is highlighted.

6 This area displays the current time. To change the time, double-click the part of the time you want to change and type the correct information.

7 To save the changes you made to the date and time, click **Save**.

*Note: To cancel your changes, click **Revert**.*

CONTINUED

CHANGE THE DATE OR TIME

Mac OS allows you to specify how you want to display the date and time on your desktop.

By default, the day and time are displayed in the menu bar in digital format. You can choose to display the date and time in a floating window or in analog format instead.

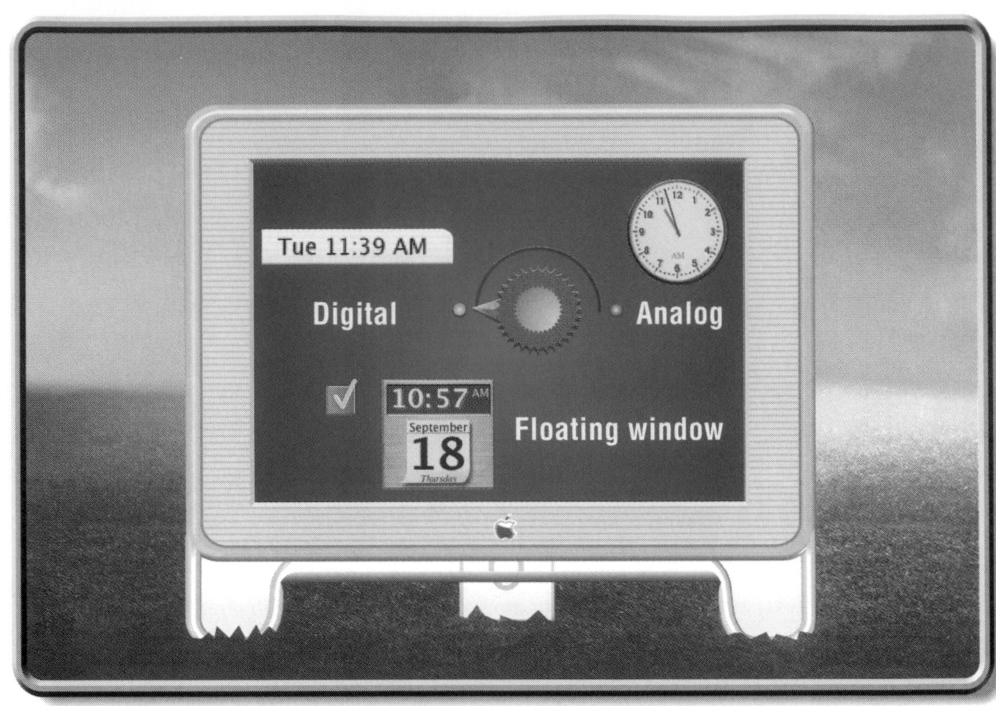

CHANGE THE DATE OR TIME (CONTINUED)

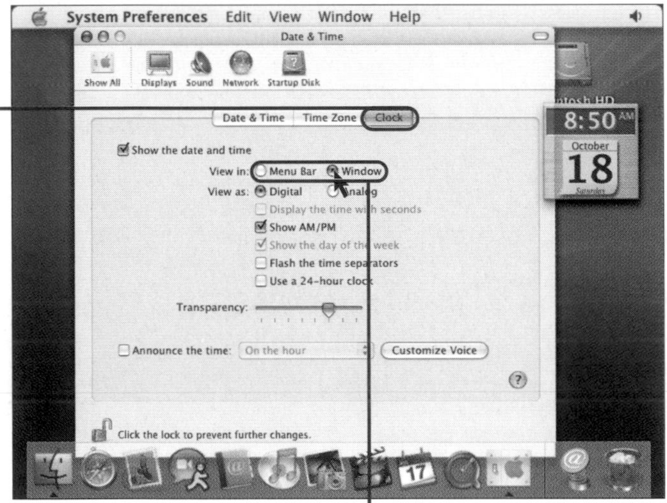

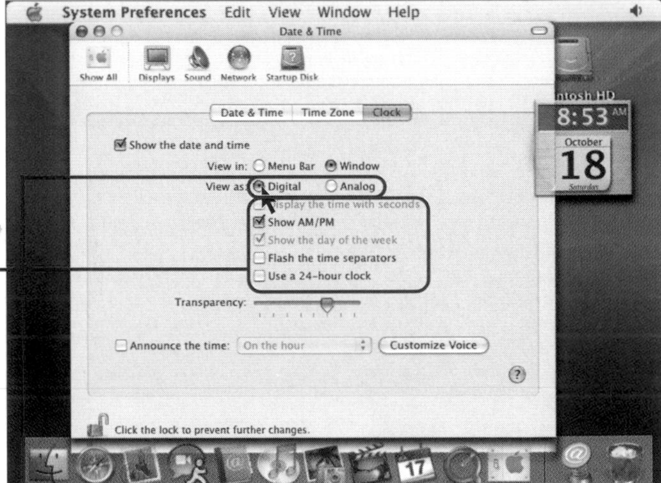

CHANGE CLOCK SETTINGS

8 Click the **Clock** tab.

9 Click an option to specify if you want to show the date and time in the menu bar or in a floating window on your desktop (◯ changes to ◉).

10 Click an option to specify if you want to view the date and time in a digital or analog format (◯ changes to ◉).

■ This area displays options that affect the appearance of the date and time. You can click an option to turn the option on (☑) or off (☐).

*Note: The available options depend on the options you selected in steps **9** and **10**.*

How can I change the time zone set in my computer?

Click the **Time Zone** tab. Drag the mouse over the text in the Closest City area and then type the first few letters of the name of a major city close to you in your time zone. Mac OS automatically completes the city name for you. Continue typing until the city name you want appears in the area and then press the return key. A grey area on the map indicates the time zone you selected.

Can I move or remove the clock that floats on my desktop?

To move the clock to a new location on your desktop, position the mouse over the floating clock and then drag the clock to a new location.

To remove the floating clock from your desktop, perform steps **1** and **2** on page 86 to display the Date & Time window. Then perform steps **8** and **9** on page 88, selecting **Menu Bar** in step **9**.

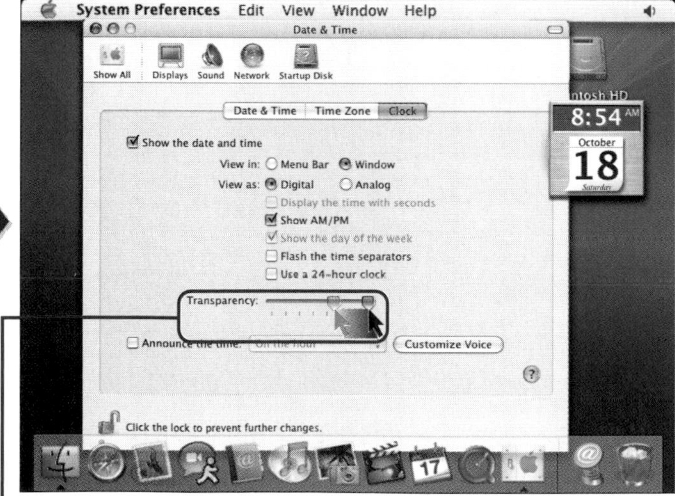

11 If you selected to show the date and time in a floating window on your desktop, you can drag this slider ( ) left or right to increase or decrease the transparency of the window.

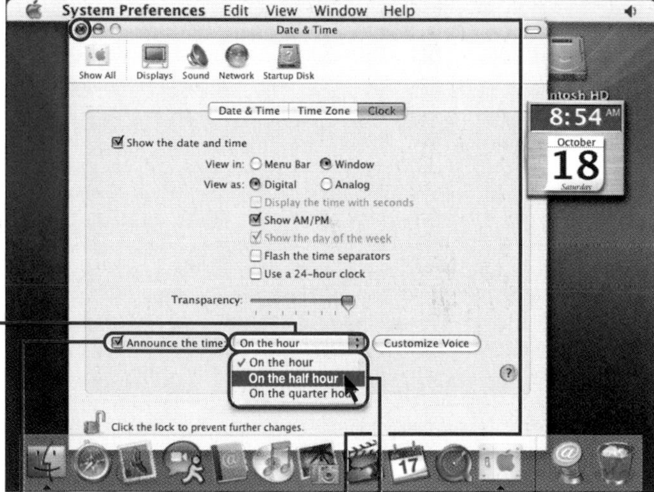

12 This option instructs your computer to say the time at specified intervals. You can click this option to turn the option on ( ) or off ( ).

13 To specify how often your computer will say the time, click this area.

14 Click an option to specify how often your computer will say the time.

15 To quit System Preferences, click .

OPEN APPLICATIONS AUTOMATICALLY AT LOG IN

If you use the same applications every day, you can have the applications open automatically each time you log in to Mac OS.

You can set up files and folders to open automatically each time you log in to Mac OS the same way you set up applications.

OPEN APPLICATIONS AUTOMATICALLY AT LOG IN

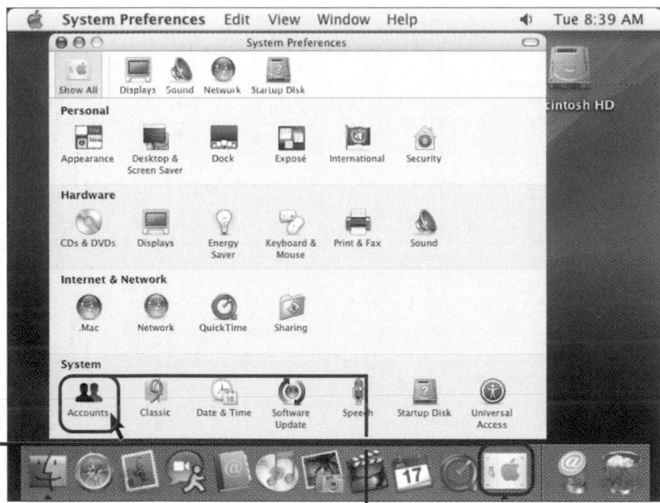

1 Click the System Preferences icon to access your system preferences.

■ The System Preferences window appears.

2 Click **Accounts** to access information for your user account.

■ The Accounts window appears.

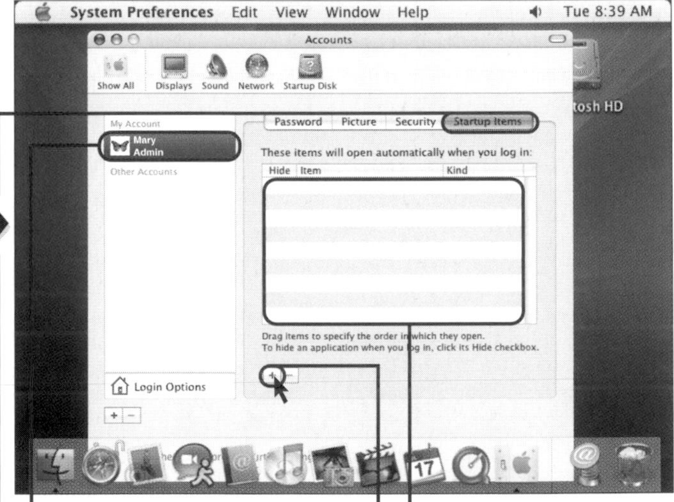

3 Click your account name.

4 Click the **Startup Items** tab to specify the applications you want to open automatically when you log in.

■ This area lists any applications that will open automatically when you log in.

5 To add an application to the list, click +.

How do I stop an application from opening automatically when I log in?

If you no longer want an application to open automatically when you log in, you must remove the application from the Accounts window.

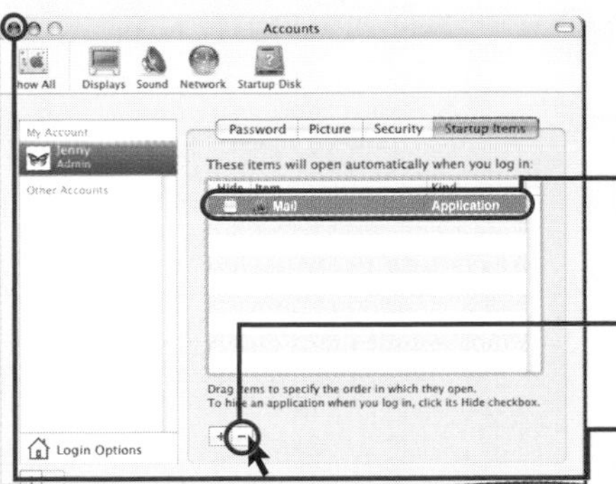

1 Perform steps **1** to **4** below to display the list of applications that open automatically.

2 Click the application you no longer want to open automatically when you log in.

3 Click − to remove the application from the window.

4 To quit System Preferences, click .

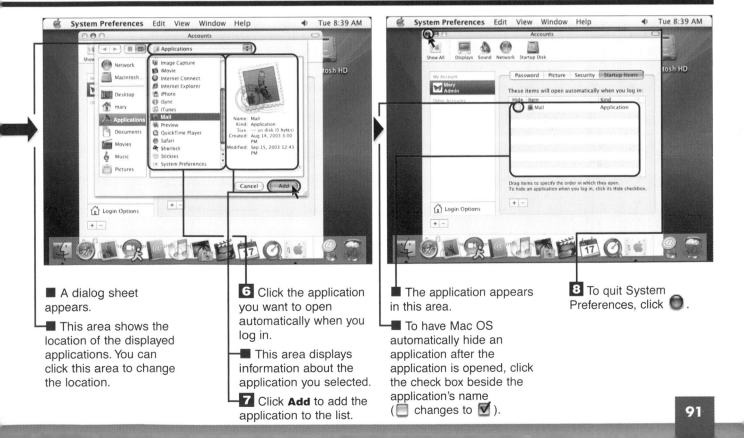

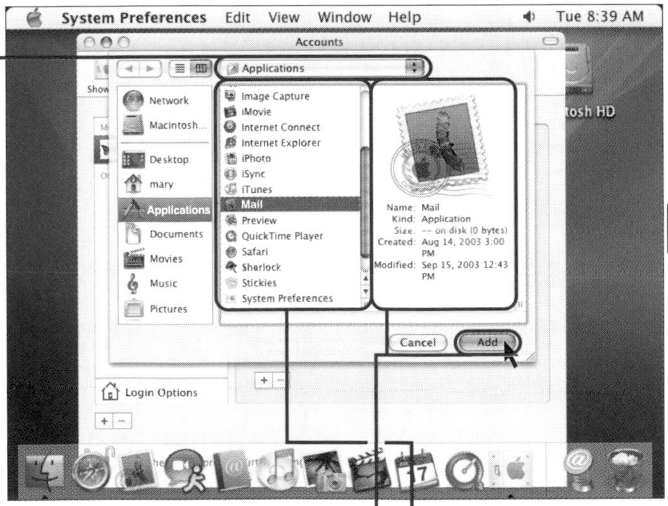

■ A dialog sheet appears.

■ This area shows the location of the displayed applications. You can click this area to change the location.

6 Click the application you want to open automatically when you log in.

■ This area displays information about the application you selected.

7 Click **Add** to add the application to the list.

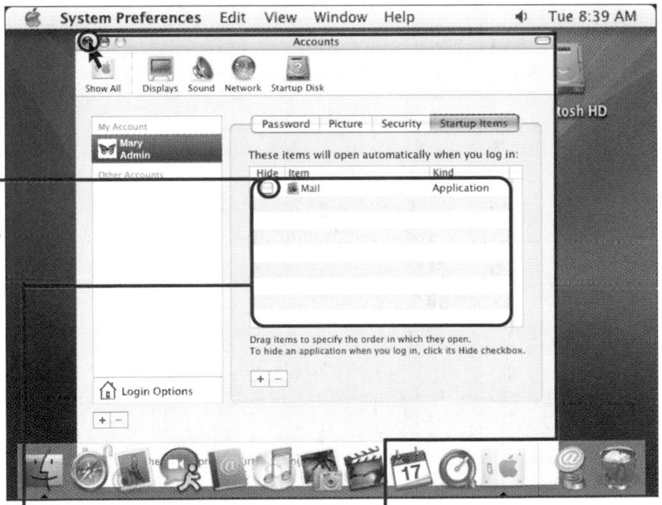

■ The application appears in this area.

■ To have Mac OS automatically hide an application after the application is opened, click the check box beside the application's name (changes to).

8 To quit System Preferences, click .

ADD A PRINTER

Before you can use a printer, you need to add the printer to your computer. You need to add a printer only once.

ADD A PRINTER

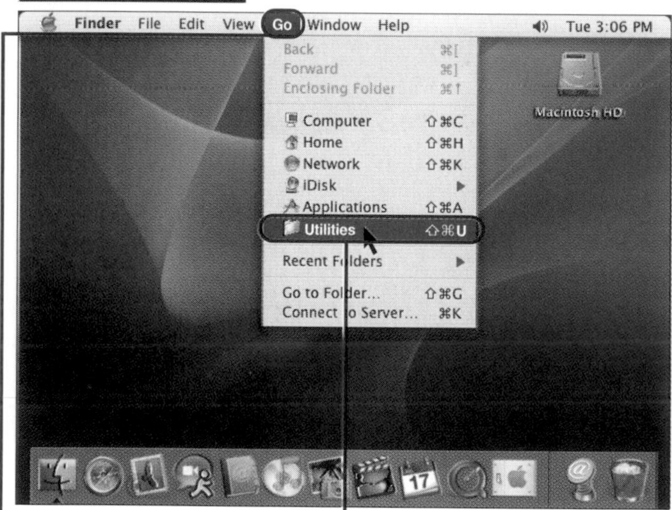

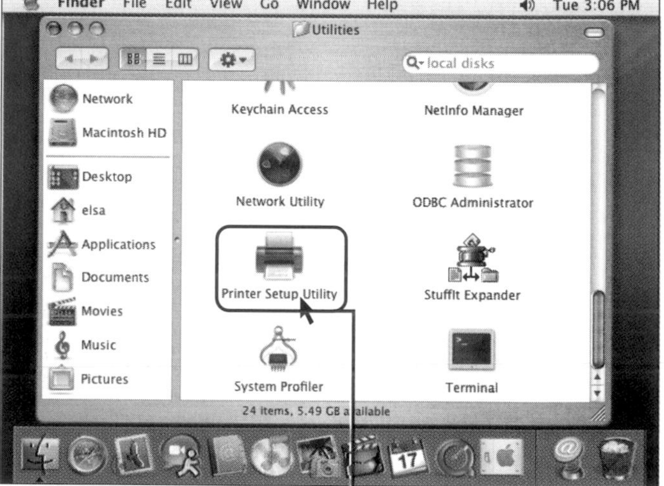

1 Click **Go**.

Note: If Go is not available, click a blank area on your desktop to display the Finder menu bar.

2 Click **Utilities** to view the utility applications available on your computer.

■ The Utilities window appears, displaying the utility applications available on your computer.

3 Double-click **Printer Setup Utility** to manage your printers.

Note: You can click ● in the Utilities window to close the window.

What are some of the connection types I can choose for my printer?

		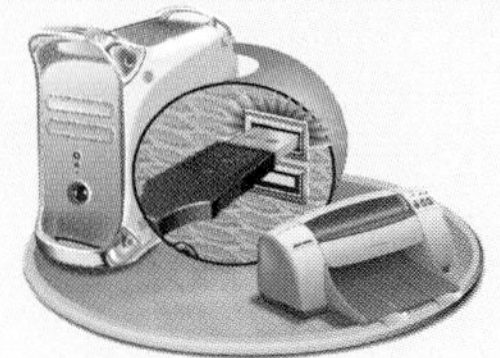	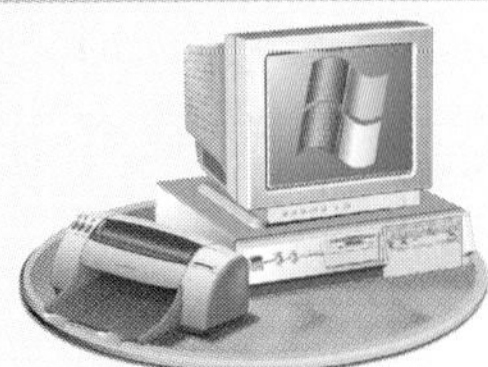
IP Printing Allows you to connect to a printer on a TCP/IP network that connects Macintosh computers or Windows-based computers. The printer will have a specific TCP/IP address, such as 192.168.253.252.	**Open Directory** Allows you to connect to a printer attached to a network server. Contact your network administrator for information on adding a printer using this connection type.	**USB** Allows you to connect to a printer plugged directly into a USB port on your computer.	**Windows Printing** Allows you to connect to a Windows printer on your network.

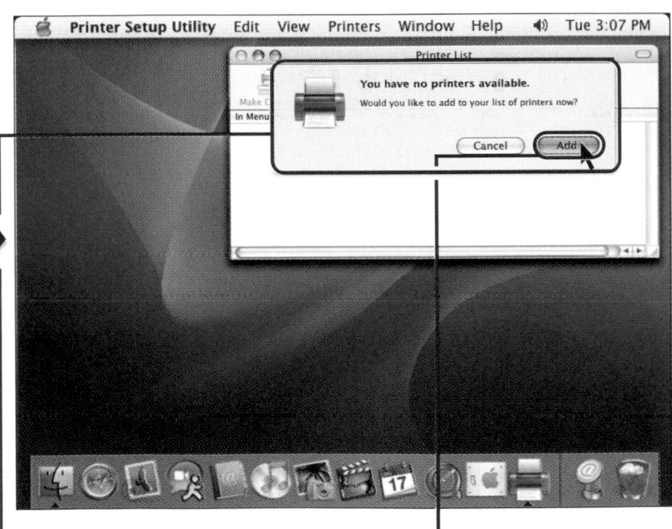

■ The Printer List window appears.

■ If you do not have any printers installed on your computer, a dialog sheet appears, stating that you have no printers available on your computer.

4 Click **Add** to add a printer.

■ If the dialog sheet does not appear, click **Add** in the Printer List window to add a printer.

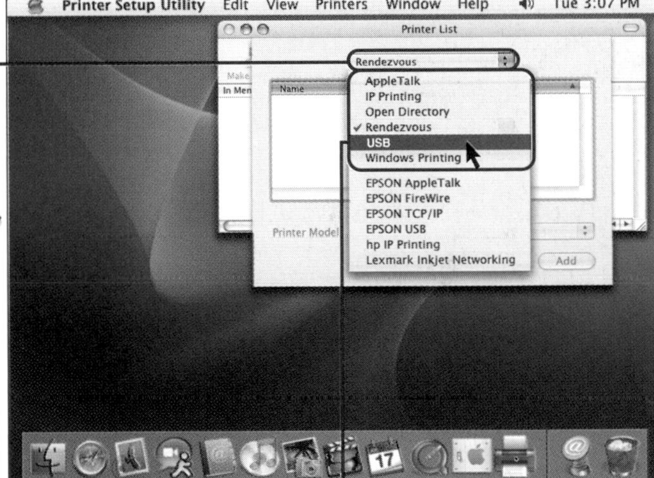

■ A dialog sheet appears.

5 To specify how the printer connects to your computer, click this area to display a list of the available connection types.

6 Click the type of connection the printer uses to connect to your computer.

*Note: A dialog box may appear if Mac OS finds new printer drivers for you. Click **OK** to continue.*

CONTINUED

When you add a printer, your computer can locate the printers available to you and then display the printers in a list for you to choose from.

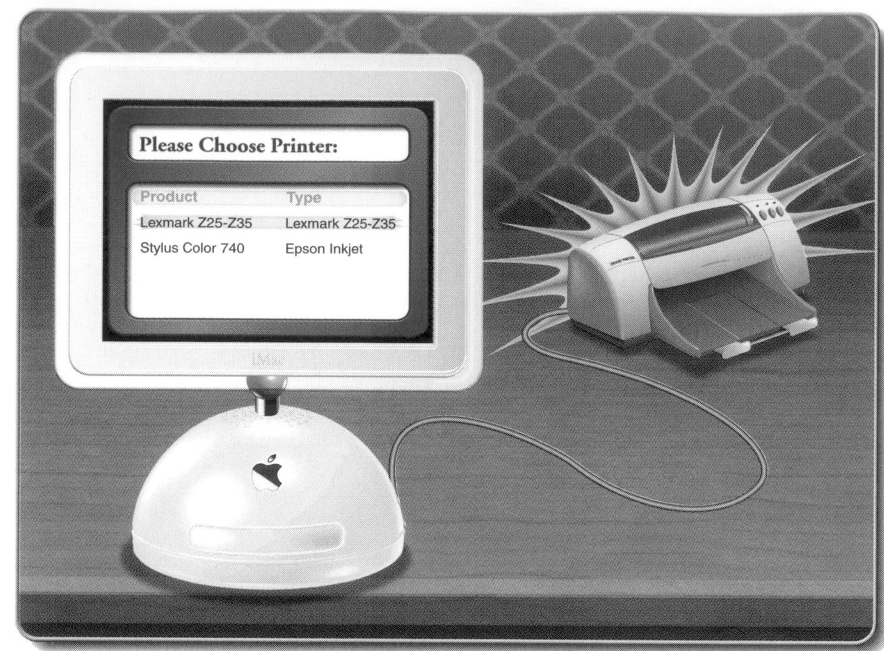

ADD A PRINTER (CONTINUED)

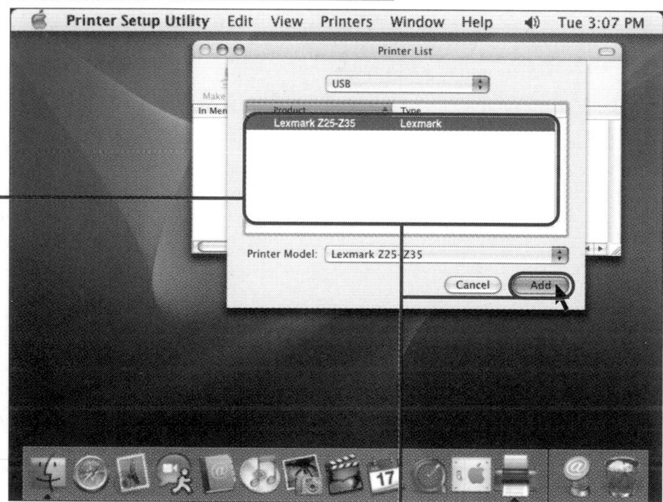

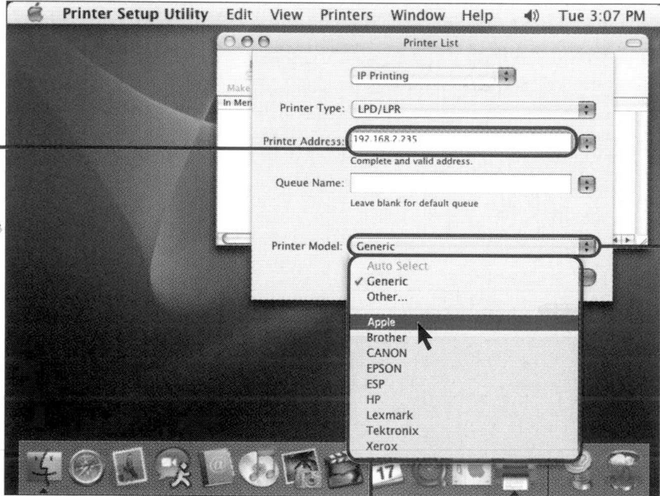

■ This area displays the names of the printers that your computer found.

*Note: If you selected Windows Printing in step **6**, double-click the workgroup name to display the names of the printers. You may also need to enter a username and password for the workgroup.*

■ If you selected IP Printing in step **6**, skip to step **9**.

7 Click the printer you want to add.

8 Click **Add** to add the printer. To continue, skip to step **14**.

9 If you selected IP Printing in step **6**, click this area and type the Internet Protocol (IP) address or domain name of the printer.

Note: If you do not know the IP address or domain name of the printer, ask your network administrator.

10 To specify the printer model for the printer, click this area to display a list of the available printer models.

11 Click the printer model for the printer.

I am having trouble adding a printer. What should I do?

If you are having trouble adding a printer, Mac OS may not have the software required to communicate with the printer. To add the printer, install the software included with the printer. If your printer did not come with software, you may be able to download the correct software from the printer manufacturer's Web site. You may also have to perform steps **1** to **15** starting on page 92 to add the printer.

How do I change the default printer?

The default printer automatically prints all your files. To change the default printer, perform steps **1** to **3** on page 92 to display the Printer List window. Click the name of the printer you want to make the default printer and then click **Make Default**. The name of the default printer appears in **bold** type.

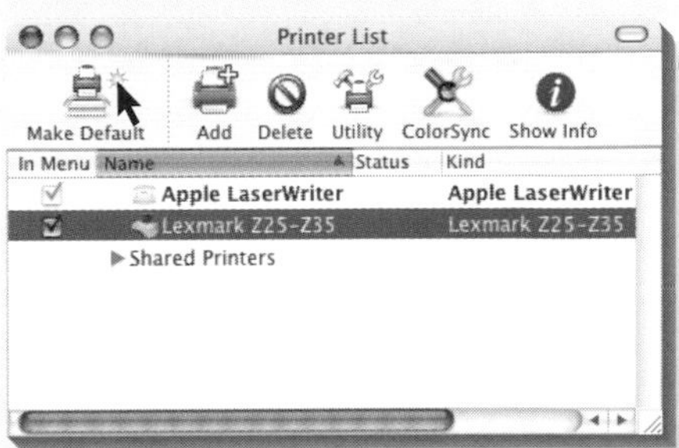

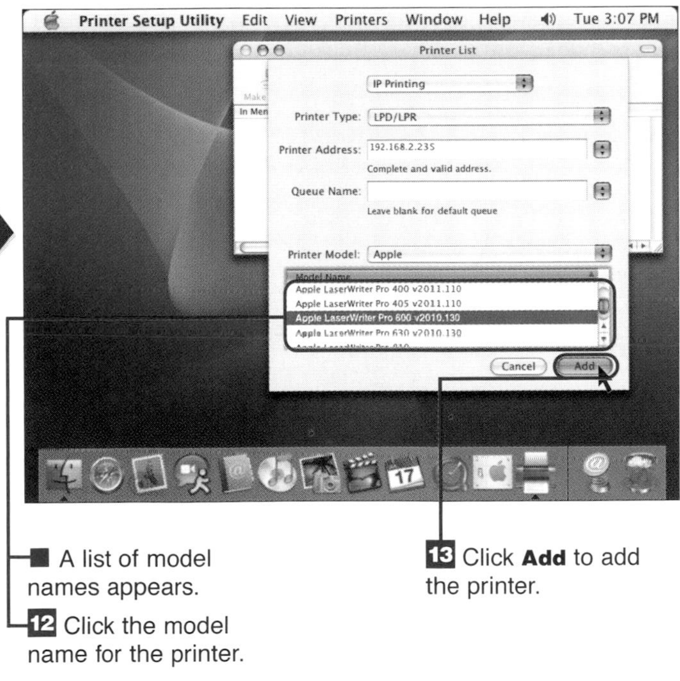

■ A list of model names appears.

12 Click the model name for the printer.

13 Click **Add** to add the printer.

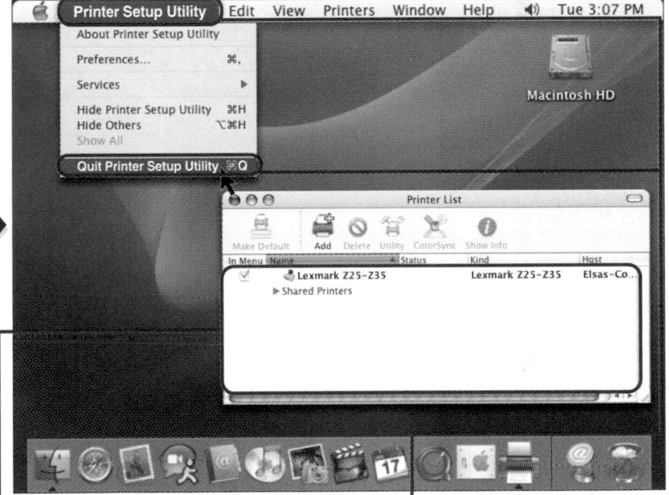

■ The printer appears in the Printer List window.

■ You can now use the printer to print documents on your computer.

14 To quit Printer Setup Utility, click **Printer Setup Utility**.

15 Click **Quit Printer Setup Utility**.

USING SPEECH RECOGNITION

You can turn on speech recognition to use spoken commands to control your computer.

Using spoken commands can help save you time when performing tasks on your computer since one spoken command often performs several steps.

TURN ON SPEECH RECOGNITION

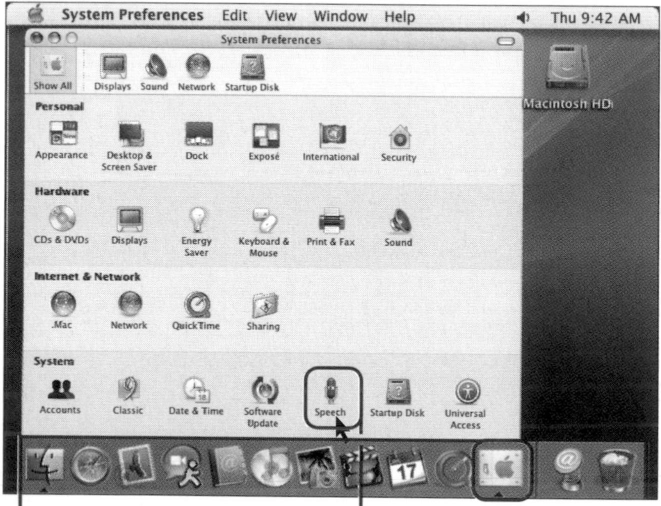

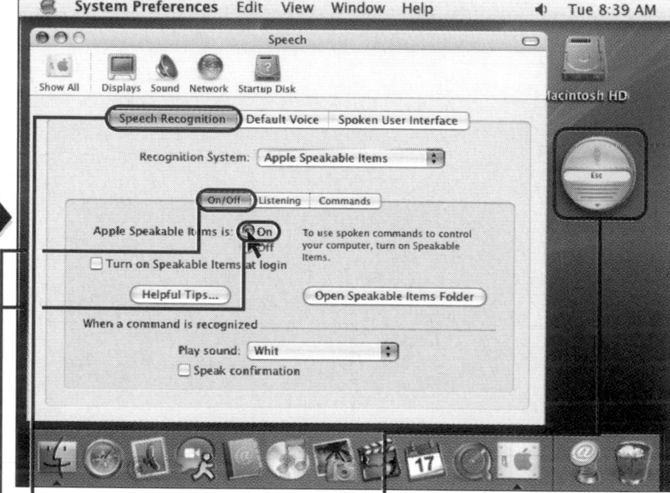

1 Click the System Preferences icon to access your system preferences.

■ The System Preferences window appears.

2 Click **Speech** to turn on speech recognition.

■ The Speech window appears.

3 Click the **Speech Recognition** tab.

4 Click the **On/Off** tab.

5 To turn on speech recognition, click **On** (○ changes to ◉).

Note: The first time you turn on speech recognition, a dialog sheet appears, displaying tips on using speech recognition. You can click ***Continue*** *to close the dialog sheet.*

■ When speech recognition is turned on, the Speech Feedback window appears on your screen.

What spoken commands can I use?

To view spoken commands you can use, perform steps **1** to **4** below and then click **Open Speakable Items Folder**. The Speakable Items window appears, displaying icons for spoken commands you can use. Each icon name represents a spoken command. The Speakable Items window also displays the Application Speakable Items folder, which contains subfolders for applications that offer additional spoken commands you can use. The commands in an application subfolder are specific to the application. To open a folder, double-click the folder.

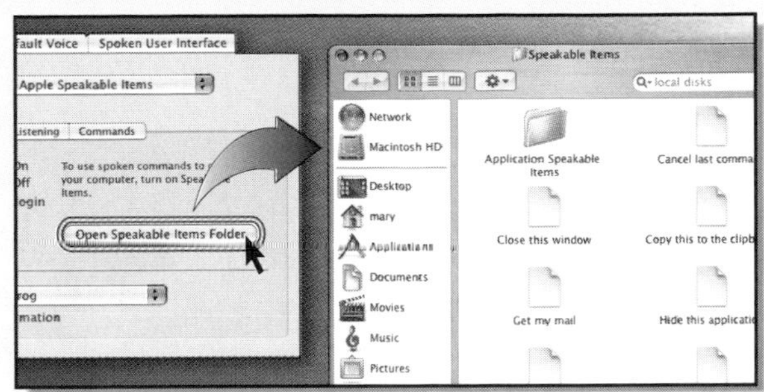

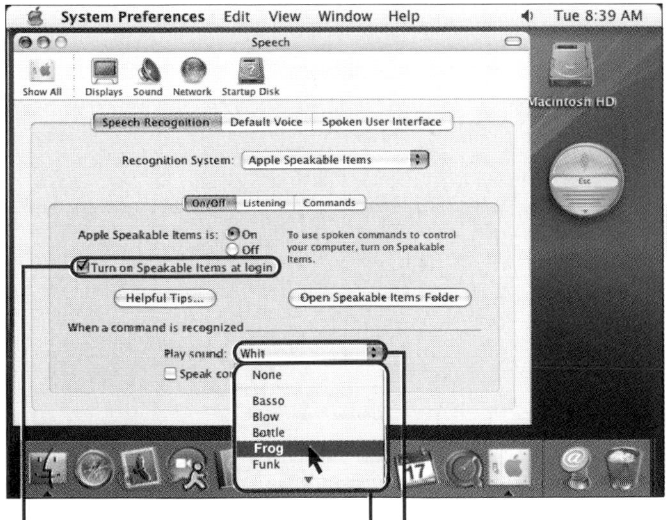

6 To turn on speech recognition each time you log in to your computer, click this option (☐ changes to ☑).

Note: Mac OS automatically turns off speech recognition each time you log out or shut down your computer.

7 To specify the sound you want to play each time your computer recognizes a spoken command, click this area to display a list of the available sounds.

8 Click the sound you want to play. The sound you selected plays.

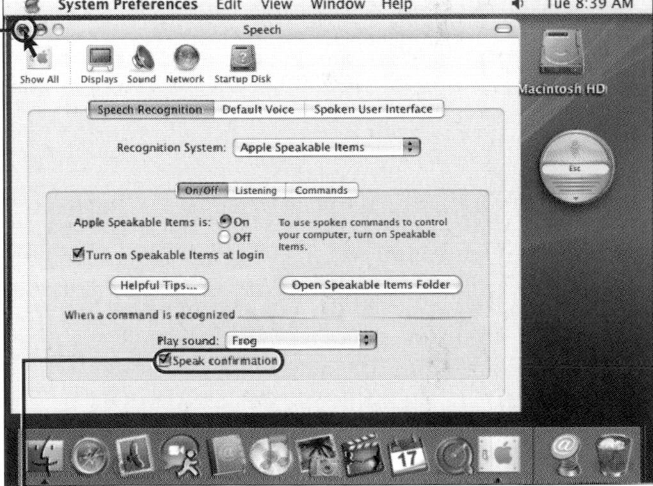

9 To have your computer repeat your spoken commands, click this option (☐ changes to ☑).

10 To quit System Preferences, click ●.

■ To turn off speech recognition, perform steps **1** to **5**, selecting **Off** in step **5**. Then perform step **10**.

■ You can now use spoken commands to control your computer. To use spoken commands, see page 98.

CONTINUED

USING SPEECH RECOGNITION

When speech recognition is turned on, you can use spoken commands to perform tasks on your computer, such as closing a window, opening an application or starting your screen saver.

You need to connect a microphone to your computer to use spoken commands to perform tasks on the computer.

USE SPOKEN COMMANDS

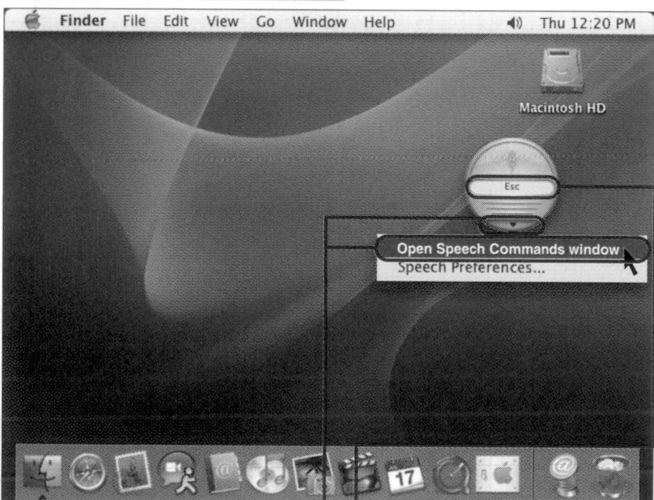

■ When speech recognition is turned on, the Speech Feedback window appears on your screen.

Note: To turn on speech recognition, see page 96.

■ This area displays the name of the key you can press and hold down to have your computer listen to your spoken commands.

1 To display a list of spoken commands you can use, click ▼.

2 Click **Open Speech Commands window**.

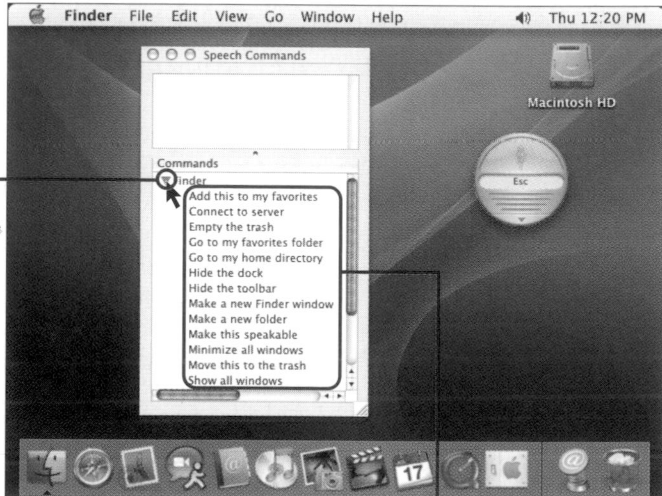

■ The Speech Commands window appears, displaying the categories of commands you can use.

Note: The available categories depend on the active application.

3 You can click ▶ beside a category to display the commands in the category (▶ changes to ▼).

■ The commands in the category appear.

■ You can click ▼ to once again hide the commands in the category.

How should I speak to my computer when using spoken commands?

You should speak to your computer in your normal tone of voice, pronouncing words clearly and not pausing between words. You should also speak at a consistent volume so the bars in the Speech Feedback window are primarily green. If you speak too softly or too loudly, the computer may not be able to recognize your commands.

Can I minimize the Speech Feedback window?

Yes. To minimize the Speech Feedback window to an icon in the Dock, double-click the window or press and hold down the esc key as you say "Minimize Speech Feedback window." To redisplay the window, click the icon for the window in the Dock.

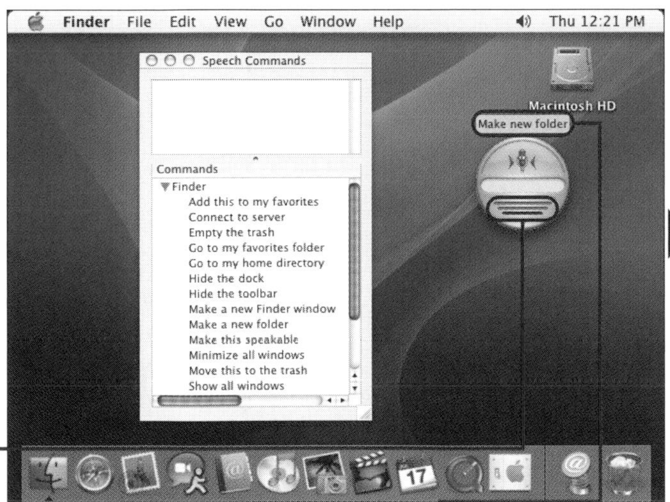

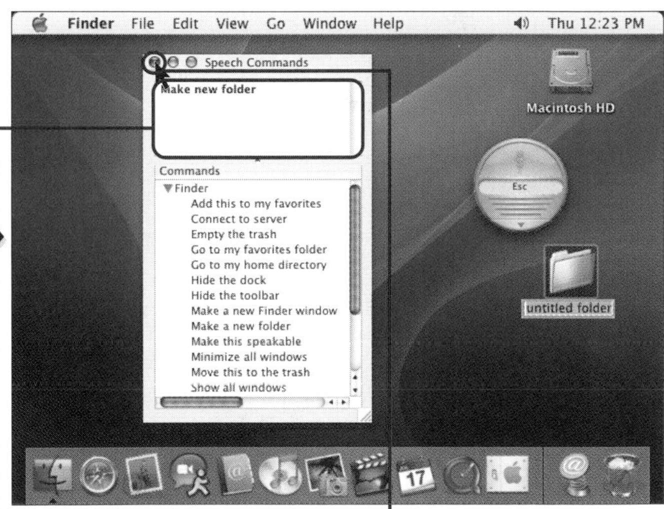

4 Press and hold down the esc key and then speak a command into your microphone.

■ While you speak, bars in the Speech Feedback window indicate the sound level of your voice.

Note: The bars should be green. If a red bar appears, you are speaking too loudly.

■ Your spoken command appears in a yellow box above the Speech Feedback window and a sound plays.

Note: Your computer may also repeat your spoken command.

■ This area of the Speech Commands window displays your spoken commands in bold.

■ You can repeat step **4** for each spoken command you want to use.

5 To close the Speech Commands window, click ●.

■ To turn off speech recognition, you can say "Quit speakable items."

CHANGE THE WAY YOUR COMPUTER SPEAKS

You can change the voice your computer uses to speak. Mac OS offers several different voices you can choose from.

You can also specify when you want the computer to speak.

CHANGE THE WAY YOUR COMPUTER SPEAKS

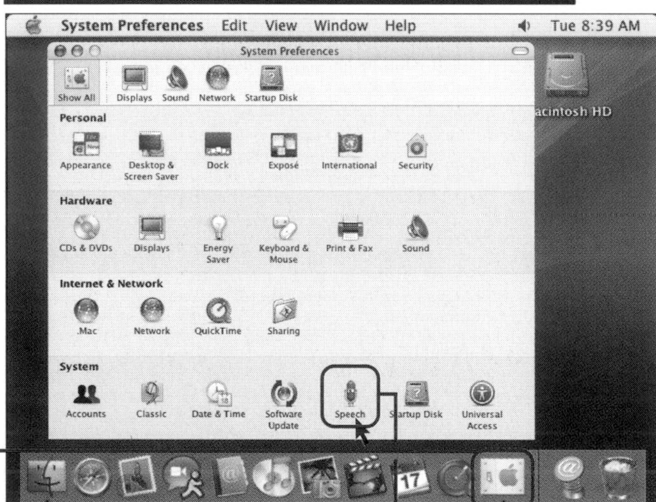

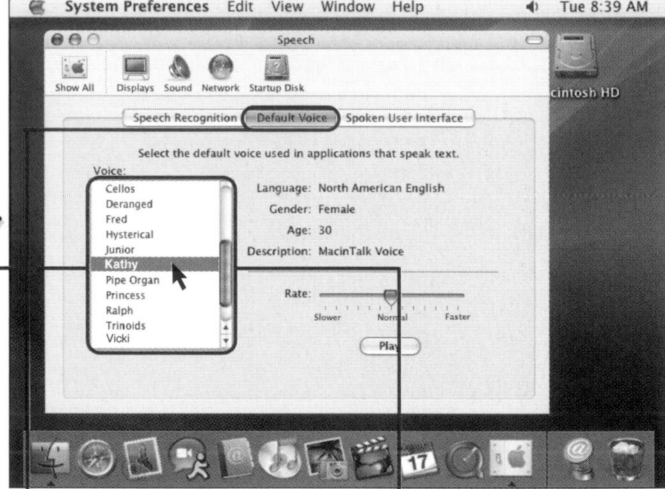

1 Click the System Preferences icon to access your system preferences.

■ The System Preferences window appears.

2 Click **Speech** to change the way your computer speaks.

■ The Speech window appears.

3 To change the voice your computer uses to speak, click the **Default Voice** tab.

■ This area displays the voices your computer can use to speak.

4 Click the voice you want your computer to use.

■ Your computer speaks using the voice you selected.

Note: To have your computer speak in another voice, repeat step ***4****.*

When will my computer use the voice I select?

Your computer will use the voice you select in step **4** below to read aloud text in applications such as TextEdit. To have your computer read aloud text in a TextEdit document, see the top of page 133. Your computer will also use the voice to speak when you use features such as speech recognition. For information on using speech recognition, see page 96.

Which phrase should I have my computer speak when an alert appears?

If you cannot decide which phrase you want your computer to speak in step **10** below, you can have your computer choose a phrase for you. Click **Next in the list** to have your computer choose a phrase in order from the list each time an alert appears. Click **Random from the list** to have your computer randomly choose a phrase from the list each time an alert appears.

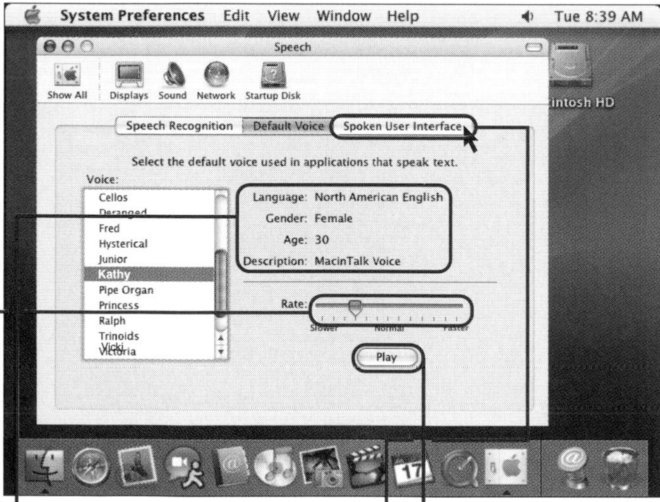

■ This area displays information about the voice you selected, including the language and gender of the voice.

5 Drag this slider ( ) left or right to have the computer speak slower or faster.

6 Click **Play** to hear your computer speak using the new speed.

7 To specify when your computer will speak, click the **Spoken User Interface** tab.

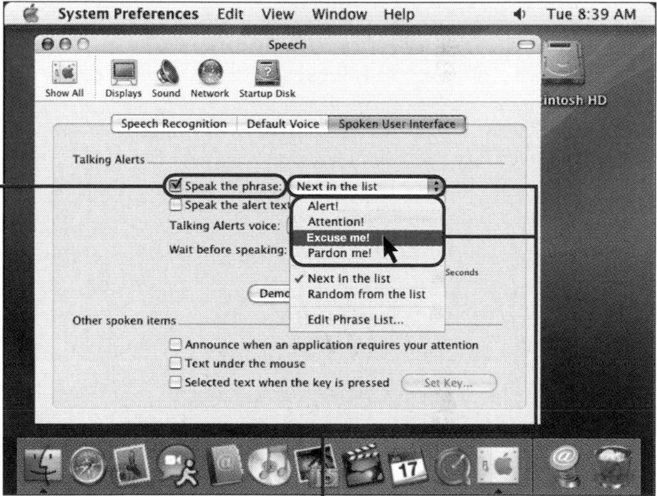

8 This option instructs your computer to speak a phrase when an alert appears. You can click the option to turn the option on ( ) or off ( ).

Note: Your computer uses alerts to get your attention or notify you of a problem.

9 If you turned the option on, click this area to display a list of phrases the computer can speak when an alert appears.

10 Click the phrase you want your computer to use.

CONTINUED

You can have your computer read the text in alerts that appear on your screen.

CHANGE THE WAY YOUR COMPUTER SPEAKS (CONTINUED)

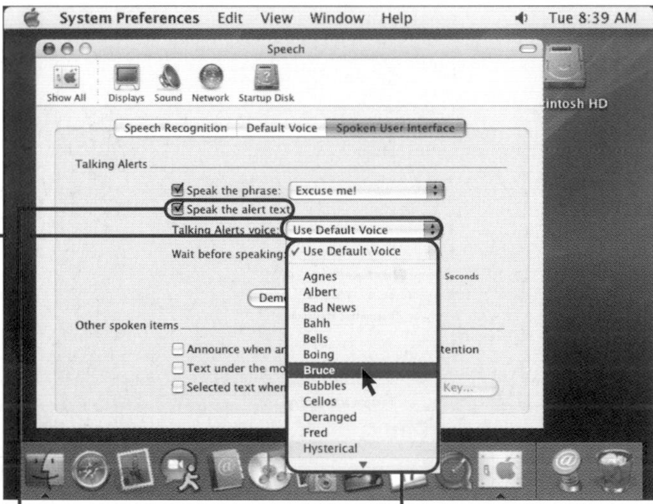

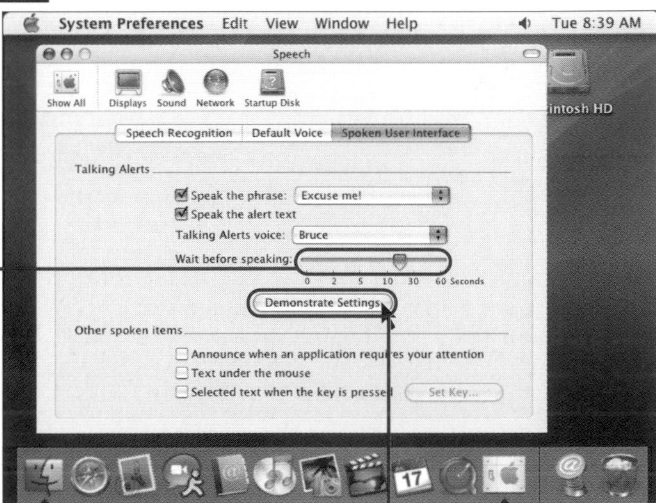

11 This option instructs your computer to read the text in alerts. You can click the option to turn the option on (☑) or off (☐).

12 To specify the voice you want your computer to use to read alerts, click this area to display a list of the available voices.

13 Click the voice you want your computer to use.

*Note: The Use Default Voice option uses the voice you selected in step **4** on page 100.*

14 To specify how long your computer should wait before speaking when an alert appears, drag this slider (▽) to a new position.

15 To have your computer demonstrate the settings you selected, click **Demonstrate Settings**.

Can my computer read aloud text I select in an application?

Yes. You can have your computer read aloud selected text in an application such as Mail when you type a specific keyboard shortcut (example: control + A). To have your computer read aloud selected text, display the Spoken User Interface tab in the Speech window and then click **Selected text when the key is pressed** (☐ changes to ☑). The first time you turn the option on, a dialog sheet appears, allowing you to type the keyboard shortcut you want to use to tell the computer to read selected text. Click **OK** in the dialog sheet to confirm the keyboard shortcut you entered.

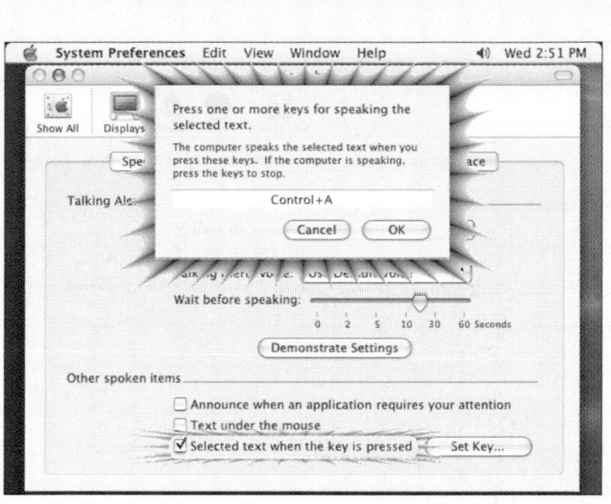

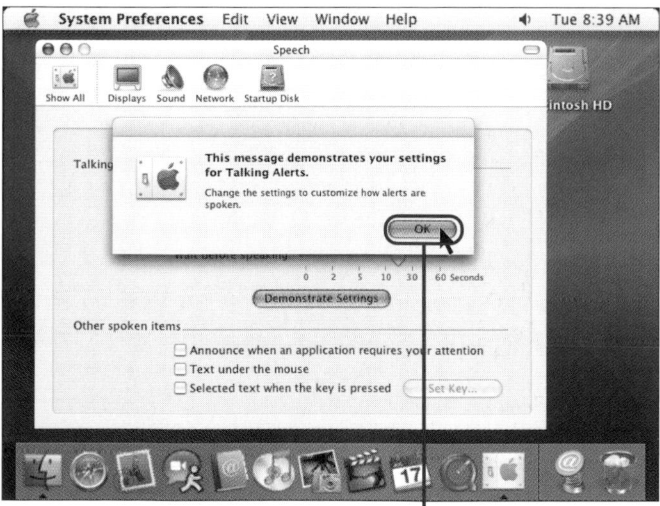

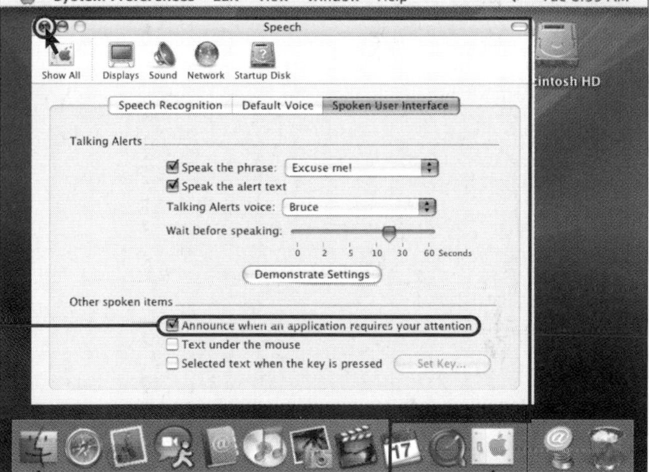

■ A dialog box appears and your computer demonstrates the settings you selected.

16 Click **OK** to close the dialog box.

17 This option instructs your computer to announce when an application needs your attention. You can click the option to turn the option on (☑) or off (☐).

18 To quit System Preferences, click ●.

UPDATE SOFTWARE

You can keep your computer up to date by having the computer automatically check for new and updated software.

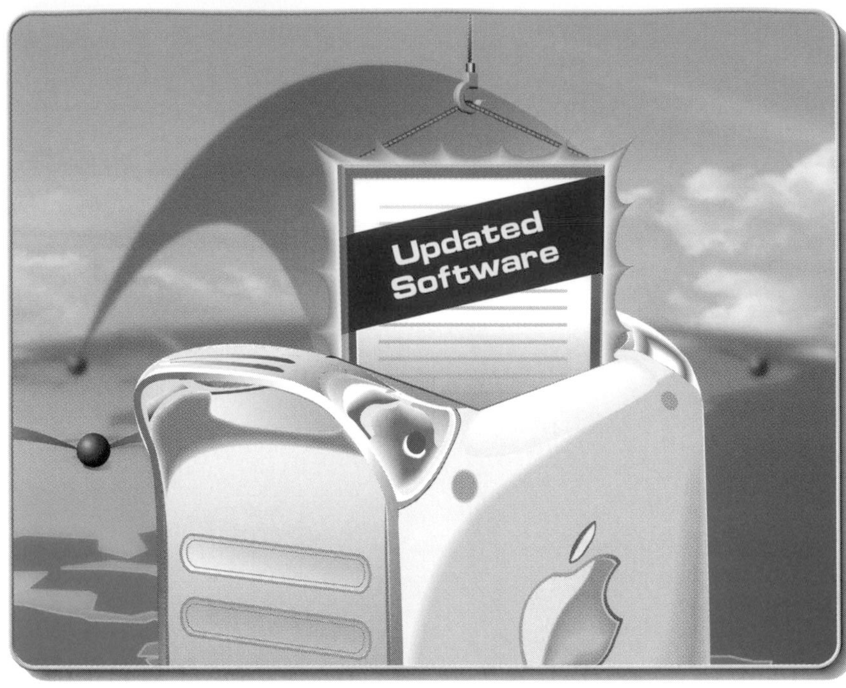

You need to be connected to the Internet to update software on your computer. To connect to the Internet, see page 236.

UPDATE SOFTWARE

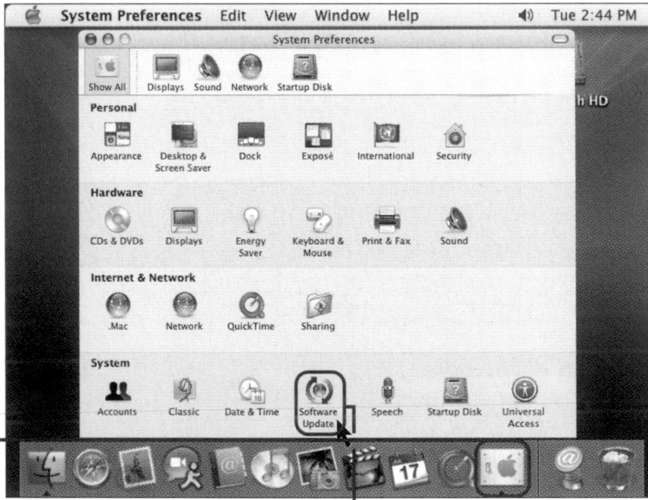

1 Click the System Preferences icon to access your system preferences.

■ The System Preferences window appears.

2 Click **Software Update** to change your software update settings.

■ The Software Update window appears.

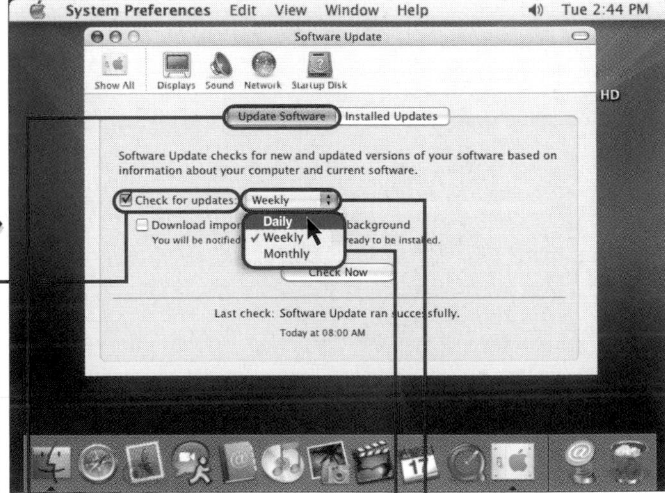

3 Click the **Update Software** tab.

4 This option automatically checks for software updates when you are connected to the Internet. You can click this option to turn the option on (☑) or off (☐).

5 To specify how often you want your computer to automatically check for software updates, click this area.

6 Click the option you want to use.

What happens if new software updates are not available?

If new software updates are not available, the message "No new software updates were available" will appear in the Software Update window. You can then click ● in the Software Update window to quit System Preferences.

Will my computer notify me when it automatically detects new software updates?

Yes. If you chose to have your computer automatically check for software updates in step **4** below, the Software Update window will appear on your screen when new software updates are available. To install the updates, perform steps **9** to **14** starting below.

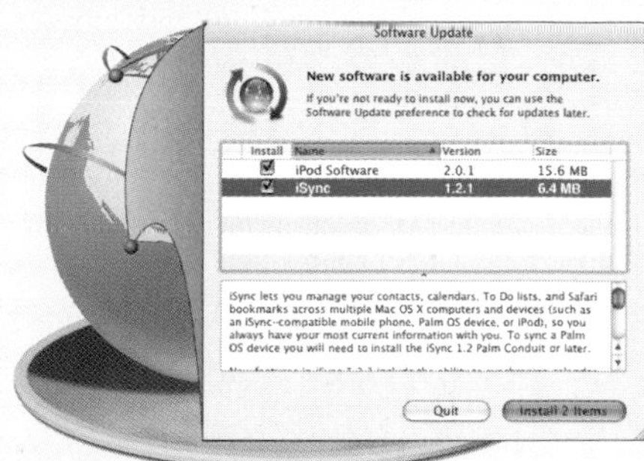

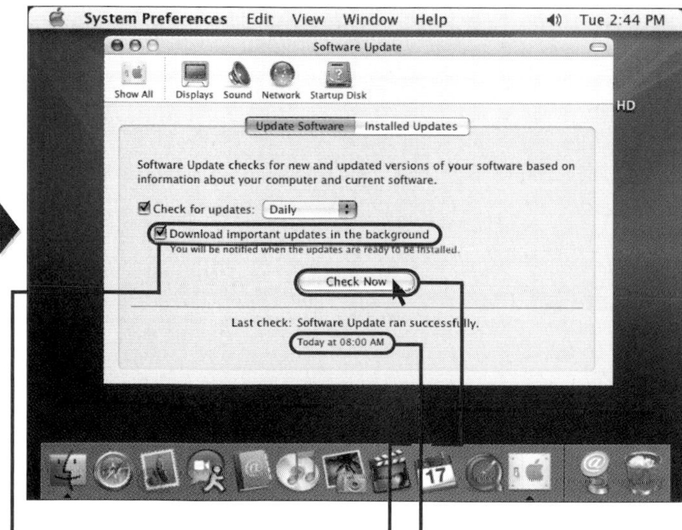

7 This option automatically downloads important updates to your computer and notifies you when they are ready to be installed. You can click this option to turn the option on (☑) or off (☐).

■ This area displays the date and time your computer last checked for software updates.

8 To immediately check for new software updates, click **Check Now**.

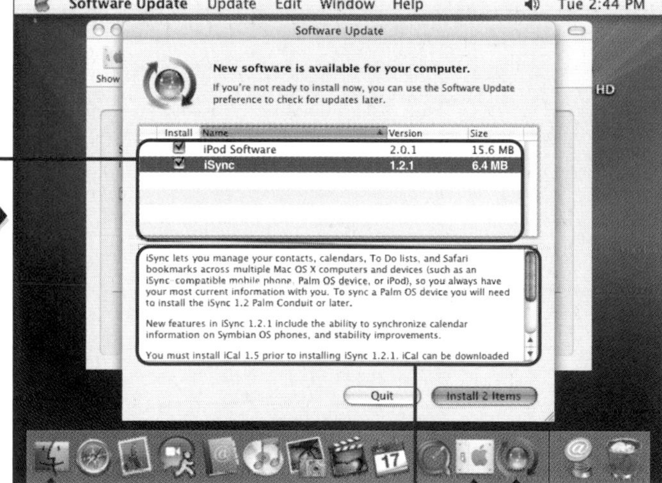

■ If software updates are available, the Software Update window appears.

9 Your computer will install each software update that displays a check mark. To add (☑) or remove (☐) a check mark for a software update, click the box (☐) beside the software update.

■ This area displays a description of the highlighted software update.

CONTINUED

UPDATE SOFTWARE

When updating software on your computer, you will need to type the password for your user account.

You must have an administrator account to update software on your computer. An administrator has greater control over a computer than a standard user.

UPDATE SOFTWARE (CONTINUED)

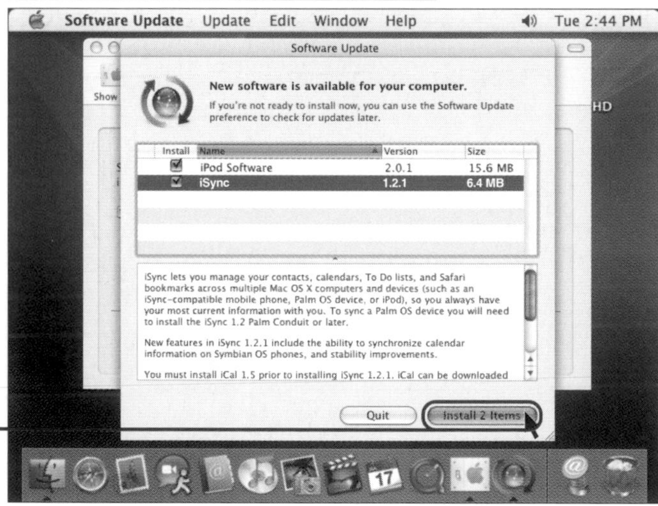

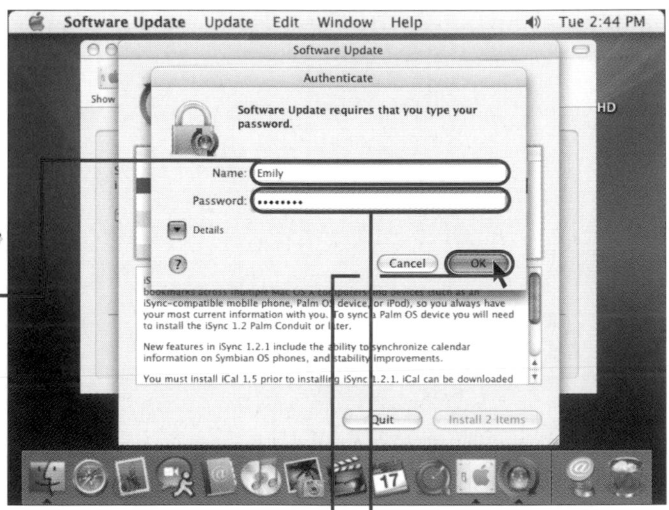

10 Click **Install** to install the software update(s).

Note: The name of the Install button depends on the number of software updates that display a check mark (✓).

■ The Authenticate dialog box appears.

■ This area displays the name of your user account.

11 Click this area and type the password for your user account.

Note: A bullet (●) appears for each character you type to prevent other people from seeing your password.

12 Click **OK** to continue.

Can I see which software updates I have installed on my computer?

Yes. Displaying the list of installed software updates is useful if you want to confirm that an update was installed correctly. To view the list of previously installed software updates, perform steps **1** and **2** on page 104 to display the Software Update window. Then click the **Installed Updates** tab.

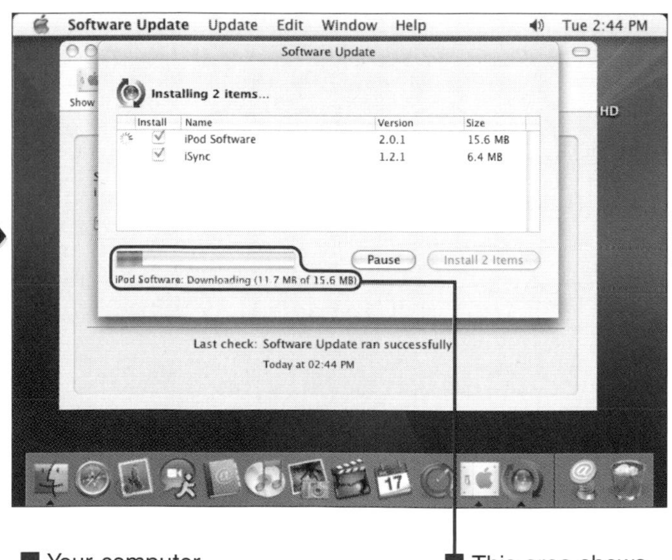

■ Your computer downloads and installs the software updates on your computer.

*Note: A dialog sheet may appear, displaying a license agreement for the software updates. To accept the agreement, click **Agree**.*

■ This area shows the progress of the installation.

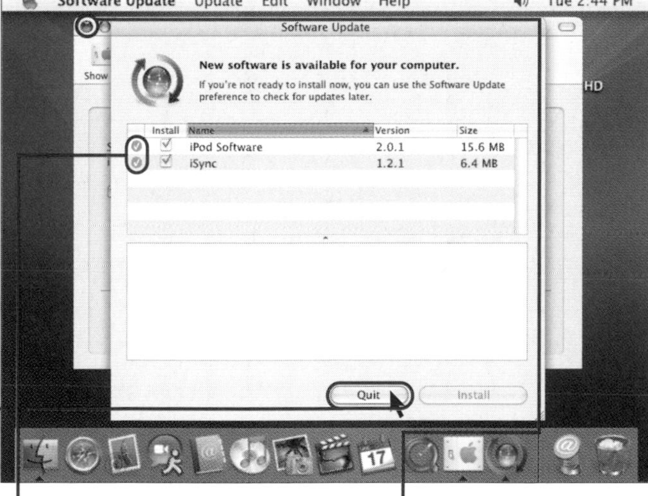

■ Software Update places a ✓ beside updates that have been installed successfully.

13 When the installation is complete, click **Quit** to close the Software Update window.

14 To quit System Preferences, click ●.

*Note: A dialog sheet may appear, asking you to restart your computer. Click **Restart** to restart your computer.*

Address Book

CHAPTER 5

Using Mac OS X Applications

You can use the applications included with Mac OS to perform many tasks on your computer. In this chapter, you will learn how to use Mac OS applications to create documents and electronic sticky notes, track your appointments in an electronic calendar, play DVD movies and more.

PLAY CHESS

You can play a game of chess on your computer.

When you play a game of chess, the computer is your opponent.

PLAY CHESS

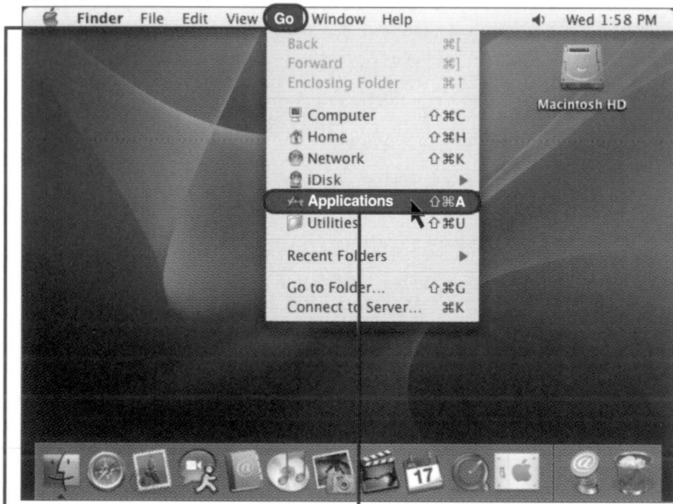

1 Click **Go**.

Note: If Go is not available, click a blank area on your desktop to display the Finder menu bar.

2 Click **Applications** to view the applications available on your computer.

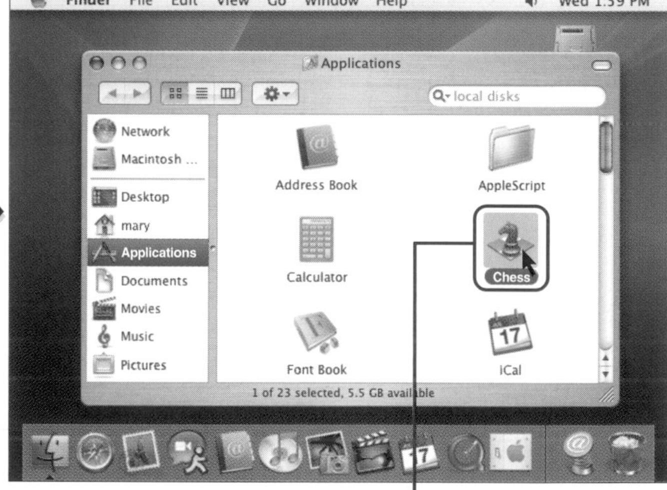

■ The Applications window appears, displaying the applications available on your computer.

3 Double-click **Chess** to play a game of chess.

Note: You can click ● in the Applications window to close the window.

How can I use spoken commands to play chess?

You must have a microphone connected to your computer to use spoken commands to play chess. To have your computer listen to your spoken commands, press and hold down the esc key as you speak into the microphone. To tell your computer where to move a chess piece, use the numbers and letters along the left and bottom edges of the chessboard, such as "Knight g1 to f3."

Can I get help with my next chess move?

If you are not sure what your next chess move should be, you can select the **Moves** menu and then click **Show Hint** to have Chess suggest a move. The move Chess suggests will appear as a red arrow on the chessboard.

■ The Chess window appears, displaying a three-dimensional chessboard.

■ The Speech Feedback window also appears, allowing you to use spoken commands to play chess.

Note: To use spoken commands to play chess, see the top of this page.

■ To start the game, you must move a chess piece.

4 To move a chess piece, drag the chess piece to a new location on the chessboard.

Note: If you move a chess piece to an invalid location, an alert will sound and the chess piece will return to its original location.

■ After you move a chess piece, the computer will automatically move a chess piece.

5 When you finish playing chess, click **Chess**.

6 Click **Quit Chess** to close the Chess window.

You can use Preview to view pictures and Portable Document Format (PDF) files on your computer.

USING PREVIEW

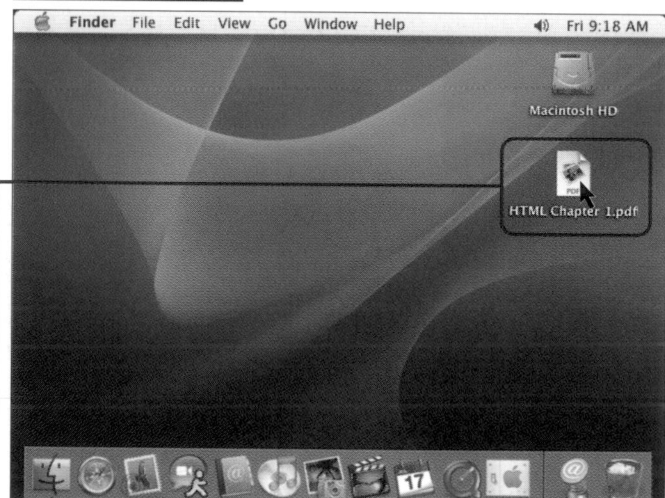

■1 Double-click the picture or PDF file you want to view.

■ A window appears, displaying the picture or a page of the PDF file.

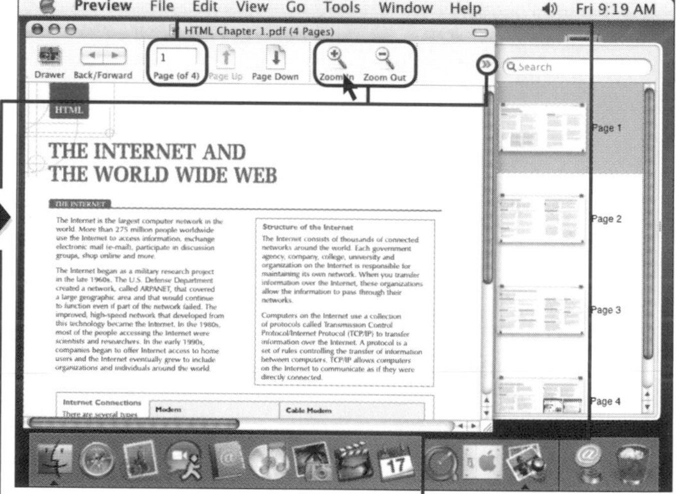

■2 To magnify or reduce the size of the picture or page, click **Zoom In** or **Zoom Out**.

■ If the button you want to use is not displayed on the toolbar, click » to display a list of the hidden buttons.

■ If you are viewing a PDF file that contains more than one page, this area displays the number of the current page and the total number of pages in the file.

What are PDF files?

A Portable Document Format (PDF) file is a popular file type that preserves a document's original layout and formatting. Books, product catalogues and support information for software are often distributed as PDF files, since this file type displays information exactly as it appears in printed form. PDF files are commonly found on the Web and on CDs included with books.

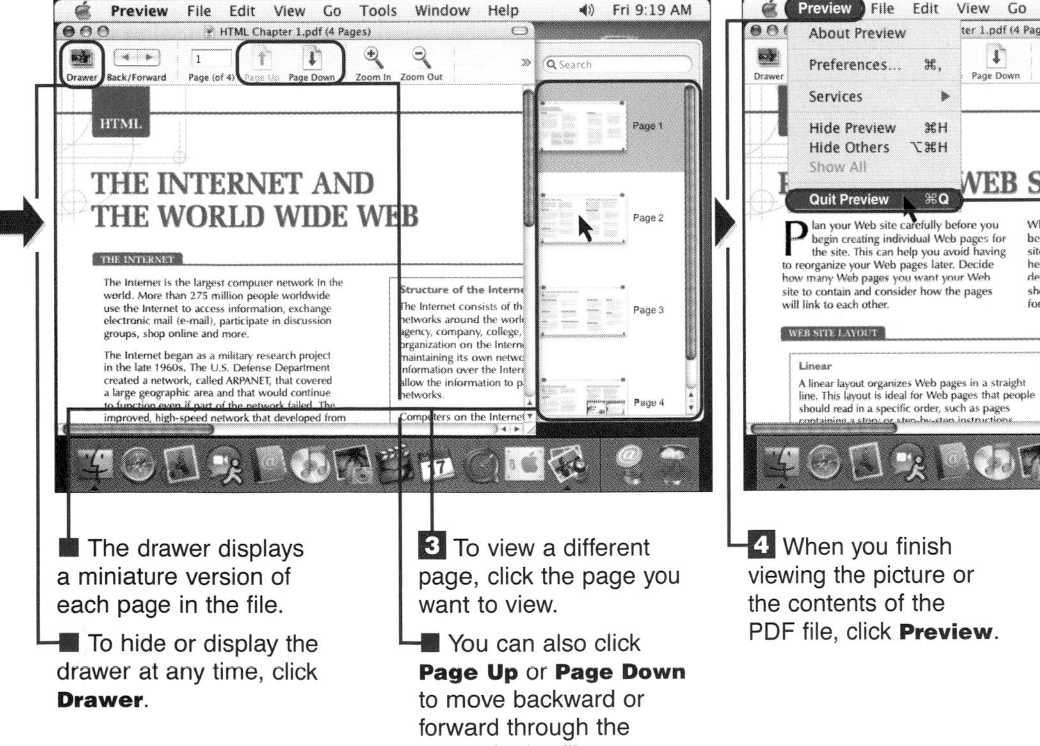

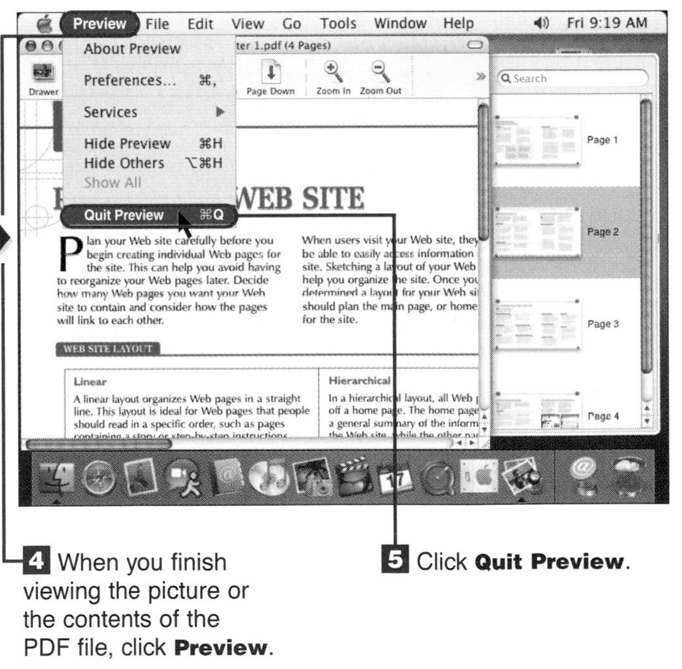

■ The drawer displays a miniature version of each page in the file.

■ To hide or display the drawer at any time, click **Drawer**.

3 To view a different page, click the page you want to view.

■ You can also click **Page Up** or **Page Down** to move backward or forward through the pages in the file.

4 When you finish viewing the picture or the contents of the PDF file, click **Preview**.

5 Click **Quit Preview**.

USING QUICKTIME PLAYER

You can use QuickTime Player to play QuickTime movies on your computer.

You can play QuickTime movies you obtained on the Internet or created using iMovie. For information on using iMovie, see pages 186 to 203.

USING QUICKTIME PLAYER

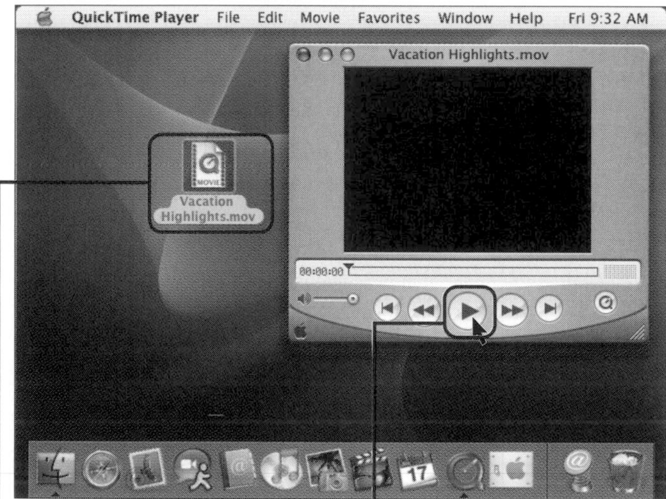

1 Double-click the QuickTime movie you want to play. QuickTime movies display the icon and .mov extension.

■ A QuickTime Player window opens.

Note: The first time you play a QuickTime movie, a dialog box appears, allowing you to purchase QuickTime Pro, an advanced version of QuickTime. You can click an option in the dialog box to continue.

2 Click ▶ to start playing the movie (▶ changes to ⏸).

■ The movie plays in this area.

■ This area displays the amount of time the movie has been playing and a slider (▼) that indicates the progress of the movie.

3 To decrease or increase the volume, drag this slider (◉) left or right.

Note: To quickly turn off the sound, click 🔊 (🔊 changes to 🔈). To once again turn on the sound, click 🔈.

Is there another way to play a QuickTime movie?

Yes. You can find QuickTime movies on the Web that you can play in your Web browser. For example, the www.apple.com/trailers and www.comingsoon.net/trailers Web sites offer QuickTime movies that you can play. When the movie is playing, you can click ⏸ to pause the movie (⏸ changes to ▶). To once again play the movie, click ▶.

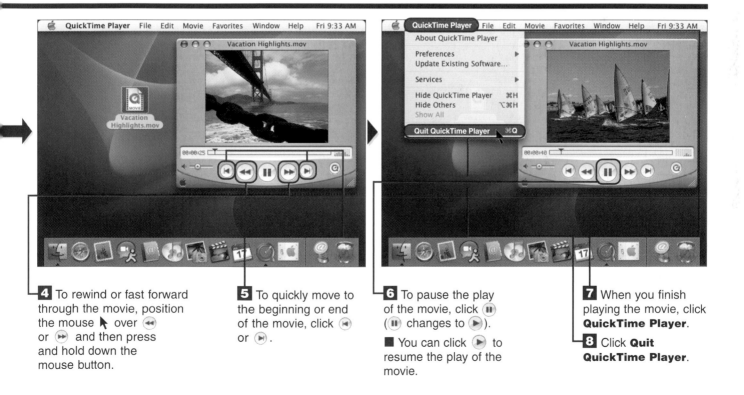

4 To rewind or fast forward through the movie, position the mouse ↖ over ⏪ or ⏩ and then press and hold down the mouse button.

5 To quickly move to the beginning or end of the movie, click ⏮ or ⏭.

6 To pause the play of the movie, click ⏸ (⏸ changes to ▶).

■ You can click ▶ to resume the play of the movie.

7 When you finish playing the movie, click **QuickTime Player**.

8 Click **Quit QuickTime Player**.

You can use Address Book to store information for people you frequently contact.

Mail and other applications can use the information in Address Book. For example, when you compose an e-mail message, Mail can quickly fill in the e-mail address of a person you have added to Address Book.

USING ADDRESS BOOK

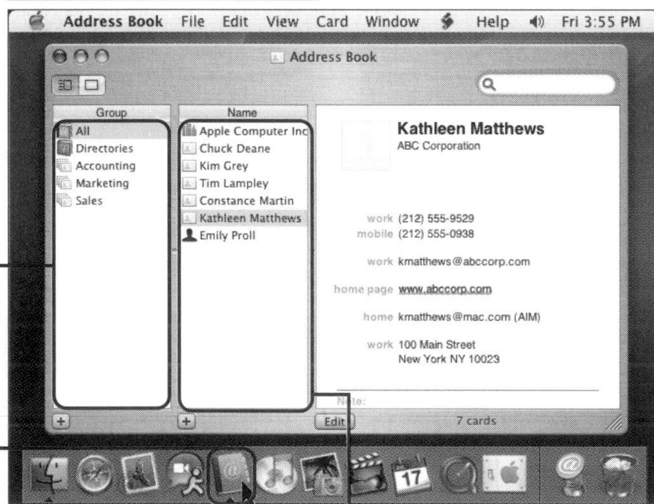

DISPLAY ADDRESS BOOK

1 Click the Address Book icon to display Address Book.

■ The Address Book window appears.

■ This area displays the groups in Address Book.

Note: To create a group, see page 120.

■ This area displays the people in the highlighted group.

Note: Your name automatically appears in the All group and displays the 👤 symbol.

ADD A PERSON

1 To add a person to Address Book, click the group you want to add the person to. The group is highlighted.

*Note: If you have not added groups to Address Book, select the **All** group.*

2 Click + to add a new person to Address Book.

Why does a plus sign (⊕) appear when I enter information for a person?

A plus sign appears if Address Book can display another area where you can enter information. To display the other area, click the plus sign (⊕). For example, after you enter a mobile phone number, you can click the plus sign (⊕) beside **mobile** to display an area where you can enter a home phone number.

When entering information for a person, can I change the label for an area?

Yes. You may want to change the label for an area to better describe the information you want to enter in the area. For example, you can change the label "mobile" to "pager."

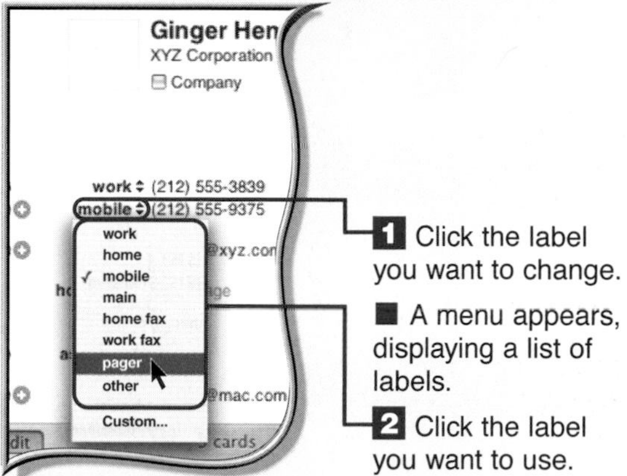

1 Click the label you want to change.

■ A menu appears, displaying a list of labels.

2 Click the label you want to use.

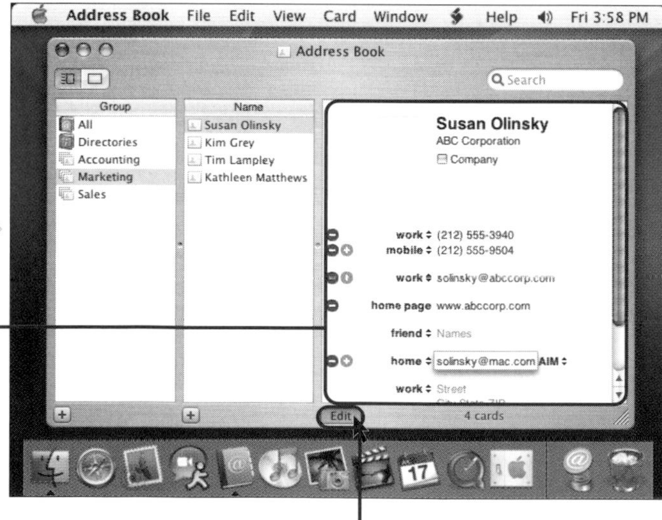

■ Address Book displays areas where you can enter information for the person.

3 Click an area and type the appropriate information for the person. Then press the return key.

4 Repeat step **3** for each area where you want to enter information for the person.

Note: You do not need to enter information into every area.

5 When you finish entering the information for the person, click **Edit** to save the information.

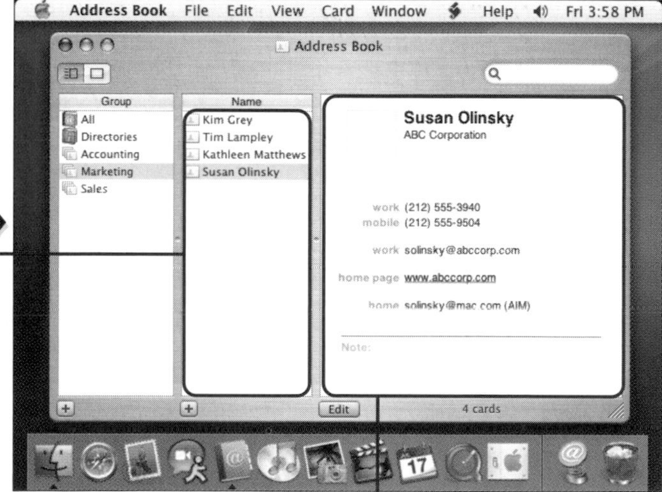

■ The name you entered for the person appears in this area.

■ This area displays the information you entered for the person.

CONTINUED

USING ADDRESS BOOK

You can browse through Address Book to find information for a specific person. You can also edit the information for a person or delete a person you no longer contact.

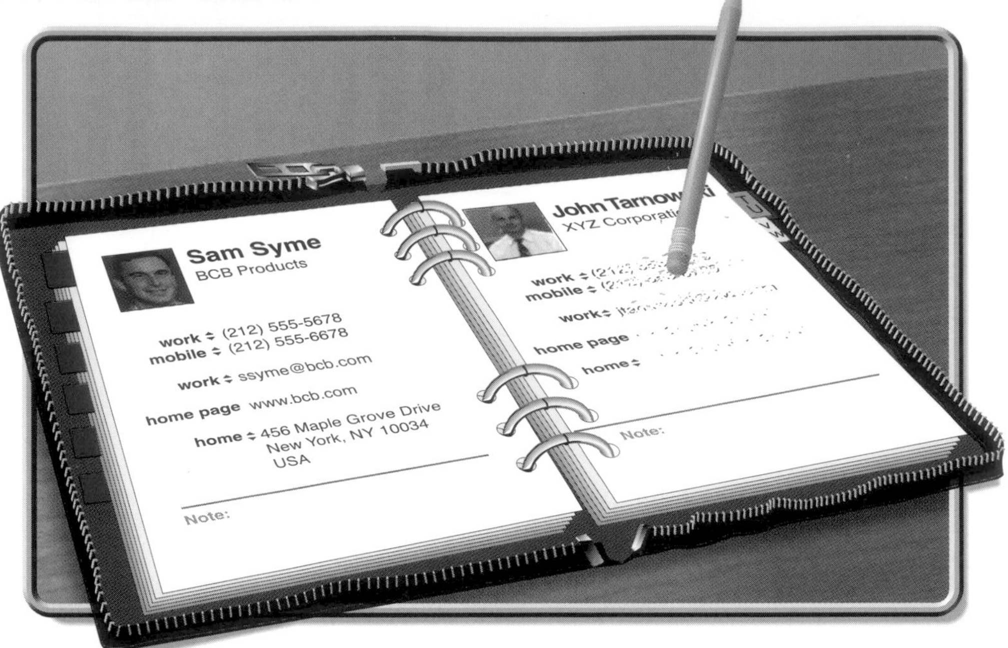

USING ADDRESS BOOK (CONTINUED)

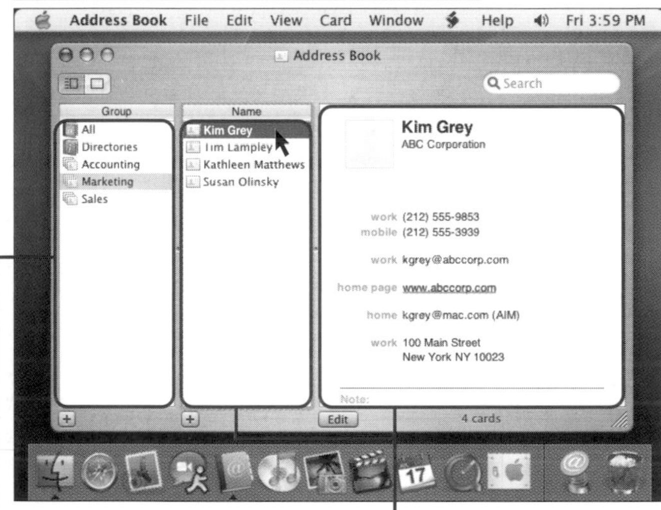

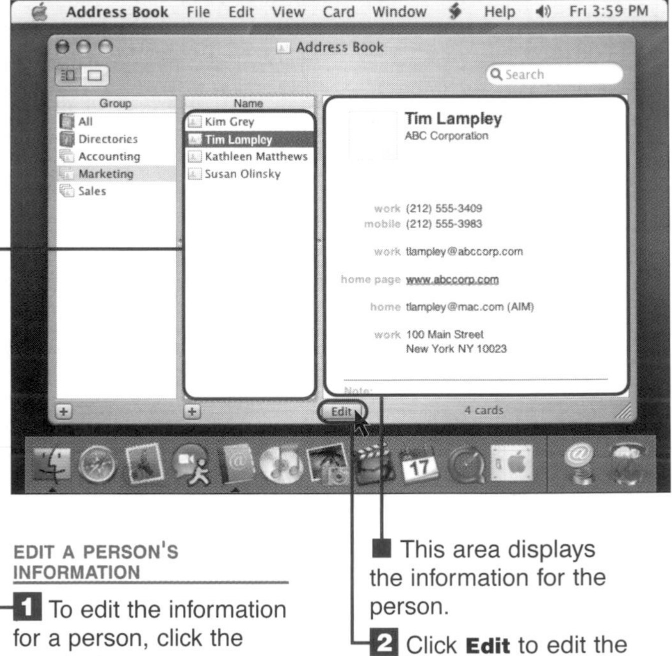

DISPLAY A PERSON'S INFORMATION

1 Click the group that contains a person of interest.

Note: The All group contains all the people you have added to Address Book.

■ This area displays the people in the group you selected.

2 Click the name of a person of interest.

■ This area displays the information for the person.

EDIT A PERSON'S INFORMATION

1 To edit the information for a person, click the name of the person.

■ This area displays the information for the person.

2 Click **Edit** to edit the person's information.

Can I add a picture to a person's information in Address Book?

Yes. Click the name of the person whose information you want to add a picture to. Locate the picture you want to add to the information and then drag the picture into the box beside the person's name in the Address Book window. A window that allows you to crop the picture may appear. Click **Set** to use the picture.

How do I search for a person in Address Book?

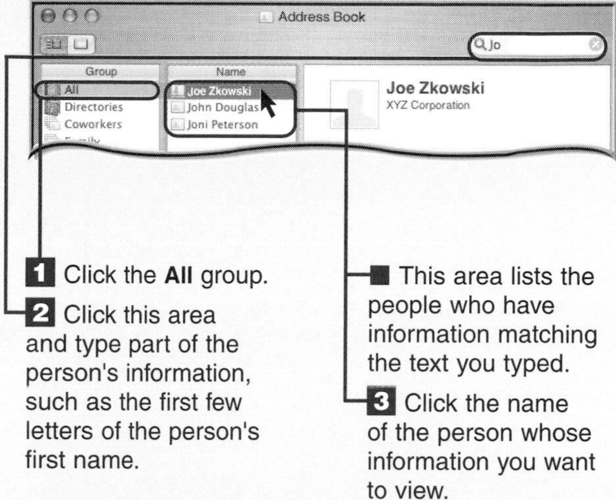

1 Click the **All** group.

2 Click this area and type part of the person's information, such as the first few letters of the person's first name.

■ This area lists the people who have information matching the text you typed.

3 Click the name of the person whose information you want to view.

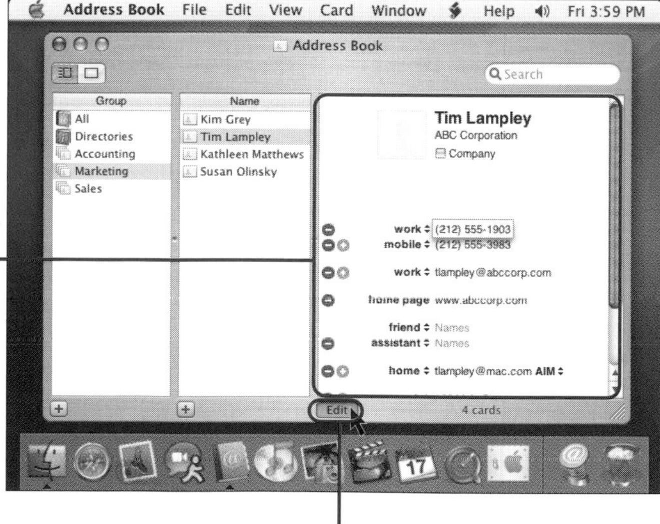

3 Click the information you want to edit. The information is highlighted.

4 Type the new information and then press the return key.

5 Repeat steps **3** and **4** for each area of information you want to edit.

6 Click **Edit** to save your changes.

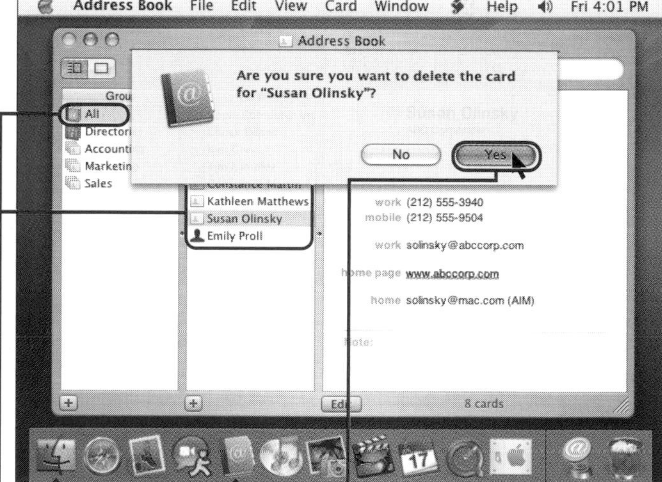

DELETE A PERSON

1 Click **All** to display all the people you have added to Address Book.

2 Click the name of the person you want to remove from Address Book.

3 Press the delete key.

■ A confirmation dialog sheet appears.

4 Click **Yes** to remove the person from Address Book.

CONTINUED

You can create groups to organize the people in Address Book. For example, you can create groups such as Family, Friends, Clients and Colleagues.

You can create as many groups as you need. A person can belong to more than one group.

Mail and other applications can use a group you create in Address Book. For example, Mail can use a group you added to Address Book to quickly address an e-mail message to each person in the group.

USING ADDRESS BOOK (CONTINUED)

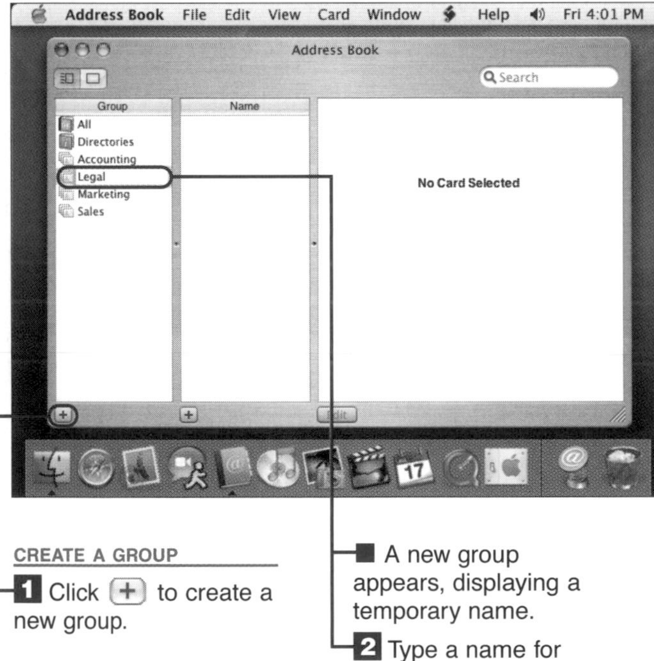

CREATE A GROUP

1 Click (+) to create a new group.

■ A new group appears, displaying a temporary name.

2 Type a name for the new group and then press the return key.

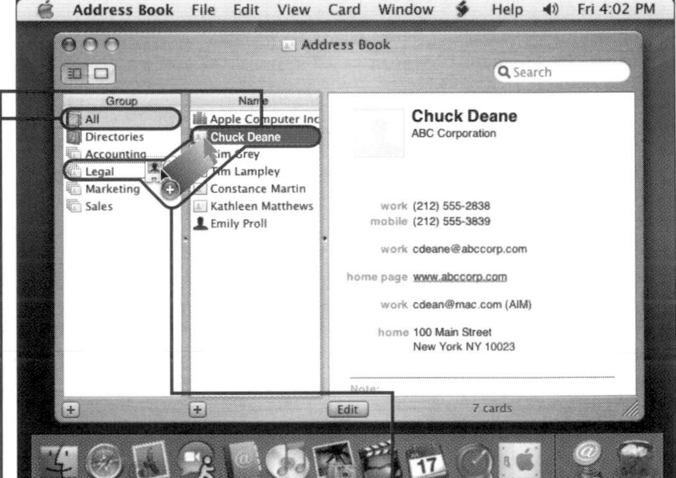

ADD PEOPLE TO A GROUP

1 Click **All** to display all the people you have added to Address Book.

2 Position the mouse over the person you want to add to a specific group.

3 Drag the person to the group (pointer changes to drag icon).

Note: When you drag a person to a group, a box appears around the group.

■ The person's information is copied to the group.

Can I remove a person from a group?

Yes. Click the group that contains a person you want to remove. Click the name of the person you want to remove from the group and then press the delete key. In the confirmation dialog sheet that appears, click **Remove from Group** to remove the person from the group without removing the person from Address Book.

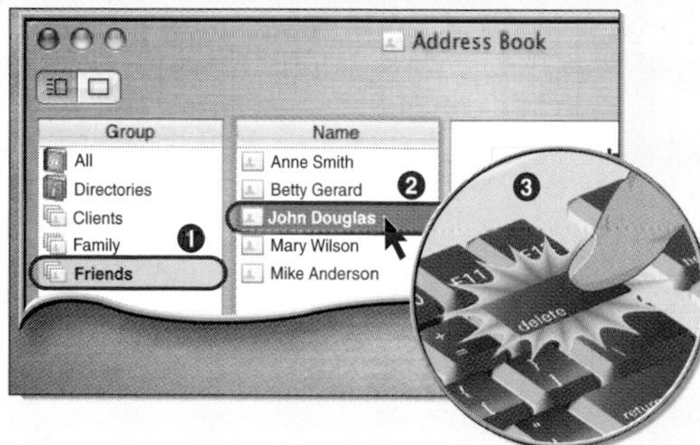

How do I rename a group in Address Book?

Double-click the name of the group you want to rename. A box appears around the name of the group. Type a new name for the group and then press the return key. You cannot rename the All group.

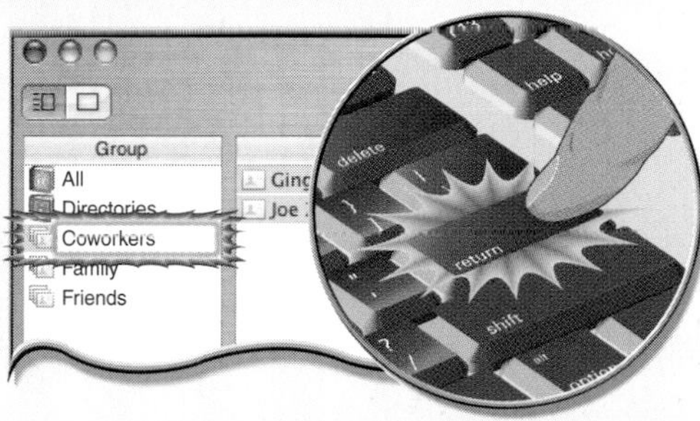

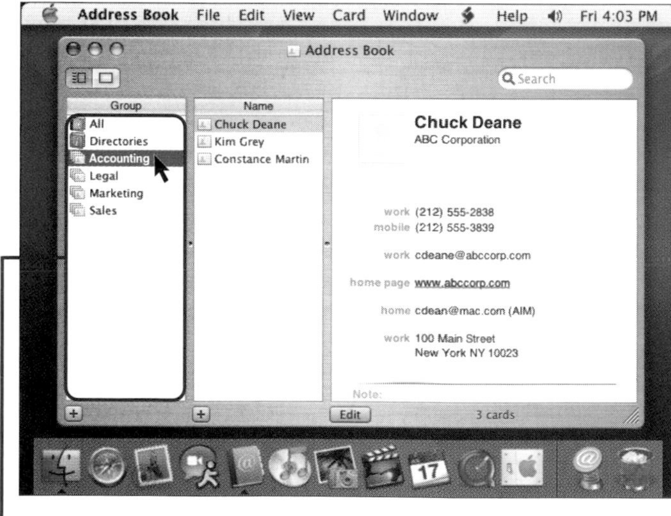

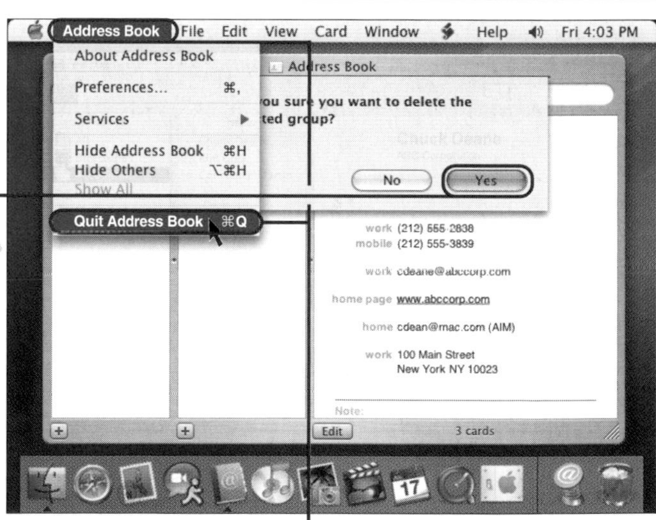

DELETE A GROUP

1 Click the group you want to remove from Address Book.

*Note: You cannot remove the **All** group.*

2 Press the delete key.

Note: Removing a group does not remove the people in the group from Address Book.

■ A confirmation dialog sheet appears.

3 Click **Yes** to remove the group from Address Book.

QUIT ADDRESS BOOK

1 When you finish using Address Book, click **Address Book**.

2 Click **Quit Address Book**.

You can use iCal™ to keep track of your appointments, such as business meetings and lunch dates.

iCal uses the date and time set in your computer to determine today's date. To change the date and time set in your computer, see page 86.

USING iCAL

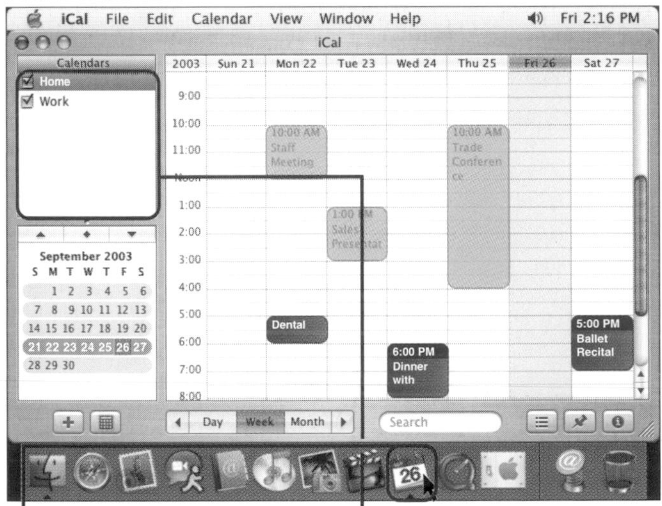

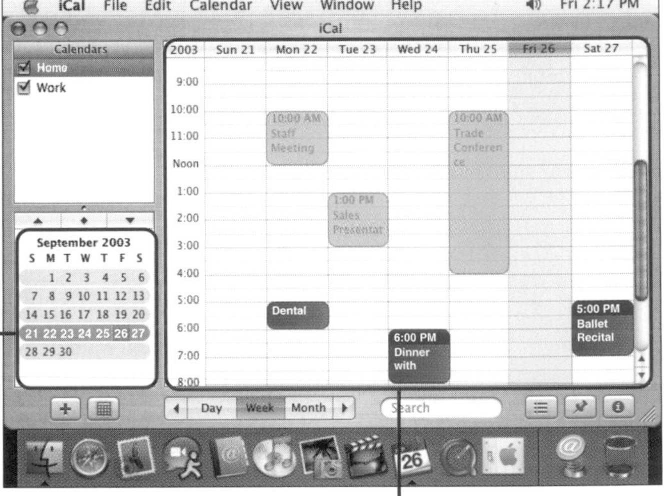

1 Click the iCal icon to start iCal.

■ The iCal window appears.

■ This area displays all your calendars. The box (☑) beside each calendar name shows the color that events in the calendar display.

■ This area displays the days in the current month. The current week is highlighted and the current day is blue.

■ This area displays events for the current week.

Note: To add an event, see page 124.

Can I create another calendar to keep track of other events?

By default, iCal creates the Home and Work calendars for you, but you can create other calendars to keep track of all your events. For example, you may want to create a calendar to keep track of your children's school events. To create a calendar, click [+]. The new calendar appears in the iCal window. Type a name for the calendar and then press the [return] key.

How can I display the events for only one calendar at a time?

A check mark (✓) appears beside the name of each calendar that displays its events in the iCal window. You can click the check box beside a calendar name to hide (☐) or display (☑) the calendar's events at any time.

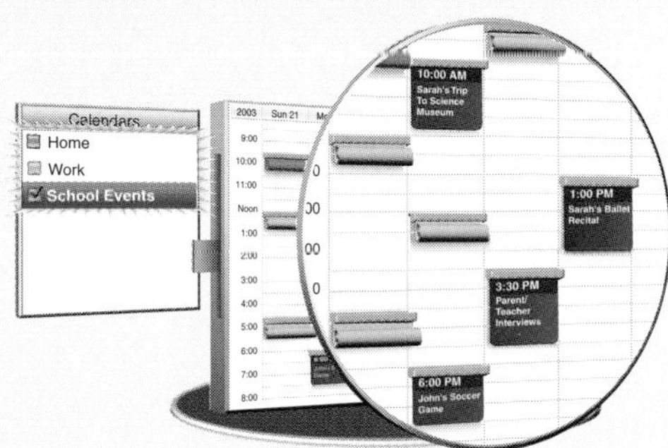

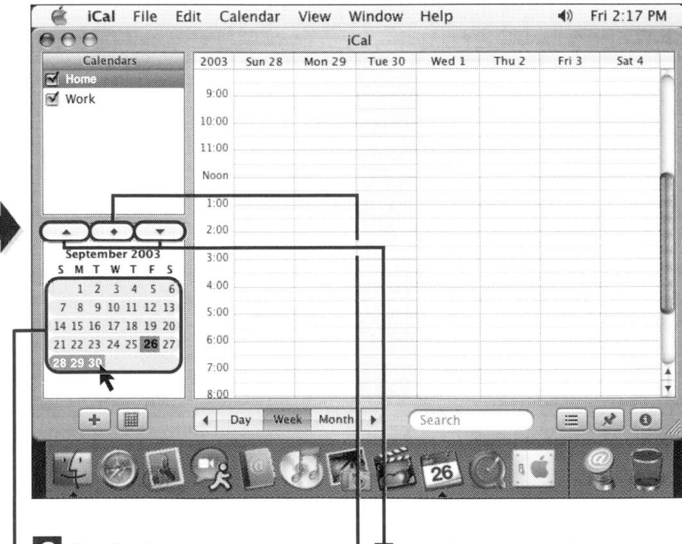

2 To display the events for another week, click a day in the week. The week you select is highlighted.

■ To display the days in another month, click [▲] or [▼] to move backward or forward through the months.

■ To quickly return to the current month, click [◆].

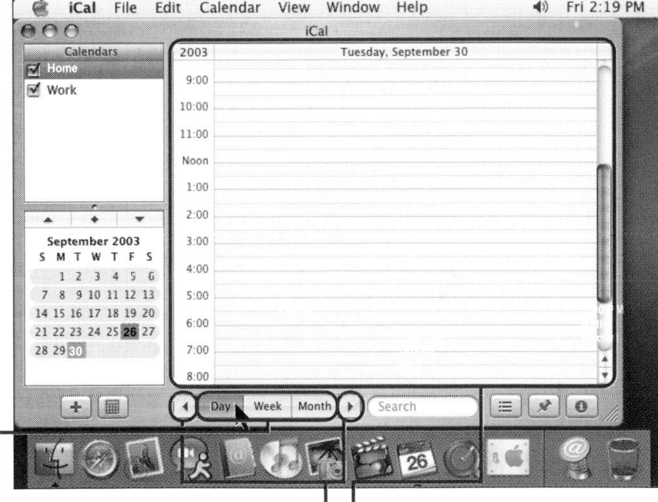

CHANGE THE VIEW OF THE CALENDAR

1 Click an option to specify if you want to display a day, week or month in the iCal window.

■ The iCal window displays the period of time you selected.

■ You can click [◀] or [▶] to display the previous or next day, week or month.

CONTINUED

You can add an event to iCal to remind you of an activity, such as a seminar or doctor's appointment.

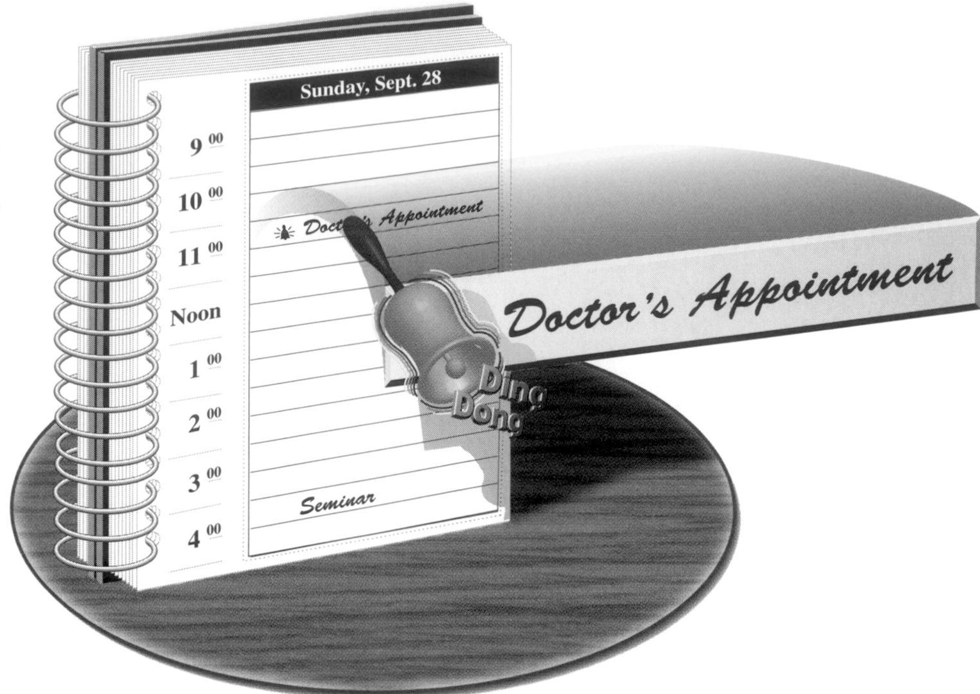

USING iCAL (CONTINUED)

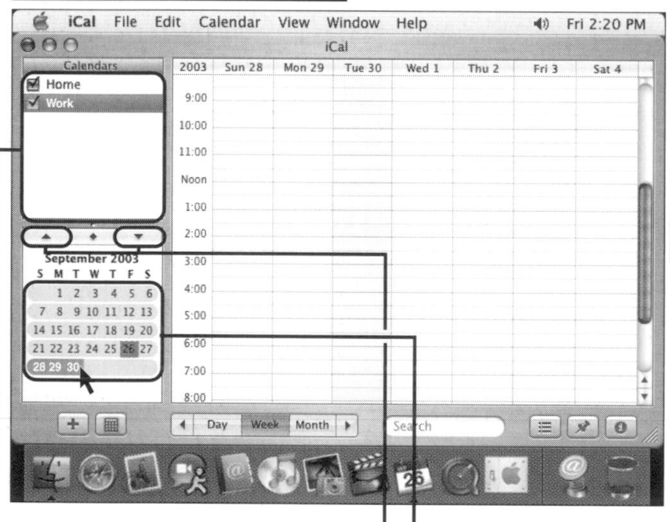

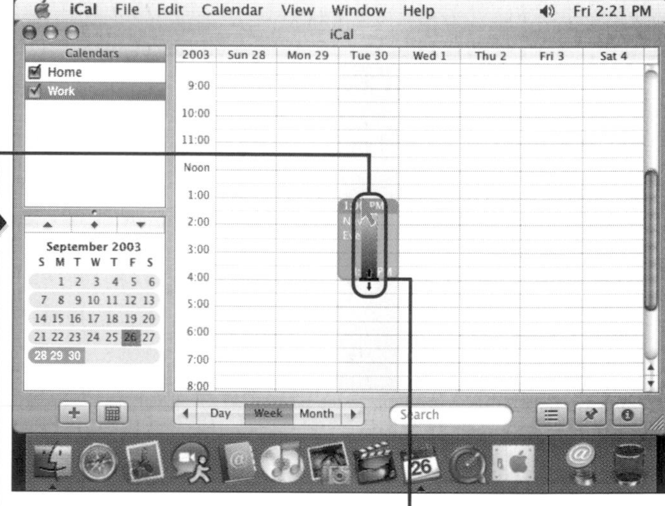

SCHEDULE AN EVENT

1 Click the calendar you want to add an event to.

Note: iCal displays the events for each calendar that displays a check mark (✓). Click the box beside a calendar name to add (☑) or remove (☐) a check mark.

2 Click the day you want to add an event to.

■ To display the days in another month, click ▲ or ▼.

3 Position the mouse over the starting time for the event.

4 Drag the mouse to select the amount of time you want to set aside for the event.

Can I search for an event in my calendar?

If you have forgotten the date or time of an event you scheduled, you can search iCal for the event.

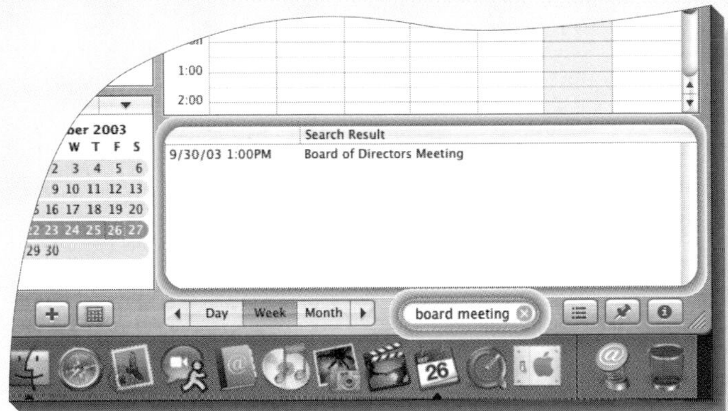

Click the Search area and type a word or phrase in the subject of the event you want to find. iCal displays all the events that contain the word or phrase in the Search Result area. To display an event on the calendar, click the event.

Note: To hide the Search Result area, drag the mouse I over the text you typed in the Search area and press the delete *key.*

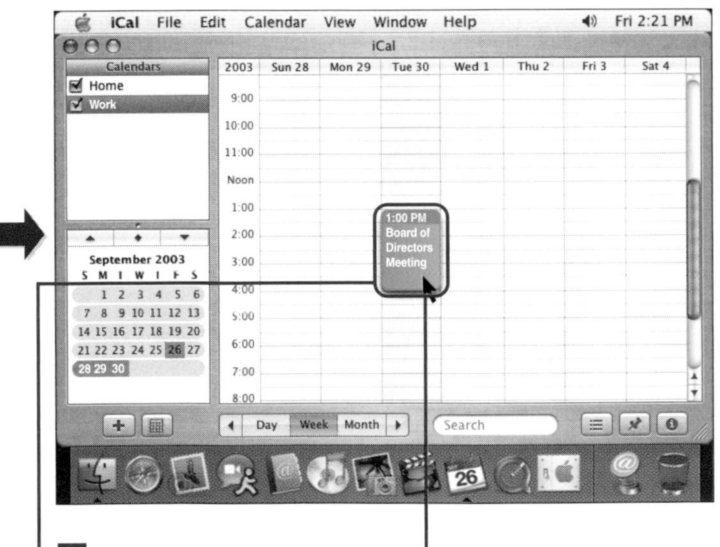

5 Type a subject for the event and then press the return key.

DELETE AN EVENT

1 To select the event you want to delete, click anywhere in the event.

2 Press the delete key to delete the event.

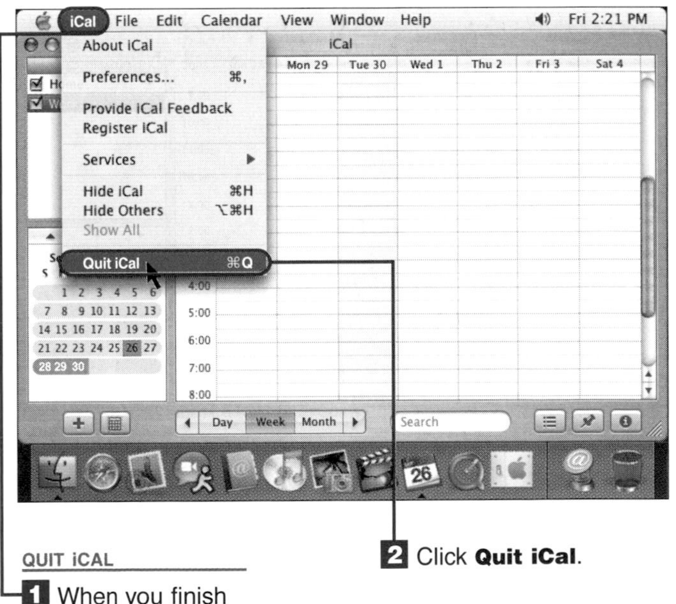

QUIT ICAL

1 When you finish using iCal, click **iCal**.

2 Click **Quit iCal**.

USING THE CALCULATOR

You can use the Calculator to perform simple mathematical calculations.

The Calculator allows you to perform the same calculations you would perform on a handheld calculator.

USING THE CALCULATOR

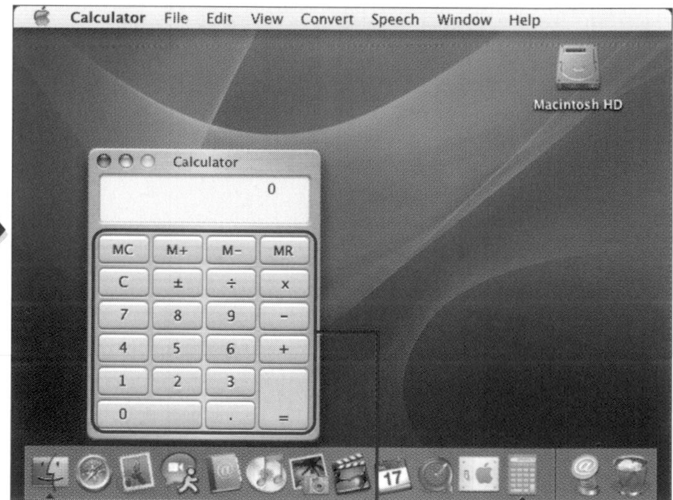

1 Click **Go**.

Note: If Go is not available, click a blank area on your desktop to display the Finder menu bar.

2 Click **Applications** to view the applications available on your computer.

■ The Applications window appears.

3 Double-click **Calculator** to start the Calculator.

■ The Calculator appears.

Note: You can click ● in the Applications window to close the window.

4 To enter information into the Calculator, click each button as you would press the buttons on a handheld calculator.

Note: You can also use the keys on your keyboard to enter information into the Calculator.

Can I use the Calculator to perform advanced mathematical calculations?

Yes. The Calculator offers an Advanced view, which allows you to perform advanced mathematical and statistical calculations.

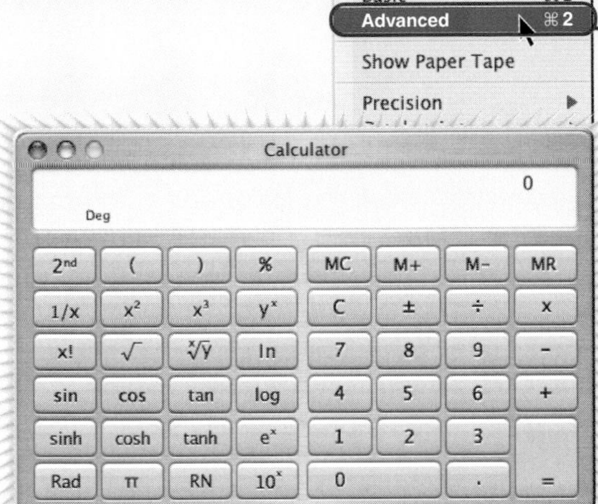

1 Click the **View** menu.

2 Click **Advanced**.

■ The Advanced view of the calculator appears.

■ To return to the Basic view, repeat steps **1** and **2**, selecting **Basic** in step **2**.

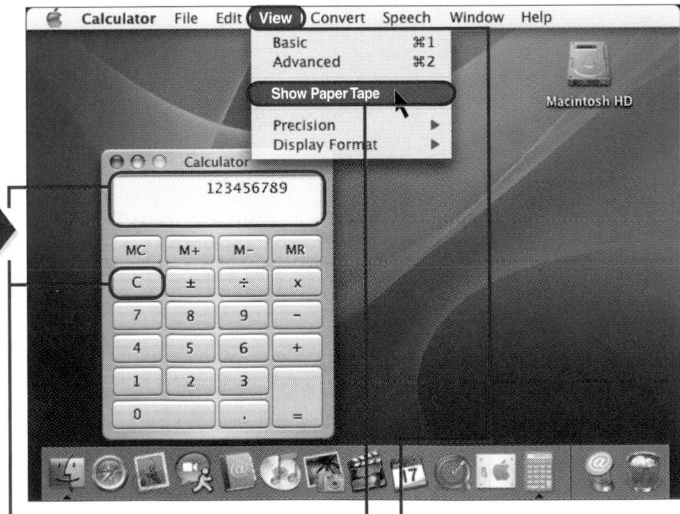

■ This area displays the numbers and operators you enter and the result of each calculation.

■ You can click C to start a new calculation at any time.

5 To display the steps for a calculation, click the **View** menu.

6 Click **Show Paper Tape**.

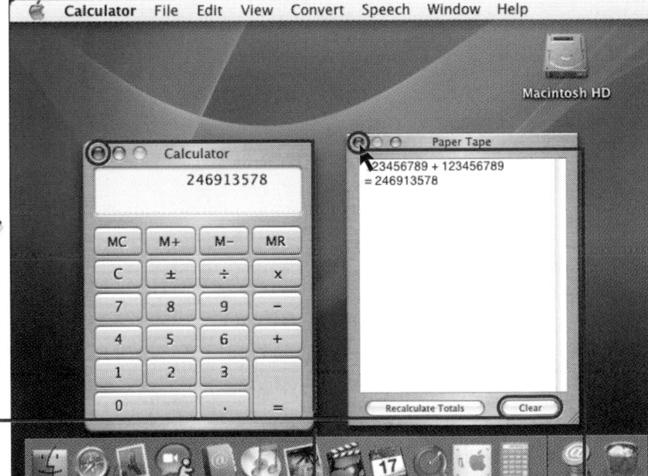

■ The Paper Tape window appears, displaying the numbers and operators you enter and the result of each calculation.

■ You can click **Clear** to clear the paper tape.

7 To close the Paper Tape window, click ● in the window.

8 When you finish using the Calculator, click ● to close the Calculator.

You can use TextEdit to create and edit documents, such as letters and memos.

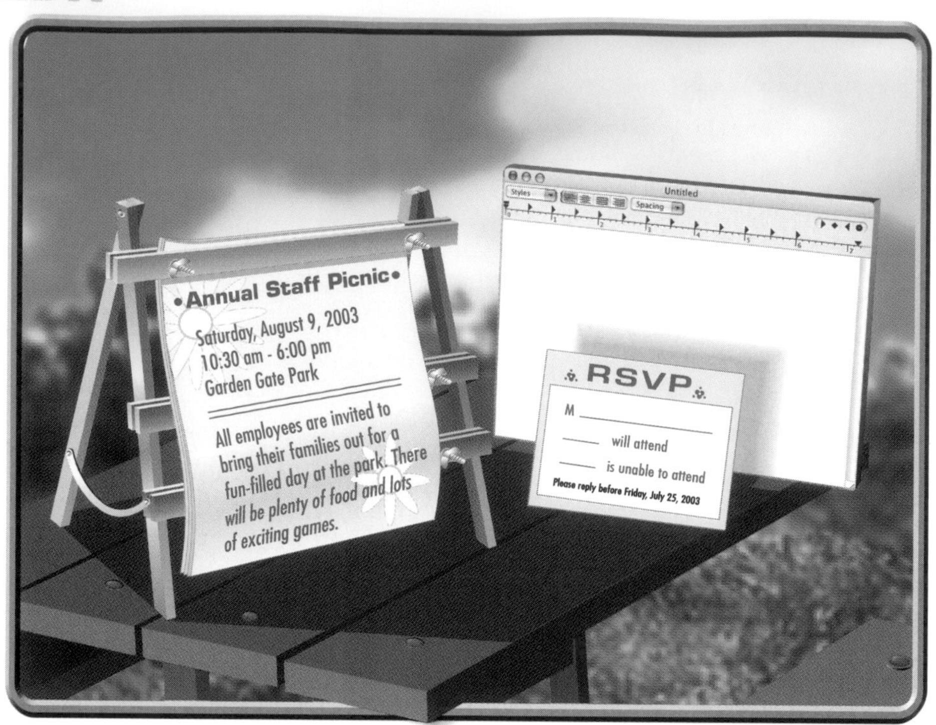

TextEdit offers only basic word processing features. If you require more advanced features, you may want to obtain a more sophisticated word processor, such as Microsoft Word.

USING TEXTEDIT

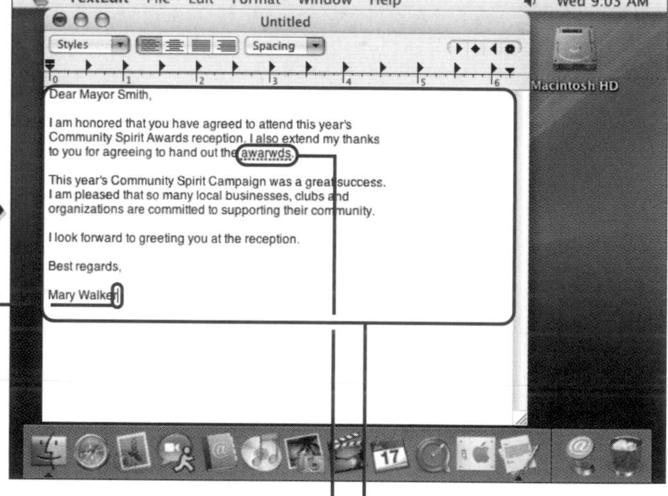

1 Click **Go**.

Note: If Go is not available, click a blank area on your desktop to display the Finder menu bar.

2 Click **Applications** to view the applications available on your computer.

■ The Applications window appears.

3 Double-click **TextEdit** to start TextEdit.

■ A new document window appears.

Note: You can click ● in the Applications window to close the window.

■ The flashing insertion point indicates where the text you type will appear.

4 Type the text for the document.

■ TextEdit checks your spelling as you type and displays a dotted red underline below potential spelling errors. The dotted red underlines will not appear when you print the document.

Can TextEdit help me correct a spelling error in a document?

Yes. To get help correcting a spelling error in a document, press and hold down the control key as you click the misspelled word. A menu appears, displaying suggestions to correct the spelling error. Click the suggestion you want to use to correct the spelling error.

Can I change how TextEdit wraps text?

Yes. By default, TextEdit wraps text based on the width of the document window. To have TextEdit wrap text based on the width of the paper you will print on, select the **Format** menu and then click **Wrap to Page**. Wrapping text to the width of the paper you will print on helps prevent unexpected results when printing a document.

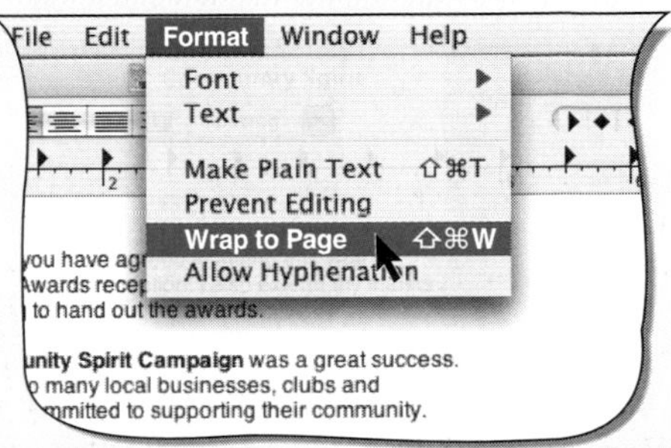

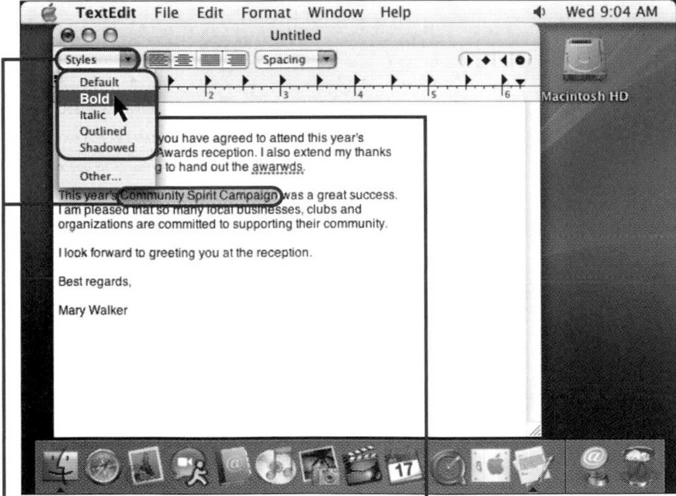

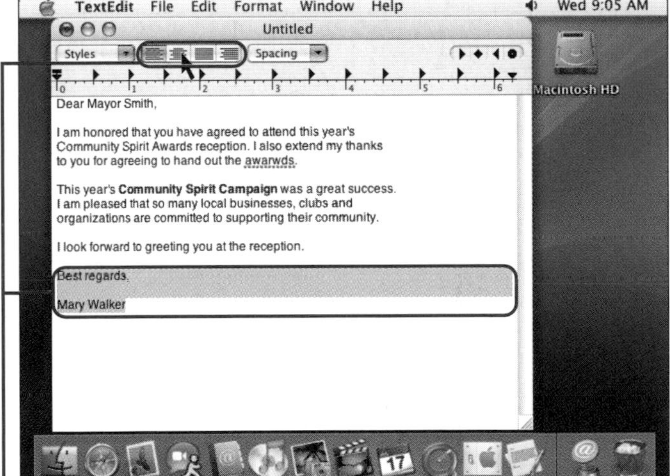

CHANGE TEXT STYLE

1 To select the text you want to change, drag the mouse I over the text until the text is highlighted.

2 Click ▾ in this area to display the available text styles.

3 Click the text style you want to use.

■ The text appears in the new style.

*Note: You can repeat steps **1** to **3**, selecting **Default** in step **3** to remove a style from text.*

CHANGE TEXT ALIGNMENT

1 To select the text you want to change, drag the mouse I over the text until the text is highlighted.

2 Click one of these options.

- Left align
- Center
- Justify
- Right align

■ The text displays the new alignment.

CONTINUED

You can change the font of text to enhance the appearance of text.

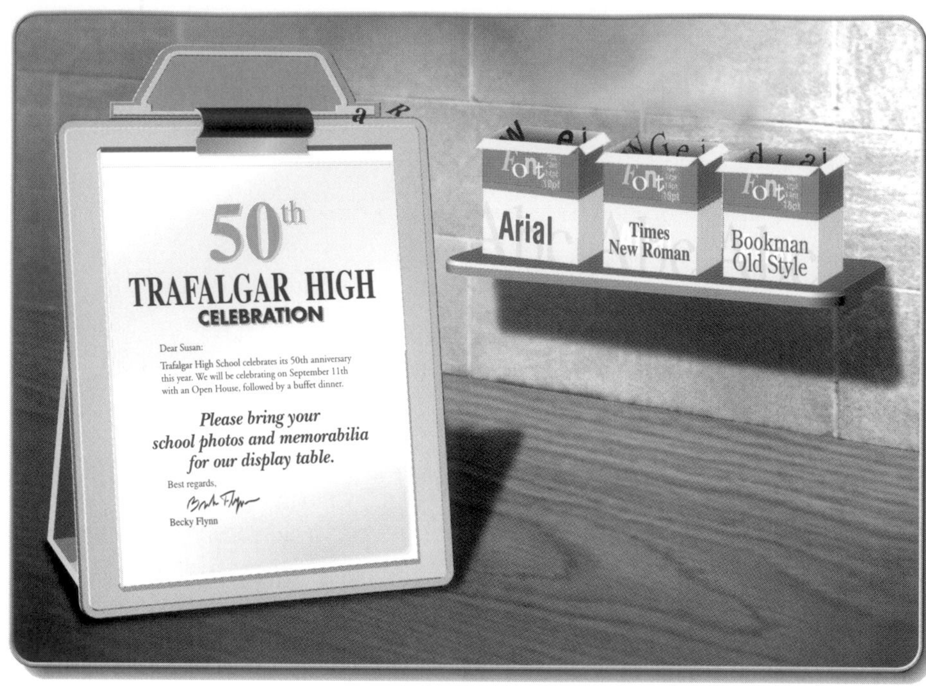

After you finish creating and making changes to your document, you can save the document.

USING TEXTEDIT (CONTINUED)

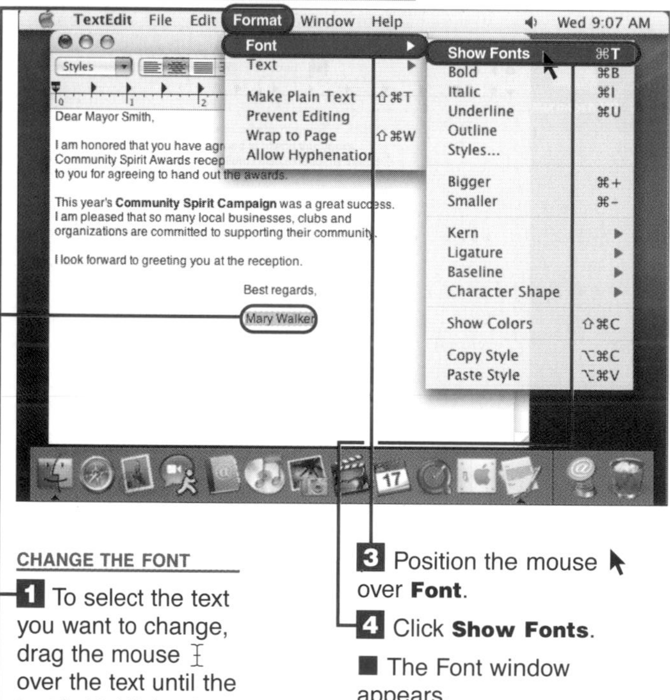

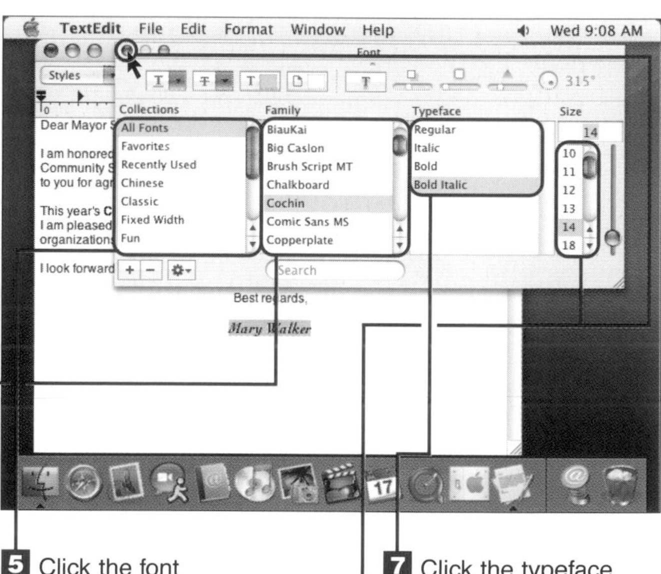

CHANGE THE FONT

1 To select the text you want to change, drag the mouse over the text until the text is highlighted.

2 Click **Format**.

3 Position the mouse over **Font**.

4 Click **Show Fonts**.

■ The Font window appears.

5 Click the font collection containing the font you want to use.

*Note: If you do not know which collection contains the font, click **All Fonts**.*

6 Click the font family you want to use.

7 Click the typeface you want to use.

8 Click the size you want to use.

9 When you finish making changes to the text, click ● to close the Font window.

Can I change the line spacing of text?

Yes. Changing the line spacing changes the amount of space between lines of text. You can choose from single or double line spacing.

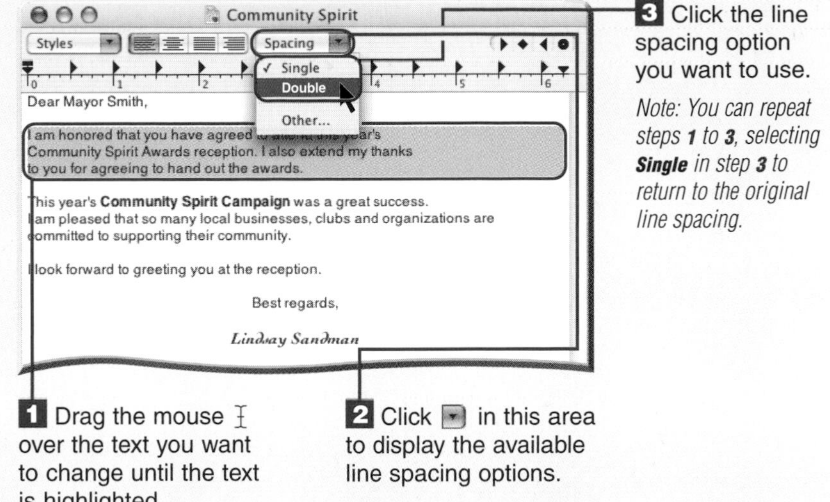

1 Drag the mouse over the text you want to change until the text is highlighted.

2 Click in this area to display the available line spacing options.

3 Click the line spacing option you want to use.

*Note: You can repeat steps **1** to **3**, selecting **Single** in step **3** to return to the original line spacing.*

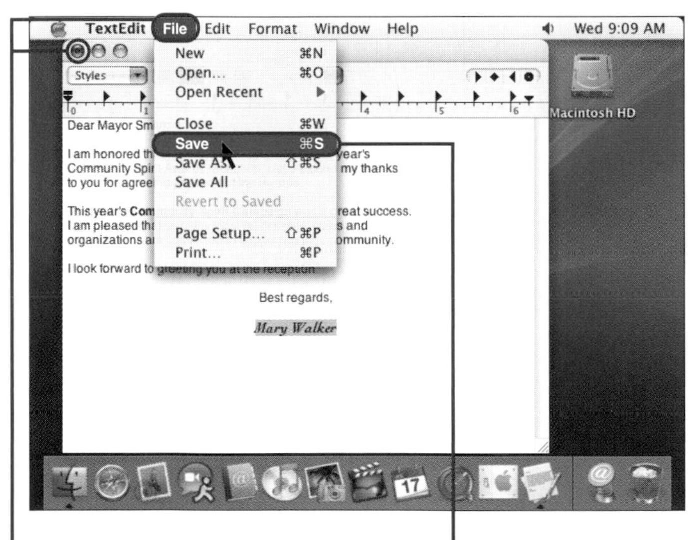

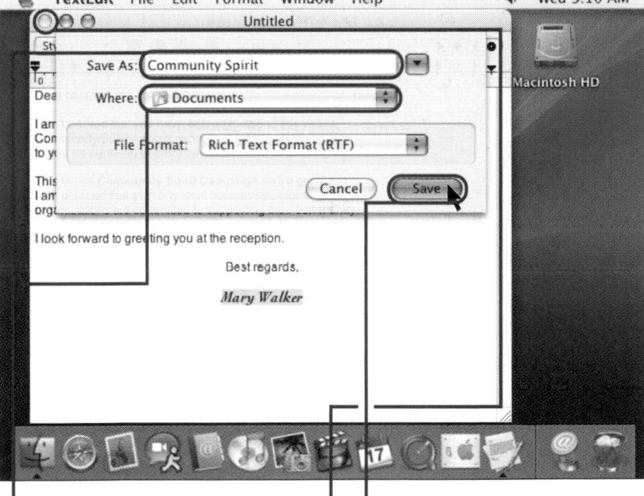

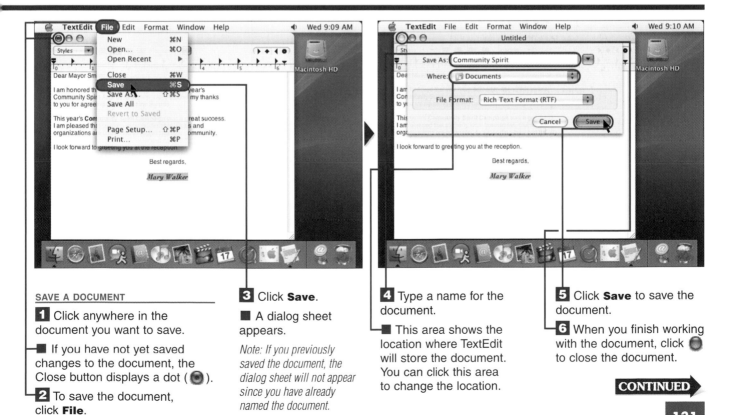

SAVE A DOCUMENT

1 Click anywhere in the document you want to save.

■ If you have not yet saved changes to the document, the Close button displays a dot ( ).

2 To save the document, click **File**.

3 Click **Save**.

■ A dialog sheet appears.

Note: If you previously saved the document, the dialog sheet will not appear since you have already named the document.

4 Type a name for the document.

■ This area shows the location where TextEdit will store the document. You can click this area to change the location.

5 Click **Save** to save the document.

6 When you finish working with the document, click to close the document.

CONTINUED

You can open a saved TextEdit document to display the document on your screen. This allows you to review and make changes to the document.

West Parkdale
AUTO SHOP
LOCATION
354 New Market Avenue, across from Jacob's Food Mart
HOURS OF OPERATION
Monday to Friday: 9:00 AM - 6:00 PM
Saturday and Sunday: 11:00 AM - 4:00 PM
We specialize in all aspects of car repair, and offer the best rates in town.
Please come and visit us for a full list of prices.

USING TEXTEDIT (CONTINUED)

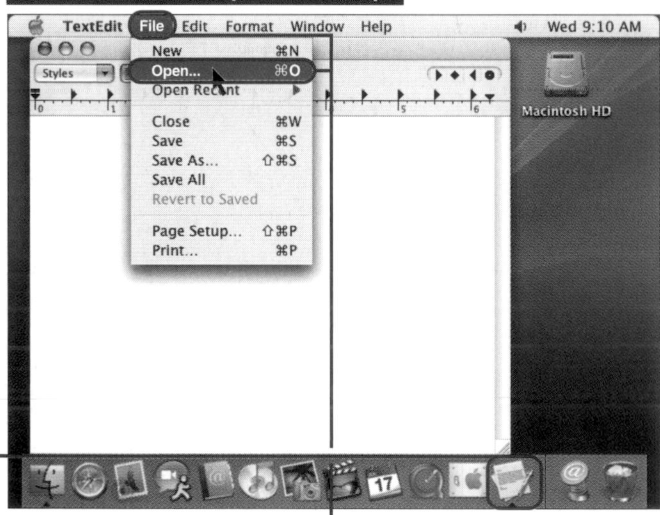

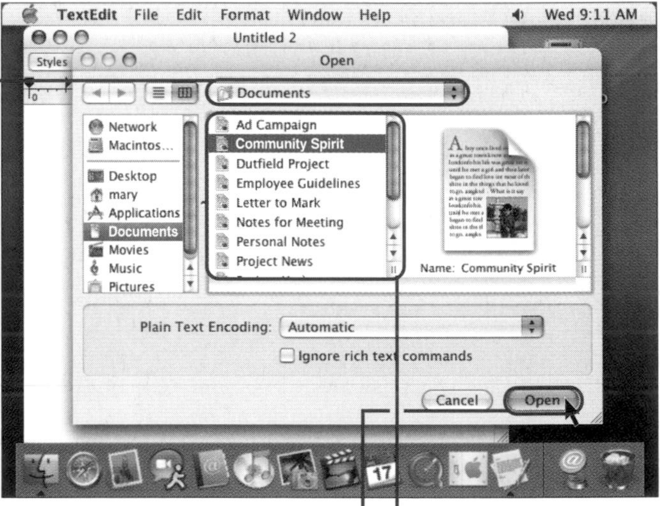

OPEN A DOCUMENT

1 Click the TextEdit icon to make TextEdit the active application.

Note: A new document window may appear.

■ If the TextEdit icon does not appear in the Dock, see page 128 to start the application.

2 Click **File**.

3 Click **Open**.

■ The Open dialog box appears.

■ This area shows the location of the displayed documents. You can click this area to change the location.

4 Click the name of the document you want to open.

5 Click **Open** to open the document.

How do I create a new TextEdit document?

To create a new TextEdit document, select the **File** menu and then click **New**. A new document window will appear on your screen.

Can TextEdit read the text in an open document aloud?

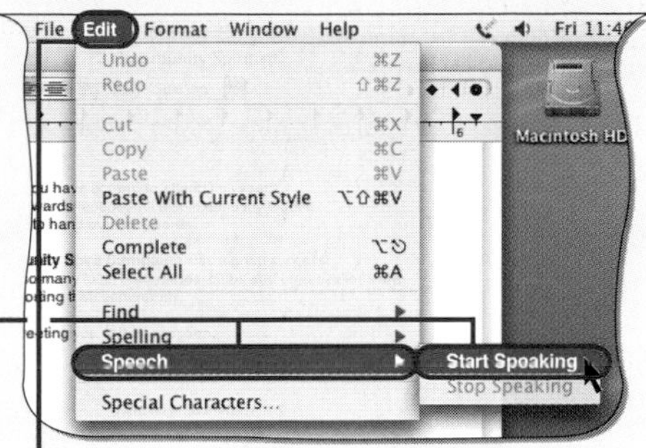

1 To have TextEdit read the text in a document aloud, click **Edit**.

2 Position the mouse over **Speech**.

3 Click **Start Speaking**.

■ TextEdit reads the text in the document aloud.

*Note: To stop TextEdit from reading the text in the document aloud, repeat steps **1** to **3**, selecting **Stop Speaking** in step **3**.*

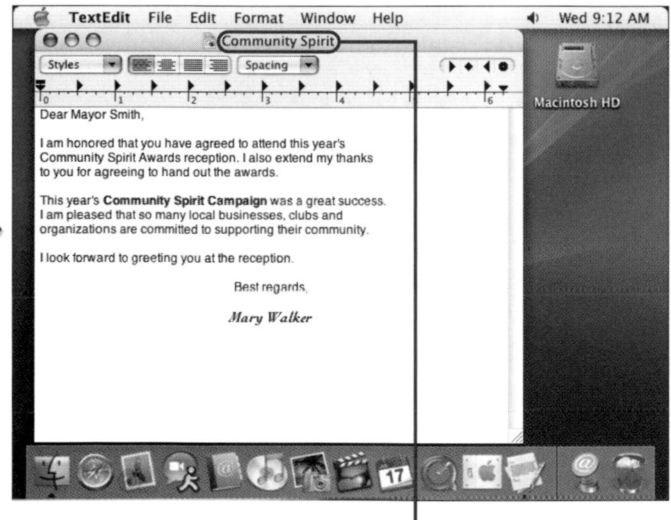

■ The document appears on your screen. You can now review and make changes to the document.

■ This area displays the name of the document.

QUIT TEXTEDIT

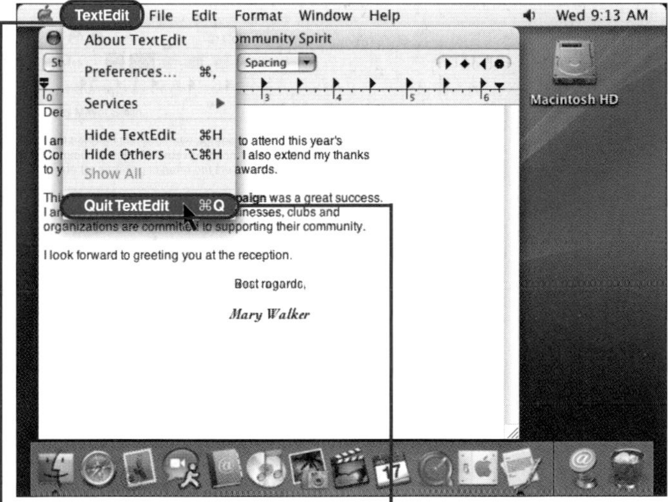

1 When you finish using TextEdit, click **TextEdit**.

2 Click **Quit TextEdit**.

You can create colorful, electronic notes that are similar to paper sticky notes.

Sticky notes are useful for storing small pieces of information, such as to-do lists, phone numbers, reminders, questions or ideas.

USING STICKIES

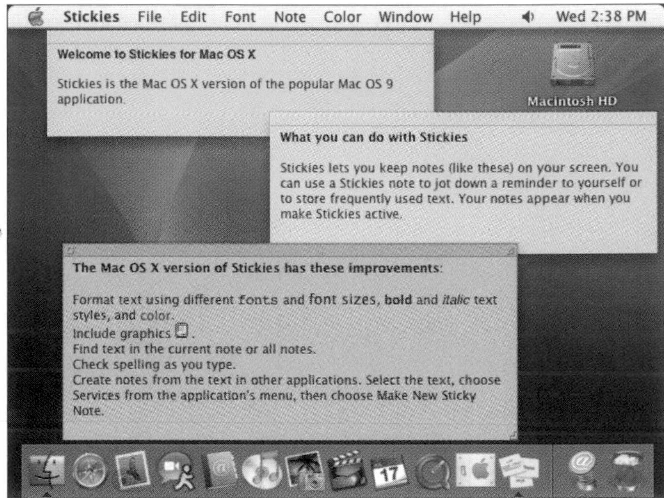

1 Click **Go**.

Note: If Go is not available, click a blank area on your desktop to display the Finder menu bar.

2 Click **Applications** to view the applications available on your computer.

■ The Applications window appears.

3 Double-click **Stickies** to start Stickies.

■ All your notes appear on your screen.

■ Stickies comes with several sample notes that describe some of the application's features. To close the sample notes, see page 136.

Note: You can click ● in the Applications window to close the window.

Can I resize a note?

Yes. Click the note you want to resize. Position the mouse over the resize handle at the bottom right corner of the note and then drag the handle until the note displays the size you want.

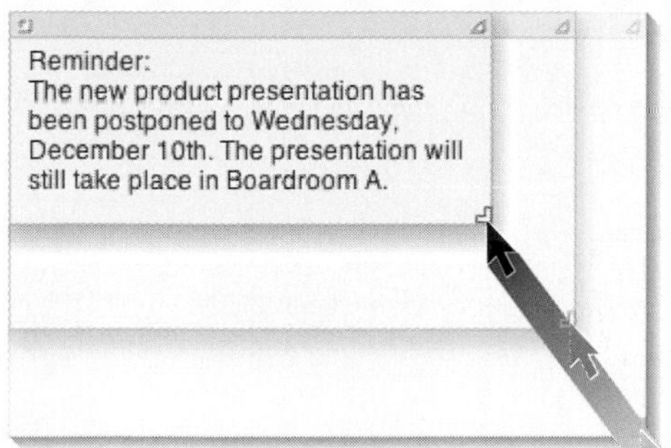

Reminder:
The new product presentation has been postponed to Wednesday, December 10th. The presentation will still take place in Boardroom A.

How can I quickly reduce the size of a note?

You can quickly collapse a sticky note to view other items on your screen more easily. Double-click the bar at the top of the note you want to collapse. The note collapses to show only the first line of text in the note. To once again display the entire sticky note, double-click the bar again.

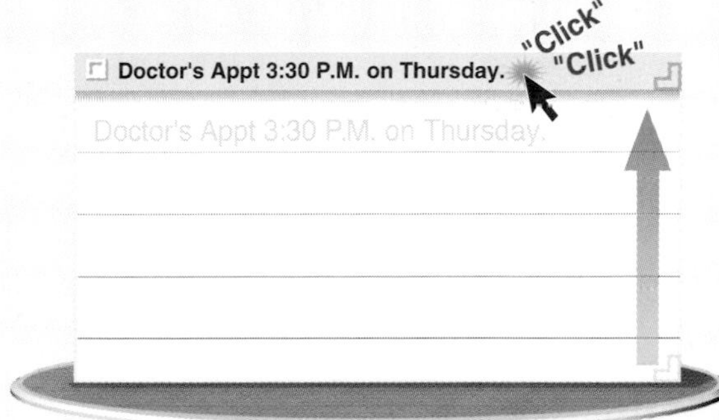

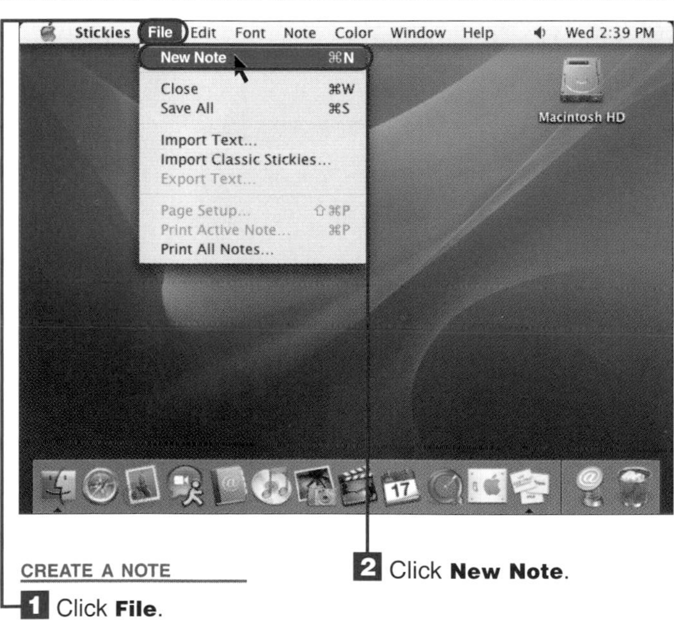

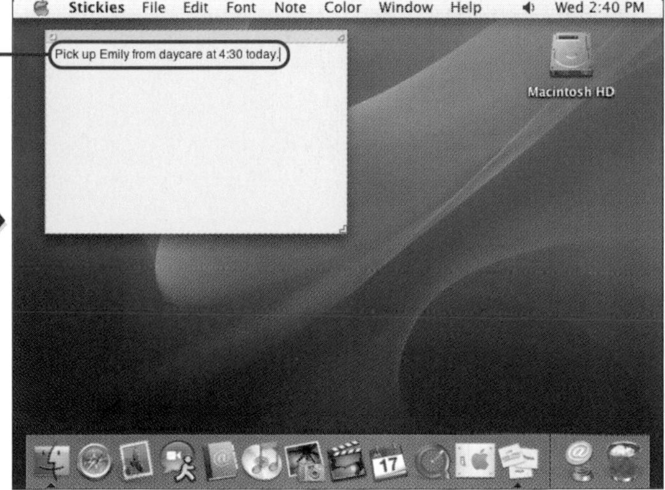

CREATE A NOTE

1 Click **File**.

2 Click **New Note**.

■ A new sticky note appears.

■ The flashing insertion point indicates where the text you type will appear in the note.

3 Type the text for the note.

Note: You do not have to save the notes you create. Each time you open Stickies, the notes you have created will be displayed for you.

CONTINUED

You can change the color of a note to help organize the notes. For example, you may want to display work-related notes in green, and personal notes in purple.

When you no longer need a note, you can close the note to remove it from your screen. You can have Stickies save the contents of the note as a text file on your computer or permanently delete the note.

USING STICKIES (CONTINUED)

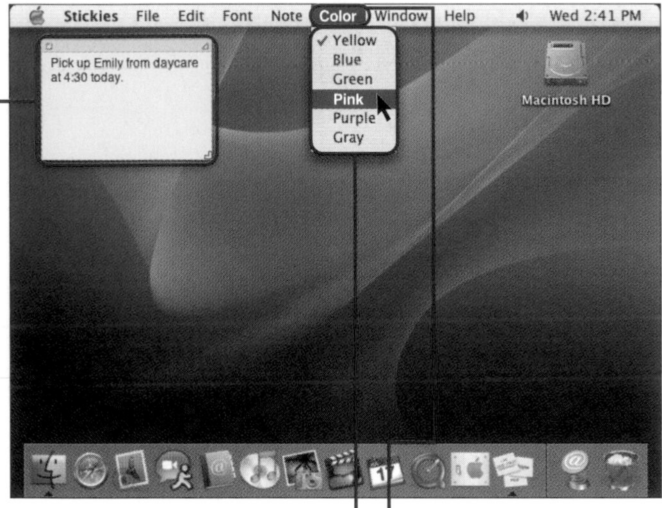

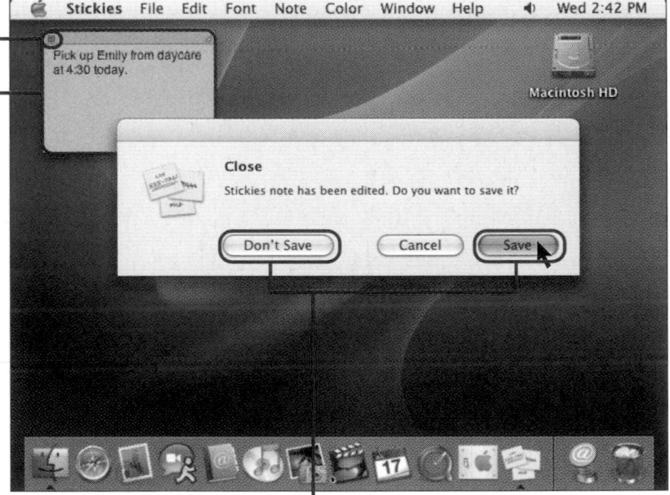

CHANGE THE COLOR OF A NOTE

1 Click the note you want to display a different color.

2 Click **Color** to display a list of the available colors.

3 Click the color you want to use for the note.

■ The note will display the color you selected.

CLOSE A NOTE

1 Click the note you want to close.

2 Click ☐ to close the note.

■ A dialog box appears, asking if you want to save the note.

3 To save the contents of the note as a text file on your computer, click **Save**.

■ To permanently delete the note, click **Don't Save**.

Can I move a note to a new location on my screen?

Yes. Click the note you want to move and then position the mouse over the bar at the top of the note. Drag the note to where you want to place the note on your screen.

Can I print a note I have created?

Yes. You can print a note to produce a paper copy of the note. To print a note, click the note you want to print. Click the **File** menu and then click **Print Active Note**. In the dialog box that appears, click **Print** to print the note.

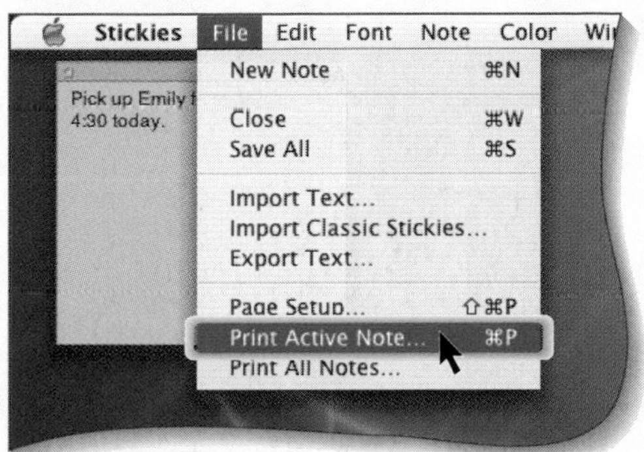

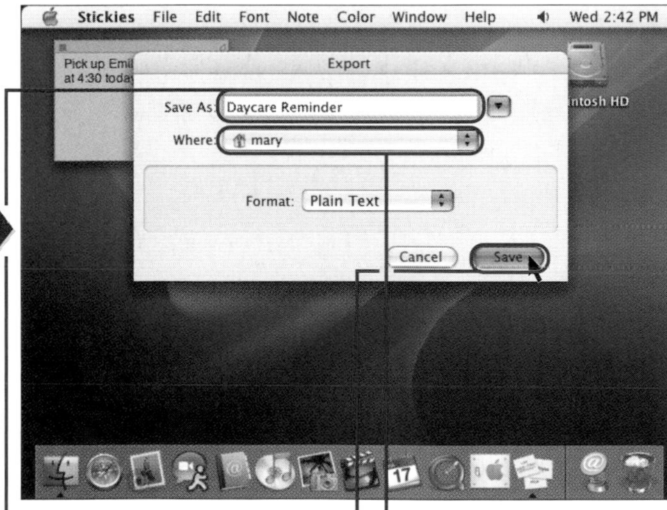

■ The Export dialog box appears, allowing you to save the contents of the note.

4 Type a name for the note.

■ This area shows the location where the note will be saved. You can click this area to change the location.

5 Click **Save** to save the note.

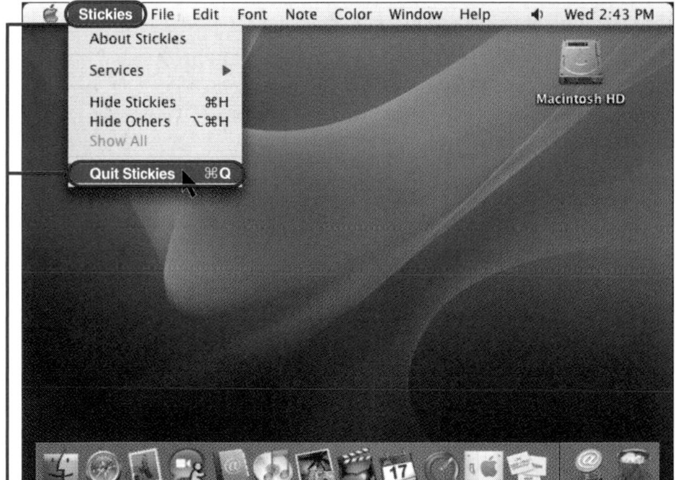

QUIT STICKIES

1 When you finish reviewing and working with your sticky notes, click **Stickies**.

2 Click **Quit Stickies**.

■ When you quit Stickies, all your notes are automatically saved on your computer and will reappear the next time you start Stickies.

You can use Font Book to view the characters that are available for each font installed on your computer.

Font Book allows you to review the characters a font offers before choosing to use the font in your documents.

USING FONT BOOK

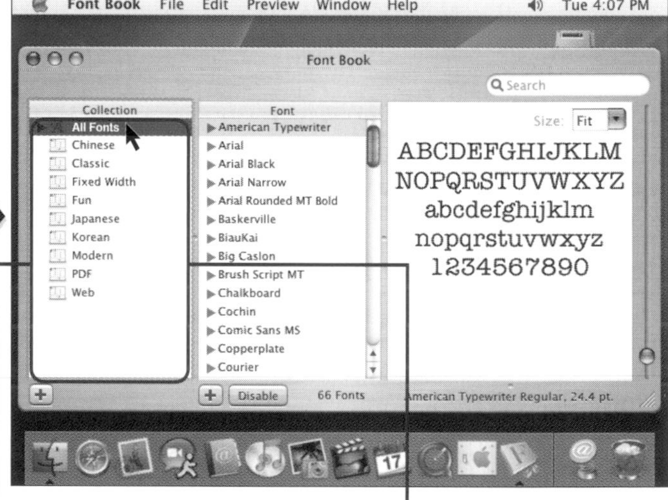

1 Click **Go**.

Note: If Go is not available, click a blank area on your desktop to display the Finder menu bar.

2 Click **Applications** to view the applications available on your computer.

■ The Applications window appears.

3 Double-click **Font Book** to start Font Book.

■ The Font Book window appears.

Note: You can click ● in the Applications window to close the window.

■ This area displays the available font collections on your computer.

4 Click a collection containing the font you want to view.

*Note: If you do not know which collection contains the font you want to view, click **All Fonts**.*

Can I search for fonts in Font Book?

Yes. You can search Font Book to find a font or font style of interest.

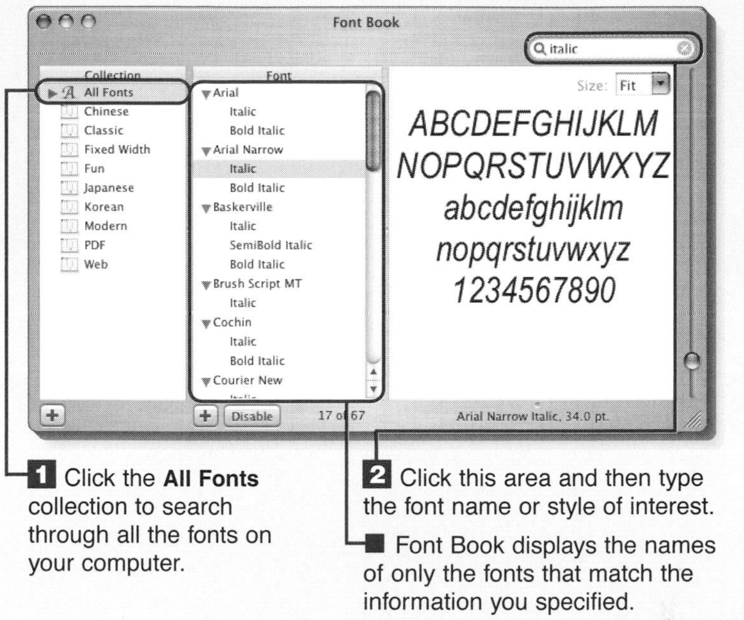

1 Click the **All Fonts** collection to search through all the fonts on your computer.

2 Click this area and then type the font name or style of interest.

■ Font Book displays the names of only the fonts that match the information you specified.

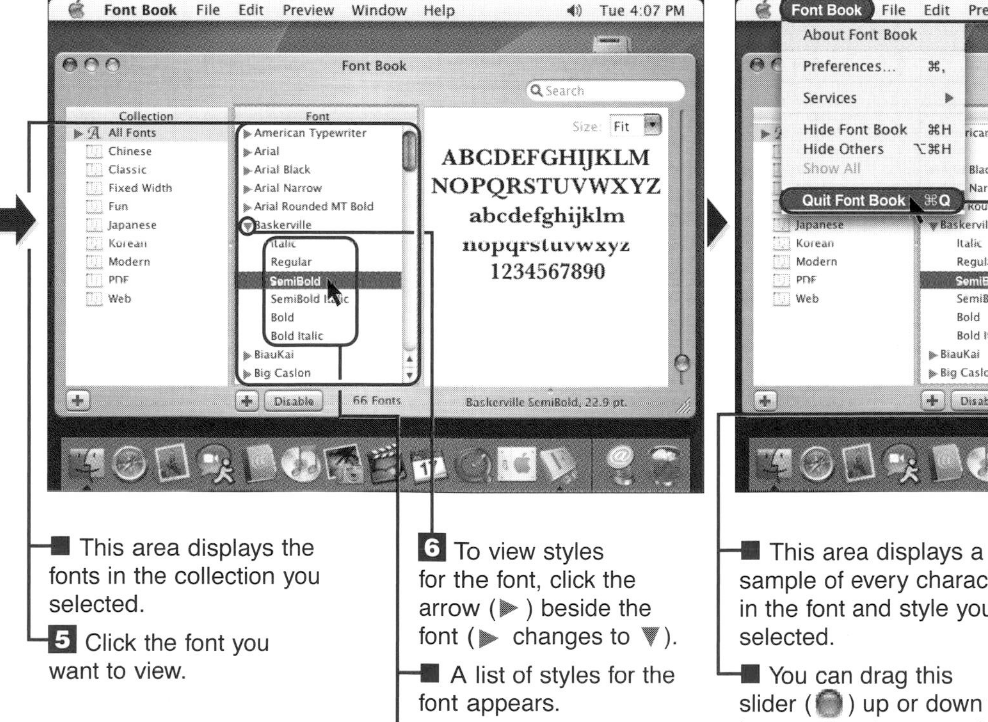

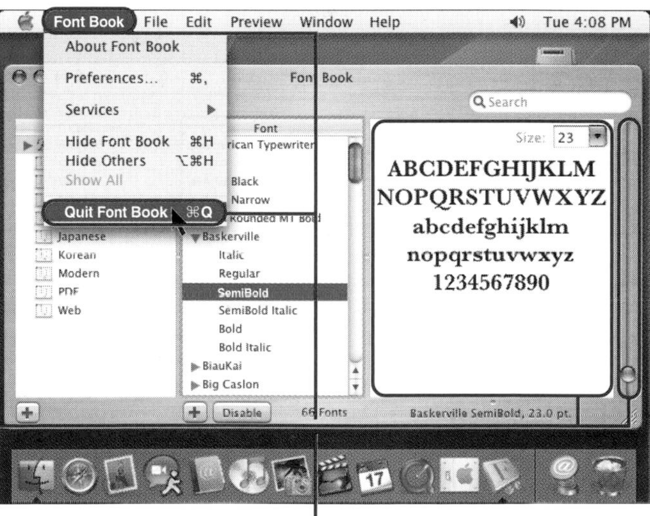

■ This area displays the fonts in the collection you selected.

5 Click the font you want to view.

6 To view styles for the font, click the arrow (▶) beside the font (▶ changes to ▼).

■ A list of styles for the font appears.

7 Click a font style of interest.

■ This area displays a sample of every character in the font and style you selected.

■ You can drag this slider (●) up or down to increase or decrease the size of the displayed characters.

8 To view other fonts of interest, repeat steps **4** to **7**.

9 To quit Font Book, click **Font Book**.

10 Click **Quit Font Book**.

USING DVD PLAYER

You can use DVD Player to play DVD movies on your computer.

Your computer must have an internal DVD drive to play DVD movies. You can usually play DVD movies only on a computer with an Apple DVD drive.

USING DVD PLAYER

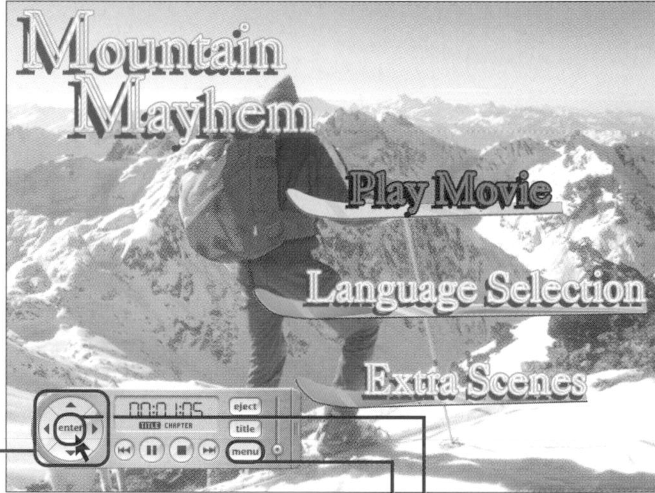

1 Insert the DVD movie you want to play into your computer's DVD drive.

■ DVD Player starts and the movie automatically begins to play.

■ You can use the playback controller to control the movie.

Note: If the playback controller does not appear, move the mouse on your desk to display the controller.

■ Most DVD movies display a main menu that lists options you can select to play the movie or access special features.

2 To select an option in the menu, click an arrow in this area to move through the options until you highlight the option you want to select.

3 Click (enter) to select the highlighted option.

Note: You can also select an option by clicking the option on your screen.

■ To return to this menu at any time, click (menu).

Can I play a DVD movie in a window?

Yes. To play a DVD movie in a window, press and hold down the ⌘ key as you press the 1 (half size), 2 (normal size) or 3 (maximum size) key. To once again play the movie using the entire screen, press and hold down the ⌘ key as you press the 0 key.

Does DVD Player offer any additional features that I can use while viewing a movie?

DVD Player allows you to perform several tasks while viewing a movie, such as viewing a movie in slow motion or displaying subtitles. The additional features may not work for some DVD movies.

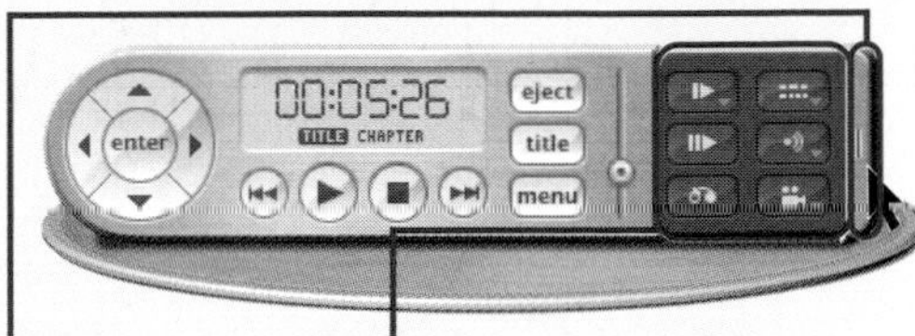

1 Double-click this area.

■ A drawer opens, displaying a button for each feature. Position the mouse over a button to display the name of the feature.

Note: To close the drawer, repeat step ***1****.*

4 To increase or decrease the volume of the movie, drag this slider ( ) up or down.

5 To rewind or fast forward through the movie, position the mouse over ⏮ or ⏭ and then press and hold down the mouse button.

6 To pause the play of the movie, click ⏸ (⏸ changes to ▶).

■ You can click ▶ to resume playing the movie.

7 To stop playing the movie at any time, click ■.

8 To eject the DVD when you finish playing the movie, click eject.

9 To quit DVD Player, move the mouse over the top of the screen and then click **DVD Player** on the menu bar that appears.

10 Click **Quit DVD Player**.

Artist = John Jones
1 Misunderstanding John Jones
2 Arbor nights Wilson Days
3 I heard it all John Jones
4 You're the one John Jones
5 Please Joan The Coppers
6 Tonight Wilson Days
7 John Jones
8
9
1 2 3 4 5 6 7 8 9 10 11 12
Smart Playlist
Title
Artist
Misunderstanding
John Jones
I heard it all
John Jones
You're the one
Cuts to the bone

CHAPTER 6

Play Music Using iTunes

In this chapter, you will learn how to use iTunes to play music CDs, listen to radio stations on the Internet, organize your songs and copy songs to a CD or MP3 player.

LISTEN TO A MUSIC CD

You can use the iTunes application to listen to music CDs on your computer while you work.

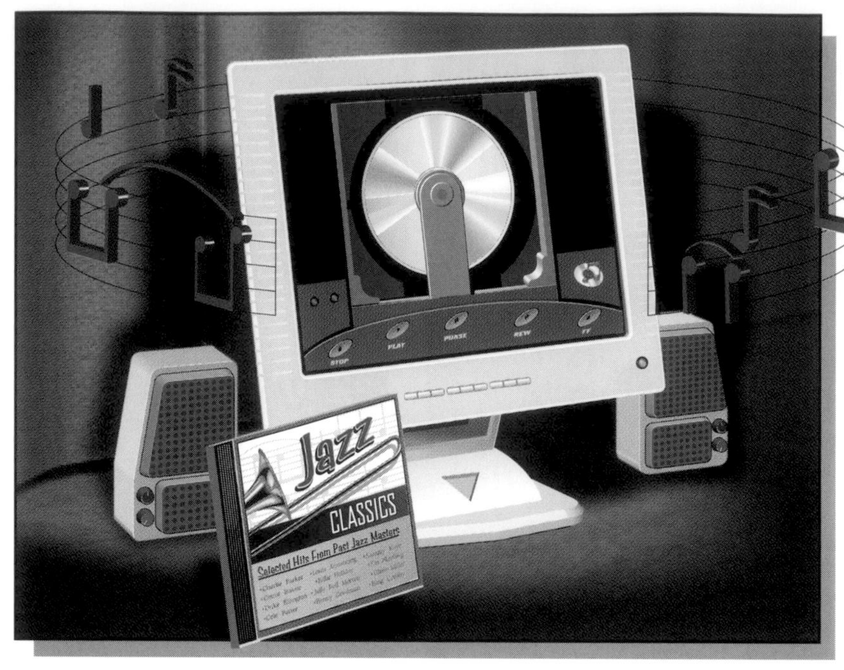

The first time you start iTunes, a license agreement appears on your screen. Click **Agree** to continue. The iTunes Setup Assistant then appears. Follow the instructions on your screen to set up iTunes.

LISTEN TO A MUSIC CD

1 Insert a music CD into your computer's CD drive.

■ After a moment, the iTunes window appears.

2 Click the name of the CD in this area.

*Note: If the name of the CD is not displayed, click **Audio CD**.*

3 Click ▶ to start playing the CD.

■ This area lists the songs on the CD and the amount of time each song will play. The song that is currently playing displays a speaker icon (🔊).

■ To play a specific song in the list, double-click the name of the song.

■ iTunes will play each song that displays a check mark. To add (☑) or remove (☐) a check mark for a song, click the box (☐) beside the song.

How does iTunes know the name of each song on my music CD?

If you are connected to the Internet when you insert a music CD, iTunes attempts to obtain information about the CD from the Internet. If you are not connected to the Internet or information about the CD is unavailable, iTunes displays the track number of each song instead. If iTunes is able to obtain information about the CD, iTunes will recognize the CD and display the appropriate information each time you insert the CD.

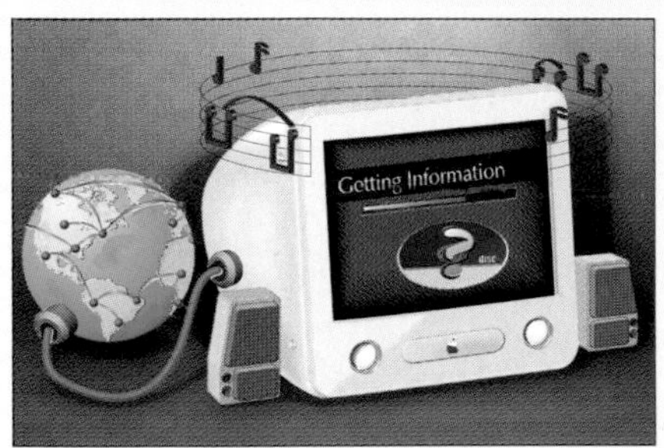

Can I play the songs on my music CD in random order?

Yes. You can shuffle the songs to play the songs in random order. Click in the iTunes window to shuffle the songs. To once again play the songs on the CD in order, click .

■ This area displays the name of the song that is currently playing and the amount of time the song has been playing.

4 To decrease or increase the volume, drag this slider ( ) left or right.

5 To pause the play of the CD, click (changes to).

Note: You can click to resume the play of the CD.

6 When you finish listening to the CD, click to eject the CD.

7 When you finish listening to CDs, click **iTunes**.

8 Click **Quit iTunes**.

LISTEN TO RADIO STATIONS ON THE INTERNET

You can listen to radio stations from around the world that broadcast on the Internet.

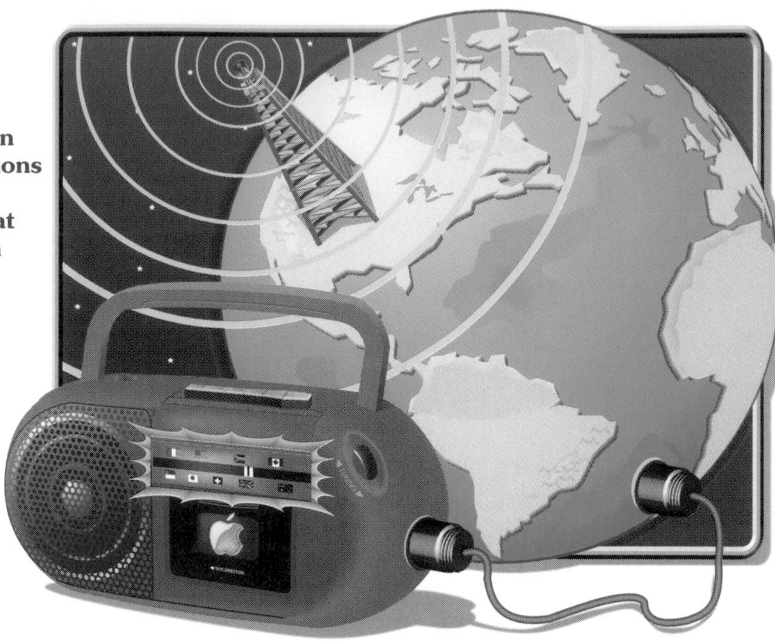

You need to be connected to the Internet to listen to radio stations that broadcast on the Internet. To connect to the Internet, see page 236.

The first time you start iTunes, a license agreement appears on your screen. Click **Agree** to continue. The iTunes Setup Assistant then appears. Follow the instructions on your screen to set up iTunes.

LISTEN TO RADIO STATIONS ON THE INTERNET

1 Click the iTunes icon to start iTunes.

■ The iTunes window appears.

2 Click **Radio** to listen to radio stations that broadcast on the Internet.

■ This area lists the categories of available radio stations.

3 To display the radio stations in a category, click ▶ beside the category (▶ changes to ▼).

■ The name, bit rate and description of each radio station in the category appear.

Note: The higher the bit rate, the better the sound quality.

■ You can click ▼ beside a category to once again hide the radio stations in the category (▼ changes to ▶).

4 Double-click the radio station you want to play.

Note: If you use a modem to connect to the Internet, you should select a radio station with a bit rate of less than 56 kbps for the best results.

How can I reduce the size of the iTunes window?

You can reduce the size of the iTunes window so you can easily view other items on your screen while listening to a radio station. Click ◯ in the top left corner of the iTunes window to reduce the size of the window. To return the iTunes window to its previous size, click ◯ again.

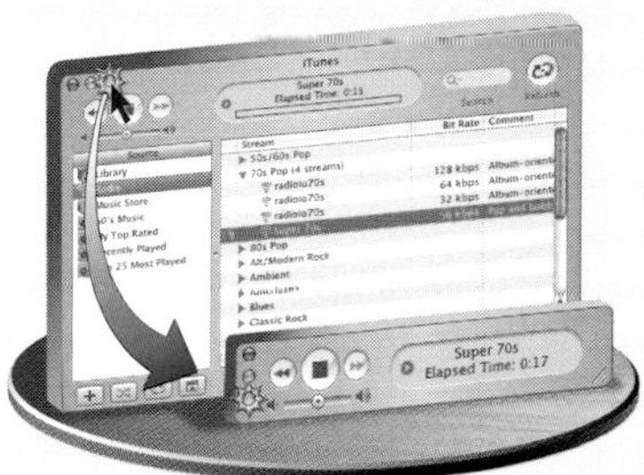

Can I use iTunes to purchase music from the Internet?

Yes. iTunes allows you to connect to Apple's Music Store and purchase songs or entire albums that you can store in your iTunes Library.

■ To use the Music Store to purchase music, click **Music Store** in the iTunes window and then follow the instructions on your screen.

Note: The Music Store is not available in all countries.

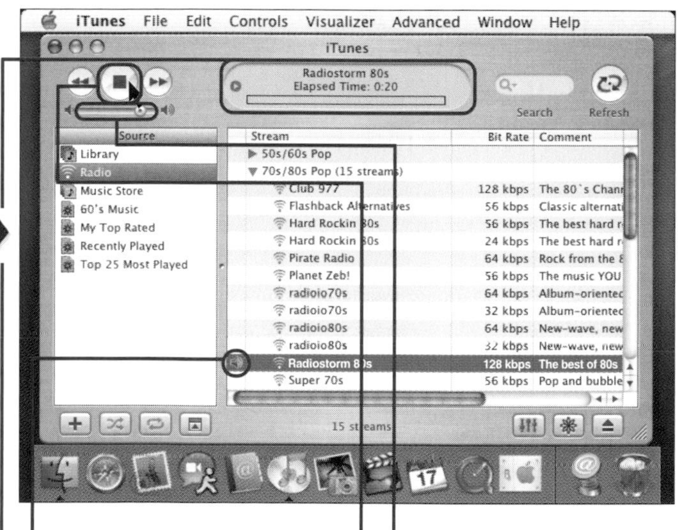

■ The radio station begins to play. The selected radio station displays a speaker icon (🔊).

■ This area displays information about the currently playing radio station and the amount of time the radio station has been playing.

5 To decrease or increase the volume, drag this slider (◉) left or right.

6 To stop playing the radio station, click ■ (■ changes to ▶).

Note: You can click ▶ to resume the play of the radio station.

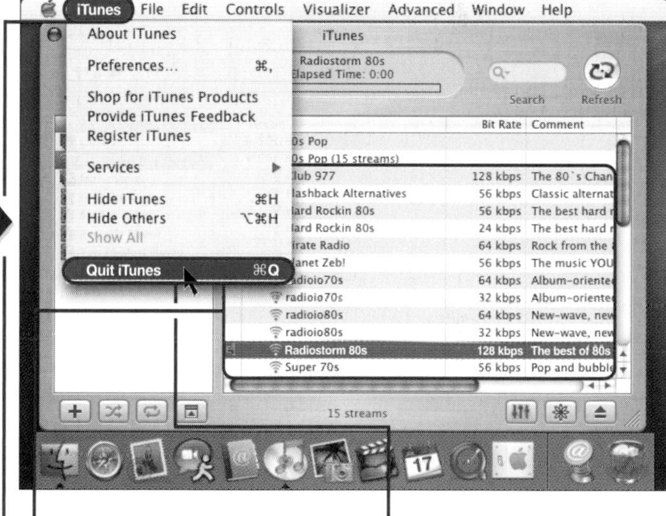

■ To play another radio station, double-click the radio station you want to play.

7 When you finish listening to radio stations on the Internet, click **iTunes**.

8 Click **Quit iTunes**.

COPY SONGS FROM A MUSIC CD

You can copy songs from your favorite music CD onto your computer.

Copying songs from a music CD allows you to play the songs at any time without having to insert the CD into your computer.

The first time you start iTunes, a license agreement appears on your screen. Click **Agree** to continue. The iTunes Setup Assistant then appears. Follow the instructions on your screen to set up iTunes.

COPY SONGS FROM A MUSIC CD

1 Insert a music CD into your computer's CD drive.

■ After a moment, the iTunes window appears.

2 Click the name of the CD in this area.

Note: If the name of the CD is not displayed, click ***Audio CD****.*

■ This area lists the songs on the CD and the amount of time each song will play.

Note: For information on how iTunes determines the name of each song on a CD, see the top of page 145.

■ iTunes will copy each song that displays a check mark. To add (☑) or remove (☐) a check mark for a song, click the box (☐) beside the song.

3 Click (Import) to copy the songs to your computer.

Where can I find the songs I copied from a music CD?

The Library

Songs you copy from a music CD are listed in the iTunes Library. You can click **Library** in the iTunes window to display all the songs in the Library. To play a song in the Library, see page 151.

The iTunes Music folder

Songs you copy from a music CD are stored in the iTunes Music folder. To view the contents of the iTunes Music folder, display the contents of the Music folder (see page 22), double-click the iTunes folder and then double-click the iTunes Music folder. The iTunes Music folder contains a folder for each artist whose songs you have copied. You can double-click a song you copied from a CD to open iTunes and play the song.

■ iTunes begins playing the first song you selected to copy.

■ This area displays the name of the song that iTunes is currently copying and the amount of time remaining to complete the copy.

■ The song that iTunes is currently copying displays the symbol. Each song that iTunes has finished copying displays the symbol.

■ To stop the copy at any time, click .

■ When iTunes has finished copying songs from the CD, a sound plays. iTunes will continue to play the songs you selected to copy.

4 To eject the CD, click .

5 When you finish copying songs from a music CD, click **iTunes**.

6 Click **Quit iTunes**.

USING THE iTUNES LIBRARY

The Library in iTunes acts like an electronic jukebox, providing a central location where you can view and play songs on your computer.

The first time you start iTunes, a license agreement appears on your screen. Click **Agree** to continue. The iTunes Setup Assistant then appears. Follow the instructions on your screen to set up iTunes.

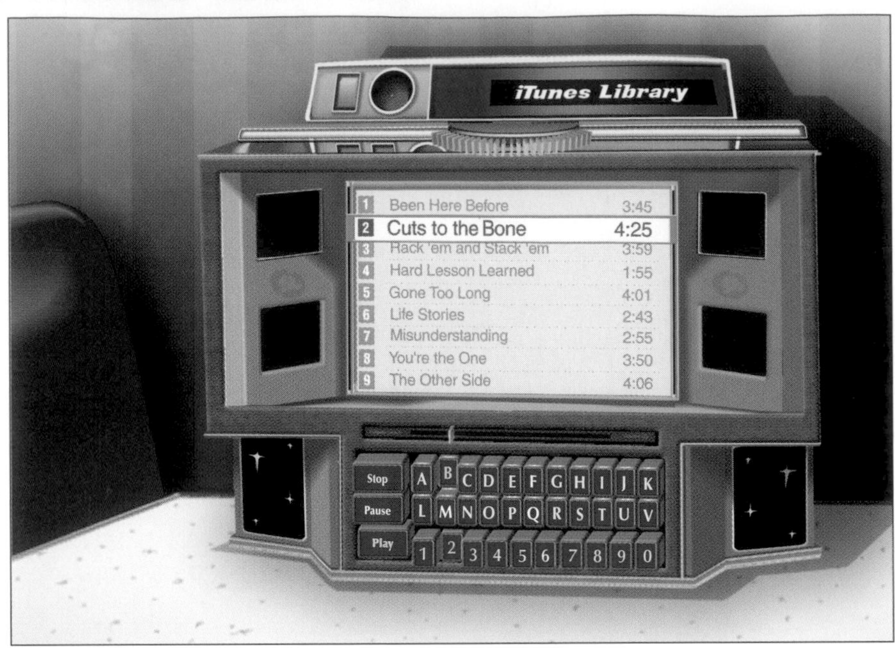

USING THE iTUNES LIBRARY

1 Click the iTunes icon to start iTunes.

■ The iTunes window appears.

2 Click **Library** to view all the songs in the Library.

■ This area lists all the songs in the Library.

Note: When you first started and set up iTunes, you may have selected to have iTunes automatically add existing songs on your computer to the Library.

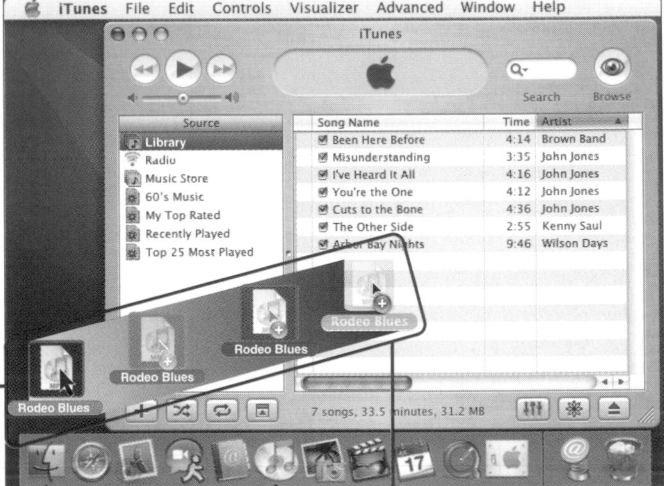

ADD A SONG TO THE LIBRARY

1 Locate the song on your computer that you want to add to the Library.

2 Position the mouse ↖ over the song.

3 Drag the song to the list of songs in the Library (↖ changes to ↖+).

■ iTunes adds the song to the Library.

Are there other ways to add songs to the iTunes Library?

Yes. When you double-click a song on your computer that plays in iTunes, iTunes automatically adds the song to the Library. Songs you copy from a music CD are also automatically added to the Library. To copy songs from a music CD, see page 148. To quickly add all the songs in a folder to the Library, position the mouse over the folder and then drag the folder to the list of songs in the Library.

How can I remove a song from the iTunes Library?

To remove a song from the Library, click the song and then press the delete key. In the confirmation dialog box that appears, click **Yes** to remove the song. An additional dialog box may appear, asking if you want to remove the song from the iTunes Music folder. Click **Yes** or **No** to specify if you want to remove the song from this folder.

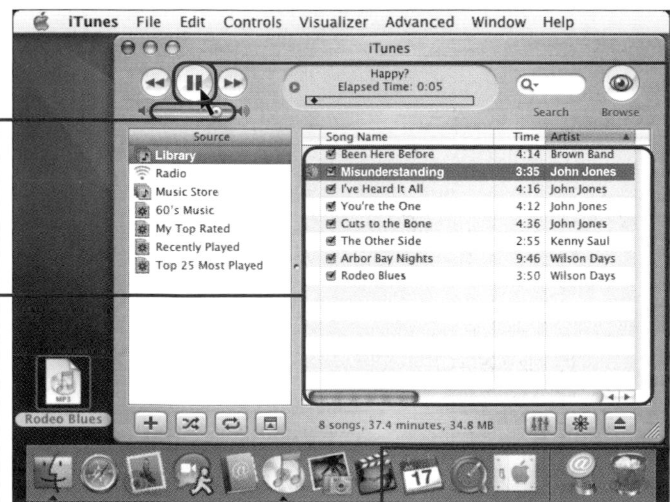

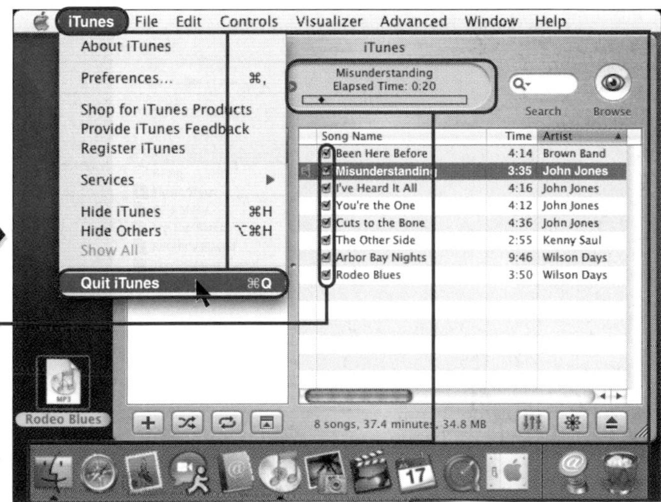

PLAY SONGS IN THE LIBRARY

1 Double-click the name of the song you want to play.

2 To decrease or increase the volume, drag this slider ( ) left or right.

Note: To quickly turn off the sound, click . To quickly turn the volume to full capacity, click .

3 To pause the play of the song, click (changes to).

■ You can click to resume the play of the song.

■ This area displays the name of the song that is currently playing and the amount of time the song has been playing.

■ When a song finishes playing, iTunes will automatically play the next song in the list that displays a check mark (✓). To add ( ) or remove ( ) a check mark for a song, click the box beside the song.

4 When you finish playing songs in iTunes, click **iTunes**.

5 Click **Quit iTunes**.

CREATE A PLAYLIST

You can create a personalized playlist that contains your favorite songs.

You can create as many playlists as you want. For example, you can create one playlist that contains your favorite jazz songs and another playlist that contains your favorite songs by a specific artist.

CREATE A PLAYLIST

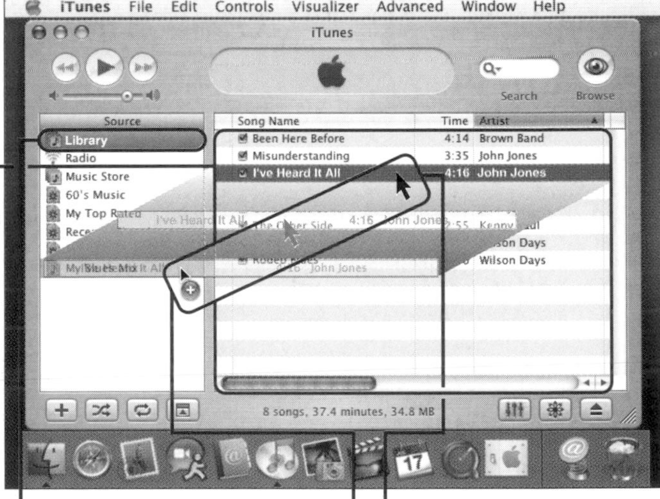

1 Click the iTunes icon to start iTunes.

■ The iTunes window appears.

2 Click + to create a new playlist.

■ A new, untitled playlist appears. Playlists display the ♪ symbol.

3 Type a name for the new playlist and then press the return key.

4 To add a song to the playlist, click **Library** to view all the songs in the Library.

■ This area lists all the songs in the Library.

Note: For information on the Library, see page 150.

5 Position the mouse over a song you want to add to the new playlist.

6 Drag the song to the playlist (pointer changes to pointer with +).

■ The song is added to the playlist.

Can I change the order in which songs will play in a playlist?

Yes. Click the icon for the playlist that contains the songs you want to reorder. Position the mouse over a song you want to move and then drag the song to a new location in the playlist. A black line indicates where the song will appear.

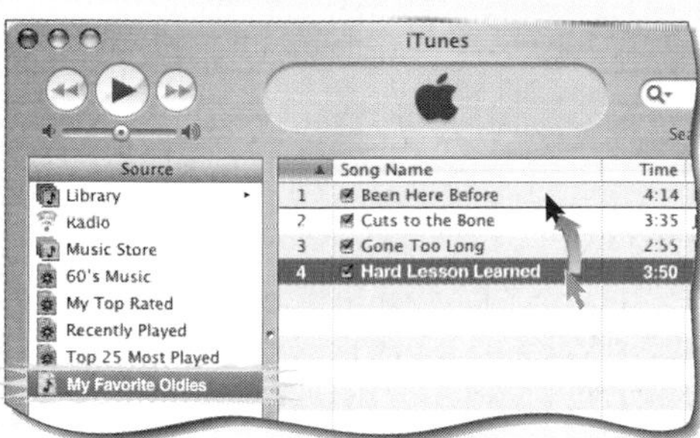

How do I delete a playlist?

To delete a playlist, click the icon for the playlist you want to delete and then press the delete key. In the confirmation dialog box that appears, click **Yes** to delete the playlist. Deleting a playlist will not remove the songs in the playlist from the Library.

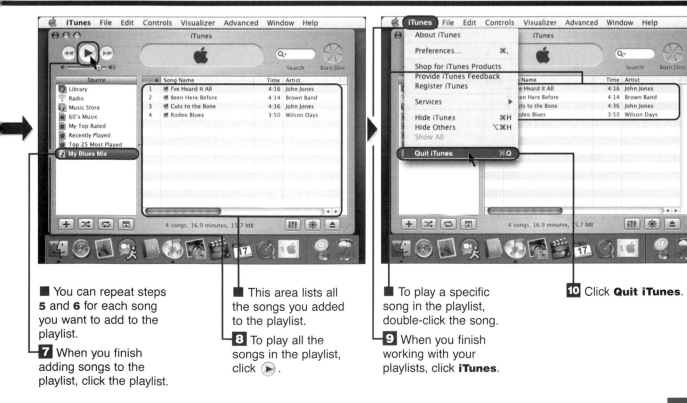

■ You can repeat steps **5** and **6** for each song you want to add to the playlist.

7 When you finish adding songs to the playlist, click the playlist.

■ This area lists all the songs you added to the playlist.

8 To play all the songs in the playlist, click ▶.

■ To play a specific song in the playlist, double-click the song.

9 When you finish working with your playlists, click **iTunes**.

10 Click **Quit iTunes**.

CREATE A SMART PLAYLIST

You can create a Smart Playlist that will automatically display songs from the iTunes Library that match information you specify.

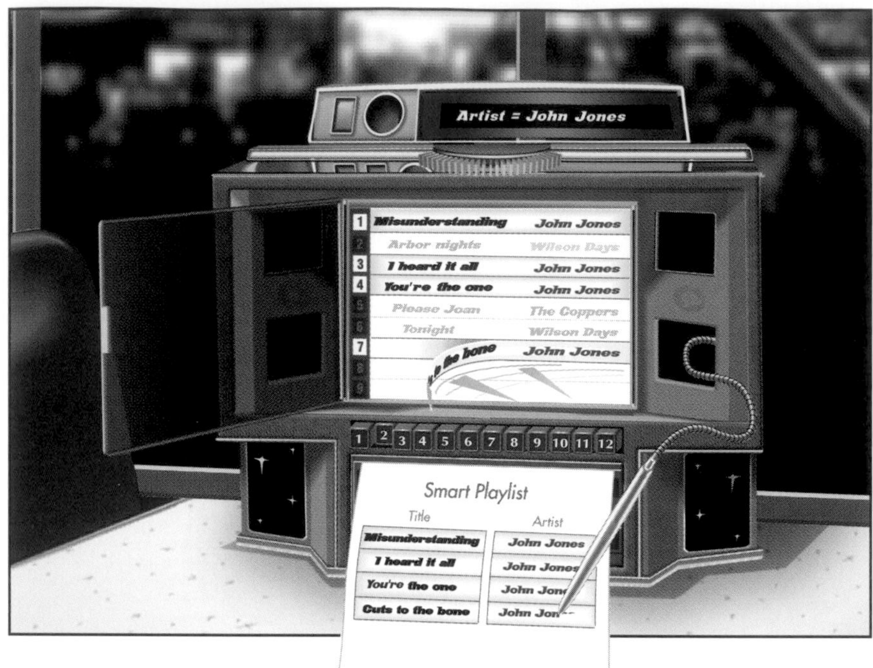

For example, you can create a Smart Playlist that displays all the songs from a specific artist or genre.

For information on the iTunes Library, see page 150.

CREATE A SMART PLAYLIST

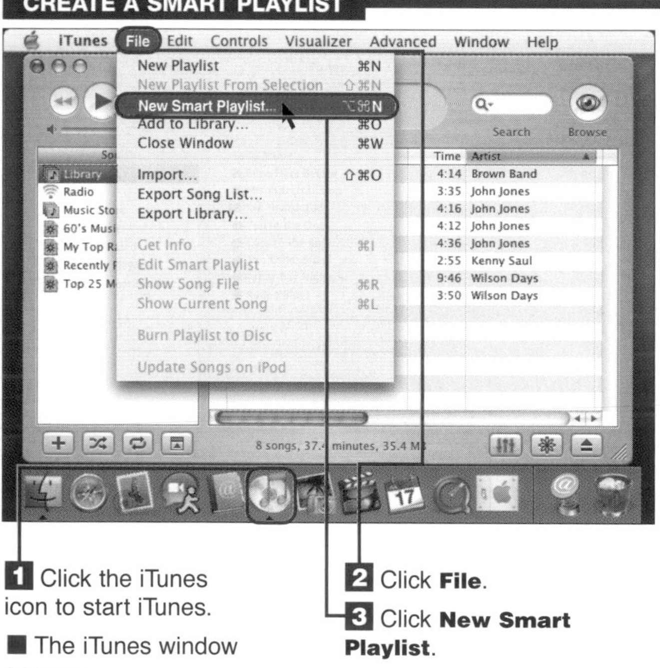

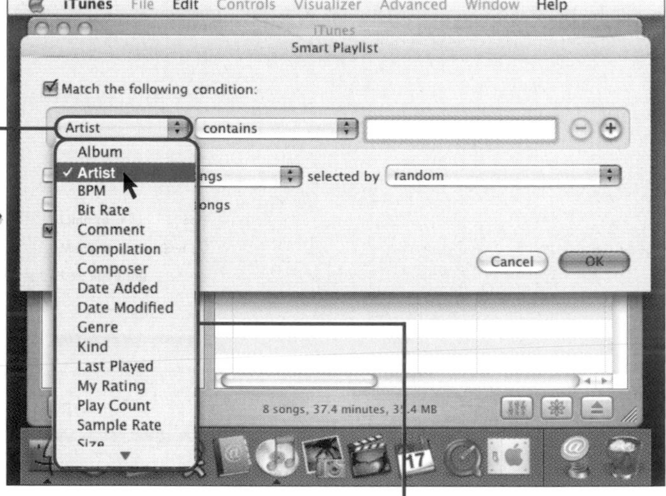

1 Click the iTunes icon to start iTunes.

■ The iTunes window appears.

2 Click **File**.

3 Click **New Smart Playlist**.

■ The Smart Playlist dialog box appears.

4 To specify the type of information you want to search for, click this area.

5 Click the type of information you want to search for.

Can I set additional conditions for a Smart Playlist?

Yes. You can have iTunes search for songs that meet more than one criteria. Click ⊕ in the Smart Playlist window to display an area where you can specify additional criteria. Then repeat steps **4** to **8** below to specify the additional criteria.

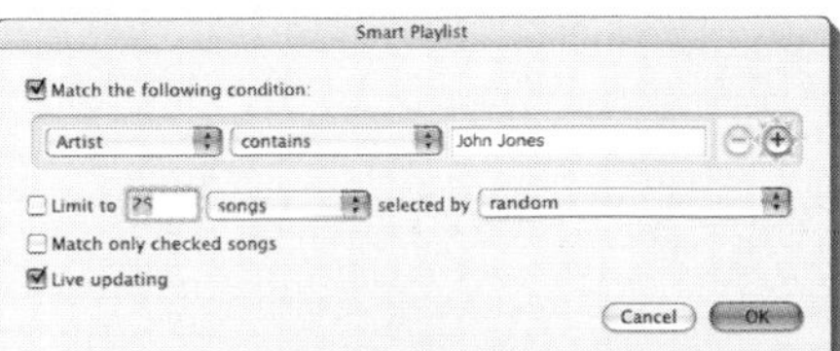

Can I limit the size of a Smart Playlist?

Yes. Instead of specifying a maximum number of songs that the Smart Playlist can include, you can specify a maximum playing time or file size for the playlist. After performing steps **1** to **10** below, click **songs** to display a list of options. Click the option you want to use to limit the size of the Smart Playlist.

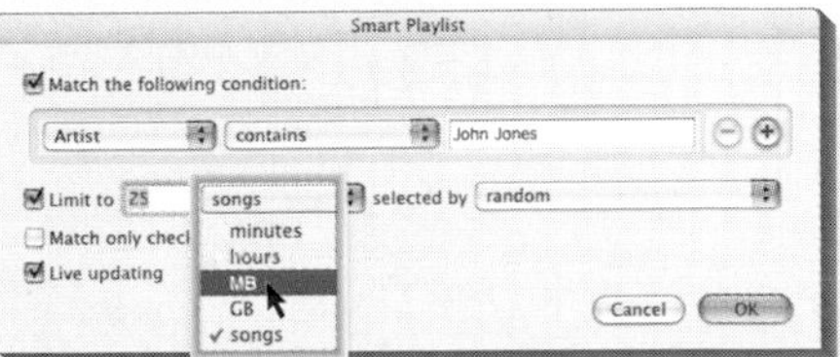

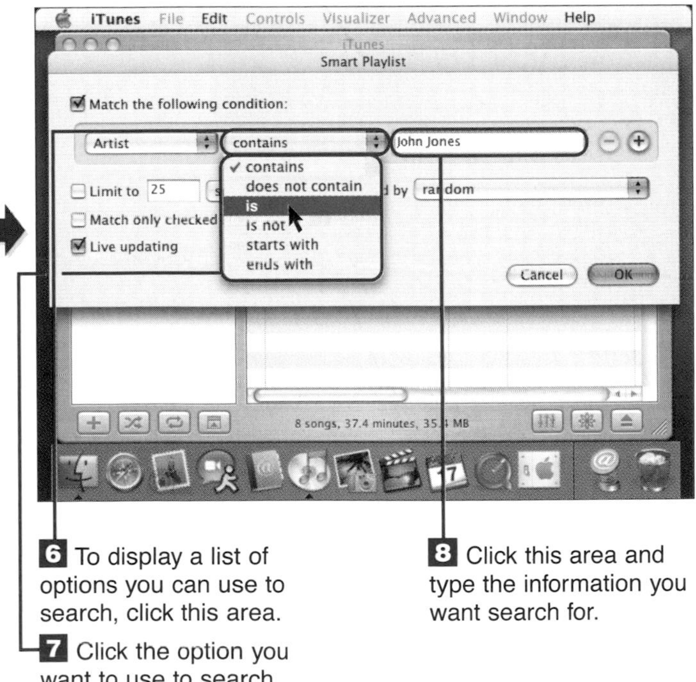

6 To display a list of options you can use to search, click this area.

7 Click the option you want to use to search.

8 Click this area and type the information you want search for.

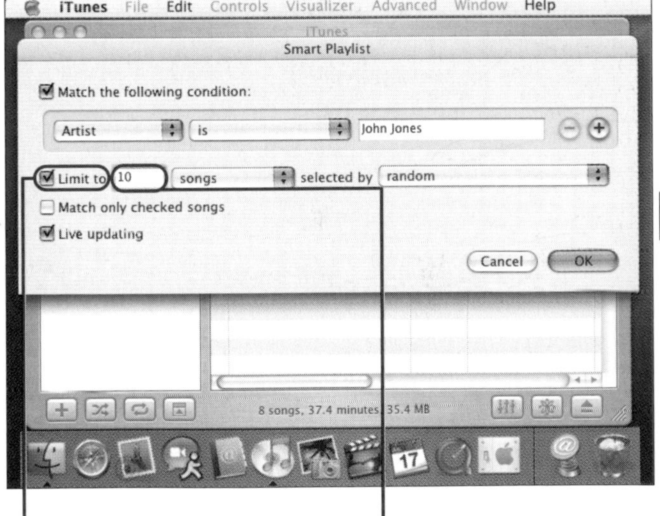

9 To limit the number of songs that will appear in the playlist, click this option (☐ changes to ☑).

10 Double-click this area and type the maximum number of songs you want to appear in the playlist.

CONTINUED

By default, iTunes will automatically update your Smart Playlists each time you add songs to the iTunes Library.

CREATE A SMART PLAYLIST (CONTINUED)

11 To specify the way you want to select the songs for the playlist, click this area.

12 Click the way you want to select the songs.

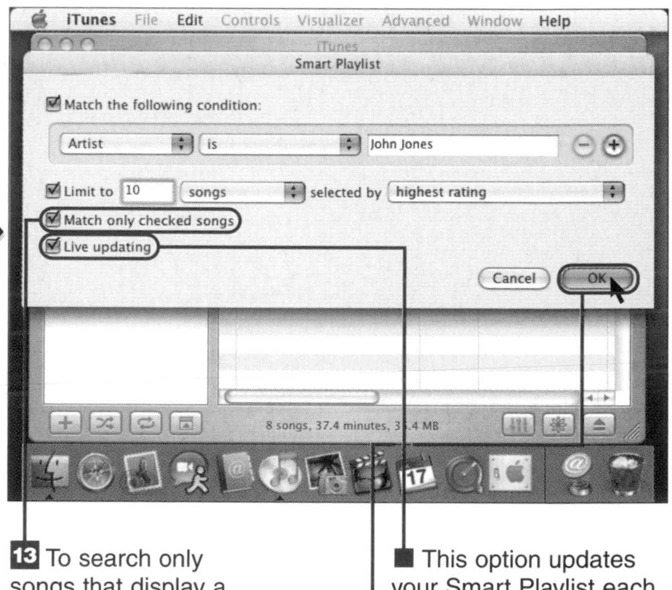

13 To search only songs that display a check mark (☑) in the Library, click this option (☐ changes to ☑).

■ This option updates your Smart Playlist each time you add songs to the iTunes Library. You can click this option to turn the option on (☑) or off (☐).

14 Click **OK** to create the Smart Playlist.

What Smart Playlists are automatically included in iTunes?

By default, iTunes includes four Smart Playlists.

Smart Playlist	Contains
60's Music	Songs recorded between 1960 and 1969.
My Top Rated	Songs rated higher than 3 stars.
Recently Played	Songs you have played within the last 2 weeks.
Top 25 Most Played	The 25 songs you have played most often.

How do I delete a Smart Playlist?

To delete a Smart Playlist, click the icon for the Smart Playlist and then press the delete key. In the confirmation dialog box that appears, click **Yes** to delete the Smart Playlist. Deleting a Smart Playlist will not remove the songs in the playlist from the iTunes Library.

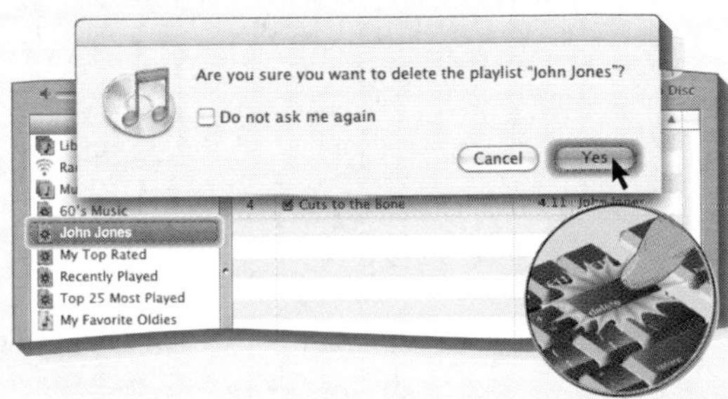

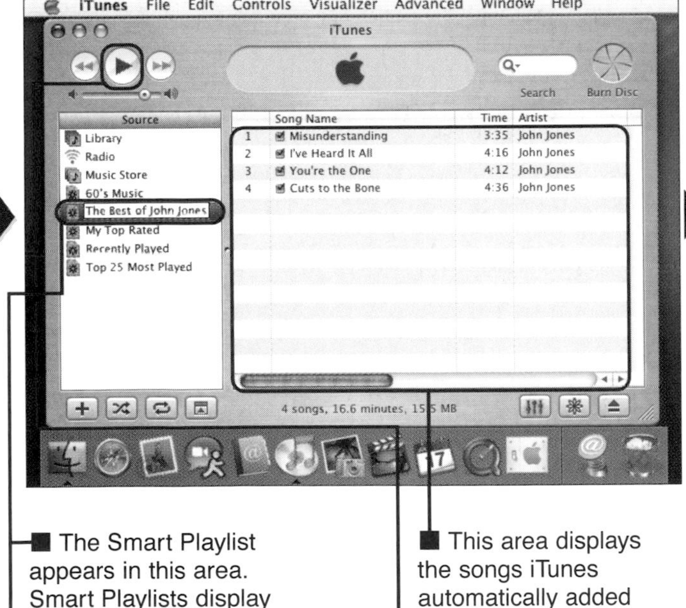

■ The Smart Playlist appears in this area. Smart Playlists display the symbol.

15 Type a name for the playlist and then press the return key.

■ This area displays the songs iTunes automatically added to the playlist. To play a song, double-click the song.

■ To play all the songs in the Smart Playlist, click ▶.

16 When you finish working with your Smart Playlists, click **iTunes**.

17 Click **Quit iTunes**.

CREATE YOUR OWN MUSIC CDS

You can create a music CD that contains your favorite songs.

You need a computer with a recordable CD drive to create your own music CDs. A CD can typically store about 74 minutes of audio, which is about 20 songs.

CREATE YOUR OWN MUSIC CDS

■ Before you can create your own music CD, you must create a playlist that contains all the songs you want to include on the CD. To create a playlist, see pages 152 to 157.

1 Click the iTunes icon to start iTunes.

■ The iTunes window appears.

2 Click the playlist that contains the songs you want to copy to a recordable CD.

■ This area lists the songs in the playlist.

3 iTunes will copy each song that displays a check mark (✓). To add (☑) or remove (☐) a check mark for a song, click the box beside the song.

4 To copy the songs you selected to a recordable CD, click ⊛ (changes to ⊛).

What type of CD should I use to create my music CD?

You should use a CD-R (Compact Disc-Recordable) to create your music CD. Most CD players can play CD-Rs. You cannot erase or change the contents of a CD-R.

If your computer has a CD-RW drive, you can also use a CD-RW (Compact Disc-ReWritable) to create your music CD, but CD-RWs may not play in some CD players. You can erase the contents of a CD-RW in order to copy new music to the disc.

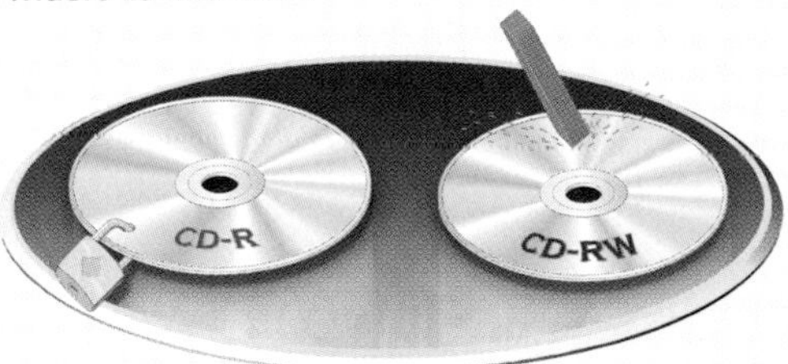

Can I stop iTunes from copying songs to a CD?

Yes. To stop iTunes from copying songs, click ⊗ in the iTunes window. In the confirmation dialog box that appears, click **Yes** to stop the copy. If you are copying songs to a CD-R, keep in mind that you can record data to a CD-R only once.

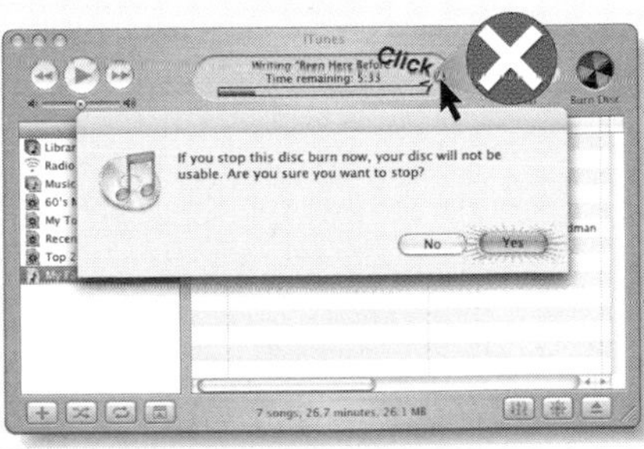

5 Insert a blank, recordable CD into your computer's recordable CD drive.

■ This area indicates the number of songs you selected and the total amount of time the songs will play.

6 Click the Burn Disc icon to start copying the songs.

■ The Burn Disc icon spins as iTunes copies the songs to the CD.

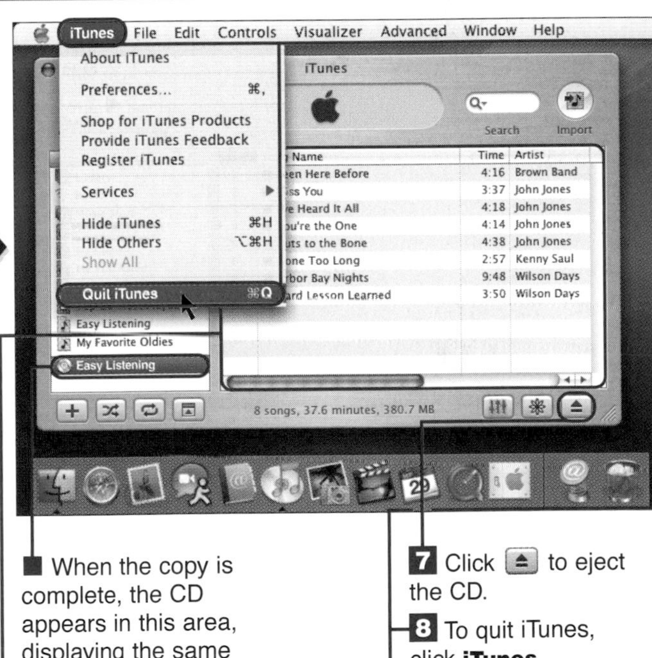

■ When the copy is complete, the CD appears in this area, displaying the same name as the playlist.

■ This area lists the songs on the CD.

7 Click the eject icon to eject the CD.

8 To quit iTunes, click **iTunes**.

9 Click **Quit iTunes**.

COPY SONGS TO AN MP3 PLAYER

You can transfer songs from the iTunes Library to a portable MP3 player.

An MP3 player is a device that can store and play MP3 files.

When you copy songs to your computer from a CD, the songs are stored on your computer in AAC format. You may need to convert songs to MP3 format before you can copy the songs to an MP3 player.

CONVERT SONGS TO MP3 FORMAT

1 Click **iTunes**.

2 Click **Preferences**.

■ A dialog box appears.

3 Click **Importing** to change your importing preferences.

4 Click this area to display a list of import formats you can use.

5 Click **MP3 Encoder**.

6 Click **OK**.

7 Click **Library** to view all the songs in the Library.

8 Press and hold down the ⌘ key as you click each song you want to convert to the MP3 format.

9 Click **Advanced**.

10 Click **Convert Selection to MP3** to make a copy of each selected song in the MP3 format.

Note: After converting songs to the MP3 format, you can return to the default import format by repeating steps ***1*** *to* ***6****, selecting* ***AAC Encoder*** *in step* ***5****.*

Can I use iTunes to remove a song from my MP3 player?

To use iTunes to remove a song from your MP3 player, perform step **1** on page 161 and then click the name of the MP3 player in the iTunes window. Click the song you want to remove and then press the delete key. In the confirmation dialog box that appears, click **Yes** to remove the song from your MP3 player.

How do I copy songs to my iPod?

When you connect the iPod to your computer, the songs in the iTunes Library are automatically transferred to the iPod. If you later change the songs in the Library, the songs on the iPod will be updated automatically the next time you connect the iPod to your computer. This ensures the songs in iTunes always match the songs on your iPod.

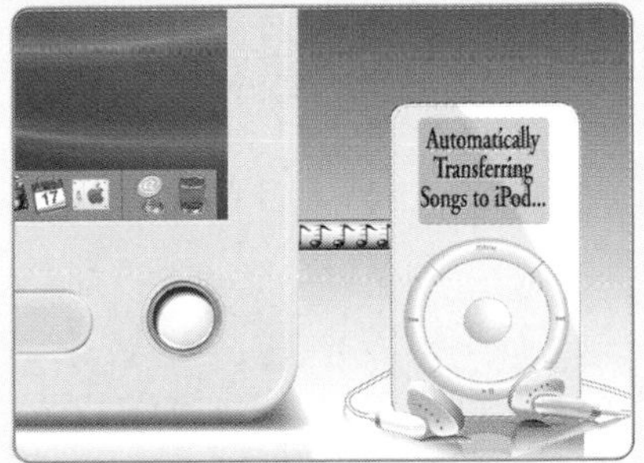

COPY SONGS TO MP3 PLAYER

1 Connect the MP3 player to your computer and turn on the player.

■ The name of the MP3 player appears in this area.

2 To copy a song in the MP3 format to your MP3 player, drag the song to the player.

■ After you drag a song to the MP3 player, this area displays the name of the song you selected and the progress of the copy.

3 You can repeat step **2** for each song you want to copy to the MP3 player.

4 When the copy is complete, click the name of the MP3 player to view all the songs on the player.

Scuba Diving in the Bahamas
The Annual Regatta

CHAPTER 7

Manage Photos Using iPhoto

This chapter teaches you how to use iPhoto to copy photos from a digital camera to your computer so you can view, organize and edit the photos.

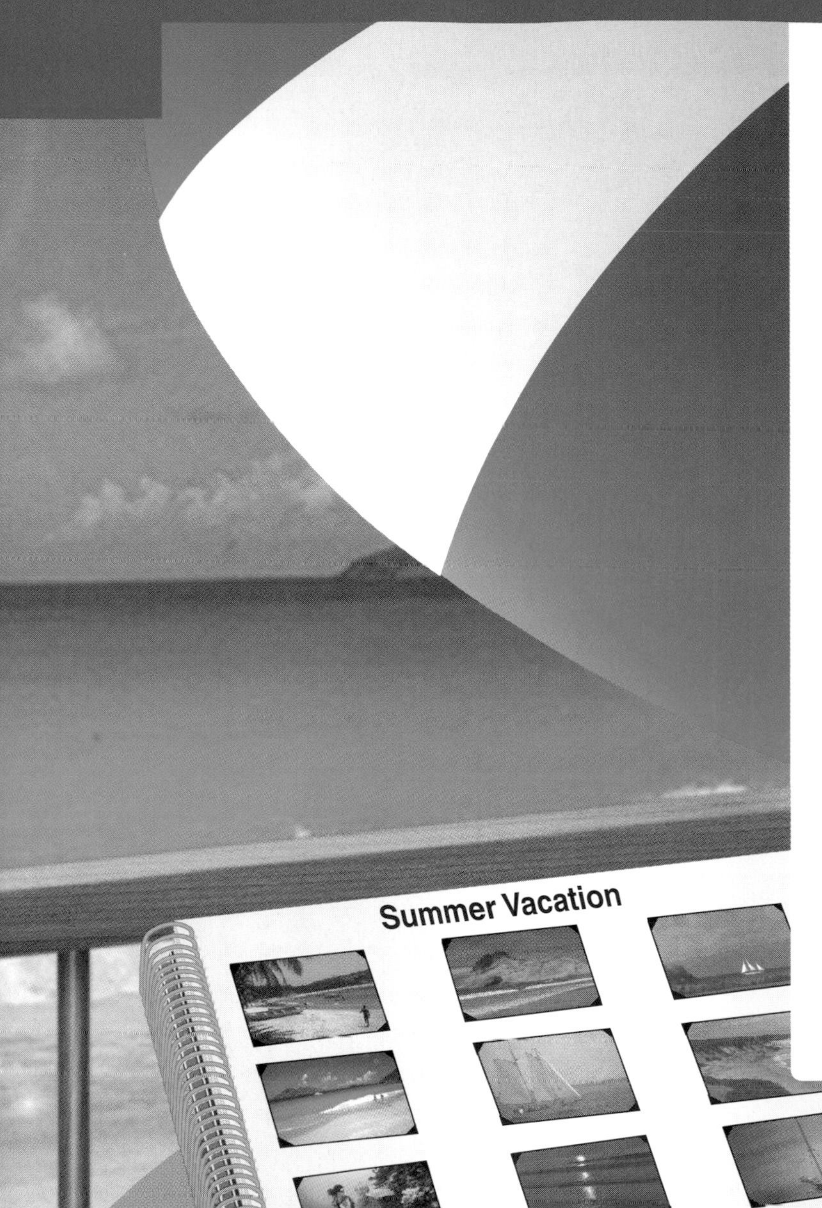

COPY PHOTOS FROM A DIGITAL CAMERA

You can copy photos from a digital camera to your computer so you can view, organize and edit the photos.

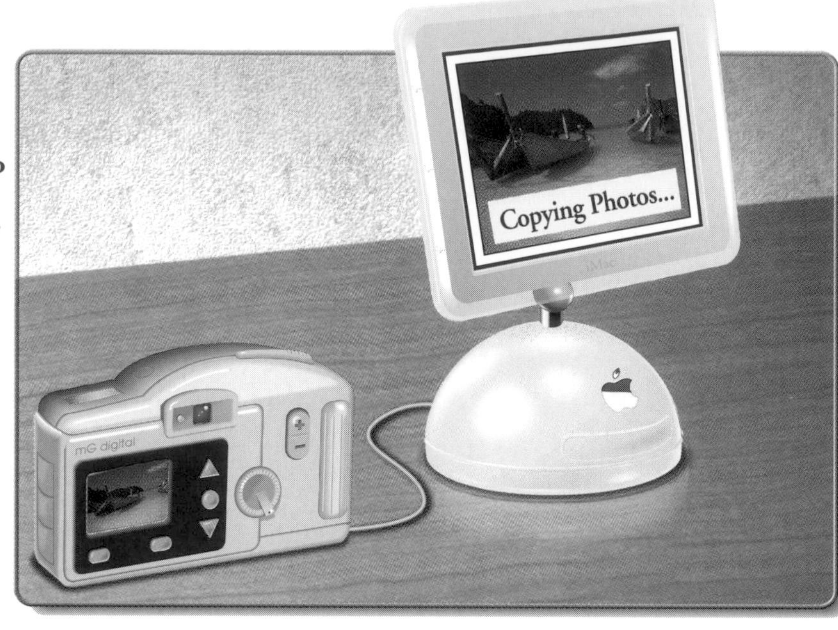

Before you start copying photos, make sure the digital camera is connected to your computer and is turned on. You may also need to set the camera to a specific mode, such as the Connect mode.

COPY PHOTOS FROM A DIGITAL CAMERA

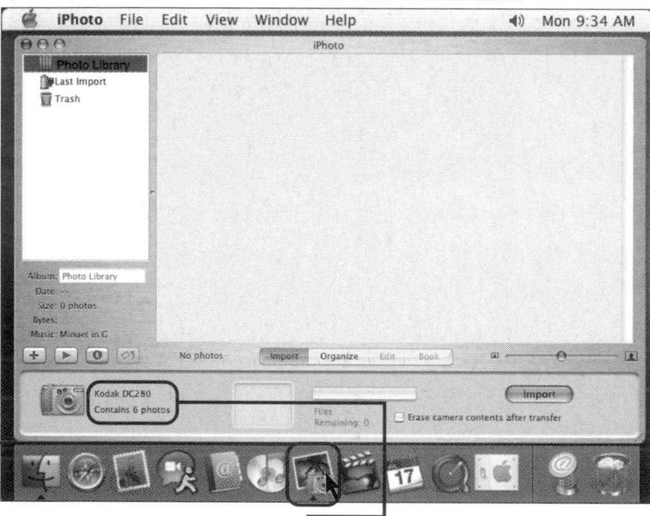

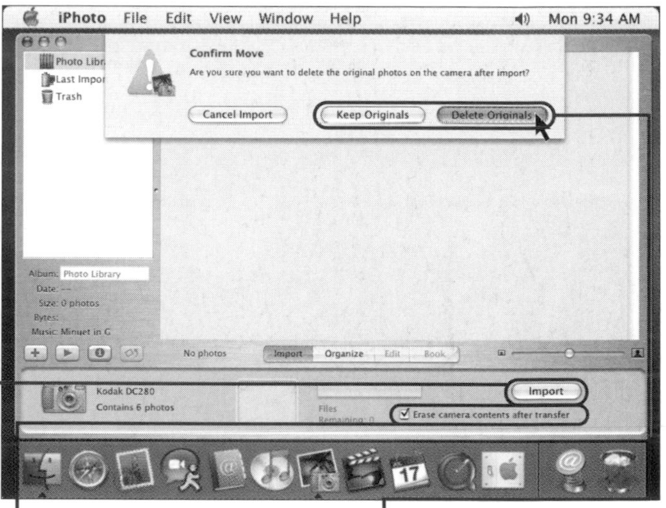

1 Click the iPhoto icon to start iPhoto.

■ The iPhoto window appears.

Note: The first time you start iPhoto, a dialog box appears, asking if you want iPhoto to open automatically when you attach a camera to your computer. Click an option in the dialog box to specify if you want iPhoto to open automatically.

■ This area displays the name of the camera and the number of photos stored on the camera.

2 This option will erase the photos on the camera after the photos are copied to your computer. You can click the option to turn the option on (☑) or off (☐).

3 Click **Import** to start copying the photos to your computer.

■ If you selected to erase the photos in step **2**, a confirmation dialog sheet appears.

4 Click an option to keep or delete the photos on the camera after the copy is complete.

How do I delete a photo I copied from my digital camera?

To delete a photo, click **Photo Library** to view all your photos. Click the photo you want to delete and then press the delete key. iPhoto will remove the photo from your photo library and from any albums that contain the photo. For information on albums, see page 166. Photos you delete from your photo library are placed in iPhoto's Trash. You must empty iPhoto's Trash to permanently remove the photos.

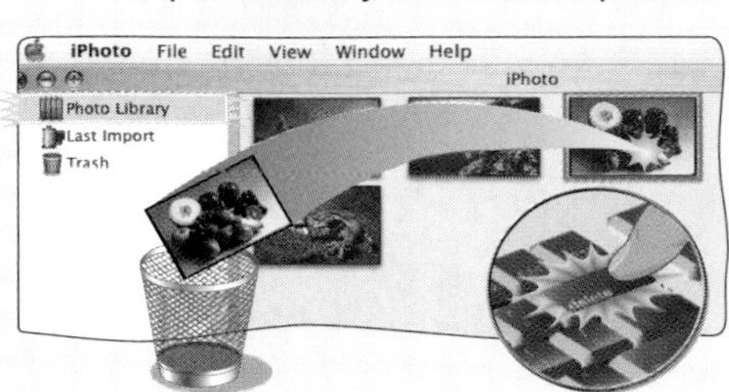

How do I empty iPhoto's Trash?

Click **Trash** in the top left corner of the iPhoto window to view the photos you have deleted. To permanently remove the photos, click the **File** menu and then click **Empty Trash**. In the confirmation dialog box that appears, click **OK** to permanently delete the photos.

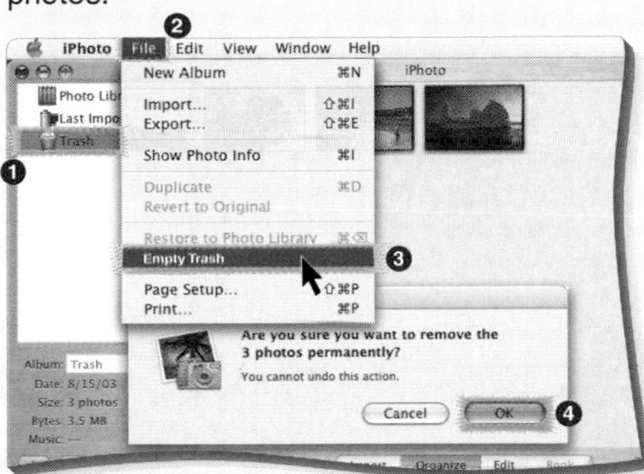

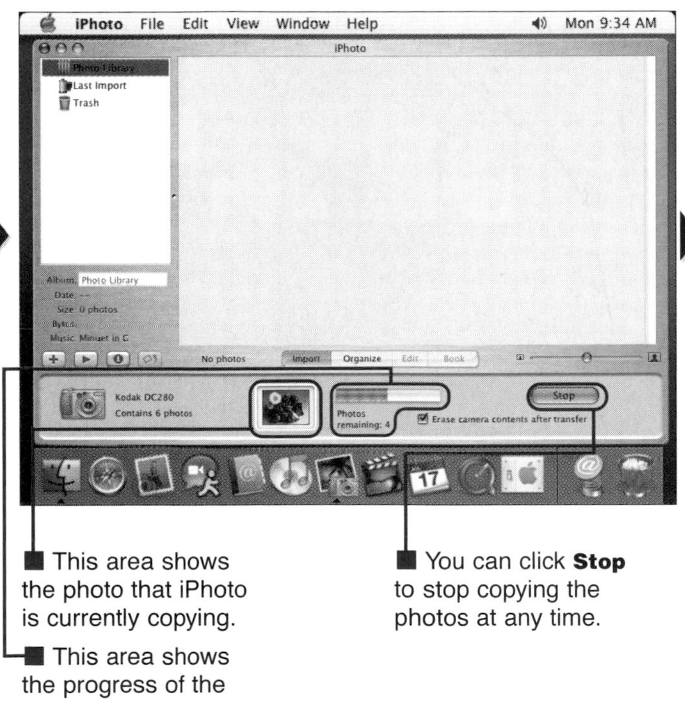

■ This area shows the photo that iPhoto is currently copying.

■ This area shows the progress of the copy.

■ You can click **Stop** to stop copying the photos at any time.

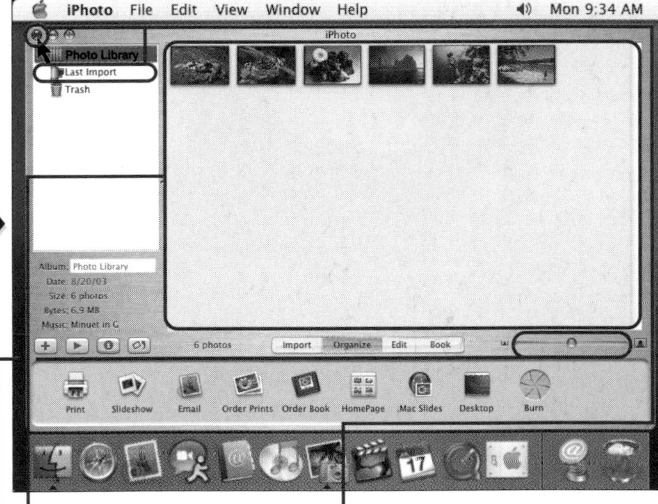

■ When the copy is complete, the photos appear in your photo library. The photo library contains all the photos you have copied to your computer.

5 To decrease or increase the size of the photos, drag this slider (●) left or right.

■ To quickly display only the last photos you copied from your digital camera, click **Last Import**.

6 When you finish working with iPhoto, click ● to close the iPhoto window.

CREATE AN ALBUM

You can create an album that contains photos you want to keep together.

You can create as many albums as you want. For example, you can create an album that contains pictures of your summer vacation and another album that contains pictures of your pet.

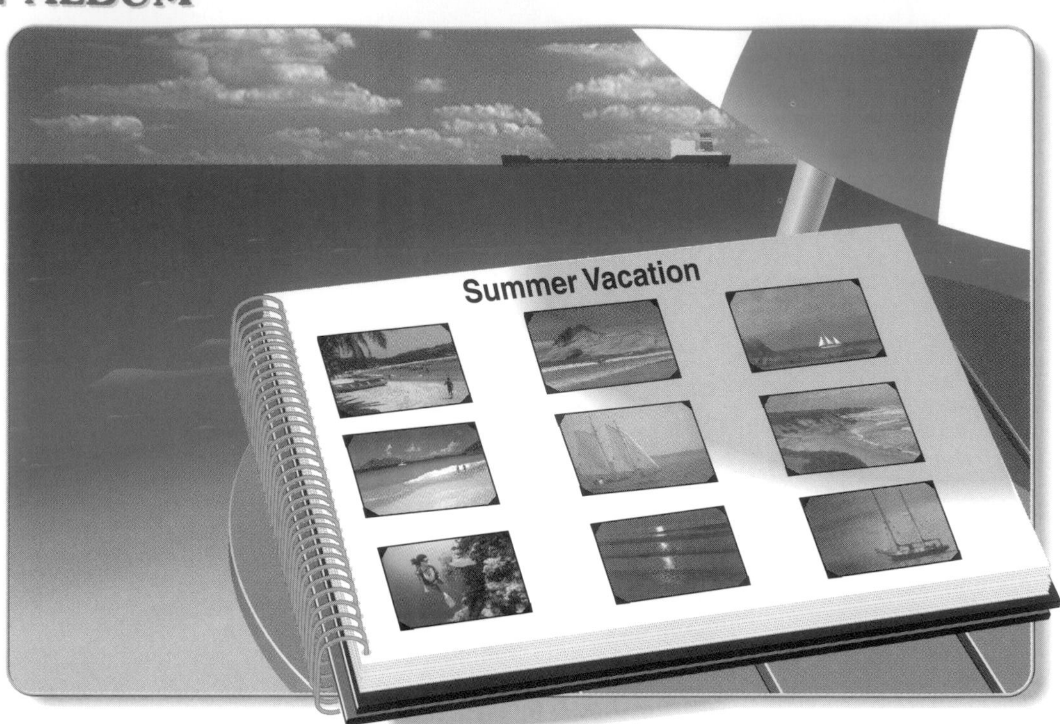

CREATE AN ALBUM

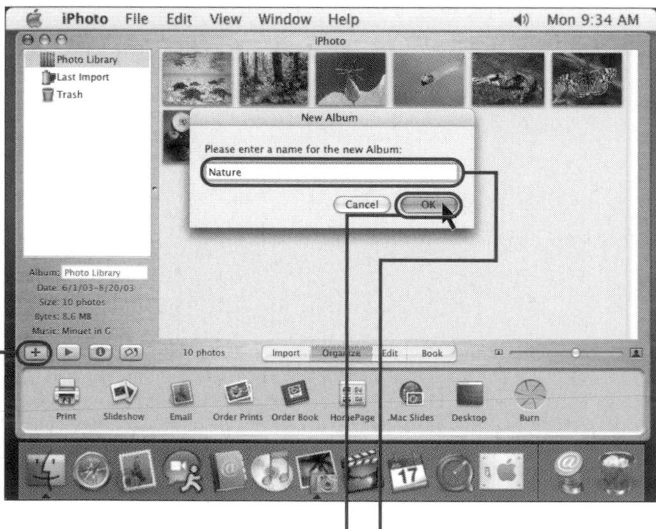

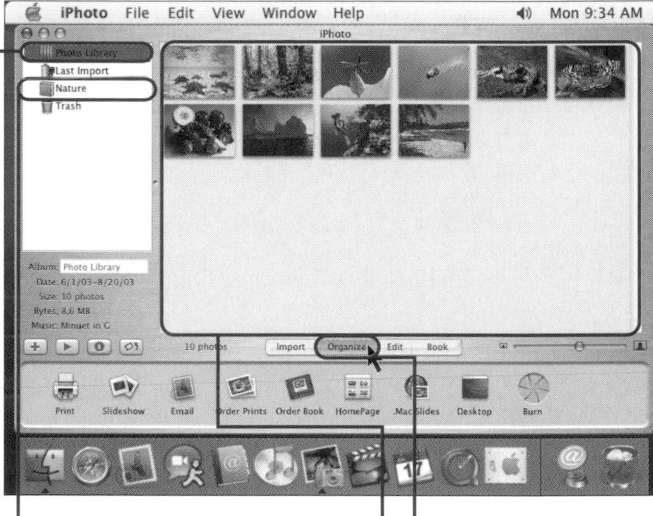

1 Click ⊞ to create a new album.

■ The New Album dialog box appears.

2 Type a name for the new album.

3 Click **OK** to create the album.

■ The album appears in this area. Albums display the ▯ symbol.

4 To add a photo to the album, click **Photo Library** to view all the photos in your photo library.

5 Click **Organize**.

■ This area displays all the photos in your photo library.

Can I change the order of photos in an album?

Yes. Click the name of the album that contains the photos you want to reorder and then click the **Organize** button. Position the mouse over a photo you want to move and then drag the photo to a new location in the album. A black line indicates where the photo will appear.

How do I delete an album?

To delete an album, click the name of the album you want to delete and then press the delete key. In the confirmation dialog box that appears, click **Remove** to delete the album. Deleting an album will not remove the photos in the album from your photo library.

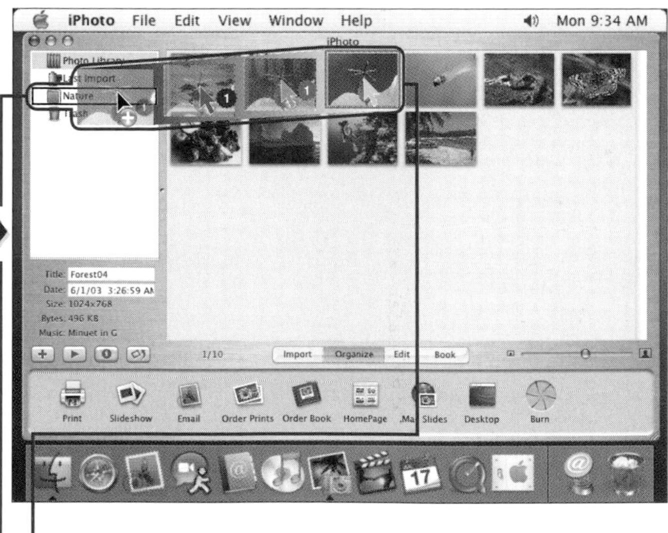

6 Position the mouse over a photo you want to add to the album.

7 Drag the photo to the album (changes to).

■ The photo is added to the album.

8 You can repeat steps **6** and **7** for each photo you want to add to the album.

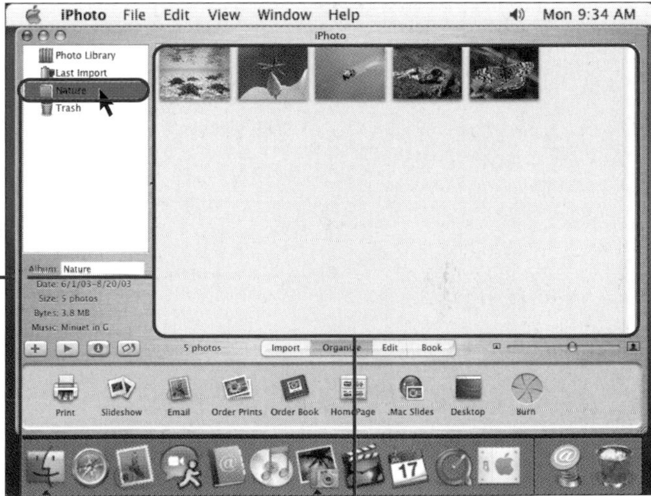

9 When you finish adding photos to the album, click the album.

■ This area displays all the photos you added to the album.

■ If you no longer want a photo to appear in the album, you can click the photo and then press the delete key to delete the photo.

Note: Deleting a photo from an album will not remove the photo from your photo library.

EDIT A PHOTO

You can edit a photo to improve its appearance. For example, you can crop a photo to remove parts of the photo you do not want to show. You can also change the brightness of a photo.

Editing a photo will change the appearance of the photo in your photo library and in every album that contains the photo.

EDIT A PHOTO

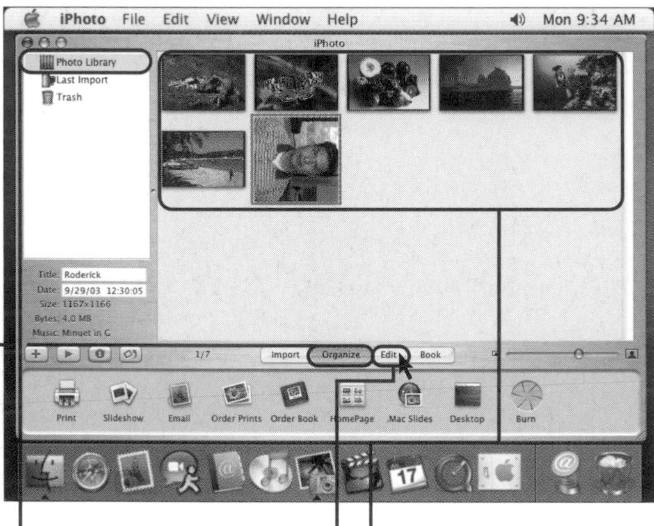

1 Click **Photo Library** to view all your photos or click the album that contains the photo you want to edit.

2 Click **Organize**.

3 Click the photo you want to change.

4 Click **Edit** to edit the photo.

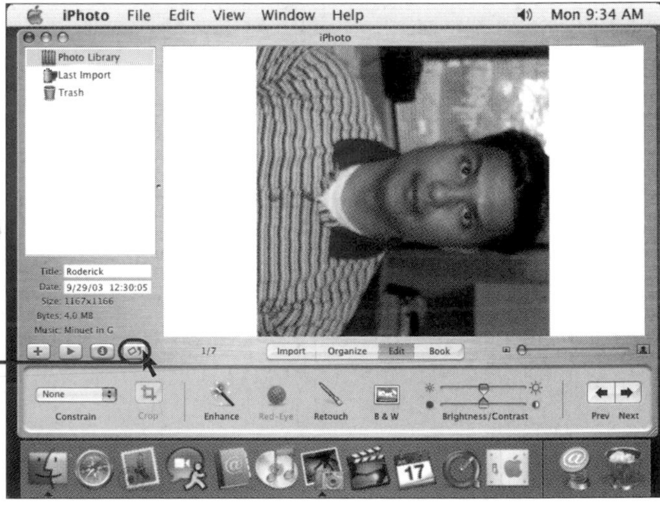

5 To rotate the photo 90 degrees, click .

■ You can repeat step **5** until the photo appears correctly.

Can I make a copy of a photo?

Yes. Making a copy of a photo before you begin editing the photo is useful if you want to edit the photo without changing the original photo. To make a copy of a photo, perform steps **1** to **3** below and then press and hold down the ⌘ key as you press the D key. If you make a copy of a photo in an album, iPhoto will also add a copy of the photo to your photo library.

Can I change a photo back to its original appearance?

If you do not like the changes you made to a photo, you can change the photo back to its original appearance. Perform steps **1** to **3** below to select the photo you want to change back to its original appearance. Click the **File** menu and then select **Revert to Original**. In the dialog box that appears, click **OK**.

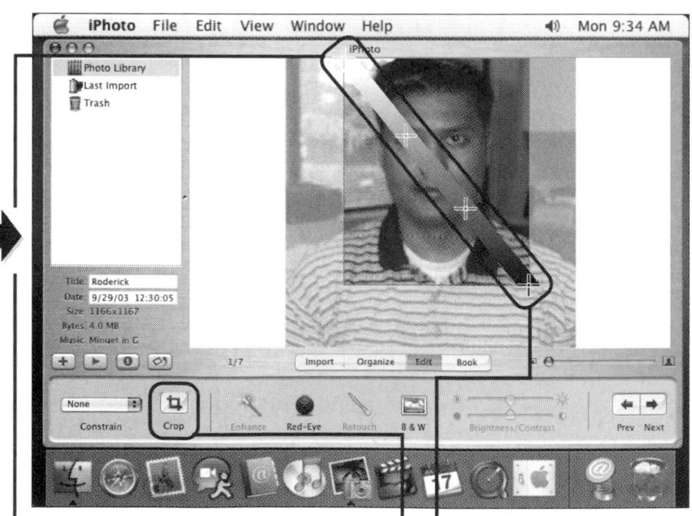

6 To show only part of the photo, position the mouse ┼ over a corner of the area you want to show.

7 Drag the mouse ┼ over the photo until you select the entire area you want to show.

8 Click **Crop** to crop the photo and show only the area you selected.

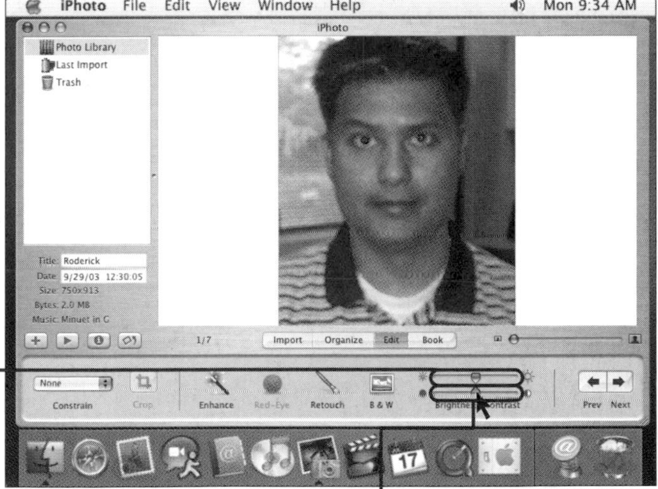

9 To decrease or increase the brightness of the photo, drag this slider (⛉) left or right.

10 To decrease or increase the contrast in the photo, drag this slider (⏶) left or right.

CONTINUED

You can use iPhoto's editing features to reduce red-eye and remove small marks or blemishes in your photos.

You can also use iPhoto to convert your photos to black-and-white images.

EDIT A PHOTO (CONTINUED)

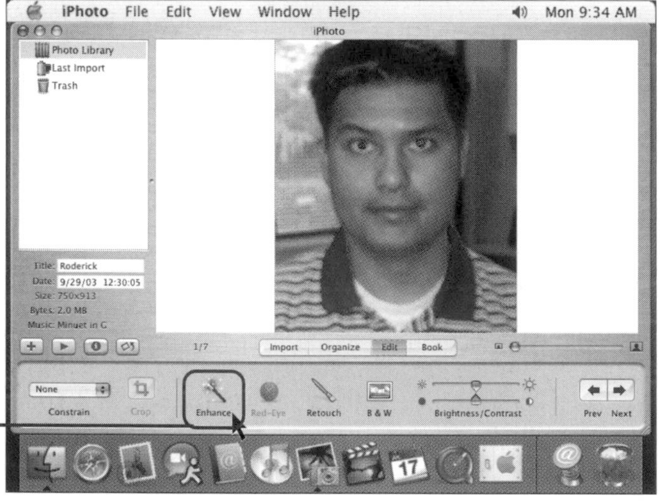

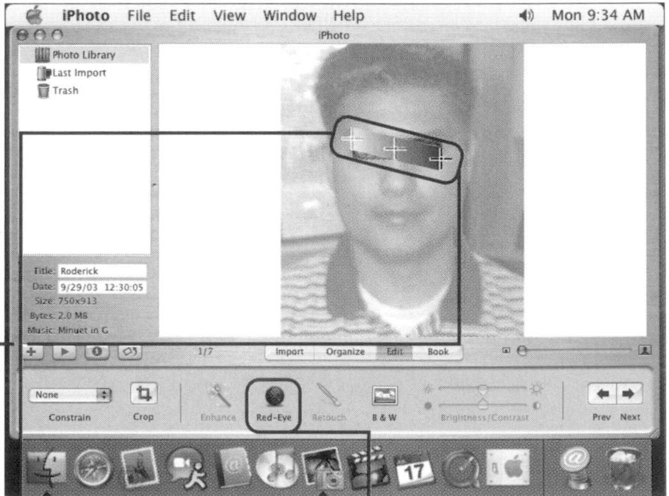

11 To have iPhoto automatically enhance the colors and clarity of the photo, click **Enhance**.

■ You can repeat step **11** to continue improving the colors and clarity.

12 To reduce red-eye for a person, position the mouse ┼ over a corner of the person's eye area.

13 Drag the mouse ┼ until you select both eyes.

*Note: The Red-Eye tool affects all shades of red in the area you select. If you make a mistake while selecting, click anywhere on the photo and repeat steps **12** and **13**.*

14 Click **Red-Eye** to remove shades of red from the person's eyes.

Can I undo a change I made without losing all of my changes?

To immediately reverse the last change you made to a photo, click the **Edit** menu and then select **Undo**. The name of the Undo command depends on the last change you made. You can repeat these actions to undo previous changes you made.

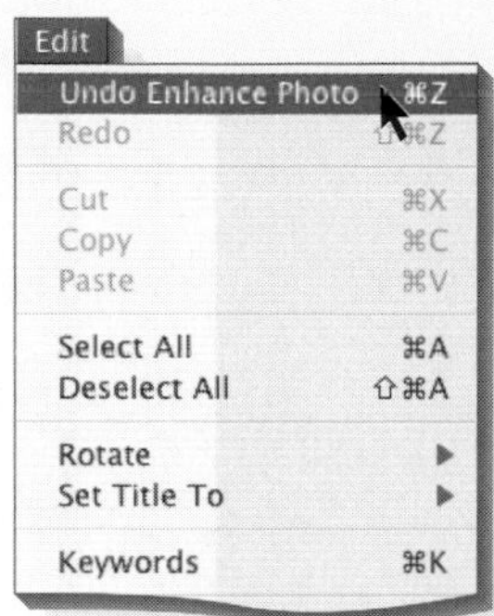

How can I enlarge the photo so I can clearly see the area I want to change?

To enlarge a photo for editing, drag the slider (●) to the right until you can clearly view the area you want to change.

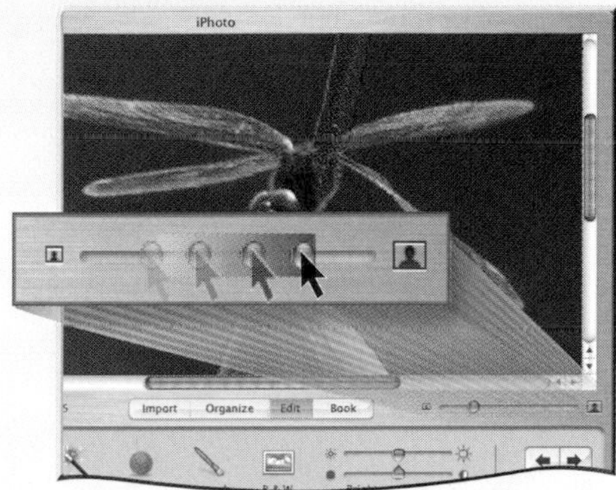

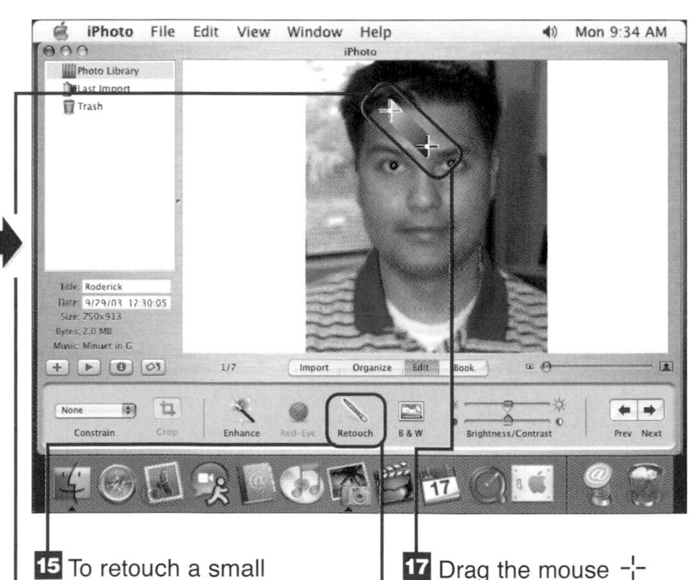

15 To retouch a small area in the photo, click **Retouch**.

16 Position the mouse -¦- over the area of the photo you want to retouch.

17 Drag the mouse -¦- away from the area using a short stroke.

18 Repeat step **17** until the area is removed from the photo.

19 When you finish retouching the photo, click **Retouch** again.

20 To change the photo to black and white, click **B & W**.

21 When you finish editing the photo, click **Organize** to return to your photo library or album.

ADD A TITLE AND COMMENTS TO A PHOTO

You can add a title and comments to a photo to provide a name and description for the photo.

iPhoto uses the film roll and photo number as a photo's title until you provide a new title. Adding a title and comments to a photo adds the information to every album that contains the photo. To create an album, see page 166.

ADD A TITLE AND COMMENTS TO A PHOTO

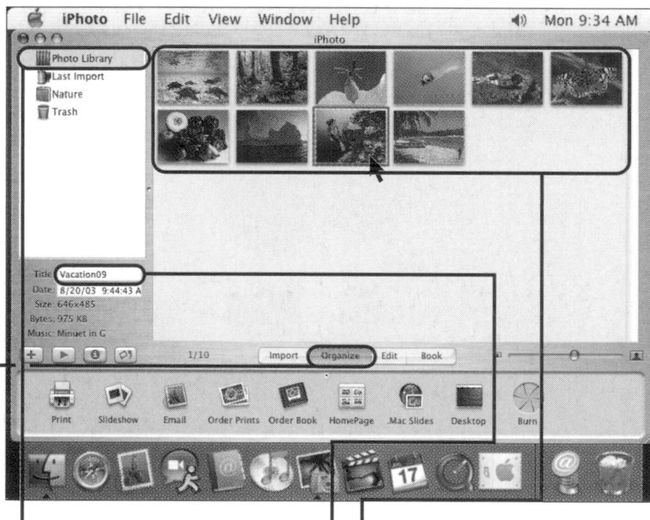

1 Click **Photo Library** to view all your photos or click the album that contains the photo you want to add a title and comments to.

2 Click **Organize**.

3 Click the photo you want to add a title and comments to.

■ This area displays the current title of the photo.

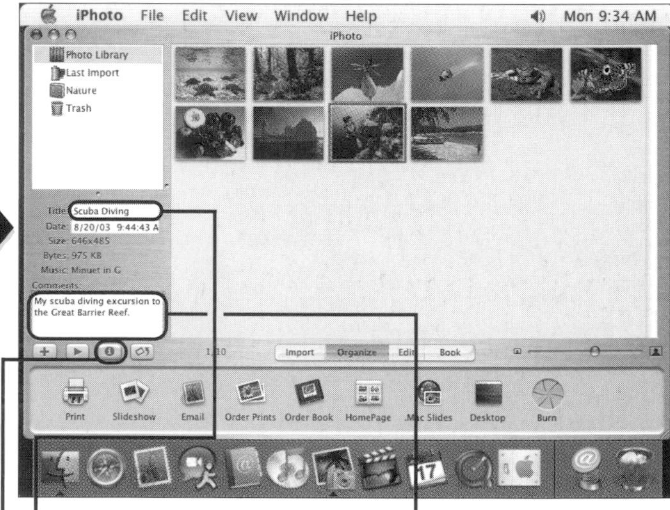

4 To change the title of the photo, drag the mouse over the current title until the title is highlighted. Then type a new title and press the return key.

5 To add comments, click ⓘ to display an area where you can enter comments.

6 Click this area and type comments for the photo.

Note: You can click ⓘ again to hide the title and comments. To redisplay the title, click ⓘ again.

VIEW A SLIDE SHOW OF YOUR PHOTOS

You can view a slide show of your photos on your computer screen. A slide show displays one photo at a time.

VIEW A SLIDE SHOW OF YOUR PHOTOS

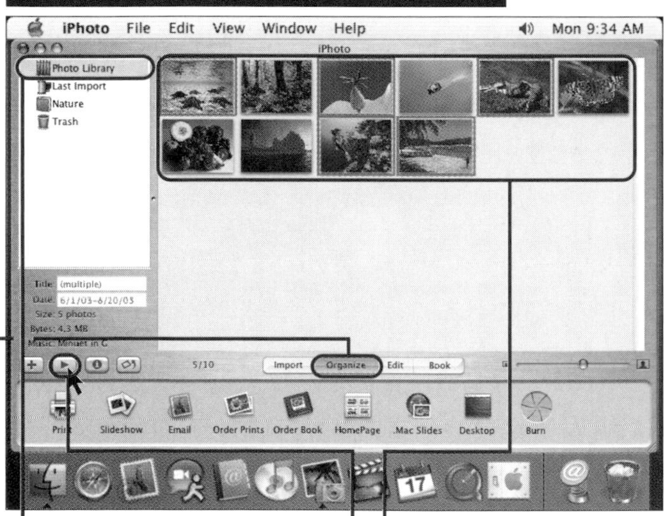

1 Click **Photo Library** to view all your photos or click the album that contains the photos you want to view in a slide show.

2 Click **Organize**.

3 Press and hold down the ⌘ key as you click each photo you want to view in a slide show.

4 Click ▶ to view a slide show of the photos you selected.

■ The slide show begins and the first photo fills your screen. iPhoto also plays background music to accompany the slide show.

5 To end the slide show at any time, click anywhere on your screen.

After you create an album, you can design a book that neatly arranges photos and text in the album.

When you create an album, iPhoto automatically assigns a standard book theme to the album. You can choose a different theme for the book and customize the design of individual pages in the book.

DESIGN A BOOK

1 Click the album that contains the photos you want to arrange in a book.

Note: To create an album, see page 166.

2 Click **Book** to design a book that arranges the photos in the album.

■ This area displays a miniature version of each page in the book.

Note: You can use the scroller to browse through the pages.

3 To view a larger version of a page, click the page.

■ This area displays a larger version of the page you selected.

How can I change the order in which photos appear on the pages in a book?

To change the order of photos in a book, you should reorder the photos in the album for the book. This is useful if you want to display a different photo on the Cover page. To change the order of photos in an album, see the top of page 167.

The photos in my book moved when I changed the design of a page. How can I make sure photos remain on a particular page?

You can lock a page to ensure the photos on the page do not move to other pages when you change the design of a page. To lock a page, click the page and then select the **Lock Page** option (☐ changes to ☑). A lock icon (🔒) appears below the locked page. You can click the **Lock Page** option again to unlock the page.

4 To select a theme for all the pages in the book, click this area.

5 Click the theme you want to use for all the pages in the book.

Note: A theme determines the way photos and text appear on the pages in a book.

■ The pages in the book immediately display the new theme.

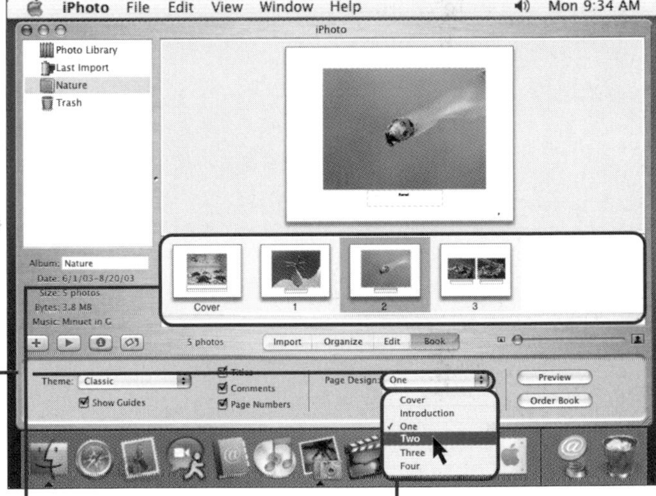

6 To change the page design of a page in the book, click the page you want to change.

Note: You cannot change the design of the Cover page.

7 Click this area to display a list of the available page designs.

8 Click the page design you want to use.

Note: The available page designs depend on the theme you selected in step ***5****.*

■ The page immediately displays the new page design.

CONTINUED

You can choose to display or hide titles, comments and page numbers on each page in a book.

You cannot hide the title on the Cover page of a book.

DESIGN A BOOK (CONTINUED)

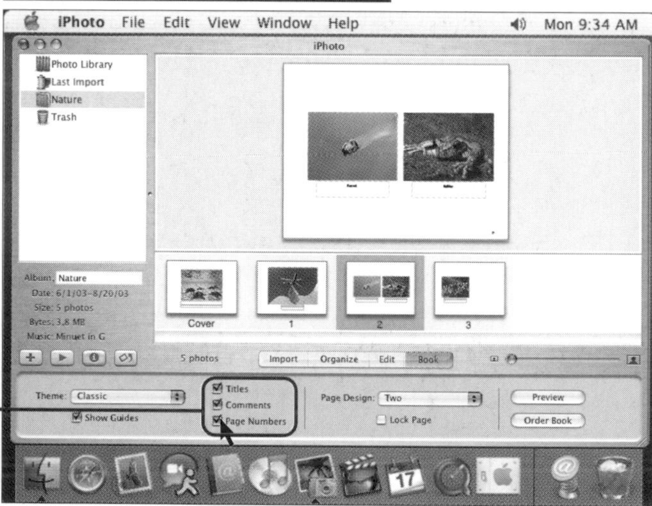

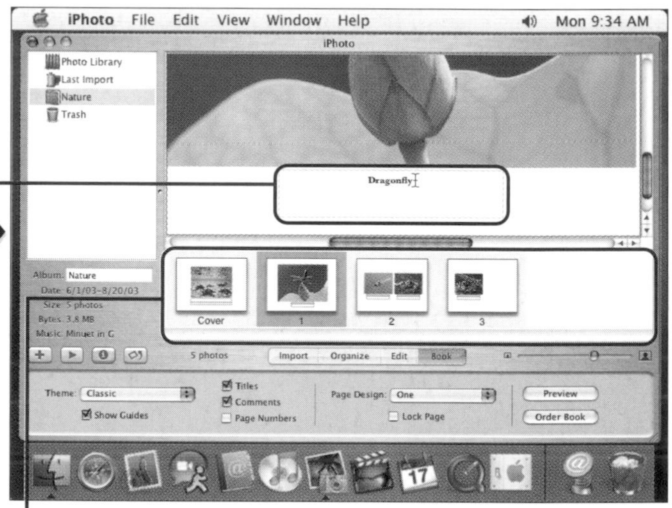

9 These options display titles, comments and page numbers on the pages in the book. You can click an option to display (☑) or hide (☐) the information on the pages.

■ The pages in the book immediately display the changes you make.

*Note: If you selected the Picture Book or Story Book theme in step **5** on page 175, selecting the Titles or Comments option will not affect the appearance of the pages in the book.*

10 To edit the title(s) or comments on a page in the book, click the page you want to edit.

11 Click in the blue box for the title or comments area.

Note: The Picture Book and Story Book themes do not display title or comments areas.

■ When you click in the title or comments area, iPhoto may automatically magnify the page so you can view the area more clearly.

Why does a ⚠ symbol appear beside a photo in my book?

The ⚠ symbol indicates a photo whose resolution is too low to print properly. A photo displaying the ⚠ symbol may appear jagged or blurry when printed. To improve the resolution of the photo, you can increase the number of photos per page in your book, so the photos will print at a smaller size.

How can I change the order of the pages in a book?

To change the order of the pages in a book, position the mouse over the page you want to move and then drag the page to a new location. You cannot move the Cover page.

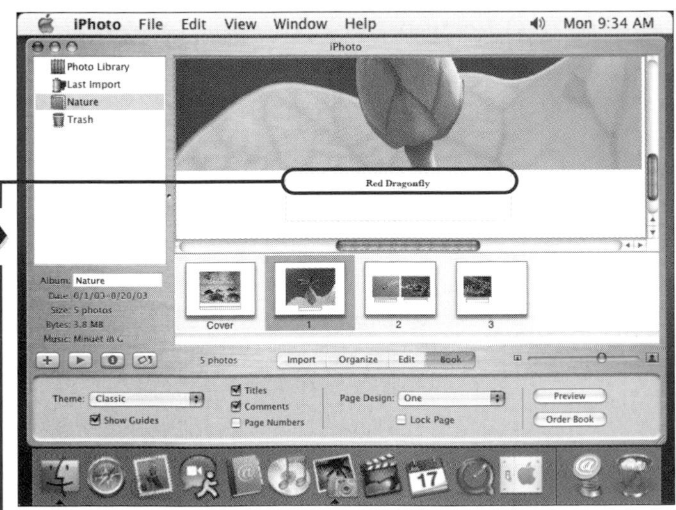

12 Type a title or comments for the photo.

Note: To delete an existing title or comments, drag the mouse over the existing text until you highlight the text. Then press the delete *key.*

13 You can repeat steps **10** to **12** for each page that contains text you want to edit.

Note: Editing a photo's title and comments changes the title and comments in your photo library and in every album that contains the photo.

14 To view the book in a separate window, click **Preview**.

■ A window appears, displaying the current page in the book.

15 To move backward or forward through the pages in the book, click ◀ or ▶.

16 When you finish viewing the pages in the book, click ● to close the window.

Note: To order a printed copy of your book, see the top of page 179.

You can produce a paper copy of your photos.

iPhoto offers many different styles you can use to print your photos.

PRINT PHOTOS

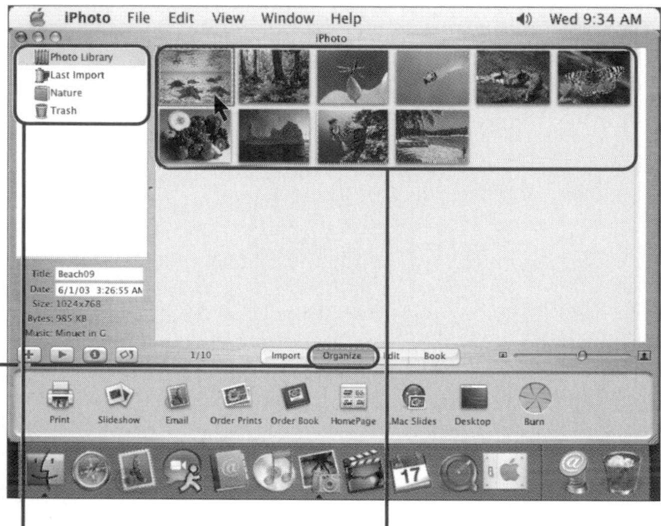

1 Click **Photo Library** to view all your photos or click the album that contains the photos you want to print.

2 Click **Organize**.

3 Click the photo you want to print.

■ To print more than one photo, press and hold down the ⌘ key as you click each additional photo you want to print.

4 Click **Print** to print the photos you selected.

■ The Print dialog box appears.

■ This area displays the printer iPhoto will use.

5 To select a print setting for your printer, click this area.

6 Click the setting you want to use.

Can I use iPhoto to order professionally printed copies of my photos?

Yes. When your computer is connected to the Internet, you can use iPhoto to order prints or a book of your photos from an online print service.

Order Prints

To order prints of your photos, perform steps **1** to **3** below to select the photos you want to order prints of. Then click **Order Prints**. The Order Prints window appears, displaying an order form you can fill out to order the prints.

Order a Book

Before ordering a book, you should design the book you want to order. To design a book, see page 174. Make sure the book contains at least 10 pages of photos. To order a book, perform steps **1** and **2** below, selecting the album you used to create the book in step **1**. Then click **Order Book**. The Order Book window appears, displaying an order form you can fill out to order the book.

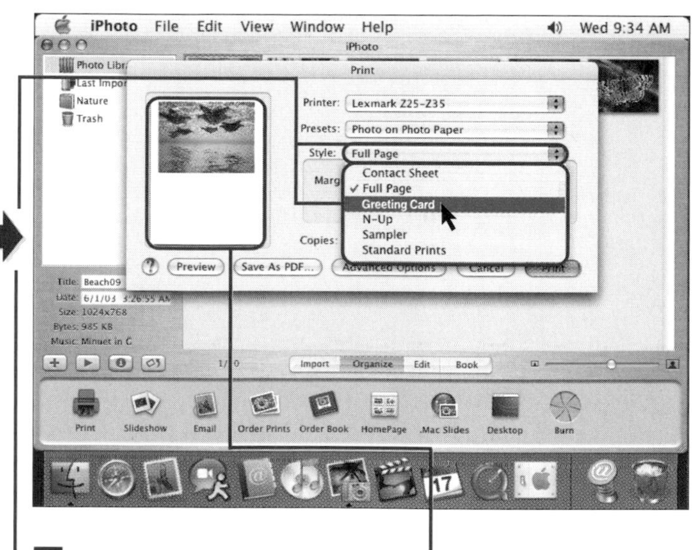

7 To select a print style, click this area.

8 Click the style you want to use.

■ This area shows a preview of how the photos will print.

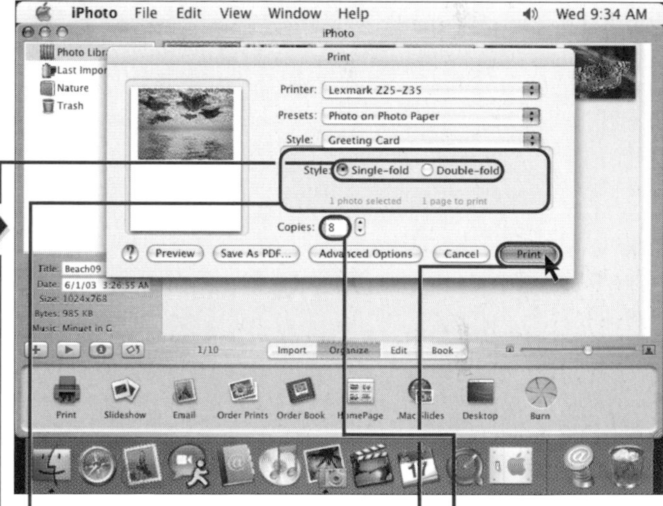

■ This area displays the options for the style you selected in step **8**. In this example, the Greeting Card options are displayed.

9 Click an option to specify if you want to use the single-fold or double-fold style for your greeting cards (○ changes to ◉).

10 To specify the number of copies you want to print, double-click this area and type the number of copies.

11 Click **Print**.

E-MAIL PHOTOS

You can e-mail your photos to a friend, colleague or family member.

You need to be connected to the Internet to e-mail your photos.

E-MAIL PHOTOS

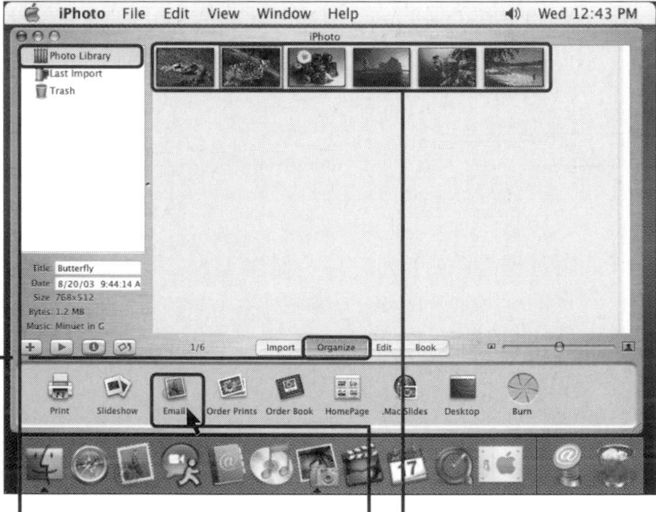

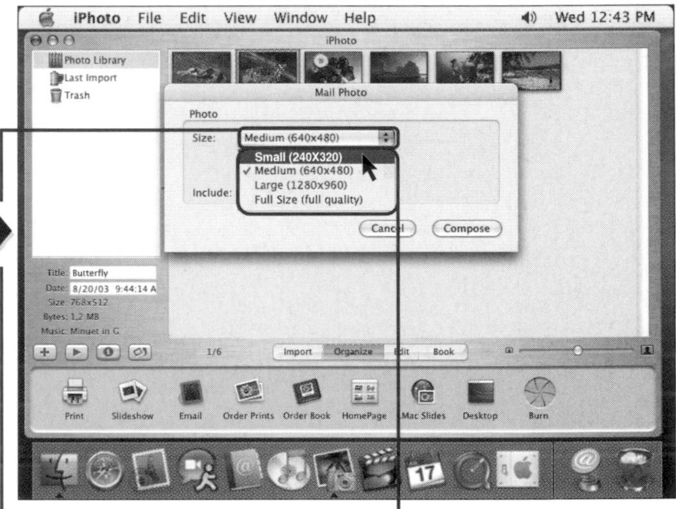

1 Click **Photo Library** to view all your photos or click the album that contains the photos you want to e-mail.

2 Click **Organize**.

3 Click the photo you want to e-mail.

Note: To e-mail more than one photo, press and hold down the ⌘ key as you click each photo you want to e-mail.

4 Click **Email** to e-mail the photo you selected.

■ The Mail Photo dialog box appears.

5 To select a size for the photos, click this area.

6 Click the size you want to use for the photos.

Note: Smaller photos transfer faster over the Internet and fit better on the recipient's screen.

Is there another way I can share my photos with other people?

You can burn your photos onto a recordable CD or DVD that you can distribute to other people.

1 Perform steps **1** to **3** below to select the photos you want to burn.

2 Click **Burn** (changes to).

3 Insert a blank, recordable CD or DVD into your computer's drive.

4 Click **Burn**.

■ The Burn Disc window appears.

5 Click **Burn**.

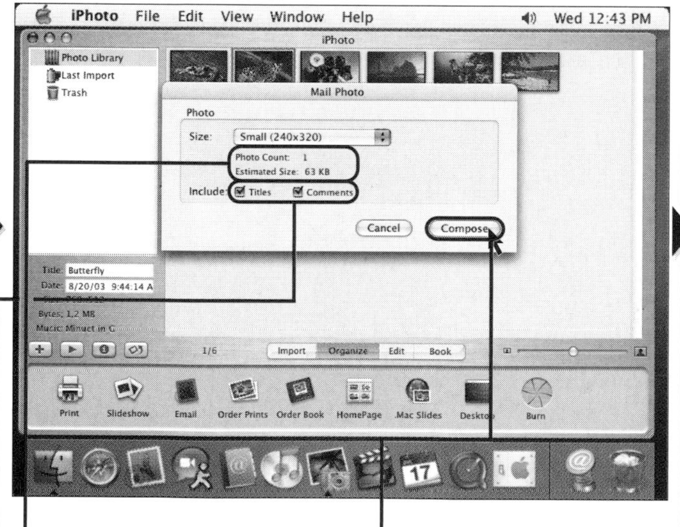

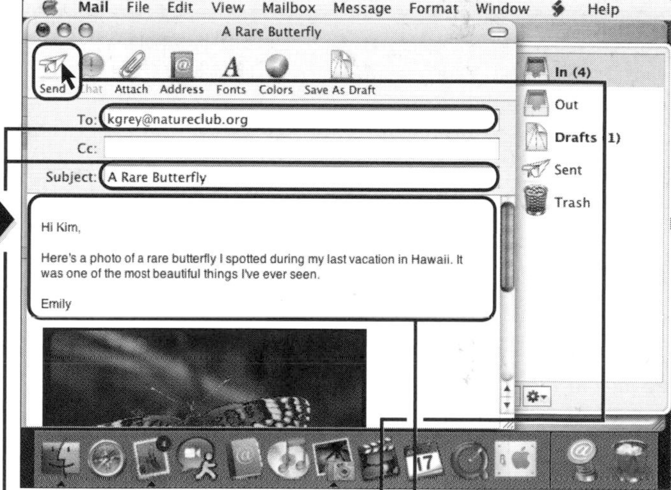

■ This area displays the number of photos you selected and the estimated file size of the photos.

7 These options display the titles and comments for the photos in the e-mail message. You can click an option to display () or hide () the titles or comments.

Note: To add titles and comments to photos, see page 172.

8 Click **Compose** to compose the e-mail message.

■ A window appears, allowing you to send the photos in an e-mail message.

9 Click this area and type the e-mail address of the person you want to receive the photos.

10 This area displays a subject for the message. To change the subject, drag the mouse over the existing subject and then type a new subject.

11 Click this area and type the message you want to accompany the photos.

12 Click **Send** to send the message.

PUBLISH PHOTOS TO THE WEB

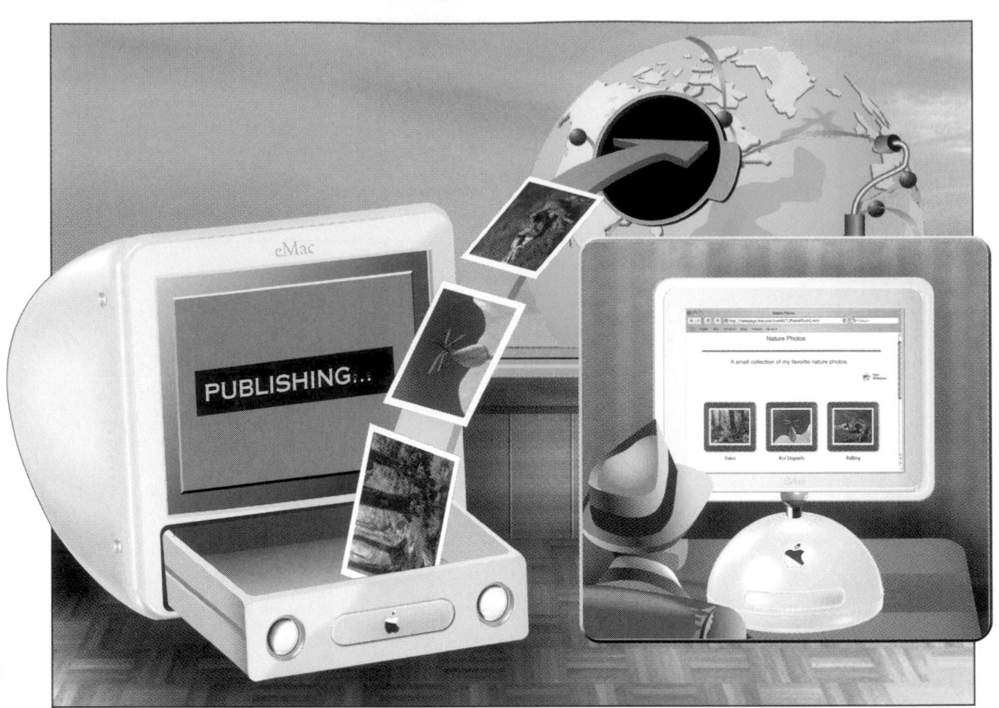

You can publish photos to the Web to allow people from around the world to view the photos. iPhoto creates a Web page called a HomePage to display your photos.

You need to be connected to the Internet and have a .Mac membership to publish photos to the Web. To connect to the Internet, see page 236.

If you do not have a .Mac membership, you can obtain a membership at the www.mac.com Web site.

PUBLISH PHOTOS TO THE WEB

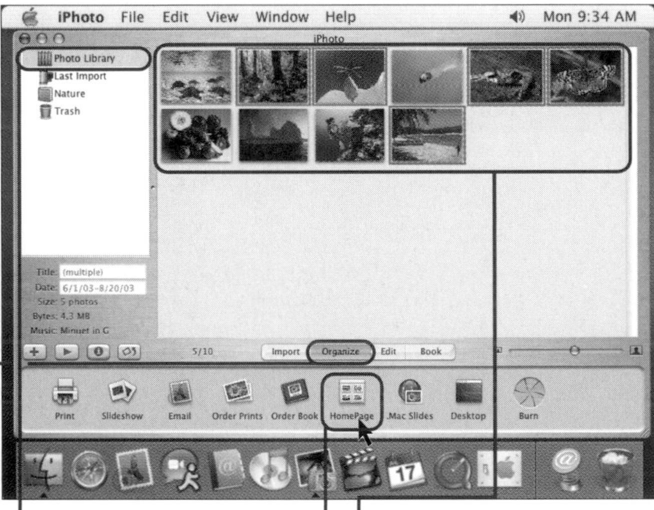

1 Click **Photo Library** to view all your photos or click the album that contains the photos you want to publish to the Web.

2 Click **Organize**.

3 Press and hold down the ⌘ key as you click each photo you want to publish.

4 Click **HomePage** to publish the photos you selected.

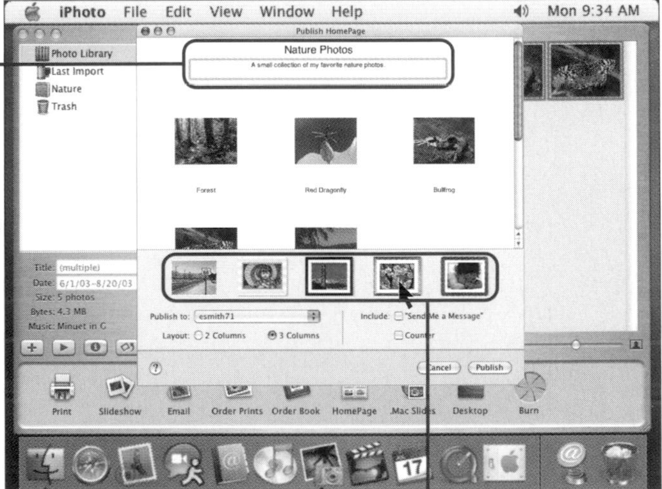

■ The Publish HomePage window appears, displaying the photos you selected to publish.

5 To edit the text that will be displayed on the Web page, drag the mouse I over the text you want to change until the text is highlighted. Then type the new text.

6 Click the border style you want to use for the photos.

■ The photos display the border style you selected.

Can I make changes to my HomePage?

Yes. When viewing your HomePage on the Web, click the **Created using .Mac** link at the bottom of the page to be able to make changes to the page. For example, you can remove photos or edit text. You may need to enter the member name and password for your .Mac membership to make changes to your HomePage.

Is there another way I can view my photos on my screen?

You can display a photo as a desktop picture on your computer. Perform steps **1** to **3** below, selecting one photo in step **3**. Then click **Desktop**. The photo you selected immediately appears on your desktop. If you select more than one photo in step **3**, Mac OS will automatically change the picture displayed on your desktop every 30 minutes. For more information on changing the desktop picture, see page 74.

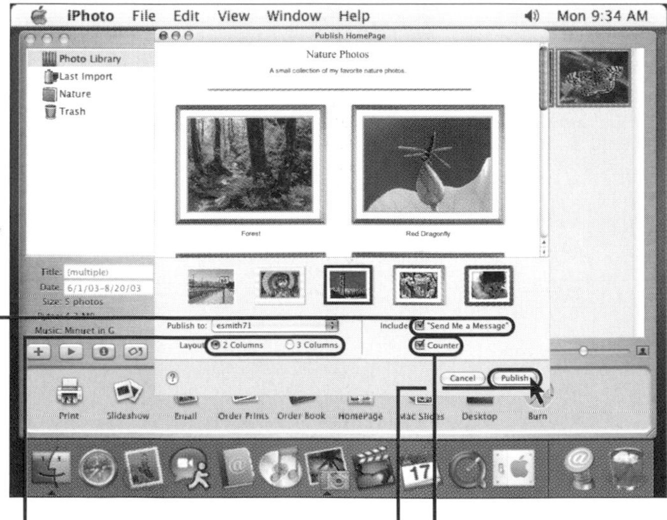

7 Click an option to specify the number of columns you want to use to display your photos on your Web page (○ changes to ◉).

8 Click this option to include a link that allows people to send you a message from your Web page (☐ changes to ☑).

9 Click this option to include a counter to record the number of people who visit your Web page (☐ changes to ☑).

10 Click **Publish** to publish the photos to the Web.

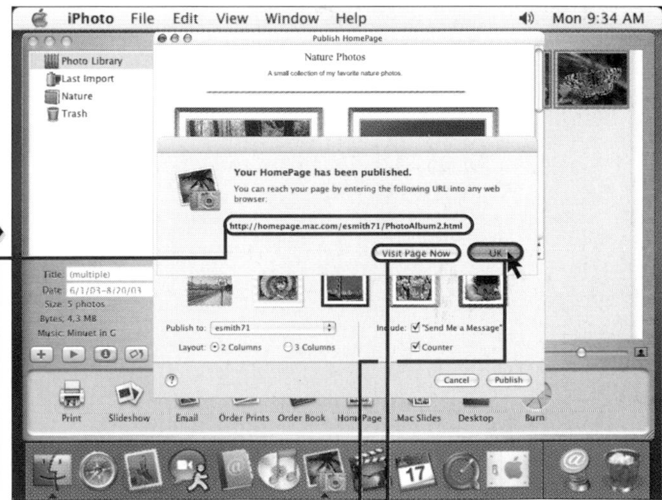

■ A dialog box appears, displaying the address where you can view the Web page.

Note: You should write down the address for future reference.

11 To view the Web page, click **Visit Page Now**.

■ To close the dialog box without viewing the Web page, click **OK**.

iMac

CHAPTER 8

Create Movies Using iMovie

Read this chapter to find out how to use iMovie to create and work with movies on your computer. You will learn how to transfer video from a digital video camera, rearrange video clips and add sound effects to your movies.

TRANSFER VIDEO FROM A DIGITAL VIDEO CAMERA

You can use iMovie to transfer video from a digital video camera to your computer. Transferring video to your computer allows you to view and edit the video on your computer.

Your screen resolution must be set to 1024 x 768 to work with a movie in iMovie. For information on changing your screen resolution, see page 76.

Before you start transferring video from a digital video camera, make sure the camera is turned on and in VTR mode. Also make sure the tape is at the point where you want to begin transferring the video.

TRANSFER VIDEO FROM A DIGITAL VIDEO CAMERA

1 Connect the video camera to your computer.

2 Click the iMovie icon to start iMovie.

■ iMovie opens on your screen.

■ The first time you start iMovie, a dialog box appears.

3 Click **Create Project** to start a new project.

*Note: If the dialog box does not appear and you want to transfer video to a new project, see page 192 to create a new project. Then skip to step **6** on page 187.*

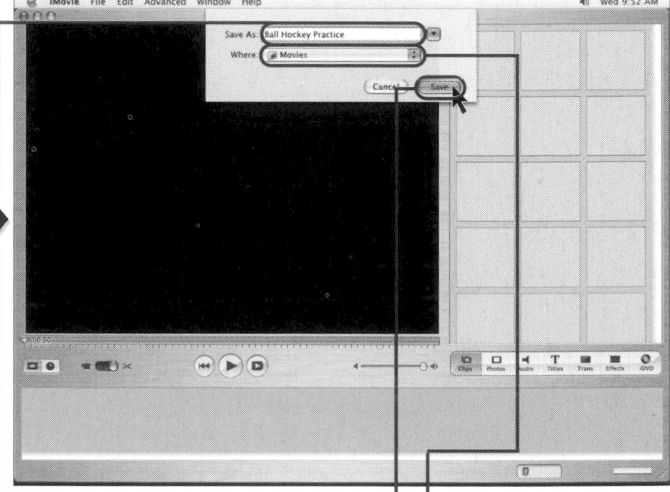

■ A dialog sheet appears.

4 Type a name for the project.

■ This area shows the location where iMovie will store the project. You can click this area to change the location.

5 Click **Save** to create the project.

What is a video clip?

A video clip is a small, manageable segment of a video you transfer to iMovie. A video clip is created each time iMovie detects a different scene in a video, such as when you switch from pause to record.

How can I delete a video clip?

To delete a video clip you do not plan to use in your movie, click the video clip and then press the delete key. The video clip will no longer appear in iMovie.

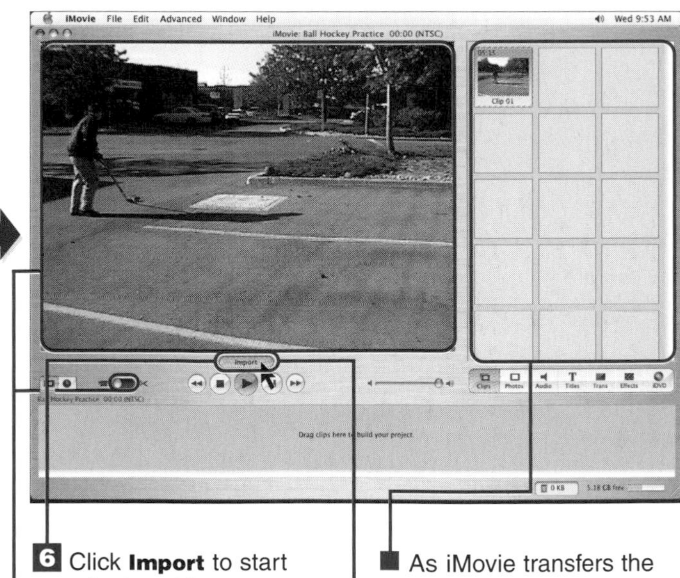

6 Click **Import** to start transferring video to your computer.

■ If Import is not displayed, drag ● to the left in this area to display the button.

■ This area displays the video iMovie is transferring.

■ As iMovie transfers the video, clips for the video appear in the Clips pane. For information on video clips, see the top of this page.

7 When you want to stop recording the video, click **Import** again.

8 To play a video clip, click the video clip.

9 Click ▶ to play the video clip.

■ The video clip plays in this area.

■ When you finish working with your video, you should save your project. See page 190 to save a project.

10 To quit iMovie, click ●.

ADD A VIDEO CLIP TO A MOVIE

You must add each video clip you want to include in a movie to the clip viewer.

The clip viewer displays the order in which video clips will play in a movie.

ADD A VIDEO CLIP TO A MOVIE

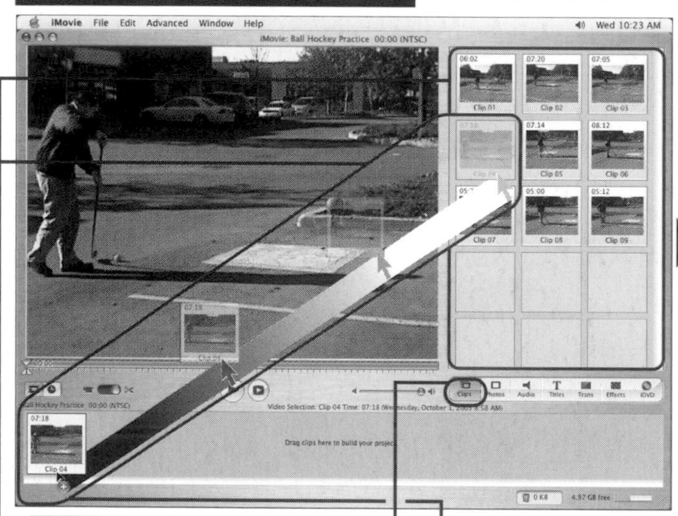

1 Click **Clips** to view all the video clips in the current project.

■ The Clips pane displays the video clips.

2 Position the mouse over the video clip you want to add to your movie.

3 Drag the video clip to the clip viewer.

Note: You can add a video clip before, after or between existing video clips in the clip viewer.

■ The video clip appears in the clip viewer.

■ You can repeat steps **2** and **3** for each video clip you want to add to your movie.

■ If you no longer want a video clip to appear in your movie, drag the video clip back to the Clips pane.

REARRANGE VIDEO CLIPS

You can change the order of video clips in the clip viewer to change the order in which the clips will play in your movie.

REARRANGE VIDEO CLIPS

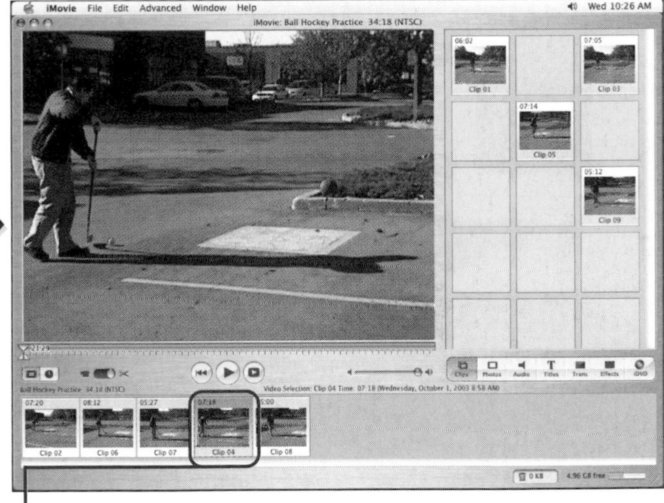

1 Position the mouse over the video clip that you want to move to a different location in your movie.

2 Drag the video clip to a new location in your movie (pointer changes to a pointer with a plus sign).

■ The video clip appears in the new location.

■ The surrounding video clips automatically move to make room for the video clip.

SAVE AND OPEN A PROJECT

You should regularly save changes you make to a project to avoid losing your work. You can also open a saved project to work with the contents of the project.

A project stores the video clips for a video you transferred from a video camera and a rough draft of your movie.

SAVE A PROJECT

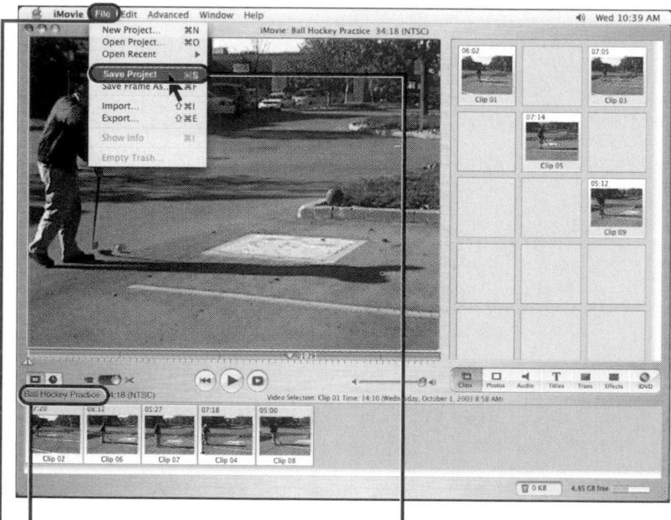

■ This area displays the name of the current project.

1 To save the project, click **File**.

2 Click **Save Project**.

■ iMovie saves the changes you made to the project.

OPEN A PROJECT

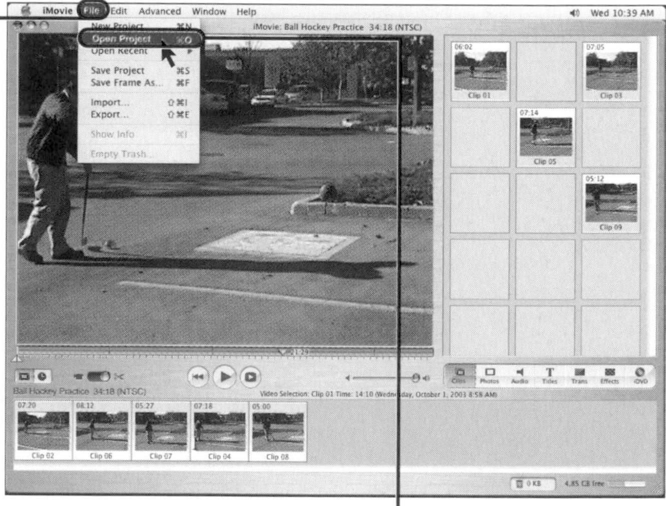

■ You can work with only one project at a time. Before opening a project, make sure you save your current project.

1 Click **File**.

2 Click **Open Project**.

■ A dialog sheet appears.

Where does iMovie store my projects?

By default, iMovie stores each project you create in a separate folder within your Movies folder. Each project folder contains a project file that opens the project, a QuickTime version of the project that you can play in QuickTime Player and a Media folder, which stores the sound and video clips for the project. For information on the Movies folder, see page 23. For information on QuickTime Player, see page 114.

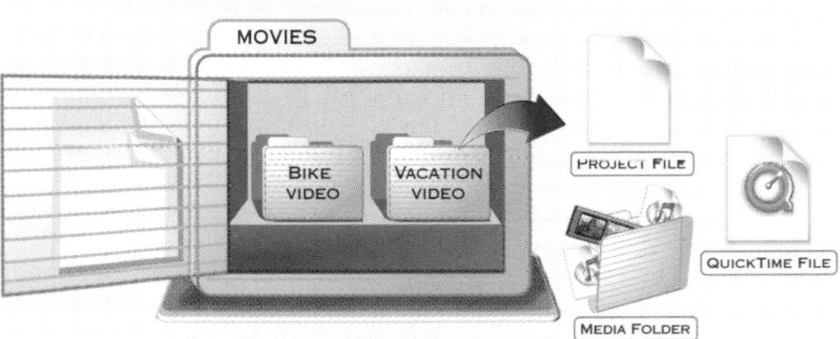

Can iMovie automatically open the last project I worked with?

Yes. When you start iMovie, the last project you worked with automatically appears on your screen. This allows you to immediately begin working with the project.

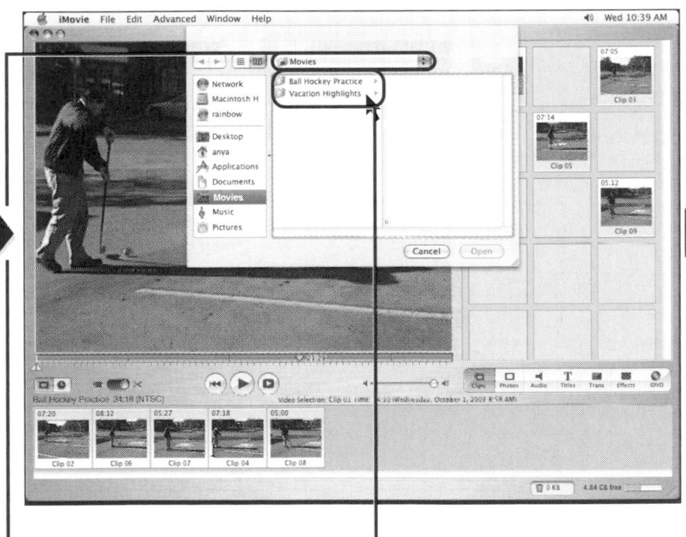

■ This area shows the location of the displayed project folders. You can click this area to select a different location.

3 Click the project you want to open.

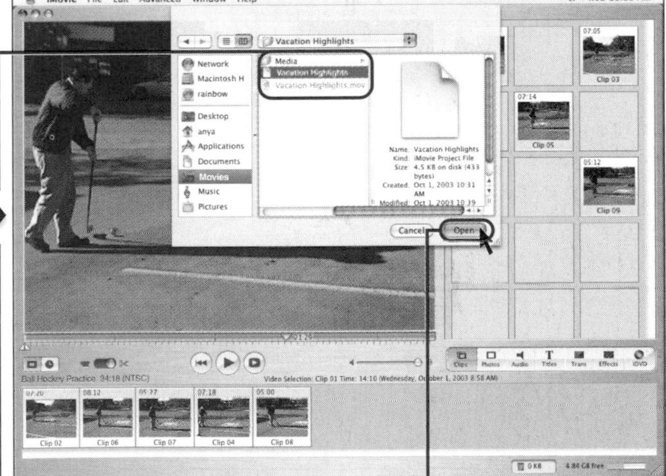

■ The contents of the project folder appear.

4 Click the project file you want to open. Project files display the ▯ symbol.

5 Click **Open** to open the project.

■ The project opens and the video clips in the project appear on your screen.

CREATE A NEW PROJECT

When you want to transfer new video from a digital video camera to your computer, you can create a new project to store the video.

A project stores the video clips for a video you transfer from a video camera and a rough draft of your movie.

CREATE A NEW PROJECT

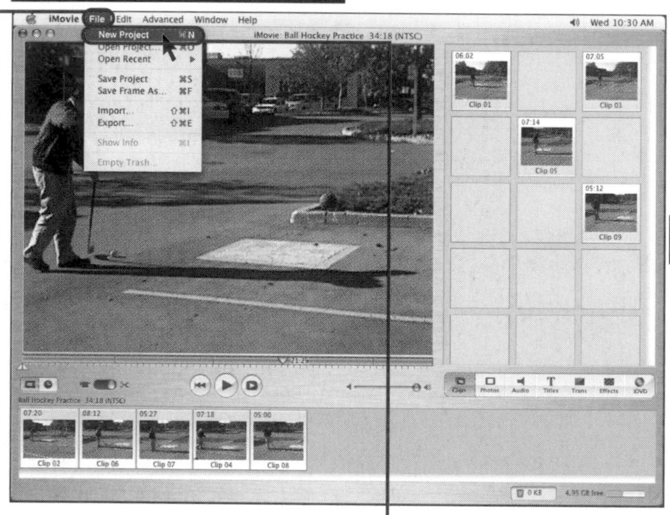

■ You can work with only one project at a time. Before creating a new project, make sure you save your current project. To save a project, see page 190.

1 Click **File**.

2 Click **New Project**.

■ A dialog sheet appears.

3 Type a name for the new project.

■ This area shows the location where iMovie will store the project. You can click this area to change the location.

4 Click **Save** to create the project.

*Note: To transfer video from a video camera into the new project, perform steps **6** and **7** on page 187.*

CROP A VIDEO CLIP

You can crop the beginning and end of a video clip to remove parts of the clip you do not want to play in your movie.

CROP A VIDEO CLIP

1 Click the video clip you want to crop.

2 To specify where you want the video clip to end, drag the end crop marker (◺) to the location in the video clip.

3 To specify where you want the video clip to start, drag the start crop marker (◿) to the location in the video clip.

■ A yellow area on the bar indicates the part of the video clip that iMovie will keep. iMovie will remove the parts of the video clip outside of the yellow area.

4 Click **Edit**.

5 Click **Crop** to crop the video clip.

ADD A TRANSITION BETWEEN VIDEO CLIPS

You can add an interesting transition from one video clip to another in your movie. Adding transitions between video clips blends the end of one video clip with the beginning of the next video clip.

ADD A TRANSITION BETWEEN VIDEO CLIPS

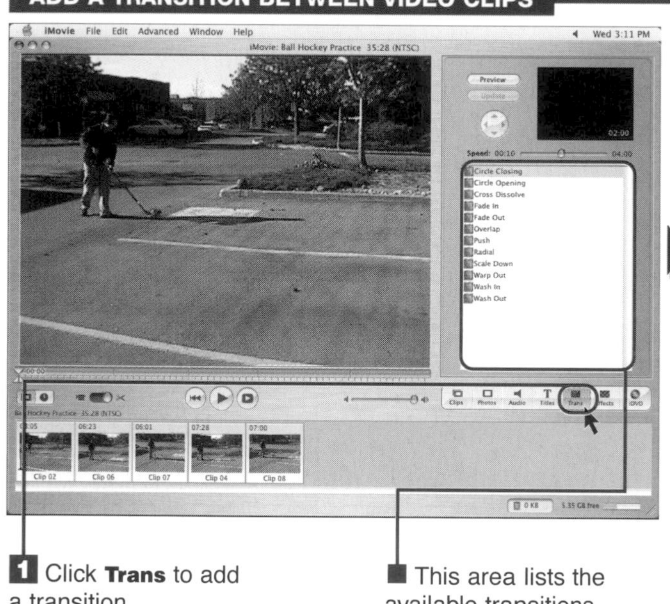

1 Click **Trans** to add a transition.

■ This area lists the available transitions.

2 Click the transition you want to add.

■ This area displays a preview of the transition you selected.

*Note: You can repeat step **2** to select a different transition.*

■ If you selected the **Push** transition, click an arrow in this area to specify the direction you want the video clip to move off the screen.

What transitions can I add to the beginning or end of my movie?

You can add the Fade In or Wash In transition to the beginning of your movie and the Fade Out or Wash Out transition to the end of your movie. To add one of these transitions, perform steps **1** to **5** below. When adding a transition to the beginning of your movie, drag the transition to the area before the first video clip in the movie in step **5**. When adding a transition to the end of your movie, drag the transition to the area after the last video clip in the movie in step **5**.

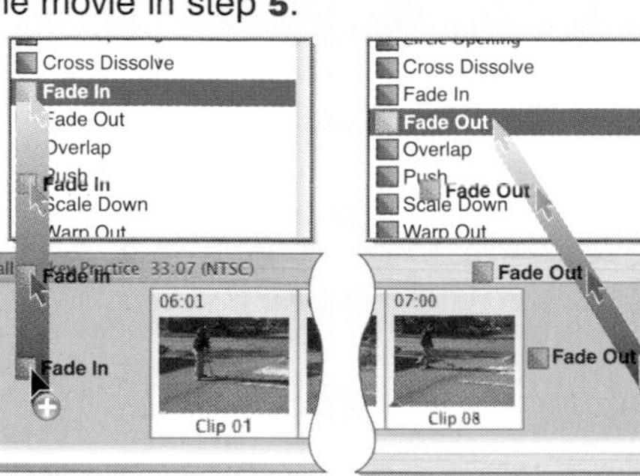

How do I remove a transition from my movie?

To remove a transition, click the transition symbol (, or) for the transition you no longer want to use. Then press the delete key to remove the transition from your movie.

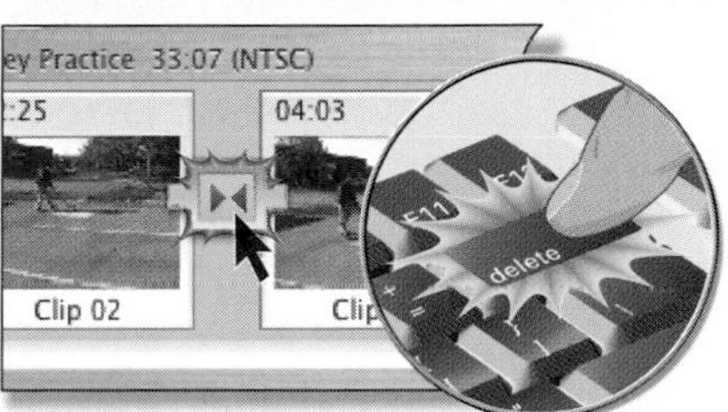

3 To change the duration of the transition, drag this slider ( ) left or right.

4 To add the transition you selected to video clips in your movie, position the mouse over the transition.

5 Drag the transition to the area between the video clips you want to use the transition (changes to).

■ A transition symbol (, or) appears between the video clips.

Note: The transition symbol indicates if the transition will affect the video clip before the transition ( ), after the transition ( ) or both ( ).

6 To play the transition between the video clips, click the transition symbol.

7 Click ( ) to play the transition.

■ The transition plays in this area.

ADD SOUNDS TO A MOVIE

You can add sounds, such as music from a CD, to your movie to enhance the movie.

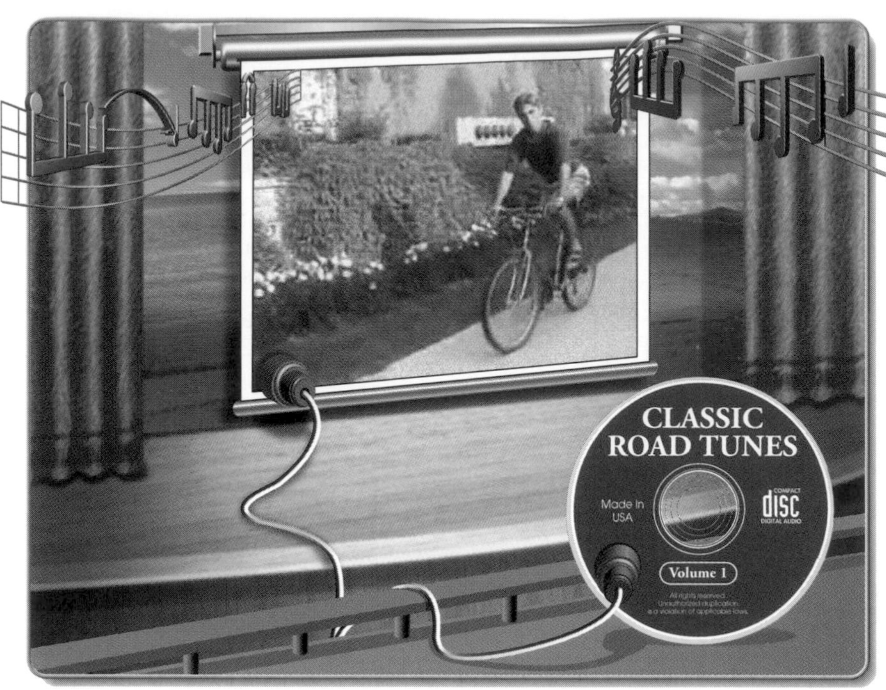

iMovie comes with two sound tracks that you can add sounds to. You can add sounds to both sound tracks to overlap sounds in your movie.

ADD SOUNDS TO A MOVIE

1 Click ◷ to display the timeline viewer.

■ The timeline viewer appears.

■ This area displays the video clips in your movie and areas for both sound tracks for the movie.

2 Drag this slider (▽) to the location in your movie where you want a sound to start playing.

3 To add music from a CD, insert a music CD into your computer's CD drive.

Note: If the iTunes window appears, click ● to close the window.

4 Click **Audio** to display the sound options for your movie.

5 Click this area to display a list of sound locations.

6 Click the name of the music CD you inserted.

Can I add songs from my iTunes Library or a playlist to my movie?

Yes. If a song you want to add to your movie is already in your iTunes Library or a playlist, you can easily add the song to your movie. Perform steps **1** to **9** below, except select **iTunes Library** or the name of the playlist containing the song in step **6**.

Note: For information on the iTunes Library, see page 150. For information on playlists in iTunes, see pages 152 to 157.

Does iMovie provide sound effects that I can add to my movie?

Yes. iMovie includes many sound effects you can use to add interest to your movie. To add a sound effect, perform steps **1** to **6** below, except select **iMovie Sound Effects** in step **6**. Double-click a sound effect to play the sound effect and then drag a sound effect to the location on a sound track where you want the sound effect to play.

- This area lists the songs on the CD and the amount of time each song will play.

7 Click the song you want to add to your movie.

8 Position the mouse over the song.

9 Drag the song to the location on the sound track where you want the song to start playing in the movie.

Note: You should line up the yellow line ( ) with the slider ( ).

- A sound you add to your movie appears as a purple or orange bar on the sound track.
- To delete a sound from your movie, click the purple or orange bar for the sound and then press the delete key.
- To once again display the clip viewer, click .

ADD A PHOTO TO A MOVIE

You can add a photo stored in your iPhoto Library to your movie.

For information on using iPhoto, see pages 164 to 183.

You can use the Ken Burns Effect to zoom in or out of a photo to add motion to a photo in your movie. The Ken Burns Effect is named after Ken Burns, an acclaimed filmmaker.

ADD A PHOTO TO A MOVIE

1 Click **Photos** to add a photo to your movie.

■ This area displays the photos in your iPhoto Library.

■ To display the photos in an album you created, click this area and then click the name of the album containing the photos you want to use.

2 Click the photo you want to add to your movie.

■ This area displays the way your photo will appear in the movie.

■ If the photo does not display motion, click the box (☐) beside **Ken Burns Effect** to add motion to the photo (☐ changes to ☑).

3 To change the starting size of the photo, click **Start** (○ changes to ◉).

4 Drag this slider (●) right or left to increase or decrease the size of the photo.

How can I remove the motion from a photo I added to my movie?

You can turn off the Ken Burns Effect to remove motion from a photo in your movie. Displaying still photos is useful if you want to create a slide show in iMovie.

1 Click the photo you want to remove motion from in the clip viewer.

2 Click **Photos** to display the photo options.

3 Click the box (☑) beside **Ken Burns Effect** (☑ changes to ☐).

4 Click **Update** to update the photo in your movie.

5 To change the finished size of the photo, perform steps **3** and **4**, selecting **Finish** in step **3**.

6 To change the duration of the motion, drag this slider (●) left or right.

7 To preview your changes, click **Preview**.

8 To add the photo to your movie, click **Apply**.

■ The photo appears after the last video clip in the clip viewer. To move the photo to a new location in the movie, see page 189.

■ To delete a photo from your movie, click the photo and then press the delete key.

PREVIEW A MOVIE

After you add the video clips you want to include in your movie, you can preview how the movie will play.

PREVIEW A MOVIE

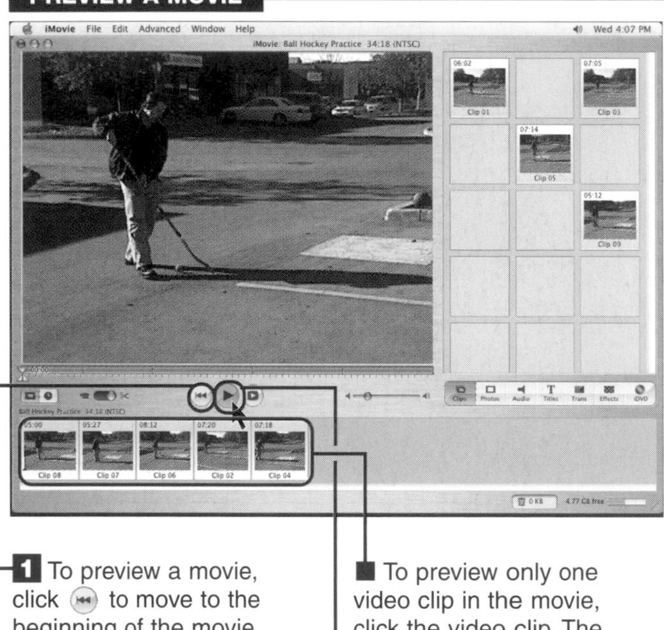

1 To preview a movie, click ⏮ to move to the beginning of the movie.

■ To preview only one video clip in the movie, click the video clip. The video clip is highlighted.

2 Click ▶ to preview the movie.

■ The movie plays in this area.

■ You can click ▶ again to stop playing the movie.

■ This slider (▽) indicates the progress of the movie. The amount of time the movie has been playing appears next to the slider.

Note: Lines on the bar indicate where each video clip begins and ends in the movie.

Can I preview my movie in QuickTime Player?

When you save your iMovie project, iMovie creates a QuickTime version of the movie that you can view in QuickTime Player. Display the contents of your Movies folder (see page 22). Double-click the folder for your movie project and then double-click the QuickTime movie. A QuickTime movie displays the icon. For more information on QuickTime Player, see page 114.

Note: When your movie is complete, you can save a QuickTime version of the movie for sharing with other people. For more information, see page 202.

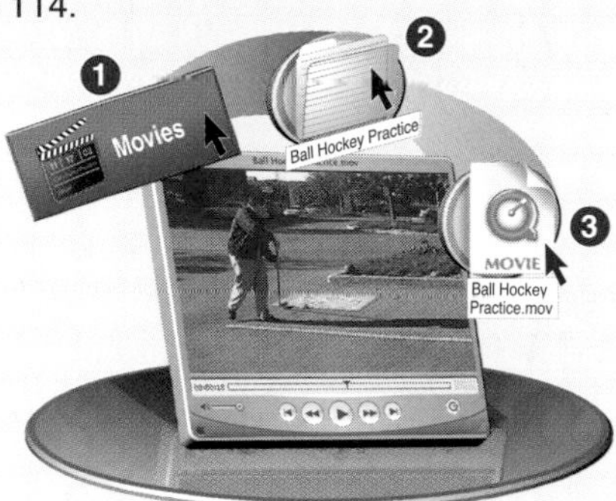

Can I preview a movie using the entire screen?

Yes. You can click to preview a movie using the entire screen. To return to iMovie, click anywhere on your screen.

3 To quickly move to a specific location in your movie, click the location on the bar.

■ The slider ( ) moves to the new location.

■ A red marker ( ) in the video clips also indicates the progress of the movie.

4 To decrease or increase the volume, drag this slider ( ) left or right.

SAVE A MOVIE AS A QUICKTIME MOVIE

After you finish creating a movie, you can save the movie as a QuickTime movie on your computer.

Saving a movie as a QuickTime movie allows you to share the movie with other people. You cannot make changes to a movie you have saved. To play a QuickTime movie, see page 114.

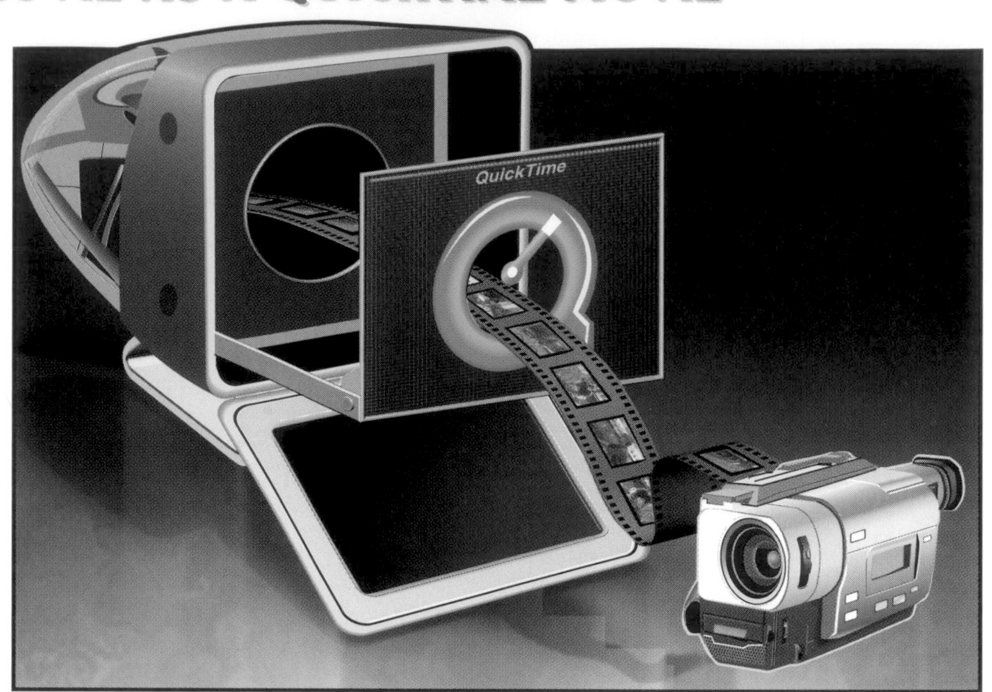

SAVE A MOVIE AS A QUICKTIME MOVIE

1 To save the video clips in the clip viewer as a QuickTime movie, click **File**.

2 Click **Export**.

■ The Export dialog box appears.

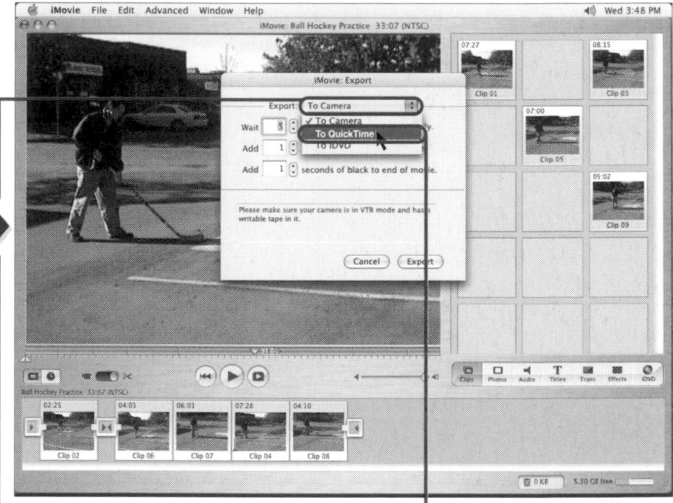

3 To specify how you want to save your movie, click this area to display a list of the available save options.

4 Click **To QuickTime** to save your movie as a QuickTime movie.

Which format should I select for my movie?

The format you should select depends on how you intend to use the movie.

Format:	Intended Use:
Email	Send the movie in an e-mail message.
Web	Publish the movie to the Web.
Web Streaming	Publish the movie to a QuickTime streaming Web server, which plays movies on the Web as they are downloading.
CD-ROM	Copy the movie to a recordable CD.
Full Quality DV	Work with the movie in another application.

Is there another way to save a movie?

Yes. In step **4** below, you can choose to save a movie to your digital video camera or for iDVD.

✓ Select **To Camera** to save a movie to the tape in your video camera. This is useful if you want to play the movie on your television.

✓ Select **For iDVD** to save a movie for the iDVD application. iDVD allows you to prepare a high-quality movie that you can copy to a recordable DVD. Some computers do not support iDVD.

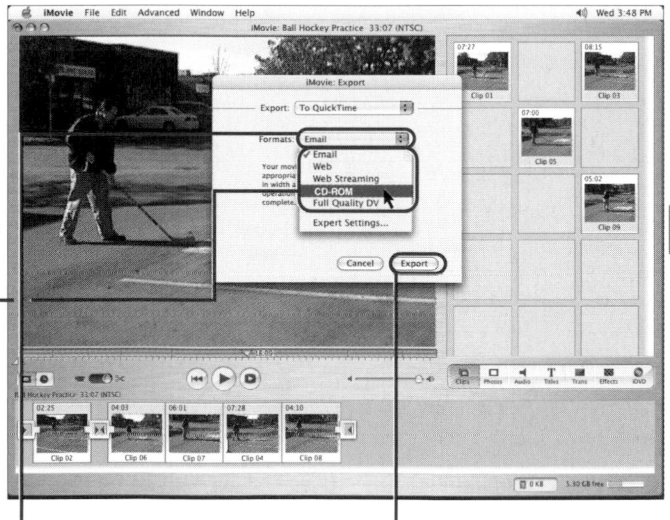

5 To specify the format you want to use for your movie, click this area to display a list of the available formats.

6 Click the format you want to use.

Note: For information on the available formats, see the top of this page.

7 Click **Export** to save the movie.

■ A dialog sheet appears.

8 Type a name for the movie.

■ This area shows the location where iMovie will store the movie. You can click this area to change the location.

9 Click **Save** to save the movie.

■ A progress dialog box will appear on your screen until iMovie has finished saving your movie.

USER ACCOUNTS
TOM
SALLY
West Parkdale
Auto Shop
JENN

Share Your Computer

If you share your computer with other people, you can create a separate user account for each person. In this chapter, you will learn how to create and manage user accounts on your computer.

ADD A USER ACCOUNT

If you share your computer with other people, you can create a separate user account for each person.

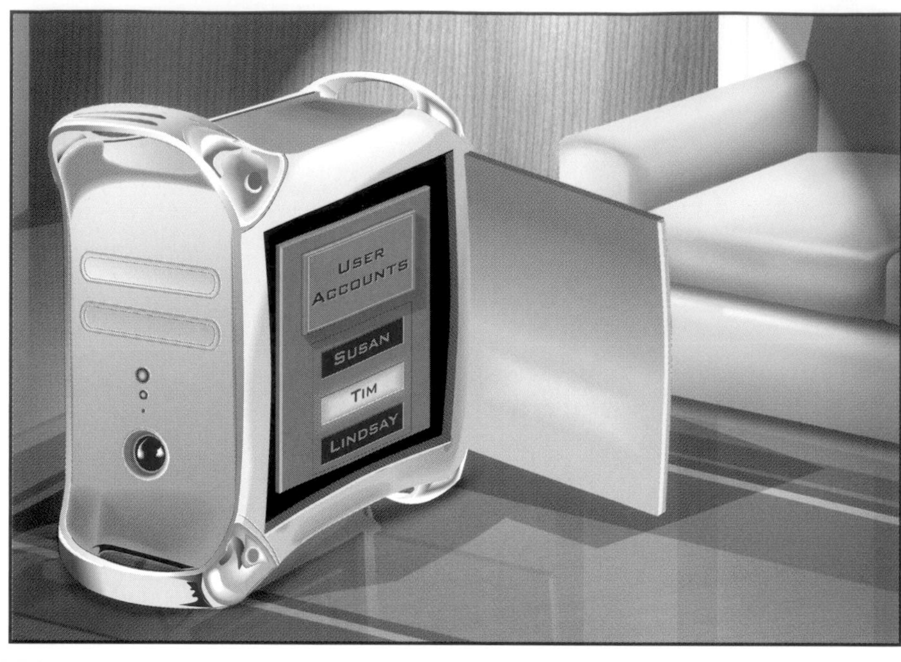

You must have an administrator account to add a user account to your computer.

ADD A USER ACCOUNT

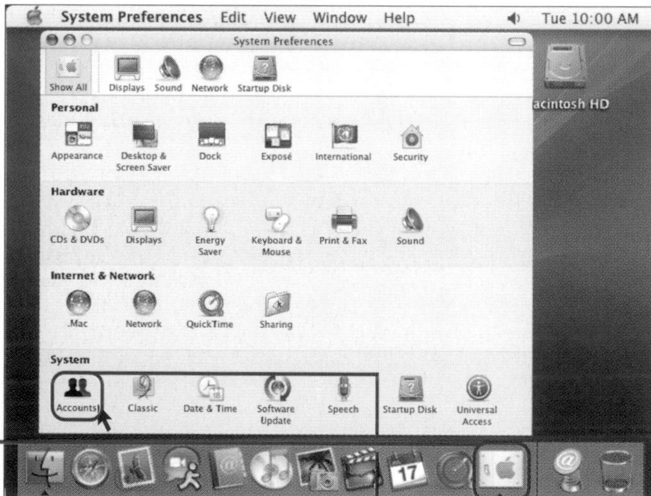

1 Click the System Preferences icon to access your system preferences.

■ The System Preferences window appears.

2 Click **Accounts** to work with the user accounts on your computer.

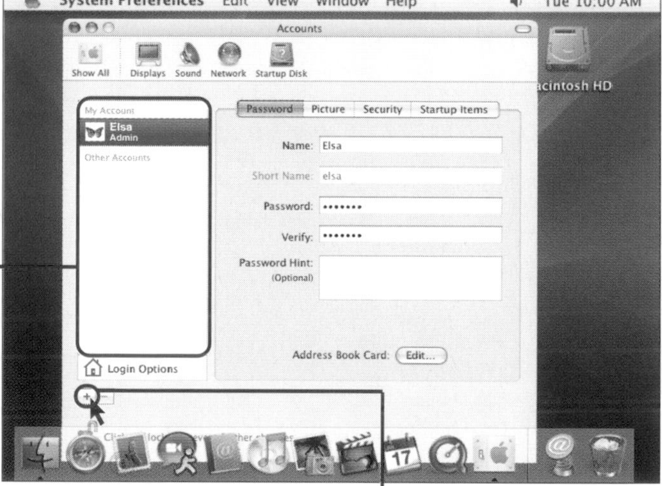

■ The Accounts window appears.

■ This area lists the names of the user accounts that are currently on your computer.

Note: When Mac OS was installed on your computer, an administrator account was created.

3 Click + to add a new user account to your computer.

Will Mac OS keep my personal files separate from the files of other users?

Yes. Mac OS will keep your personal files separate from the personal files created by other users. For example, your home folder contains only the files you have created.

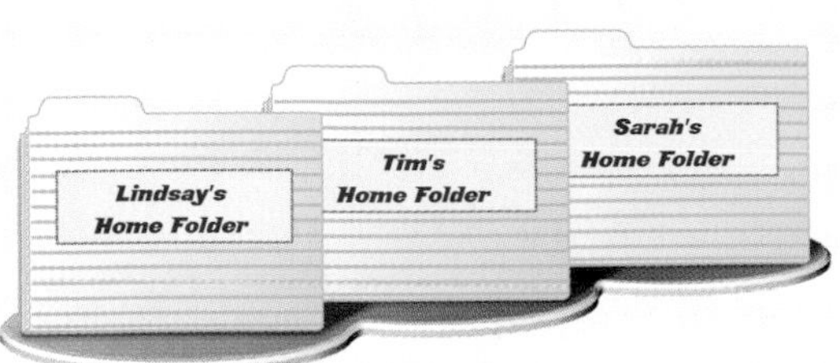

How can I personalize Mac OS for my user account?

You can personalize the appearance of Mac OS for your user account by changing the screen saver, desktop picture, appearance of the Dock and many other computer settings.

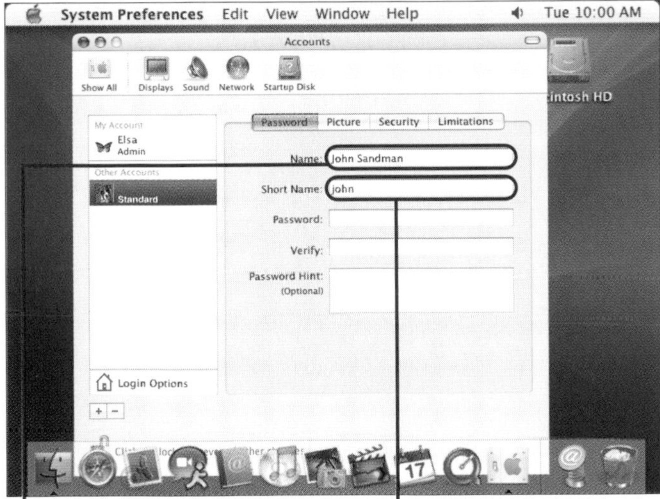

4 Click this area and type the full name of the person who will use the new user account. Then press the return key.

5 This area displays a short name for the person. To change the short name, drag the mouse I over the name until the name is highlighted and then type a new short name.

Note: A short name cannot contain spaces.

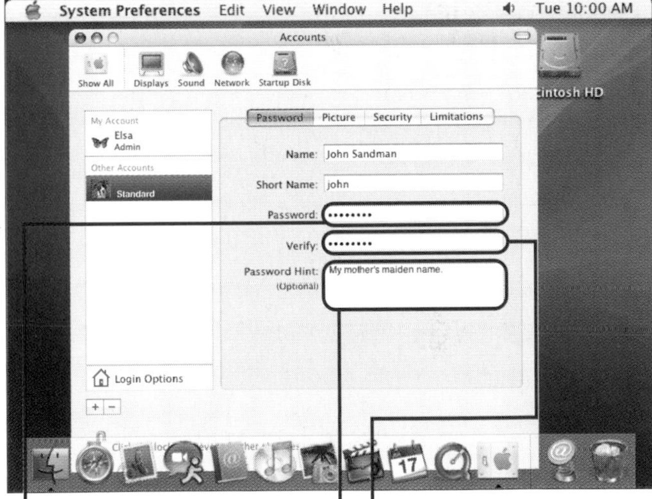

6 Click this area and type a password for the user account.

Note: A password will prevent unauthorized people from accessing the user account.

7 Click this area and type the password again to confirm the password.

8 Click this area and type a password hint that can help the person remember the password.

Note: Typing a password hint is optional.

CONTINUED

ADD A USER ACCOUNT

When adding a user account to your computer, you can select the picture you want to use for the account.

The picture you select for a user account will appear on the login window each time you log in to Mac OS. The picture will also appear with the user's information in Address Book and iChat. For more information on Address Book, see page 116. For more information on iChat, see page 286.

ADD A USER ACCOUNT (CONTINUED)

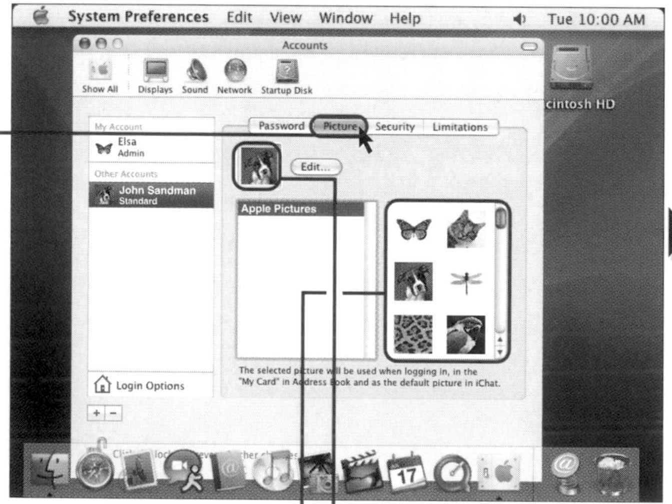

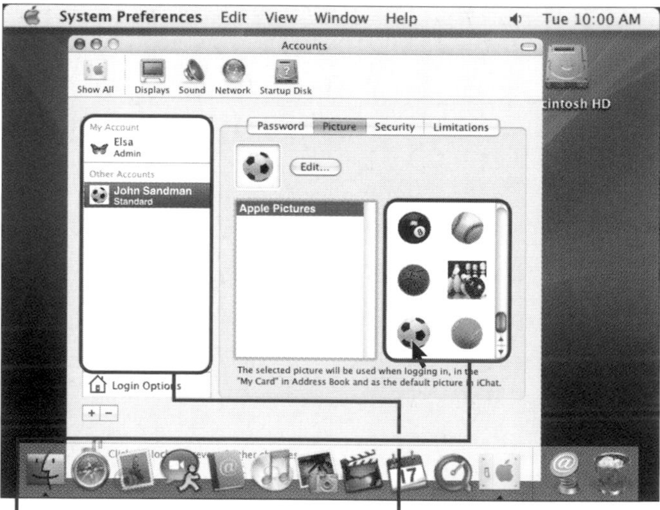

CHOOSE A PICTURE

9 To choose a picture you want the user account to display, click the **Picture** tab.

■ This area displays the current picture for the user account.

■ This area displays the pictures you can use for the user account.

10 Click the picture you want to use for the user account.

■ This area displays the user's name and the picture for the user account.

Can I edit the information for a user account?

If you have an administrator account, you can make changes to any user account on your computer. To edit the information for a user account, perform the steps starting on page 206, selecting the name of the user account you want to edit in step **3**. You cannot change the short name for a user account. If you change the password for a user account, a dialog sheet will appear. Click **OK** to change the password and close the dialog sheet.

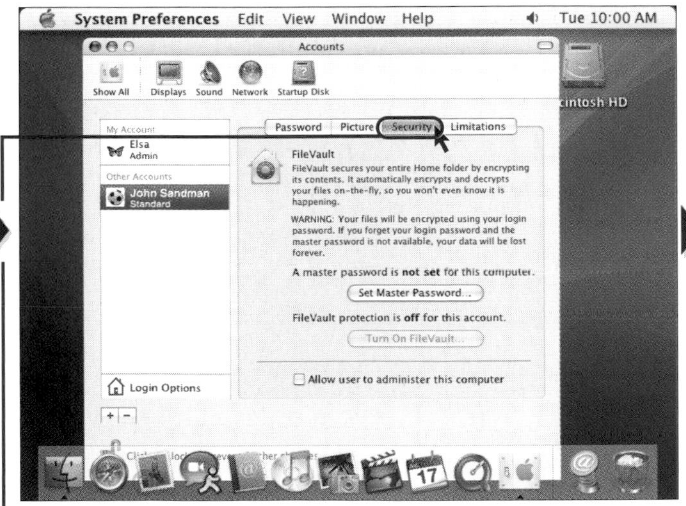

ALLOW ADMINISTRATIVE TASKS

11 To set the account as an administrator account and allow the person to perform administrative tasks on the computer, click the **Security** tab.

Note: An administrator can perform any task on the computer, such as installing new programs and adding user accounts. A standard user can perform only limited tasks on the computer, such as personalizing some settings.

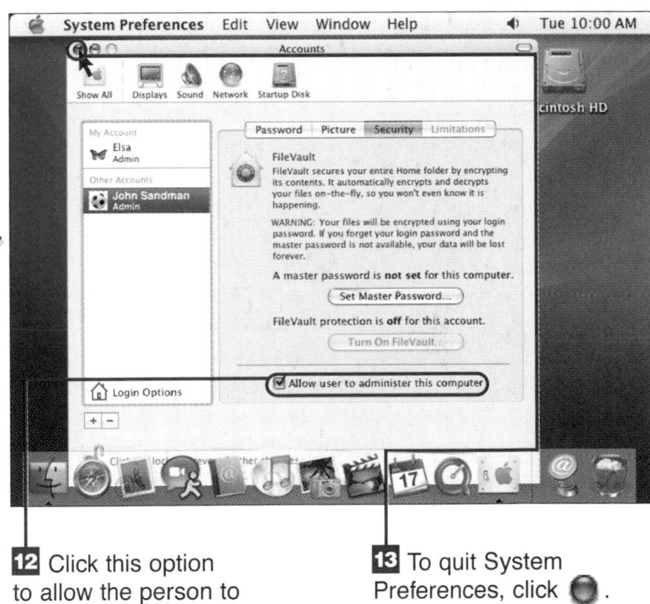

12 Click this option to allow the person to perform administrative tasks (☐ changes to ☑).

13 To quit System Preferences, click ●.

DELETE A USER ACCOUNT

If a person no longer uses your computer, you can delete the person's user account from the computer.

You must have an administrator account to delete a user account.

DELETE A USER ACCOUNT

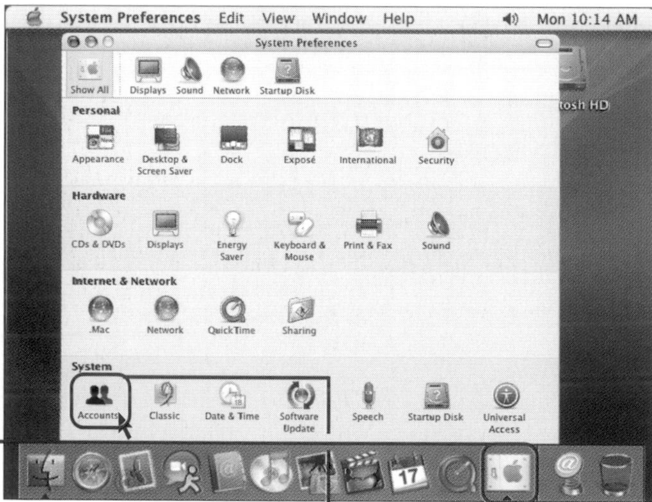

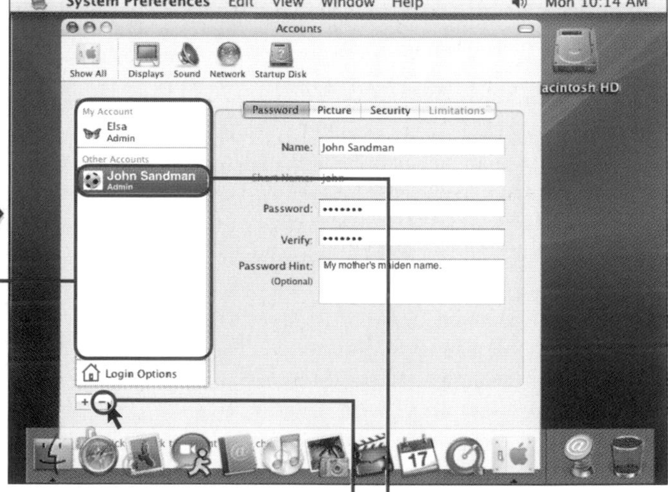

1 Click the System Preferences icon to access your system preferences.

■ The System Preferences window appears.

2 Click **Accounts** to work with the user accounts on your computer.

■ The Accounts window appears.

■ This area lists the names of the user accounts on your computer.

3 Click the name of the user account you want to delete.

4 Click [-] to delete the user account.

If I choose to keep the contents of the home folder for a deleted user account, how can I later access the contents of the folder?

If you choose to save the contents of the home folder for a deleted user account, the contents will be saved in the Deleted Users folder. To open the folder, double-click the hard disk icon on your desktop. In the window that appears, double-click the **Users** folder and then double-click the **Deleted Users** folder.

In the Deleted Users folder, double-click the icon for the deleted user account to open a window displaying the user's folders. Mac OS also places a disk icon for the deleted user account on your desktop. You can double-click the disk icon to access the contents of the home folder for the user account at any time.

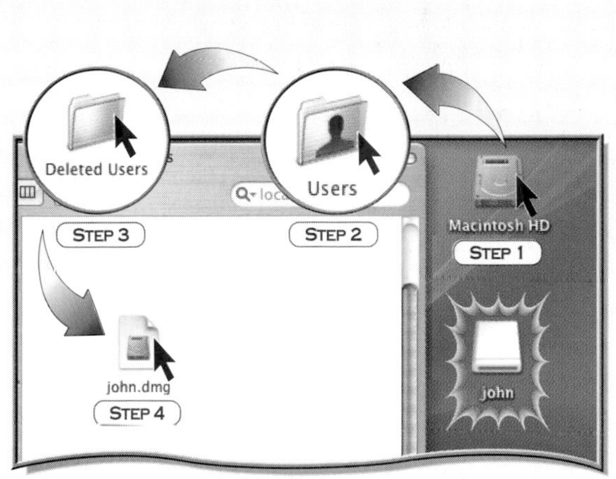

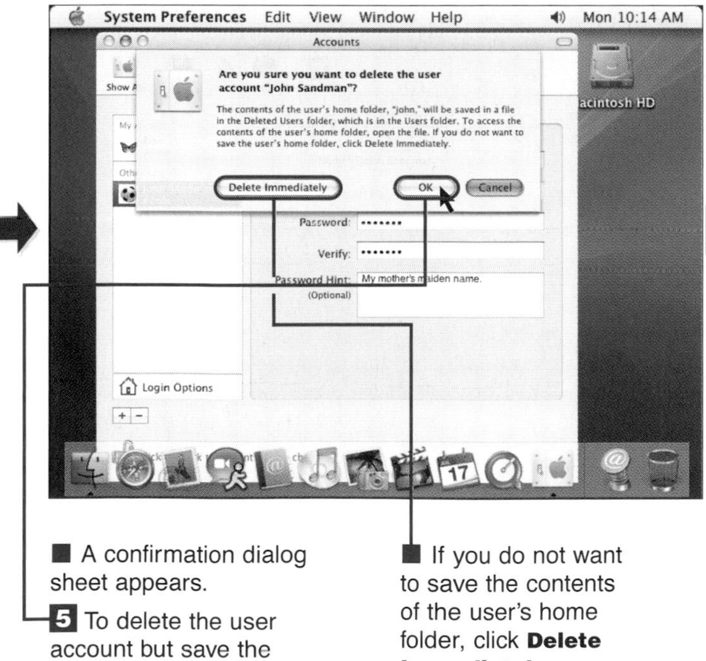

■ A confirmation dialog sheet appears.

5 To delete the user account but save the contents of the user's home folder on the computer, click **OK**.

■ If you do not want to save the contents of the user's home folder, click **Delete Immediately**.

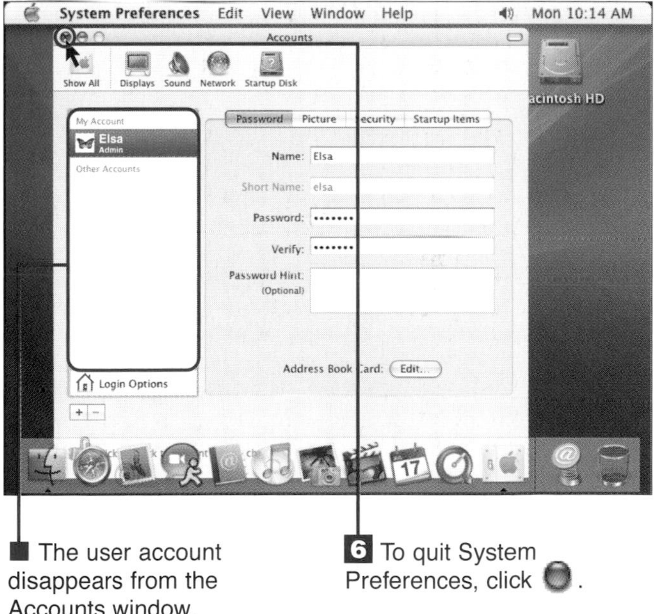

■ The user account disappears from the Accounts window.

6 To quit System Preferences, click ●.

LOG OUT OR LOG IN

When you finish using your computer, you can log out so another person can log in to use the computer.

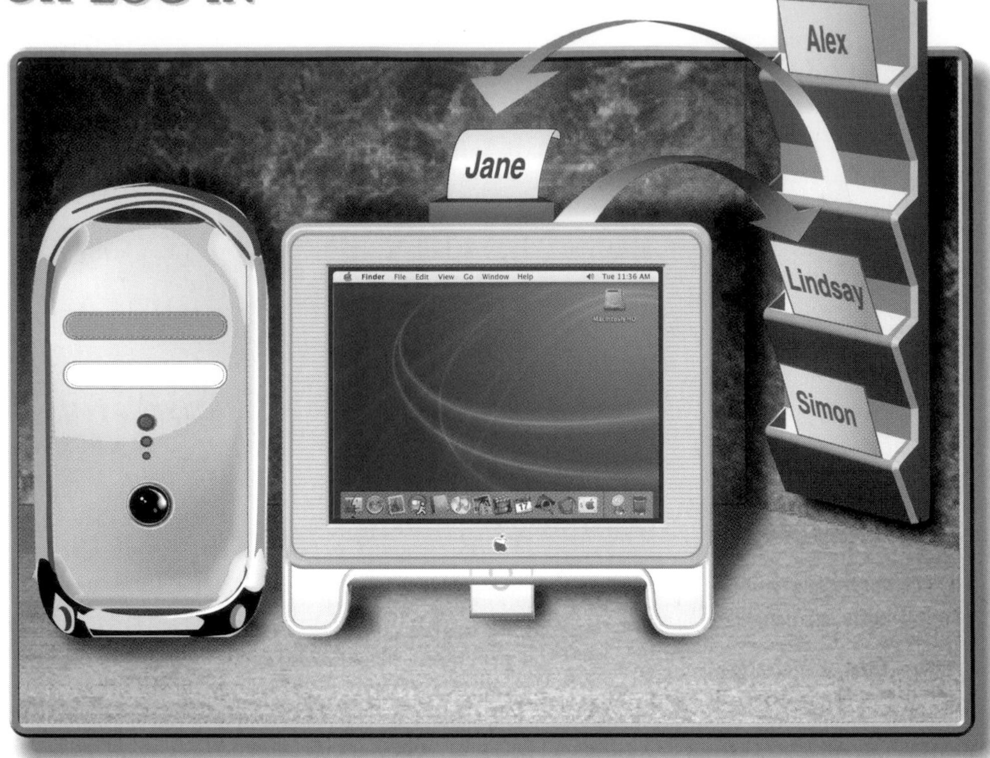

Logging out leaves the computer on, but exits your user account. Logging in allows you to specify the user account you want to use when Mac OS starts.

LOG OUT

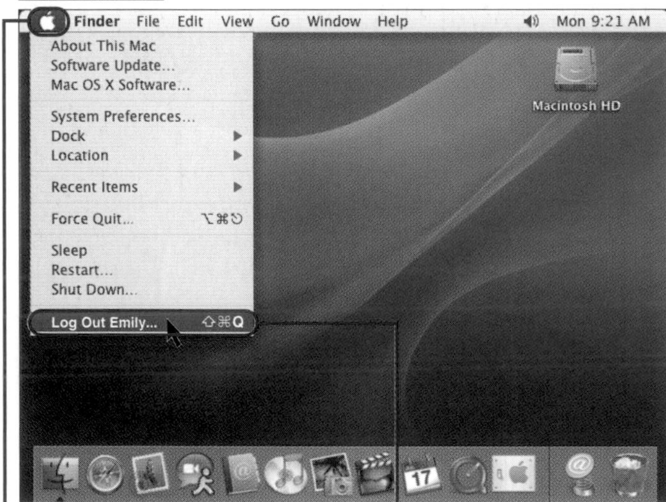

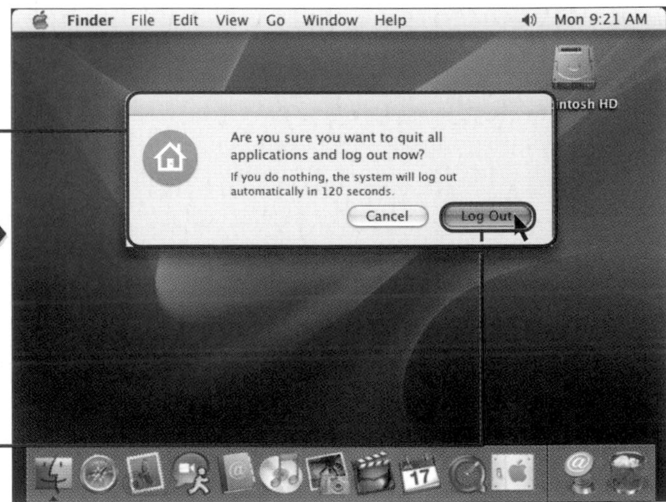

■ Before you log out, make sure you close any applications you have open.

1 Click to display the Apple menu.

2 Click **Log Out** to log out.

Note: The name of the Log Out command depends on the name of the current user.

■ A dialog box appears, confirming that you want to log out.

3 Click **Log Out** to log out.

*Note: If you do not perform step **3** within 120 seconds, your computer will log you out automatically.*

■ The login window appears, allowing another person to log in to use the computer.

Why does my login window look different than the login window shown below?

Your login window will look different if you chose to have each user enter both their account name and password to log in. For information on changing the login options, see page 214.

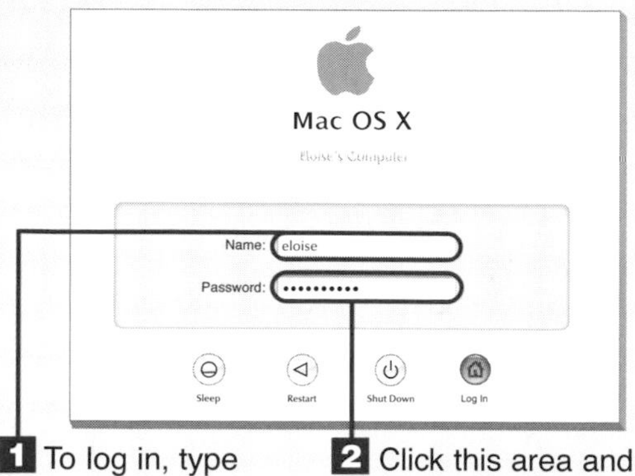

1 To log in, type the name of your user account.

2 Click this area and type the password for your user account. Then press the return key.

Why did the login window shake when I tried to log in?

The login window shakes when you enter an incorrect password. If you enter an incorrect password three times, your password hint may appear. After reading the password hint, try entering your password again.

LOG IN

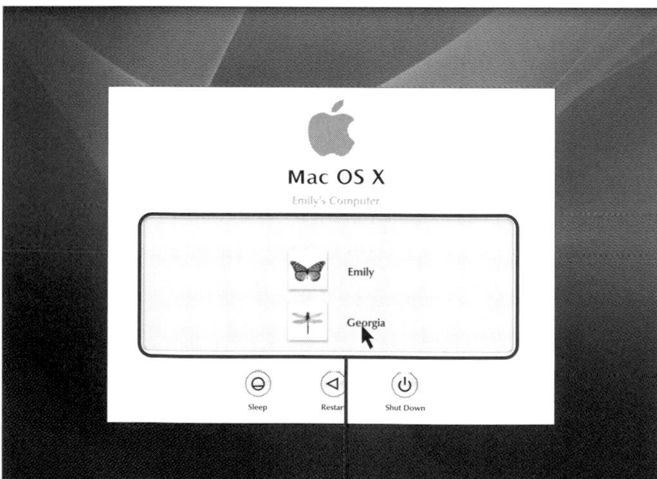

■ When you log out, the login window appears.

Note: The login window also appears each time you turn on your computer if the automatic login option is turned off. To turn off the automatic login option, see the top of page 215.

■ This area displays the names of the user accounts on your computer.

1 Click the name of your user account.

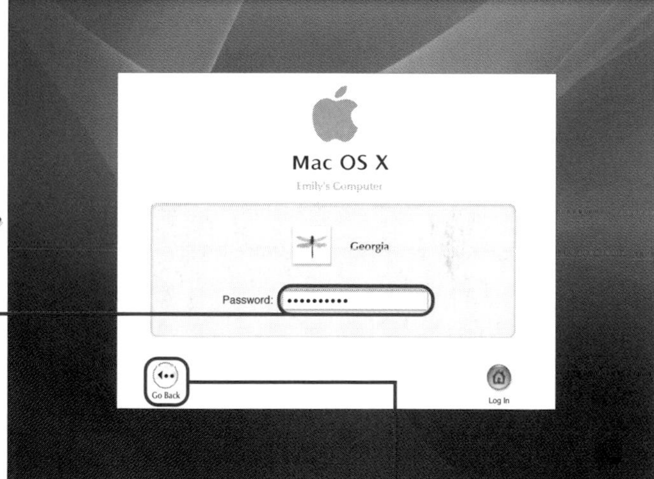

■ A box appears that allows you to enter the password for your user account.

2 Type your password and then press the return key.

Note: A bullet (●) appears for each character you type to prevent other people from seeing your password.

■ If you accidentally selected the wrong name, you can click **Go Back** to select another name.

■ Mac OS starts, displaying your personalized settings.

CHANGE THE LOGIN OPTIONS

You can change the login options to customize the way you log in to Mac OS.

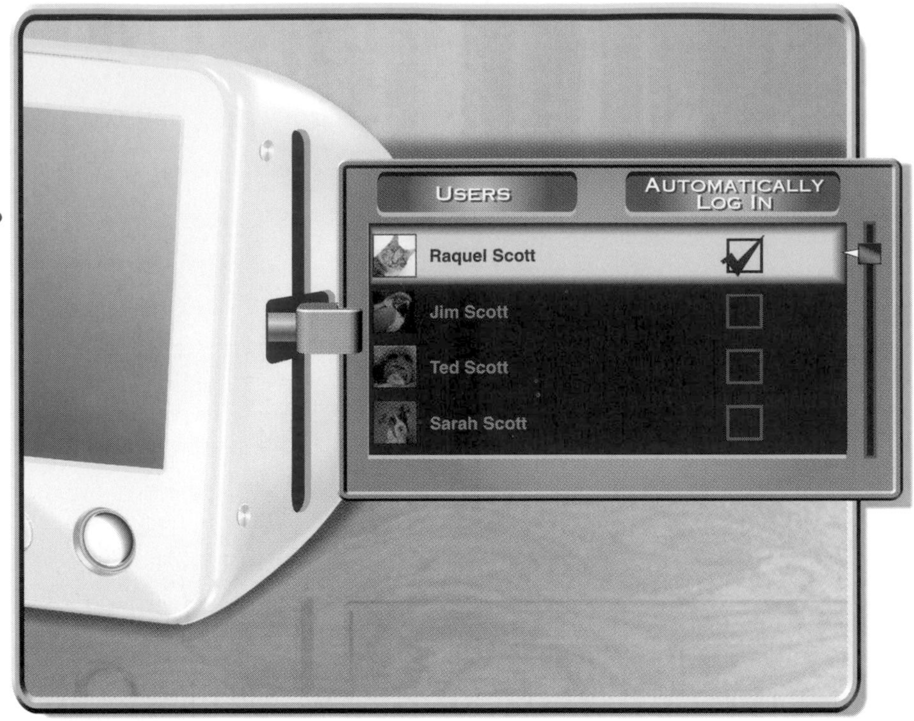

If you have more than one user account on your computer, you can specify which account you want your computer to use to automatically log in to Mac OS each time you turn on the computer.

You must have an administrator account to change the login options.

CHANGE THE LOGIN OPTIONS

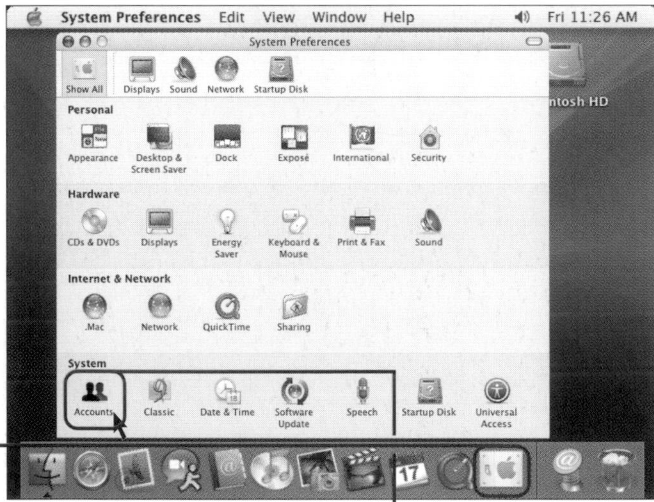

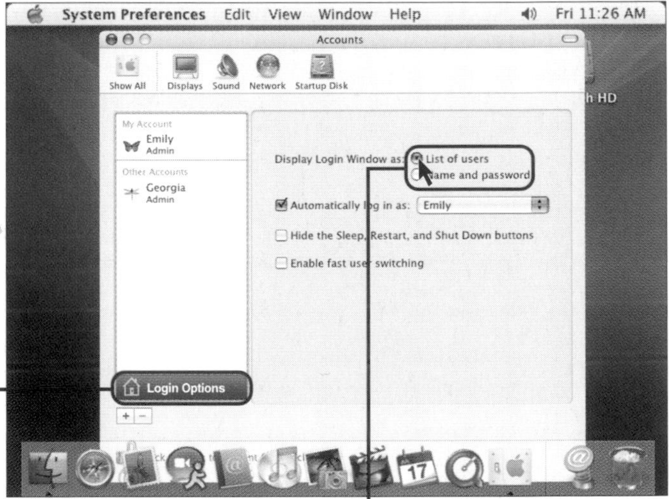

1 Click the System Preferences icon to access your system preferences.

■ The System Preferences window appears.

2 Click **Accounts** to work with the user accounts on your computer.

■ The Accounts window appears.

3 Click **Login Options** to change the login options.

4 Click an option to specify if you want each user to log in by selecting their account name from a list or by entering their account name and password (changes to).

Can I turn off the automatic login option?

Yes. You can turn off the automatic login option so that every user must specify their account name and password to log in before being able to use the computer. Requiring every user to log in helps ensure that users can access and modify only their own files and computer settings. To turn off the automatic login option, perform steps **1** to **3** below and then click **Automatically log in as:** (☑ changes to ☐).

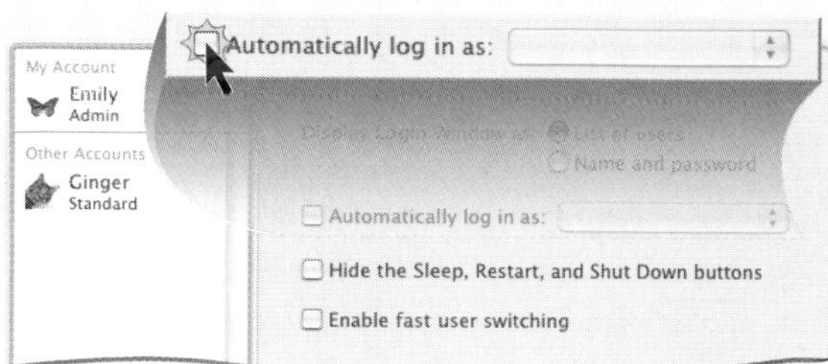

If the computer uses my account to automatically log in, how can other users log in using their accounts?

When you finish using the computer, you can log out so another user can log in using their account. Logging out exits your user account, but leaves the computer on and ready for another user to log in. For information on logging in or out, see page 212.

You can also switch between users without logging out. For information on switching between users, see page 217.

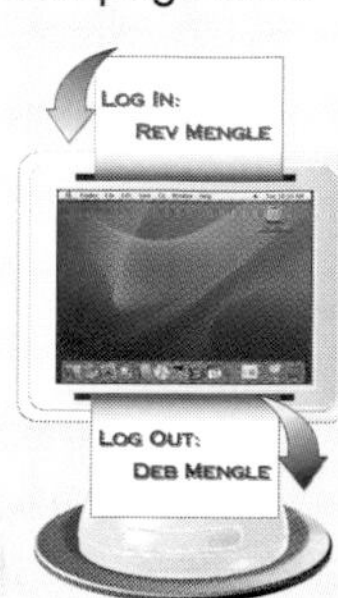

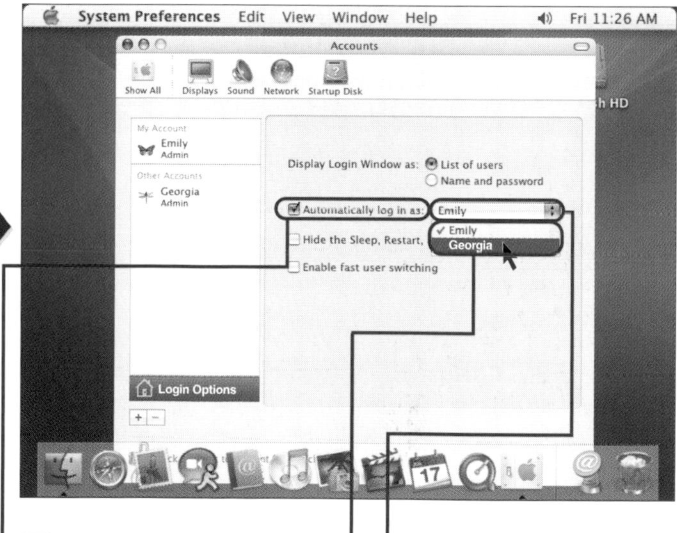

5 To have a user account automatically log in to Mac OS each time you turn on the computer, click this option (☐ changes to ☑).

6 To specify the user account you want to use to automatically log in, click this area.

7 Click the user account you want to use.

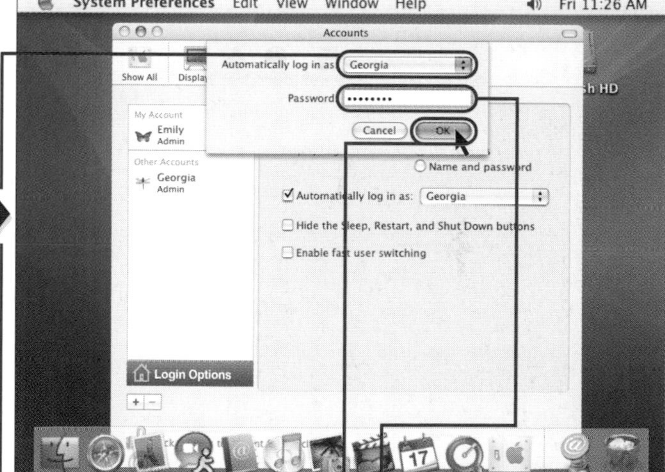

■ A dialog sheet appears.

■ This area displays the name of the user account you selected.

8 Type the password for the user account.

9 Click **OK** to confirm the information you entered.

CONTINUED

CHANGE THE LOGIN OPTIONS

You can disable the Sleep, Restart and Shut Down buttons in the login window to help prevent unauthorized access to your computer.

You can also enable the fast user switching option to allow you to quickly switch between users without logging out of the computer.

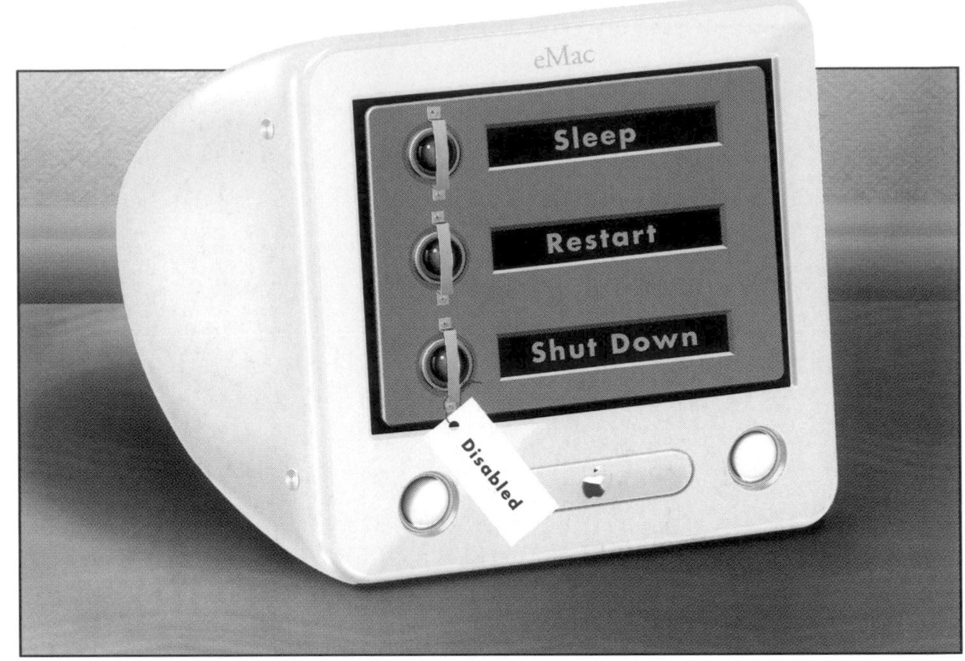

CHANGE THE LOGIN OPTIONS (CONTINUED)

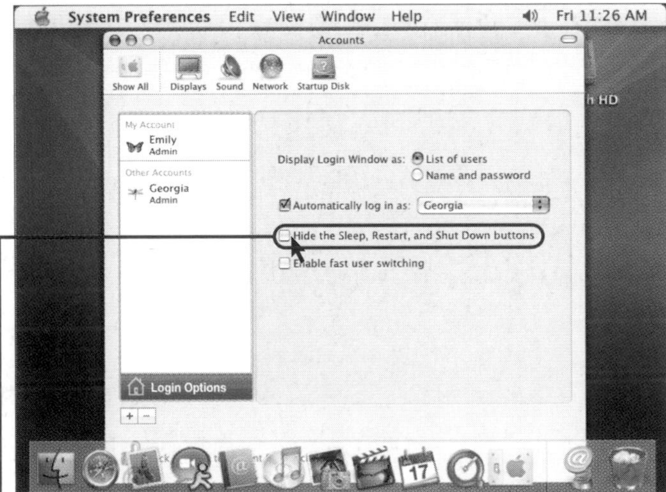

10 This option disables the Sleep, Restart and Shut Down buttons in the login window. You can click this option to turn the option on (☑) or off (☐).

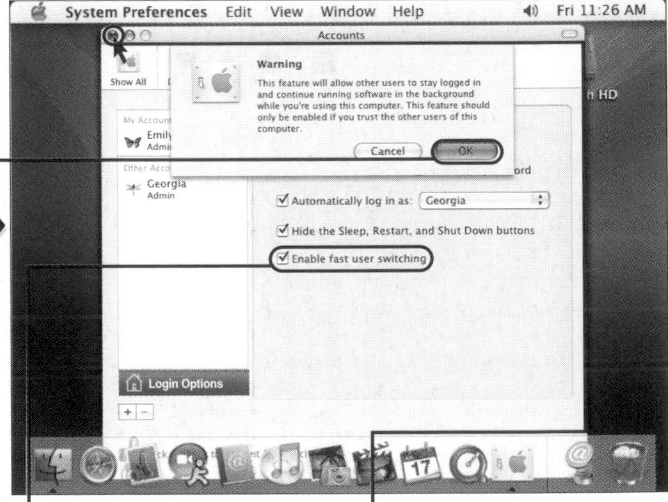

11 This option allows you to quickly switch between users without quitting your applications. You can click this option to turn the option on (☑) or off (☐).

■ A dialog sheet appears when you turn the option on. Click **OK** to continue.

Note: For information on quickly switching between users, see page 217.

12 To quit System Preferences, click .

QUICKLY SWITCH BETWEEN USERS

Mac OS allows you to quickly switch between users on the computer. This lets you keep your applications and files open while another person uses the computer.

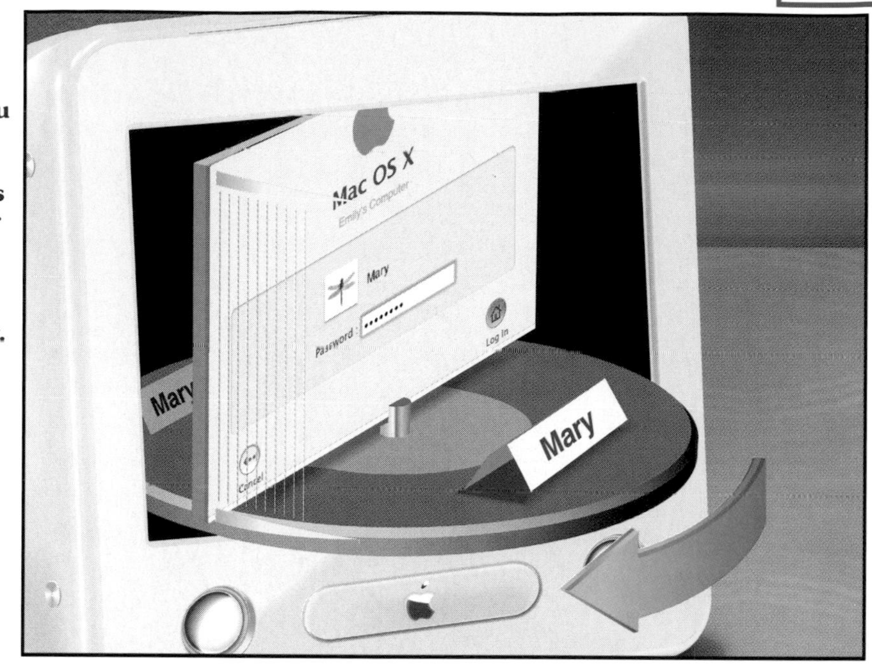

Switching between users allows you to quickly return to your applications and files after another person finishes using the computer.

QUICKLY SWITCH BETWEEN USERS

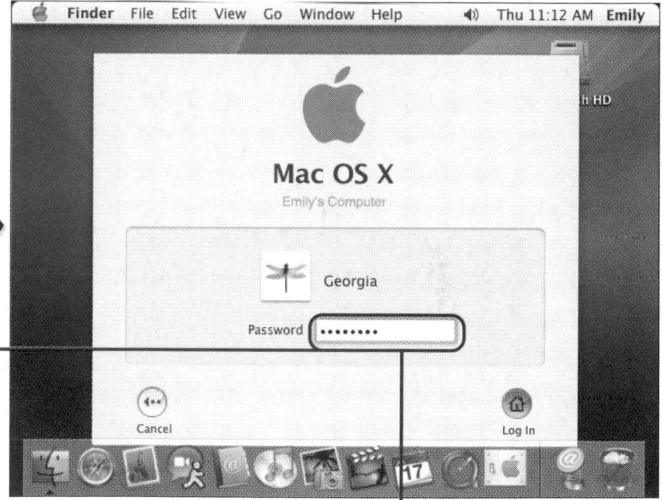

■ Before you can quickly switch between users, you must turn on the fast user switching feature. Perform steps **1** to **3** on page 214 and steps **11** and **12** on page 216 to turn on the feature.

1 Click the name of the current computer user in this area.

■ A list of user names appears.

2 To switch to your user account, click the name of your user account.

■ If you assigned a password to your user account, the login window appears, displaying an area where you can enter your password.

3 Type the password and then press the return key.

■ Mac OS displays your own personalized files and computer settings.

SET LIMITS FOR A STANDARD USER

You can set limits for a standard user to specify the tasks the user can perform on your computer.

Setting limits for a user is useful when you share your computer with a person, such as a child, who you do not want to be able to access all the features and applications on the computer.

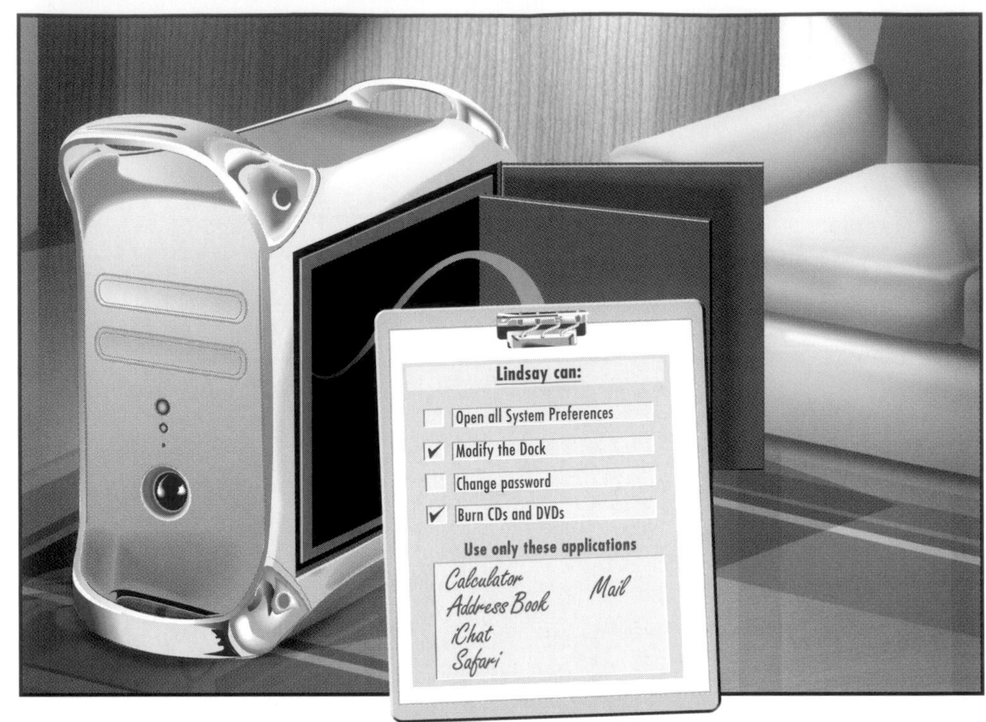

Lindsay can:
Open all System Preferences
Modify the Dock
Change password
Burn CDs and DVDs
Use only these applications
Calculator
Mail
Address Book
iChat
Safari

SET LIMITS FOR A STANDARD USER

1 Click the System Preferences icon to access your system preferences.

■ The System Preferences window appears.

2 Click **Accounts** to work with the user accounts on your computer.

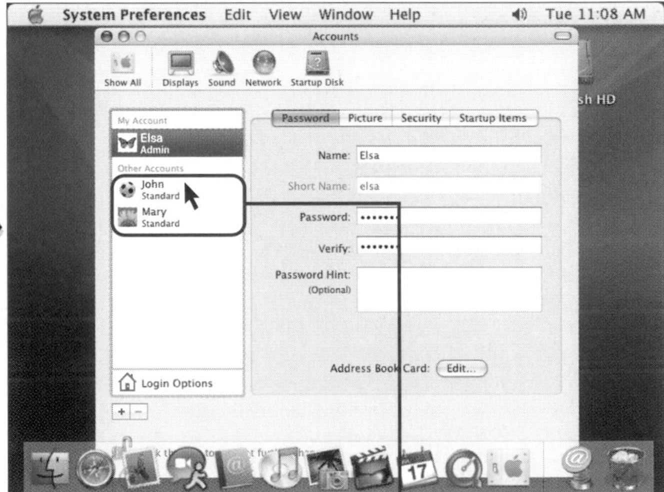

■ The Accounts window appears.

3 Click the name of the standard user account you want to set limits for.

*Note: You cannot set limits for an administrator account. Administrator accounts display the word **Admin**.*

How can I set the most limits for a standard user account?

Simple Finder allows you to set the most limits for a user account by limiting the items available in the Finder menu bar and the Dock. To set up Simple Finder, perform steps **1** to **5** below, selecting **Simple Finder** in step **5**. Then perform steps **11** to **13** on page 221 to specify the applications the user can access.

When a user is limited to Simple Finder, the Dock displays the following icons.

Finder

Displays the Finder menu bar, which includes limited versions of the Apple, Finder and File menus.

My Applications

Provides access to the applications available to the user.

Documents

Provides a place for the user to store files.

Shared

Stores files shared by other users of the computer.

Trash

Stores files the user deletes.

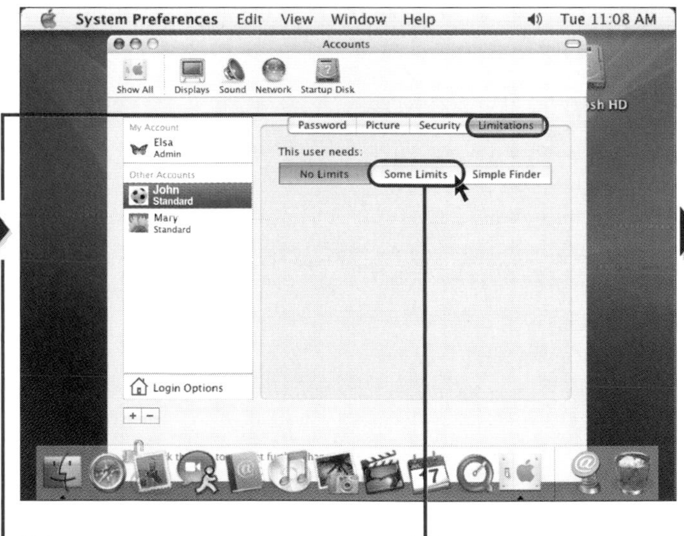

4 Click the **Limitations** tab.

5 Click **Some Limits** to specify the limits you want to set for the user account.

*Note: To set no limits for the user, click **No Limits** and then skip to step **13** on page 221. To set the most limits for the user, see the top of this page.*

6 This option allows the user to access all the features available in the System Preferences window. You can click this option to turn the option on (☑) or off (☐).

7 This option allows the user to add and remove items on the Dock. You can click this option to turn the option on (☑) or off (☐).

CONTINUED

SET LIMITS FOR A STANDARD USER

You can specify the applications you want a standard user to be able to access on your computer.

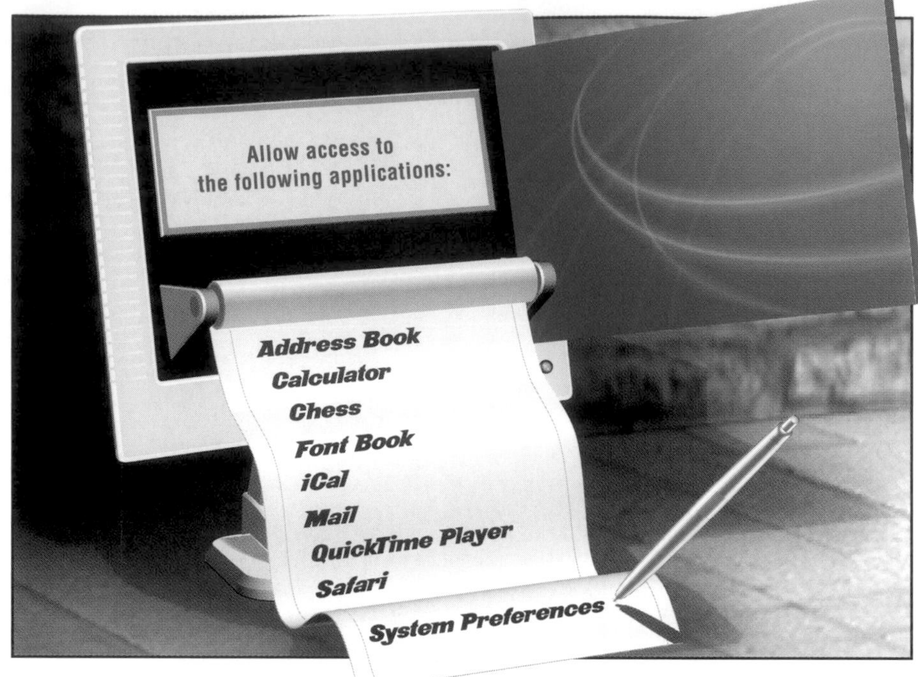

SET LIMITS FOR A STANDARD USER (CONTINUED)

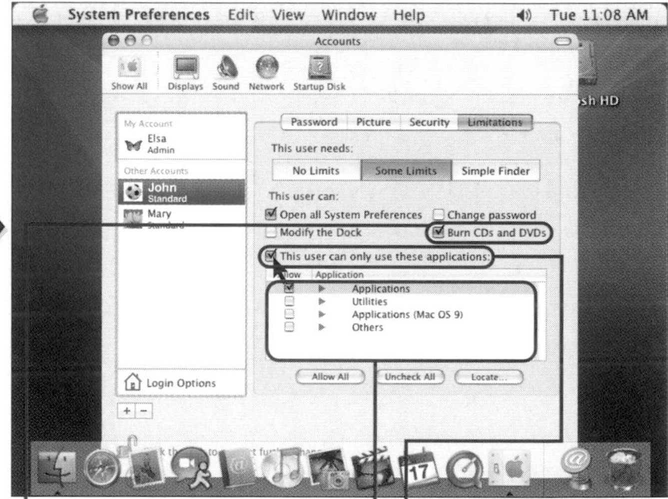

8 This option allows the user to change the password for their own account. You can click this option to turn the option on (☑) or off (☐).

*Note: Change password is available only if you selected Open all System Preferences in step **6**.*

9 This option allows the user to copy files to CDs or DVDs. You can click this option to turn the option on (☑) or off (☐).

10 This option allows the user to access only the applications you specify. You can click this option to turn the option on (☑) or off (☐).

■ This area displays categories of applications the user can access.

Can I change a standard user account to an administrator account?

Yes. If you want a standard user to be able to perform any task on your computer, you can change the user's account to an administrator account. Perform steps **1** to **5** starting on page 218, selecting **No Limits** in step **5**. Then click the **Security** tab and click the **Allow user to administer this computer** option (☐ changes to ☑).

How can I add (☑) or remove (☐) check marks for all the applications at once?

To add check marks to all the applications, click **Allow All**. To remove the check marks from all the applications, click **Uncheck All**. You may want to remove the check marks from all the applications so you can quickly select only a few applications.

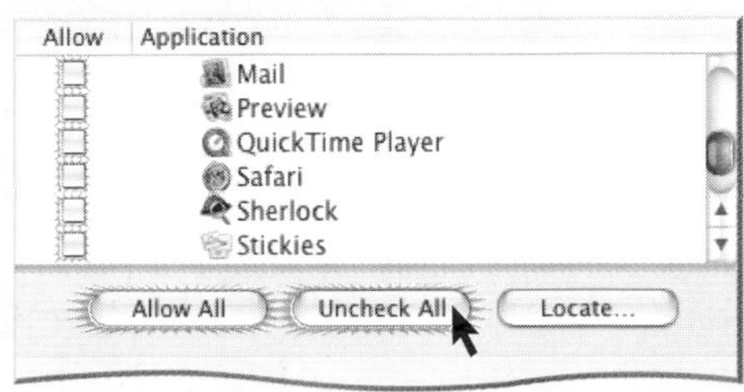

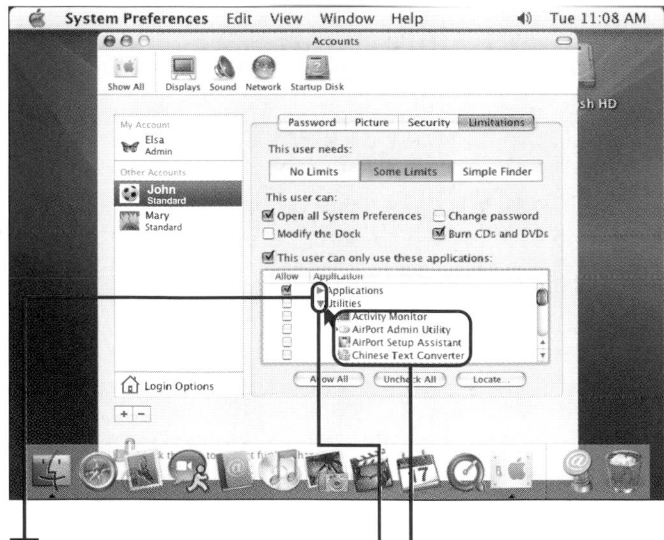

11 You can click ▶ beside a category to display the applications in the category (▶ changes to ▼).

■ The applications in the category appear.

■ You can click ▼ to once again hide the applications in the category (▼ changes to ▶).

12 The user will be able to access each application that displays a check mark. To add (☑) or remove (☐) a check mark, click the box beside the application.

13 To quit System Preferences, click ●.

You can view the files shared by every user on your computer.

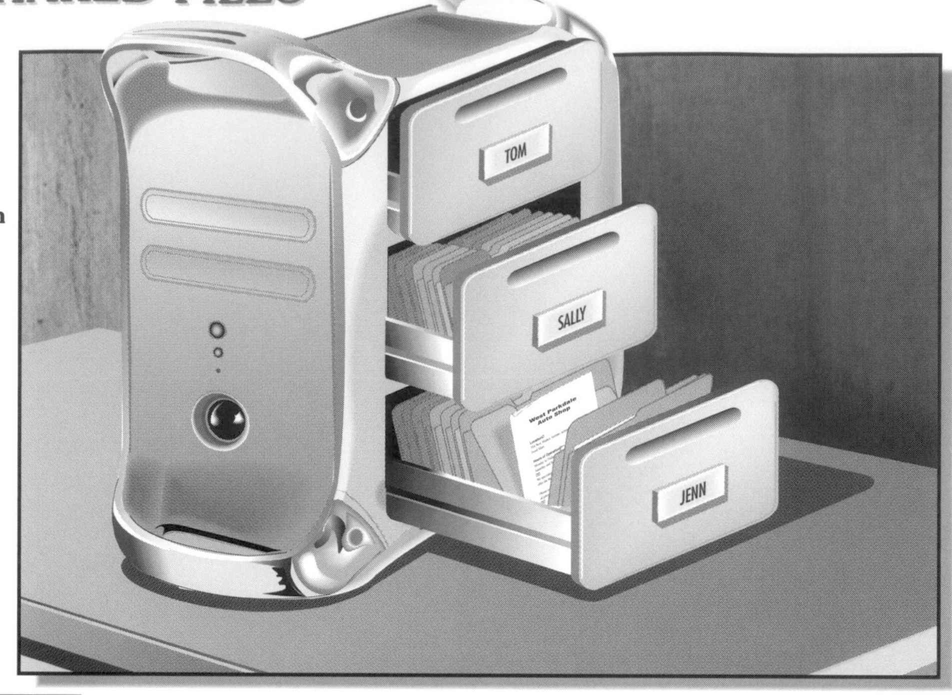

VIEW SHARED FILES

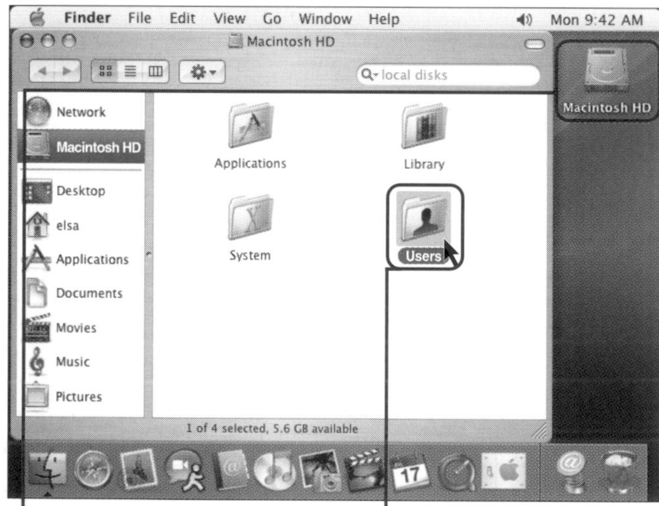

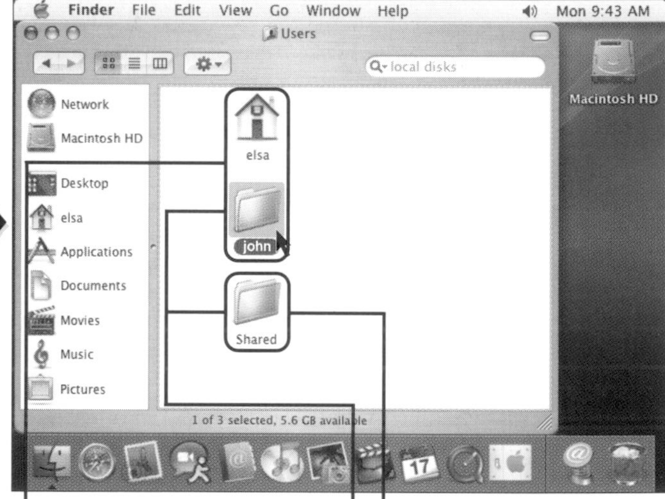

1 Double-click your hard disk icon on the desktop to view the contents of your hard disk.

■ A window appears, displaying the contents of your hard disk.

2 Double-click **Users** to display the contents of the Users folder.

■ The Users window appears, displaying the home folder for each user account on your computer. The home folder for your user account displays a house icon (🏠).

■ The Shared folder contains files shared by the users on your computer. Every user can use this folder to share files.

3 To display the contents of a folder, double-click the folder.

How can I share my files with other users?

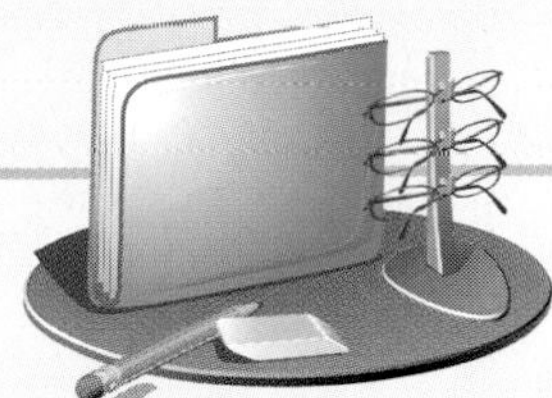

Shared Folder

To share files with every user on your computer, press and hold down the option key as you drag the files to the Shared folder within the Users folder. Every user can view, add and change files stored in this folder. You cannot delete files that other users have added to this folder.

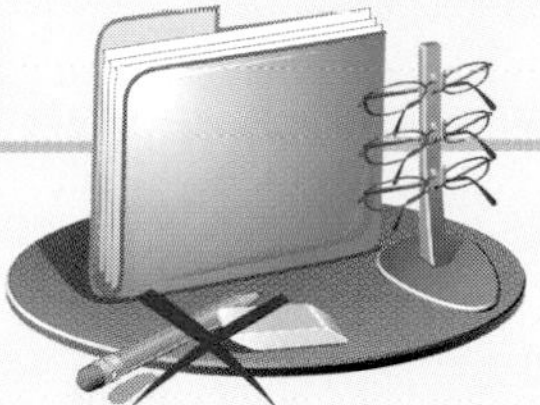

Public Folder

To allow every user on your computer to view files, but prevent other users from changing or deleting the files, press and hold down the option key as you drag the files to the Public folder within the home folder for your user account. You cannot add files to another user's Public folder.

Note: For more information on the Public folder, see page 228.

Drop Box

To share files with a specific user, press and hold down the option key as you drag the files to the Drop Box folder within the home folder for the user's account. Only the user who owns the Drop Box folder can open the folder to view, change or delete the files.

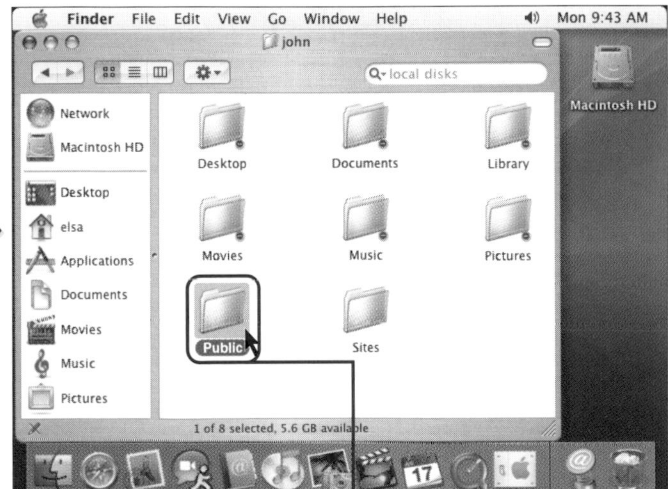

■ In this example, the personal folders for the **john** user account appear.

Note: If you are viewing the personal folders for a user account other than your own, you can access only the contents of the Public and Sites folders. You cannot access folders that display the ⊖ symbol.

■ The Public folder contains files shared by the owner of the current user account.

4 To display the contents of the Public folder, double-click the folder.

■ The contents of the Public folder appear.

■ The Drop Box folder contains files other users have shared with the owner of the current user account. Only the owner of the Drop Box folder can open this folder.

■ You can click ◀ or ▶ to move backward or forward through the folders you have viewed.

5 When you finish browsing through the shared files on your computer, click ● to close the window.

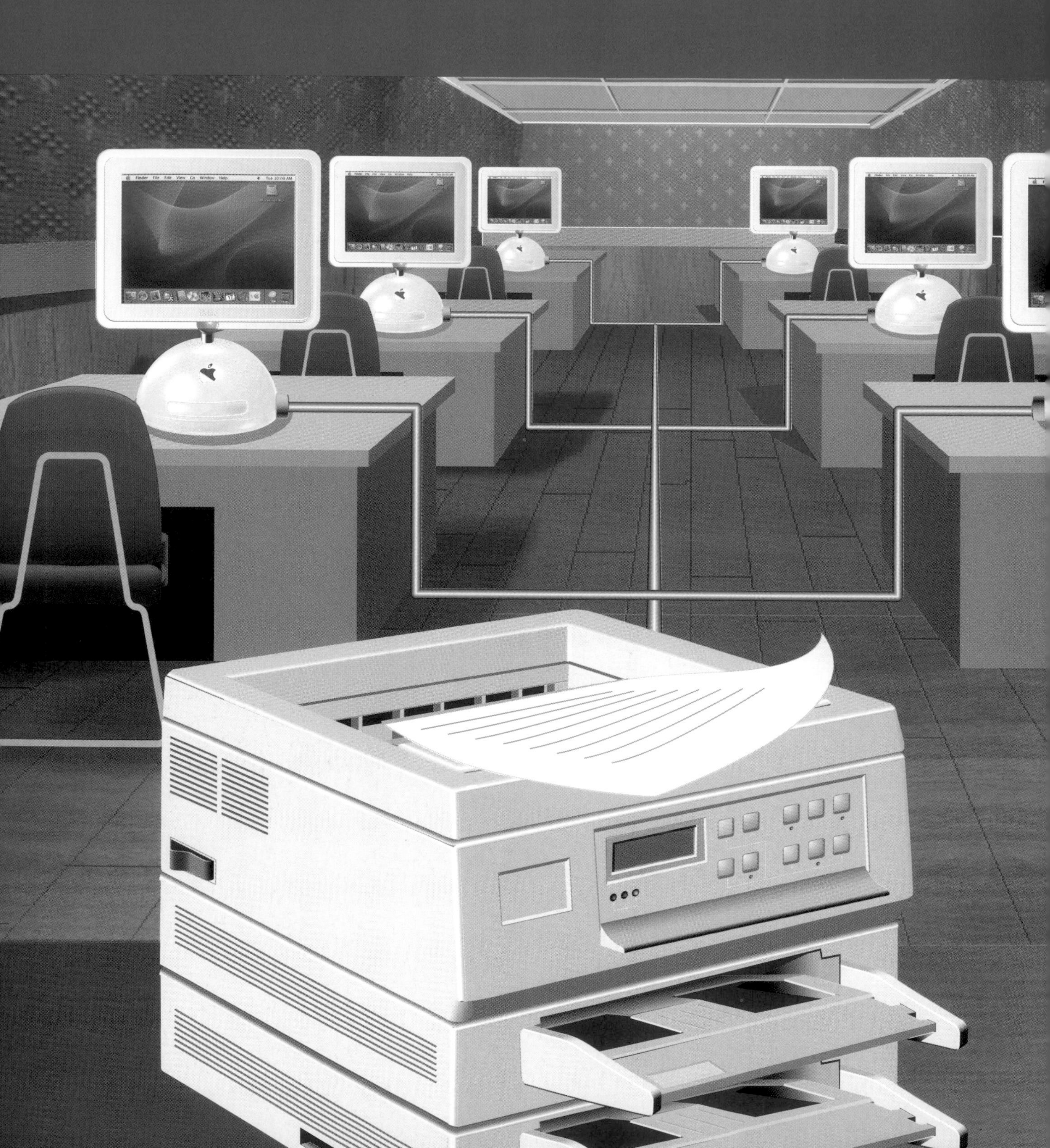

Finder File Edit View Go Window Help Tue 10:00 AM

CHAPTER 10

Work on a Network

A network is a group of connected computers. This chapter teaches you how to share files and printers on a network.

TURN ON FILE AND PRINTER SHARING

If you want to share your files and printer with other people on your network, you must turn on file and printer sharing.

Sharing files is useful when other people on your network need to access your files. Sharing a printer allows you to reduce costs since several people on a network can use the same printer.

TURN ON FILE AND PRINTER SHARING

1 Click the System Preferences icon to access your system preferences.

■ The System Preferences window appears.

2 Click **Sharing** to share your files and a printer connected to your computer.

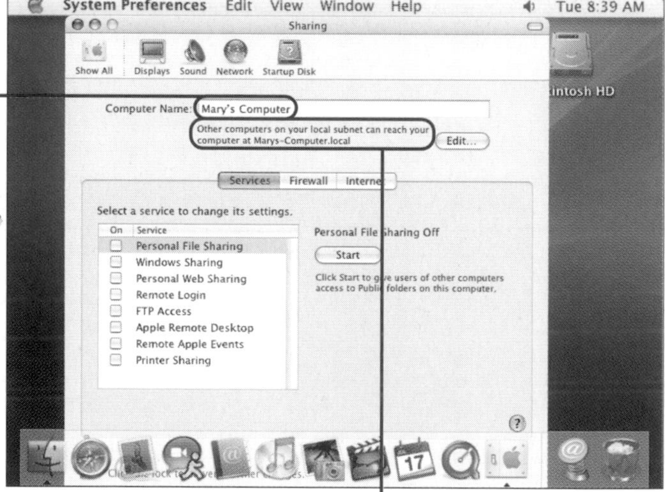

■ The Sharing window appears.

■ This area displays your computer name. To change the name, drag the mouse I over the current name until the name is highlighted. Then type a new name.

■ This area displays the name used to identify your computer to Rendezvous-compatible services and applications, such as iChat.

How can I print files using a shared printer on my network?

You can print files to a shared printer on your network as if the printer was directly connected to your computer. When you print a file, the shared printer will automatically appear in the list of available printers. To print a file, see page 54.

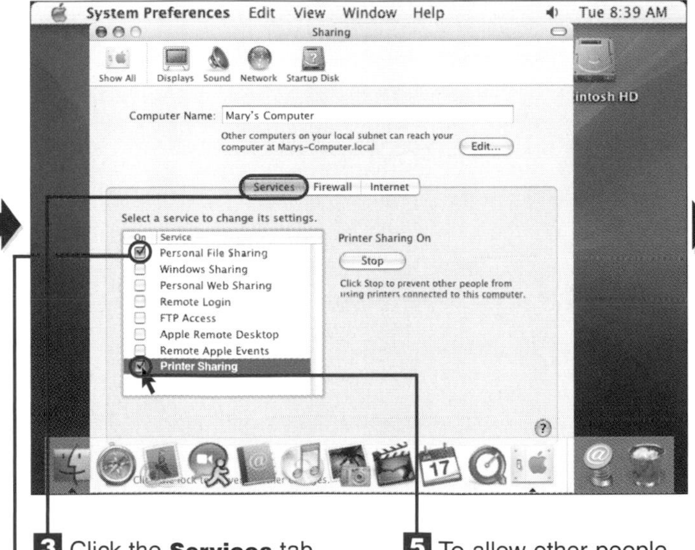

3 Click the **Services** tab.

4 To allow other people on the network to access files you share on your computer, click the box (☐) beside **Personal File Sharing** (☐ changes to ☑).

5 To allow other people on the network to use a printer connected to your computer, click the box (☐) beside **Printer Sharing** (☐ changes to ☑).

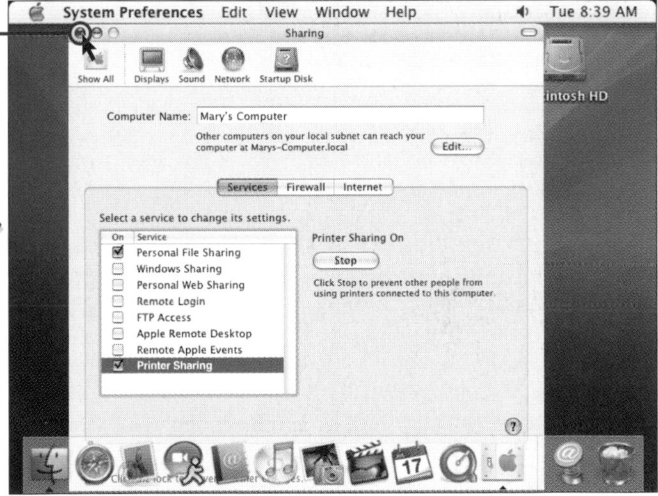

■ Everyone on the network can now access files in the Public folder on your computer and use your printer to print documents.

Note: To add files you want to share to your Public folder, see page 228.

6 To quit System Preferences, click ●.

■ To turn off file and printer sharing, perform steps **1** to **6** (☑ changes to ☐ in steps **4** and **5**).

SHARE FILES ON A NETWORK

You can share files with other people on your network by adding the files to the Public folder on your computer. Everyone on the network can access files stored in your Public folder.

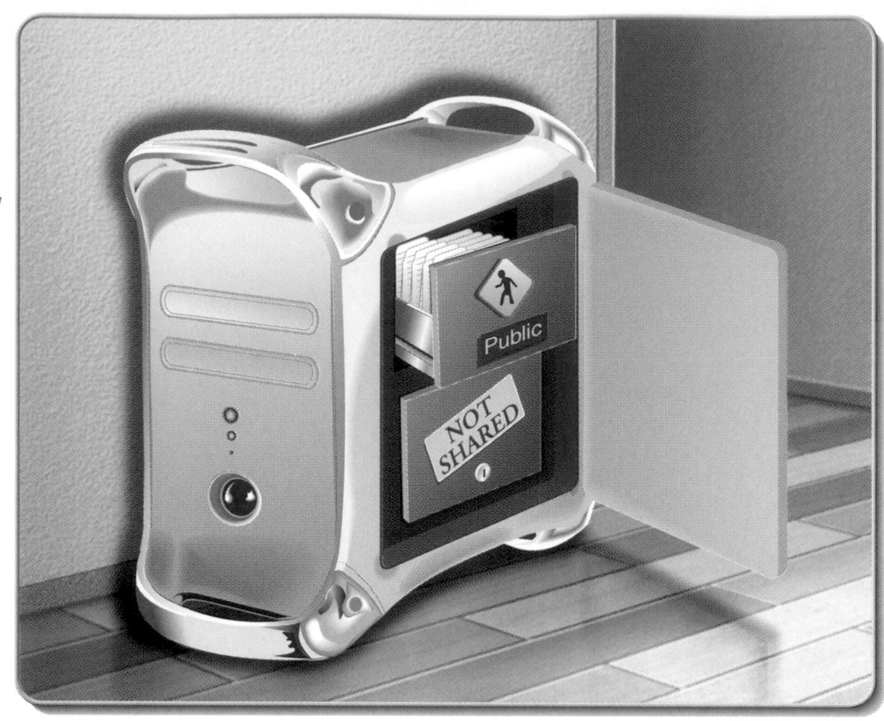

Everyone on the network can open and copy, but not change or delete files in your Public folder.

SHARE FILES ON A NETWORK

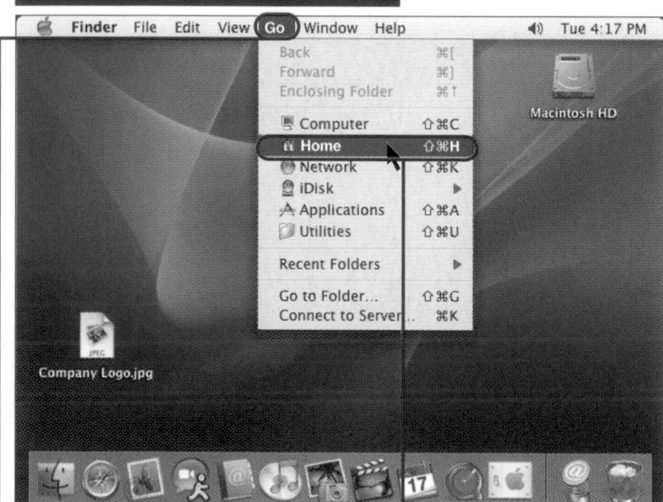

■ To allow other people on your network to access files you share on your computer, you must turn on file sharing. To turn on file sharing, see page 226.

1 Click **Go**.

Note: If Go is not available, click a blank area on your desktop to display the Finder menu bar.

2 Click **Home** to view your personal folders.

■ A window appears, displaying your personal folders.

3 Double-click the **Public** folder to display the contents of the folder.

What is the purpose of the Drop Box folder in my Public folder?

The Drop Box folder provides a location where other people on the network can place files they want to share with you. You are the only person who can open your Drop Box folder to view and work with its contents.

How can I stop sharing a file?

To stop sharing a file, you must remove the file from your Public folder. To display the contents of your Public folder, perform steps **1** to **3** below. Position the mouse over the file you no longer want to share and then drag the file out of the Public window.

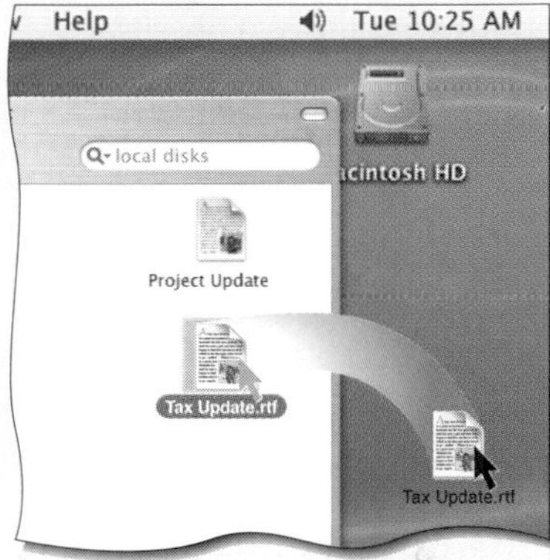

■ The Public window appears, displaying the contents of your Public folder.

4 Locate the file on your computer that you want to share with other people on your network.

5 Position the mouse over the file.

6 Press and hold down the option key as you drag the file to the Public window (changes to).

■ A copy of the file appears in the Public window.

■ You can repeat steps **4** to **6** for each file you want to share.

Note: You can copy folders to your Public folder the same way you copy files.

7 When you finish copying the files you want to share to your Public folder, click to close the Public window.

ACCESS SHARED FILES ON A NETWORK

You can view the files shared by other people on your network.

ACCESS SHARED FILES ON A NETWORK

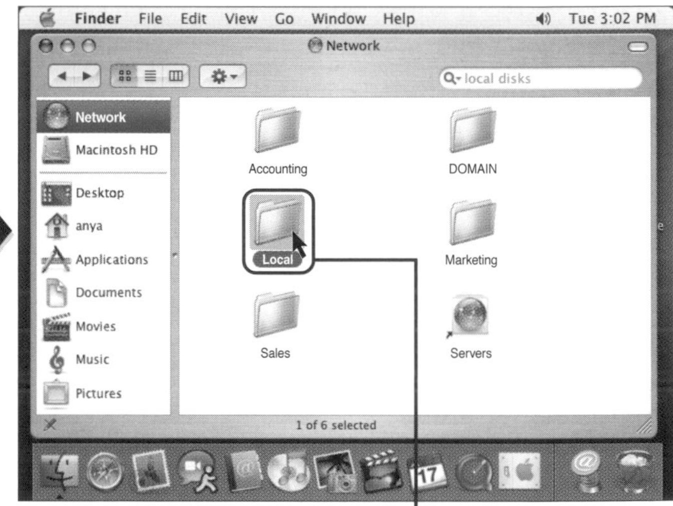

1 Click **Go**.

Note: If Go is not available, click a blank area on your desktop to display the Finder menu bar.

2 Click **Network**.

■ The Network window appears.

3 Double-click the **Local** folder to display the computers on your local network.

What files can I access on my network?

You can access files that other users on your network have added to their Public folders. To access the shared files in a user's Public folder, the computer that stores the files must be turned on and have file sharing turned on. For information on adding files to the Public folder, see page 228. For information on turning on file sharing, see page 226.

Can I quickly access the computers on my network while I'm working in a Finder window?

You can click **Network** in the Sidebar of any open Finder window on your computer to quickly display the Network window. You can then perform steps **3** to **10** starting on page 230 to access the computers and shared files on the network. For more information on using the Sidebar, see page 8.

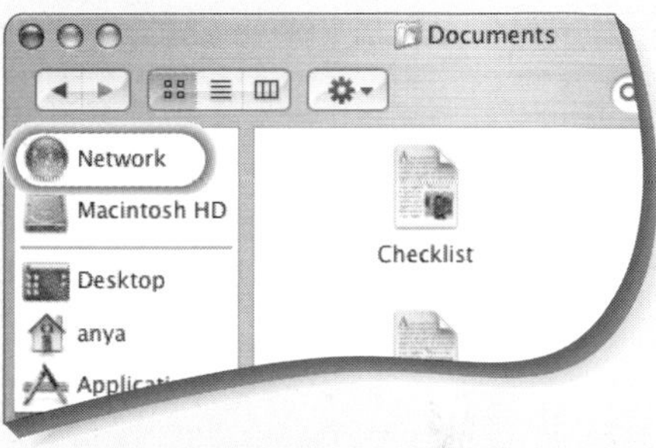

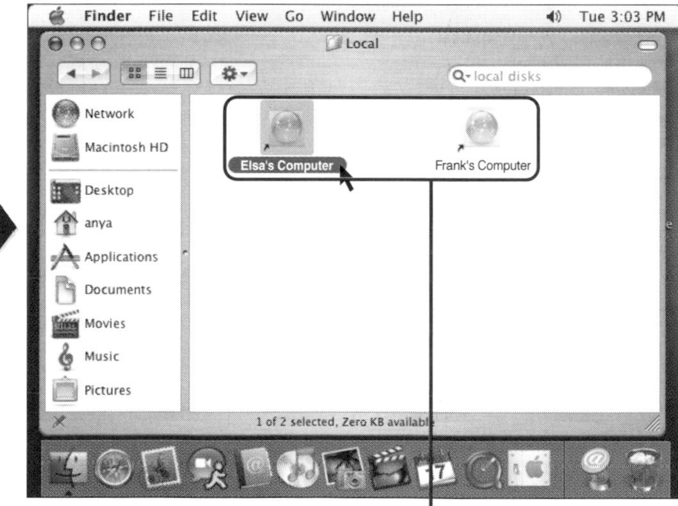

■ The computers on your network that have file or printer sharing turned on appear.

Note: For information on turning on file or printer sharing, see page 226.

4 Double-click the computer that contains the shared files you want to access.

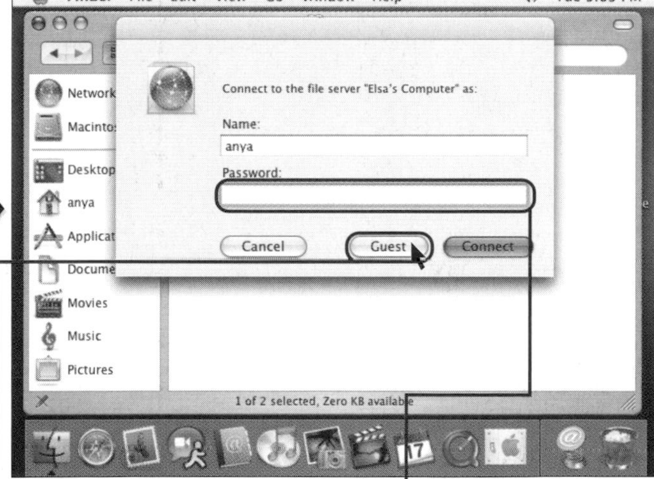

■ A dialog box appears.

5 To connect to the computer as a guest, click **Guest**.

■ To connect to the computer as a registered user, type your password and then press the return key.

CONTINUED

ACCESS SHARED FILES ON A NETWORK

When viewing shared files on a computer on your network, you can open the files, but you cannot change or delete the files.

ACCESS SHARED FILES ON A NETWORK (CONTINUED)

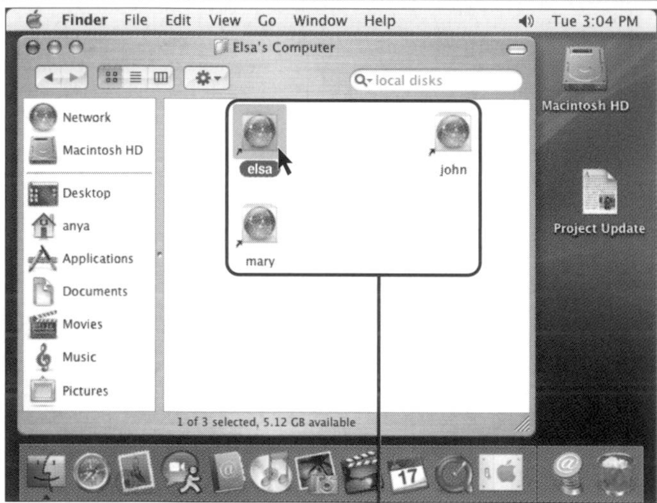

■ A window appears, displaying a folder for each user account on the computer.

6 Double-click the name of the user account that shared the files you want to access.

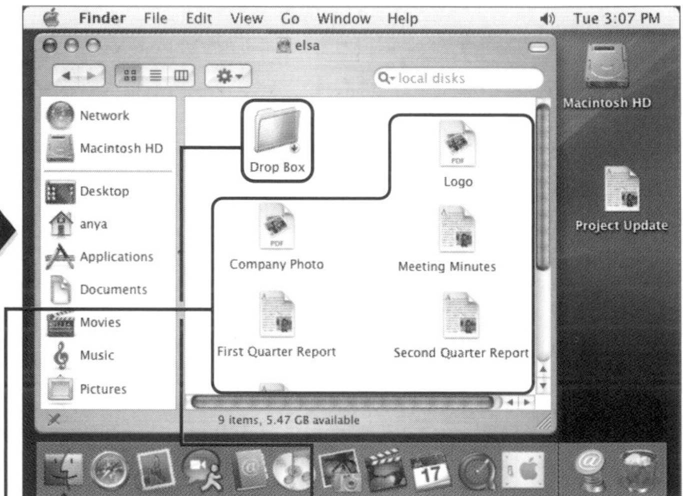

■ The files shared by the user account appear.

■ To open a file, double-click the file.

ADD FILES TO THE DROP BOX FOLDER

■ The Drop Box folder provides a location where you can place files you want to share with the owner of the user account.

Note: Only the owner of the user account can view and work with the contents of the Drop Box.

How can I make changes to a shared file on my network?

You cannot make changes to a shared file on the network, but you can create a copy of the file on your computer and then work with the copy on your computer. To make a copy of a shared file, position the mouse ↖ over the file you want to copy and then drag the file to your desktop.

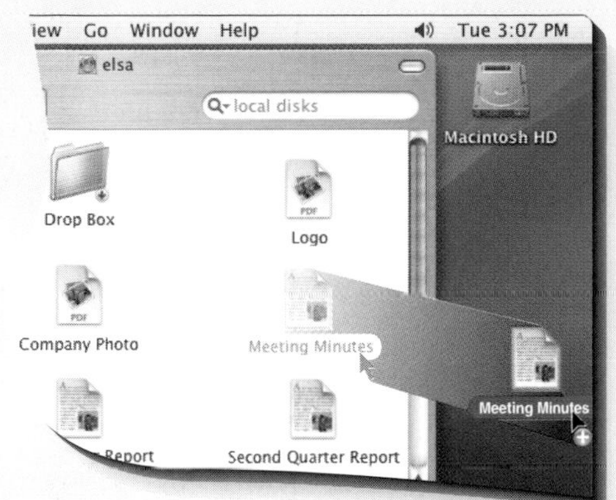

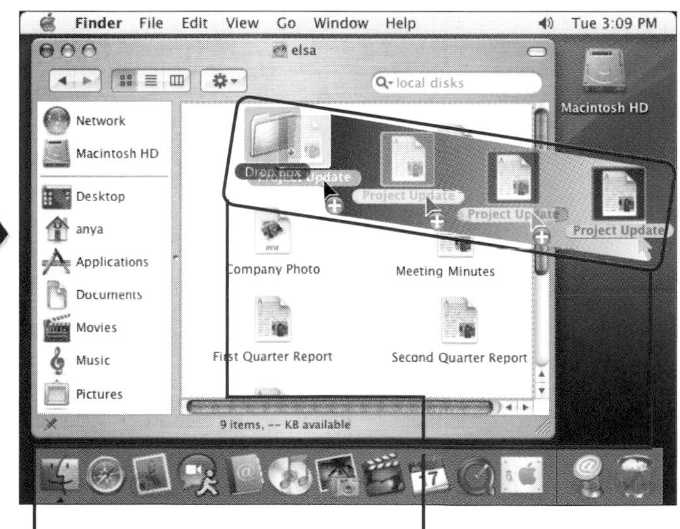

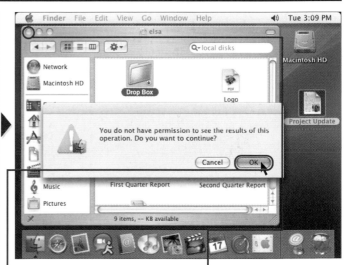

7 To share a file on your computer with the owner of the user account, position the mouse ↖ over the file.

8 Drag the file to the Drop Box folder (↖ changes to ↖+).

■ A dialog box appears, stating that you do not have permission to see the results of the copy.

9 Click **OK** to copy the file to the Drop Box folder.

10 When you finish working with the shared files, you can click ● to close the window.

Welcome to Discovery.com
http://www.discovery.com/
Apple .Mac Amazon eBay Yahoo! News
Google
Discovery.com
Explore our Web Universe.
All Our TV Schedules
Free Newsletter!
Discovery News
Search
Peacock Beauty Secrets Revealed
NETWORKS
Discovery Channel
TLC
Animal Planet
Discovery Health
Travel Channel
Discovery Times
Discovery Kids
BBC America
Science Channel
Home & Leisure
On TV: Friday at 9 p.m. ET/PT
We're Busting Myths
Discovery Channel
Google
Smithsonian
LOVE YEARNING
EXPLORE & LEARN
Online resources from the Smithsonian Institution
ART & DESIGN
HISTORY & CULTURE
whymilk - Home
got milk?
6767

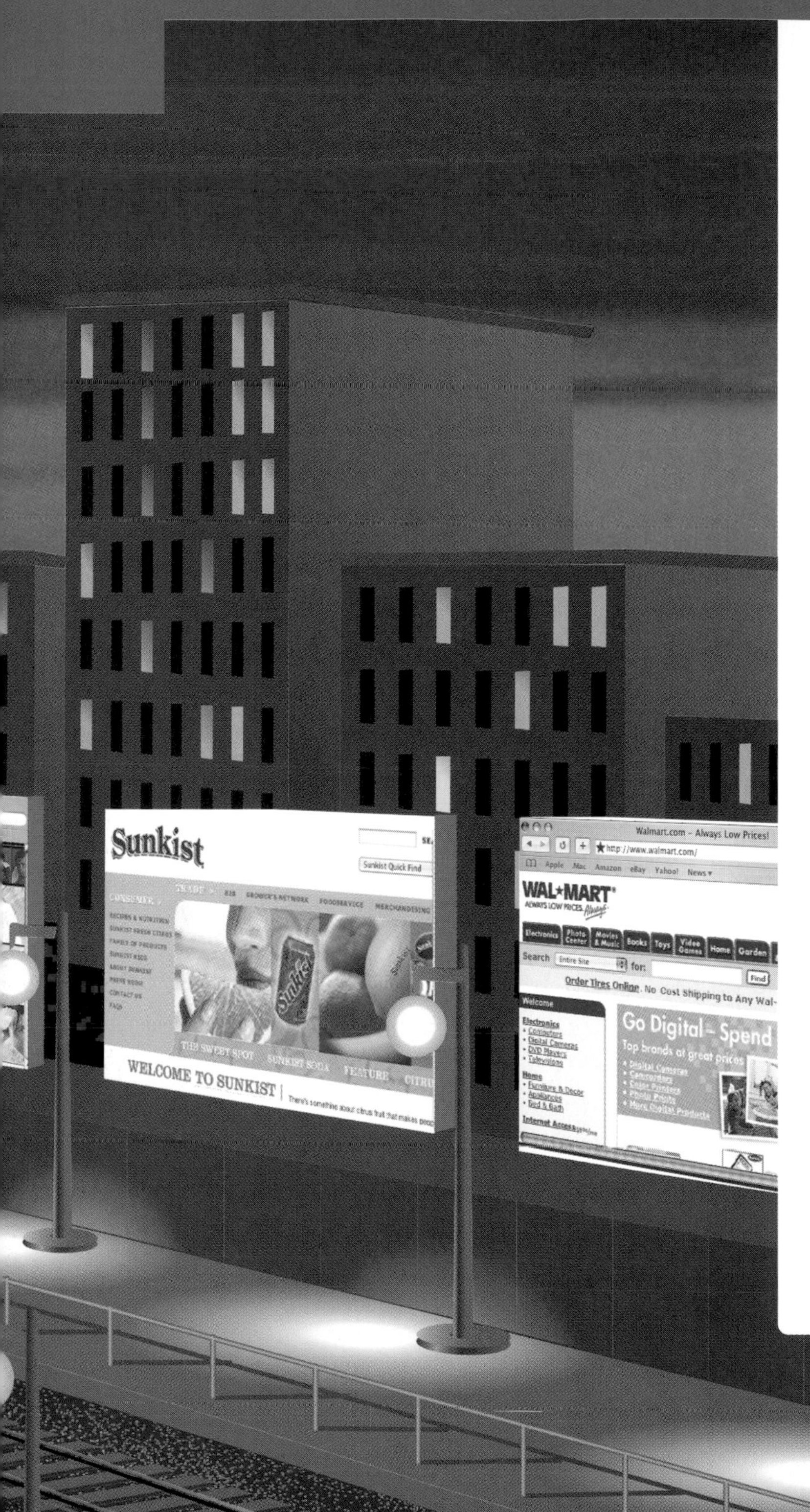

CHAPTER 11

Browse the Web Using Safari

This chapter explains how to use Safari™ to view and work with Web pages. Learn how to save a picture displayed on a Web page, block unwanted pop-up windows, change your home page and more.

CONNECT TO THE INTERNET

If you use a modem to connect to the Internet, you will need to connect to the Internet before you can access information on the Web.

When you connect to the Internet, your modem dials into a computer at your Internet Service Provider (ISP), which gives you access to the Internet.

Your Internet connection is usually set up when you install Mac OS on your computer.

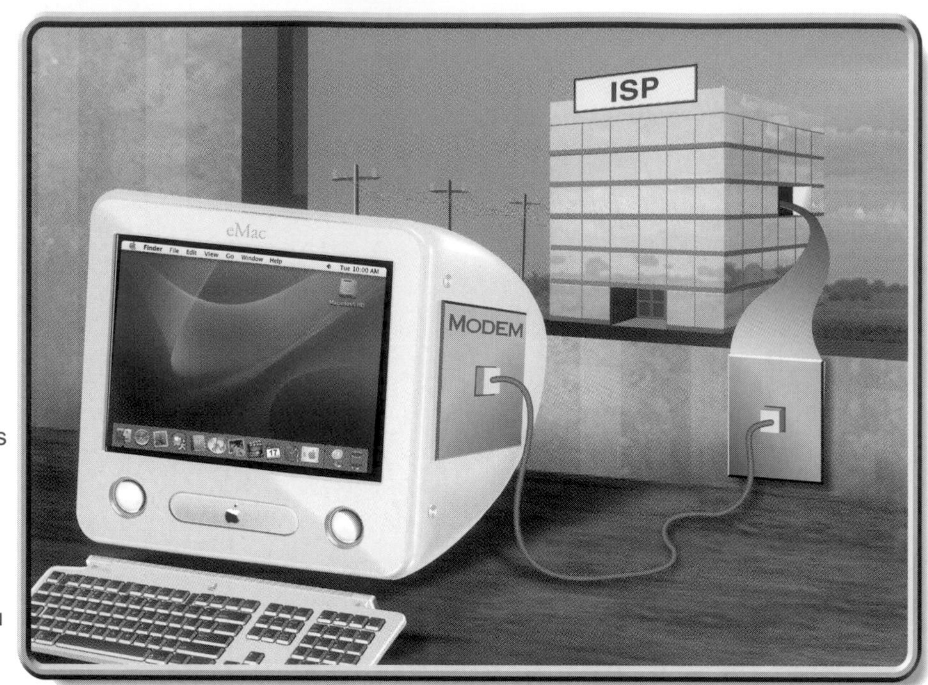

CONNECT TO THE INTERNET

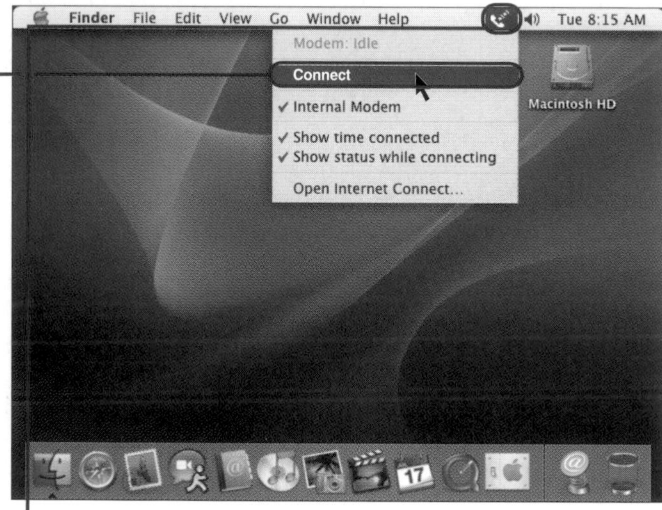

1 Click when you want to connect to the Internet.

2 Click **Connect**.

Note: A dialog box may appear, asking you to enter your password to connect to the Internet. Type the password for your Internet account and then press the return *key.*

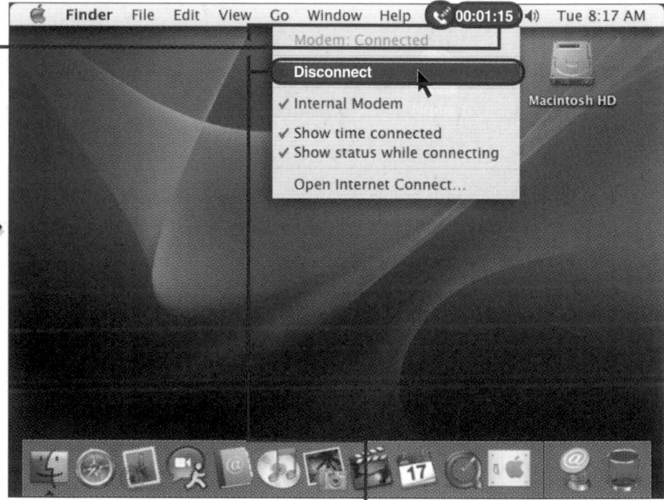

■ After a few moments, you are connected to the Internet. You can now browse the Web and exchange information on the Internet.

■ This area displays the amount of time you have been connected to the Internet.

DISCONNECT FROM THE INTERNET

1 Click when you want to disconnect from the Internet.

2 Click **Disconnect**.

START SAFARI

You can start Safari™ to browse through pages of information on the Web. Web pages can include text, pictures, sounds and videos.

Web pages also contain links, or hyperlinks, that connect text or pictures on one Web page to another Web page. When you select the text or picture, the linked Web page appears.

START SAFARI

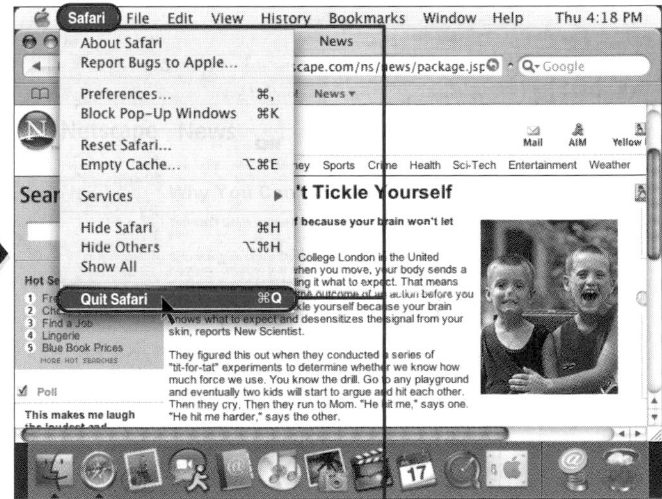

■ You must be connected to the Internet to work with Safari. To connect to the Internet, see page 236.

1 Click the Safari icon to start Safari.

■ A window appears, displaying your home page.

■ When you position the mouse over a link, the mouse changes to a hand pointer.

2 To select a link, click the link.

■ The linked Web page appears.

■ You can repeat step **2** to continue browsing through information on the Web.

QUIT SAFARI

1 When you finish browsing through the information on the Web, click **Safari**.

2 Click **Quit Safari**.

DISPLAY A SPECIFIC WEB PAGE

You can display a page on the Web that you have heard or read about.

You need to know the address of the Web page that you want to display. Each page on the Web has a unique address, called a Uniform Resource Locator (URL).

You do not need to type **http://** when typing a Web page address. For example, you do not need to type **http://** in front of www.walmart.com

DISPLAY A SPECIFIC WEB PAGE

1 Click the icon in this area to highlight the current Web page address.

2 Type the address of the Web page you want to display.

■ As you type the Web page address, Safari displays a list of matching addresses. You can click an address for a Web page you want to display.

Note: If you do not want to select one of the displayed addresses, continue typing the address you want.

3 Press the return key to display the Web page.

■ This area displays the progress of the transfer.

■ The Web page appears on your screen.

STOP TRANSFER OF A WEB PAGE

If a Web page is taking a long time to appear on your screen, you can stop the transfer of the page.

You may also want to stop the transfer of a Web page if you realize the page contains information that does not interest you.

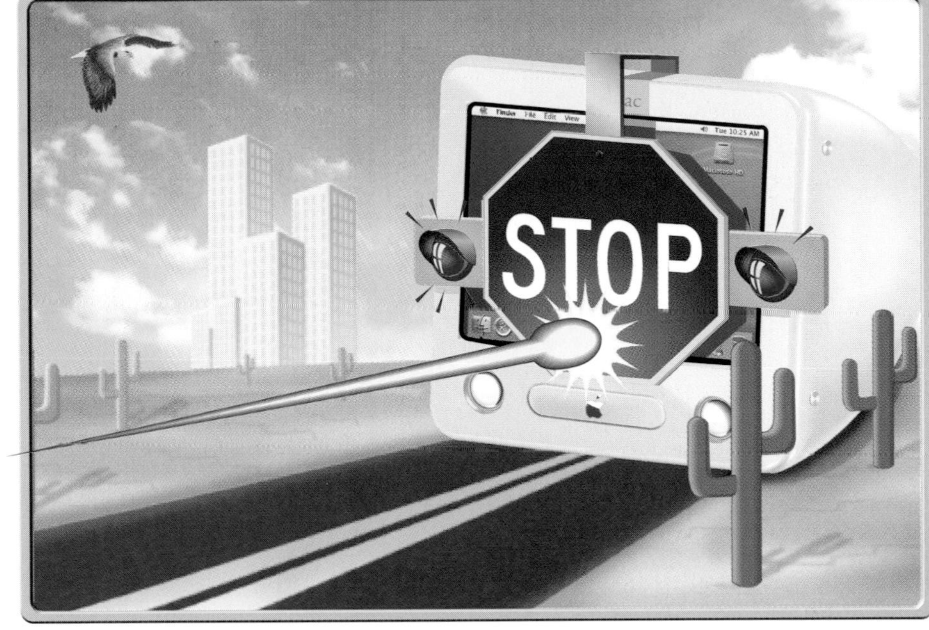

STOP TRANSFER OF A WEB PAGE

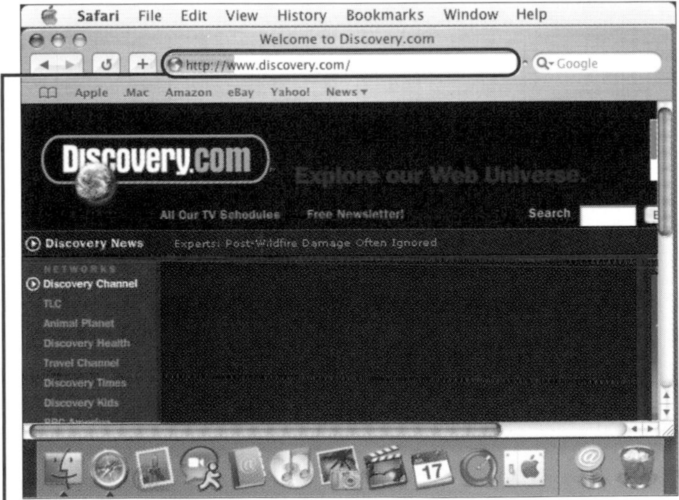

■ This area shows the progress of the transfer of a Web page to your computer.

1 Click ☒ to stop the transfer of the Web page (☒ changes to ↻)

Note: The ☒ button is available only while a Web page is transferring to your computer.

■ If you stopped the transfer of the Web page because the page was taking too long to appear, you may want to try displaying the page at a later time.

MOVE THROUGH WEB PAGES

You can easily move backward and forward through the Web pages you have viewed since you last started Safari.

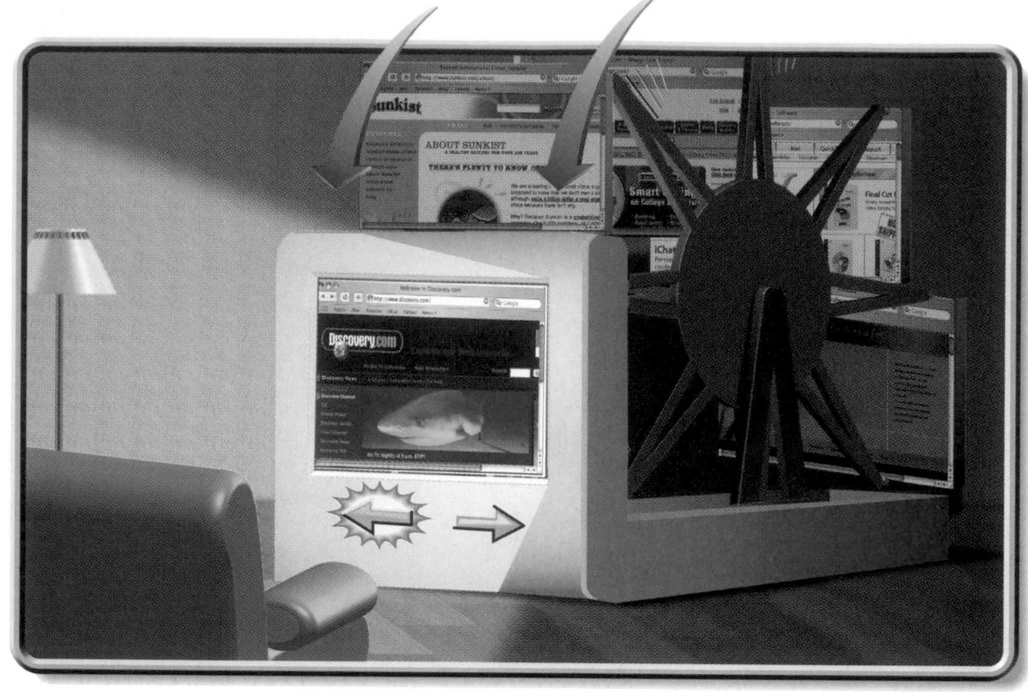

MOVE THROUGH WEB PAGES

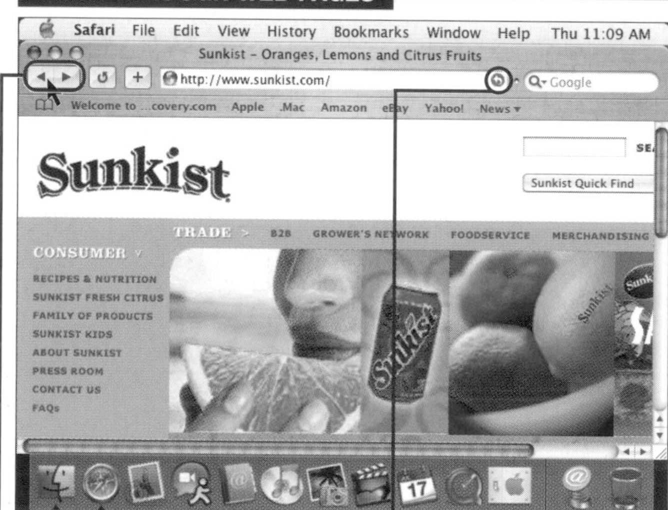

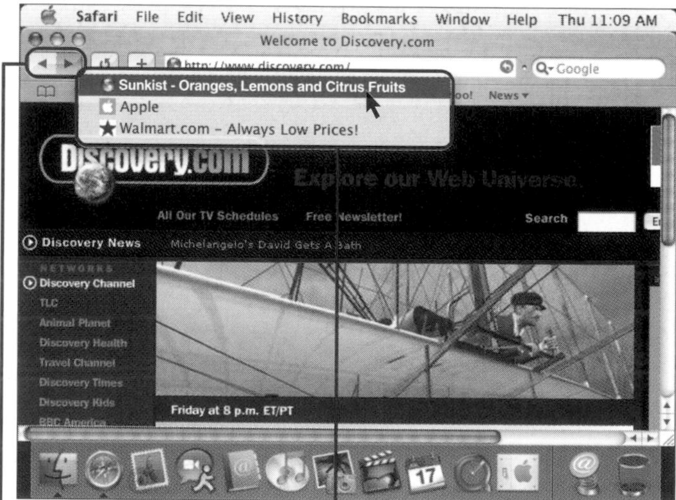

1 Click ◄ or ► to move backward or forward through the Web pages you have viewed.

Note: The ► button is only available after you use the ◄ button to return to a Web page.

■ To quickly return to the last Web page whose address you typed or whose bookmark you selected, click ↺.

Note: For information on bookmarks, see page 246.

DISPLAY A LIST OF VIEWED WEB PAGES

1 To display a list of the Web pages you have viewed, position the mouse ↖ over ◄ or ► and then press and hold down the mouse button.

■ A list appears, displaying the names of the Web pages you have viewed.

2 Still holding down the mouse button, position the mouse ↖ over the name of the Web page you want to view again. Then release the mouse button.

BLOCK POP-UP WINDOWS

You can prevent pop-up windows from appearing when you open or close a Web page.

Some Web pages use pop-up windows to display advertisements, while other Web pages use pop-up windows to display legal information or request login information.

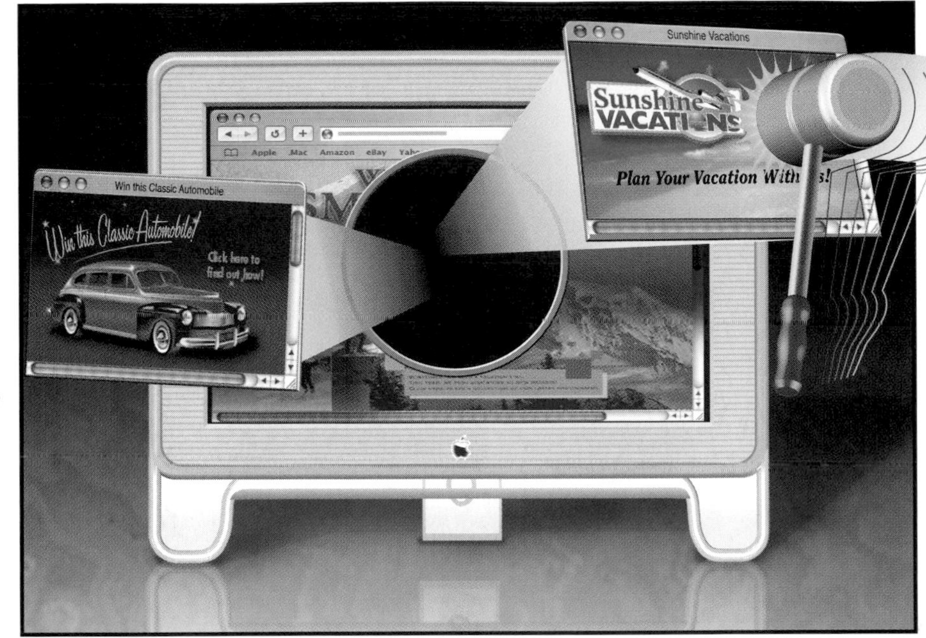

Keep in mind that if you block all pop-up windows, you may not see important information for some Web pages.

BLOCK POP-UP WINDOWS

1 To prevent pop-up windows from appearing on your screen, click **Safari**.

2 Click **Block Pop-Up Windows**.

■ Pop-up windows will no longer appear when you open or close a Web page in Safari.

*Note: To once again allow pop-up windows to appear, repeat steps **1** and **2**.*

DOWNLOAD A PICTURE OR FILE FROM A WEB PAGE

You can download a picture displayed on a Web page so you can view and work with the picture on your computer. You can also download a file stored on a Web page.

DOWNLOAD A PICTURE OR FILE FROM A WEB PAGE

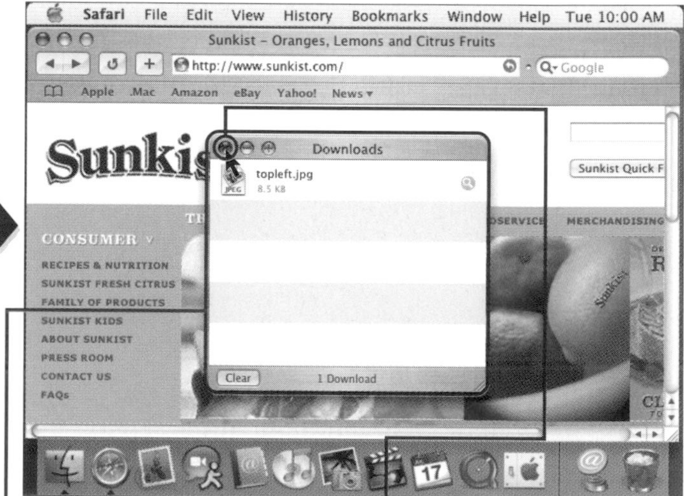

1 To download a picture displayed on a Web page, press and hold down the control key as you click the picture you want to save.

■ To download a file from a Web page, click the link for the file you want to download. Then skip to step **3**.

2 Click **Download Image to Disk**.

■ The Downloads window appears, displaying the name and size of the item you selected to download.

■ Safari saves the item on your desktop.

Note: If the picture or file you downloaded is compressed, Safari automatically decompresses the item for you.

3 To close the Downloads window, click ●.

DISPLAY HISTORY OF VIEWED WEB PAGES

Safari uses the History list to keep track of the Web pages you have recently viewed. You can display the History list at any time to redisplay a Web page in the list.

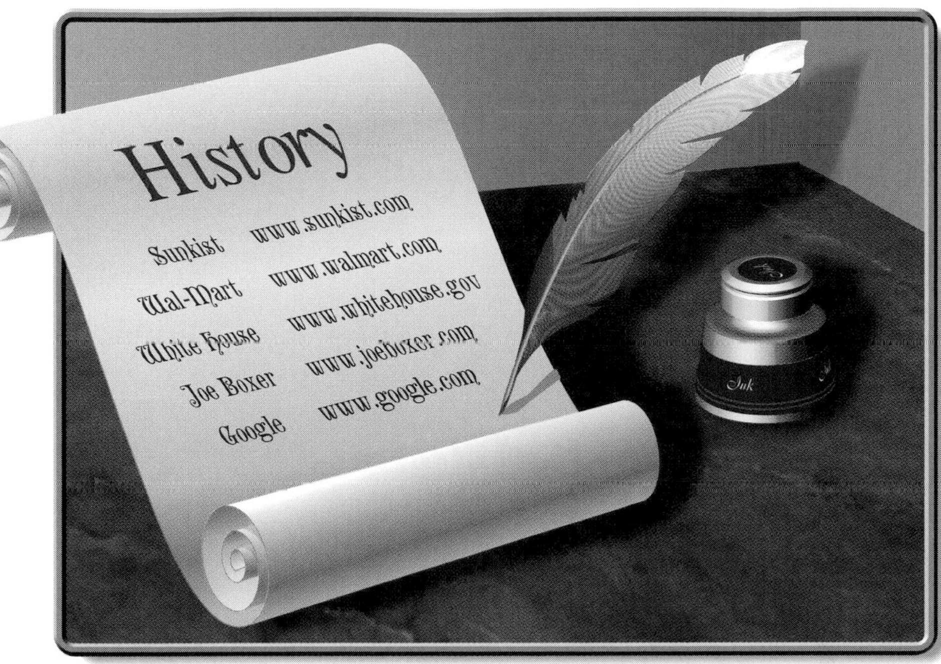

DISPLAY HISTORY OF VIEWED WEB PAGES

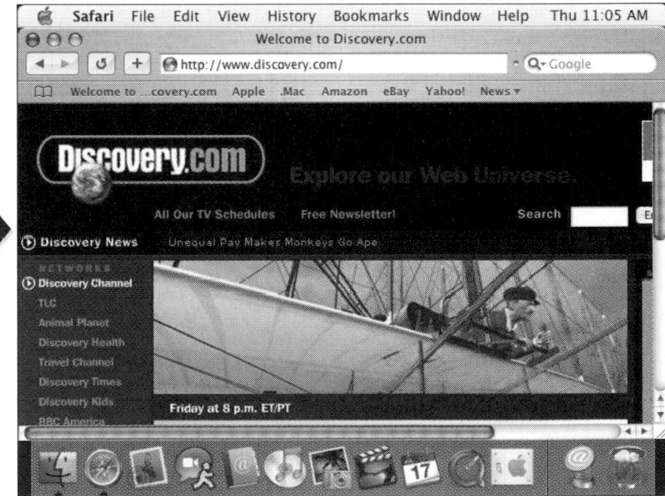

1 Click **History** to display a list of Web pages you have recently viewed.

■ This area displays the Web pages you have recently viewed.

2 To display a list of the Web pages you viewed earlier today or on a specific day, position the mouse over the option you want in this area.

3 Click the Web page you want to view.

■ The Web page you selected appears.

DISPLAY AND CHANGE YOUR HOME PAGE

You can display and change the Web page that appears each time you start Safari. This page is called your home page.

DISPLAY AND CHANGE YOUR HOME PAGE

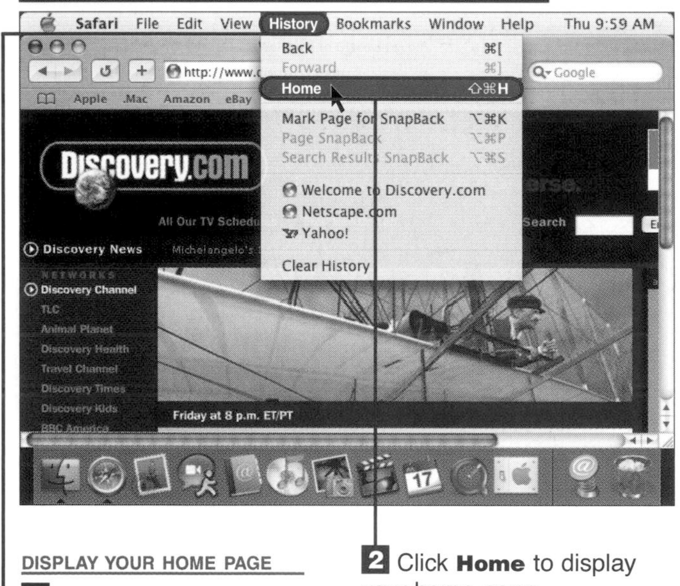

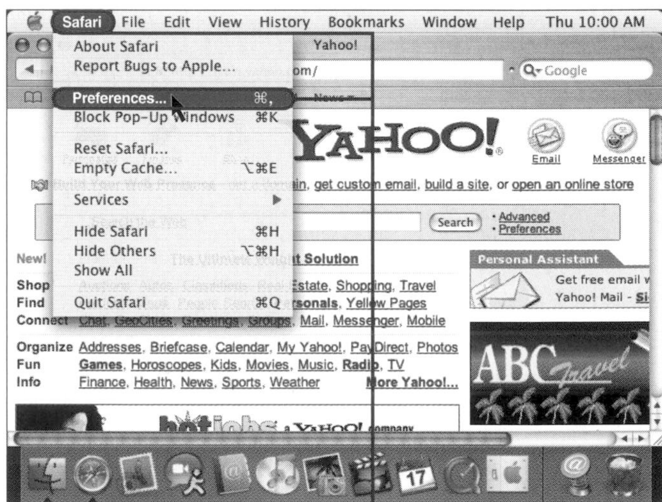

DISPLAY YOUR HOME PAGE

1. Click **History**.
2. Click **Home** to display your home page.

CHANGE YOUR HOME PAGE

1. Display the Web page you want to set as your home page.

Note: To display a specific Web page, see page 238.

2. Click **Safari**.
3. Click **Preferences**.

■ A window appears.

Which Web page should I set as my home page?

You can set any page on the Web as your home page. The page you choose should be a page you want to visit frequently. You may want to choose a page that provides a good starting point for exploring the Web, such as www.yahoo.com, or a page that provides information about your personal interests or work.

Can I add a button for my home page to the toolbar?

You can add a button to the toolbar to allow you to quickly display your home page at any time. Click **View** on the menu bar and then click **Home**. A Home button (⌂) appears on the toolbar. You can click the button to display your home page at any time.

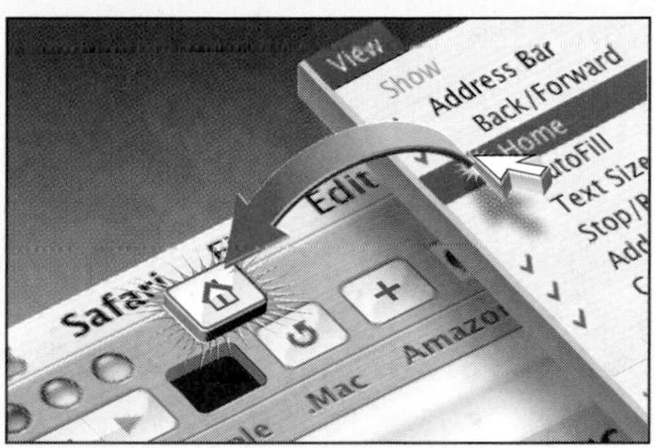

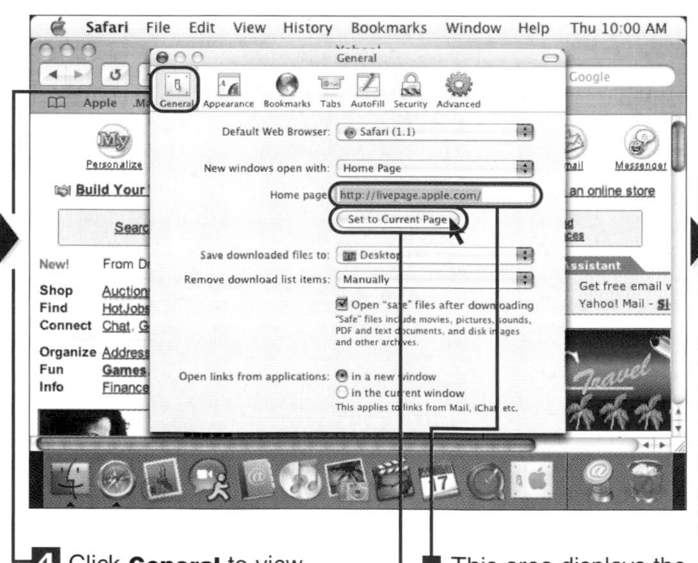

4 Click **General** to view settings for your Web browser.

■ This area displays the address of your current home page.

5 Click **Set to Current Page** to set the Web page displayed on your screen as your new home page.

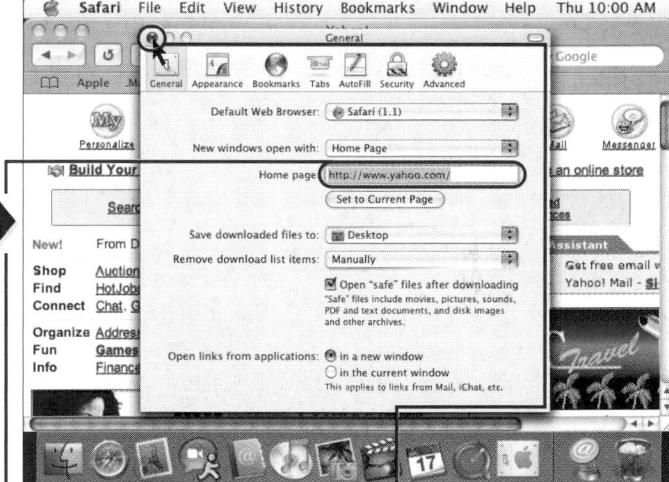

■ This area displays the address of your new home page.

6 Click ● to close the window.

CREATE A BOOKMARK

You can use the Bookmarks feature to create a list of Web pages you frequently visit. The Bookmarks feature allows you to quickly display a favorite Web page at any time.

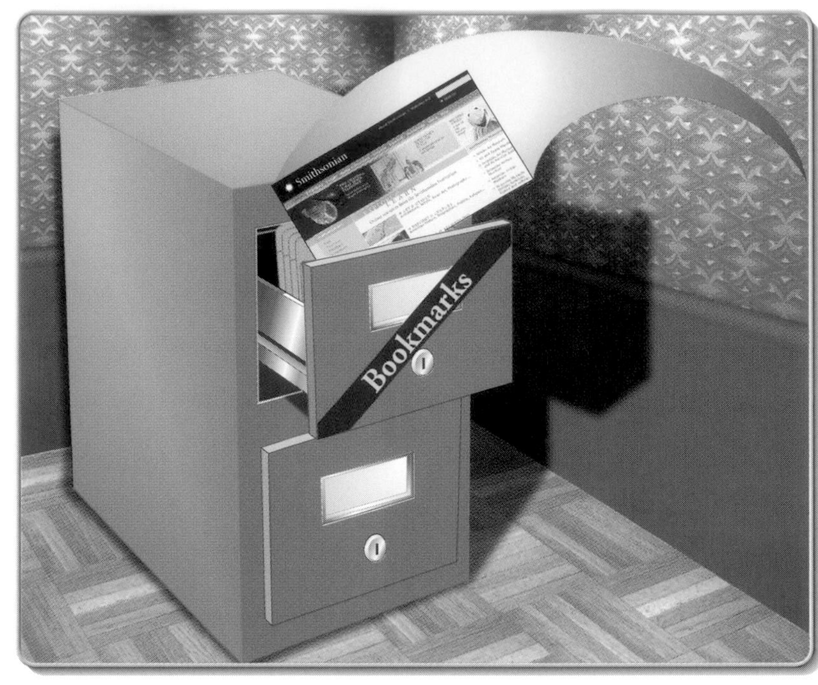

Selecting Web pages from your list of bookmarks saves you from having to remember and constantly retype the same Web page addresses.

You can store a bookmark on the Bookmarks Bar at the top of your screen or in one of the many bookmarks folders Safari provides.

CREATE A BOOKMARK

1 Display the Web page you want to add to your list of bookmarks.

Note: To display a specific Web page, see page 238.

2 Click .

■ A dialog sheet appears.

■ This area displays the name of the Web page. To use a different name for your bookmark, type the name.

■ This area displays the location where the bookmark will be stored. You can click this area to specify a different location.

3 Click **Add** to create the bookmark.

Does Safari automatically create bookmarks for me?

Yes. Safari automatically creates bookmarks for several popular Web pages and creates folders to help organize all the bookmarks. You can use bookmarks created by Safari as you use bookmarks you add yourself.

How do I remove a bookmark?

To remove a Web page from your list of bookmarks, click (bookmarks button) to display all your bookmarks. Click the bookmark you want to remove and then press the delete key. Removing bookmarks you no longer visit can help keep your bookmarks list from becoming cluttered.

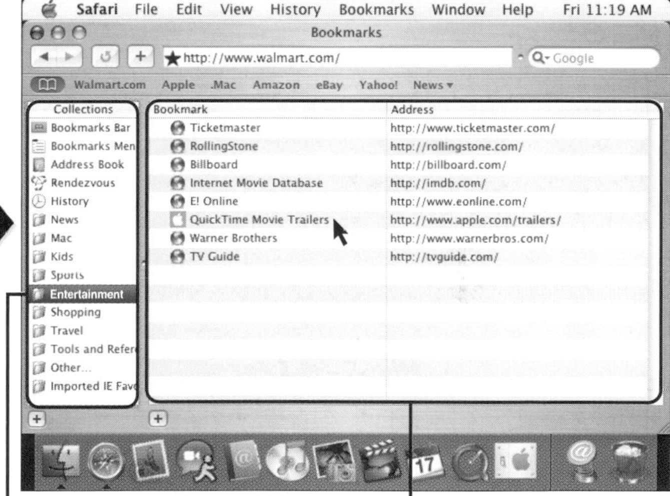

USING BOOKMARKS

■ This area displays the names of bookmarks that have been added to the Bookmarks Bar. You can click the name of a bookmark to quickly display the Web page.

1 To view all your bookmarks, click (bookmarks button).

■ Your bookmarks appear.

■ This area displays folders for all your bookmark collections.

2 To view the bookmarks in a folder, click the name of the folder.

■ The bookmarks in the folder appear in this area.

3 To display a Web page, double-click its bookmark in this area.

You can search for Web pages that discuss topics of interest to you.

Safari uses the Google search tool to help you find Web pages. A search tool is a service on the Web that catalogs Web pages to help you find pages of interest.

SEARCH THE WEB

1 Click this area and then type the information you want to search for.

Note: If this area contains text, drag the mouse over the text to highlight the text. Then type the information you want to search for.

2 Press the return key to start the search.

■ The Google Web page appears, displaying a list of matching Web pages and their descriptions.

3 Click a Web page of interest.

How can I narrow my search and find more relevant results?

To narrow your search, use specific rather than general words whenever possible. For example, if you want to find Web pages about porsches, type **porsche** instead of **car**.

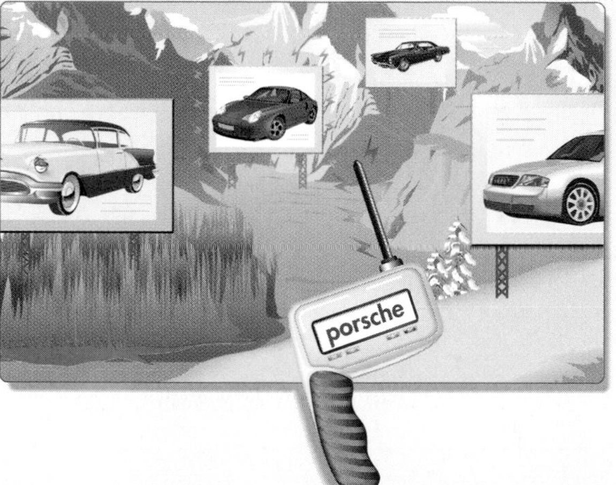

You can also use quotation marks ("") to find words that are side-by-side on a Web page. For example, if you are searching for Thomas Edison, surround the name in quotation marks (example, "Thomas Edison") to ensure that Google will find only Web pages that contain the entire name.

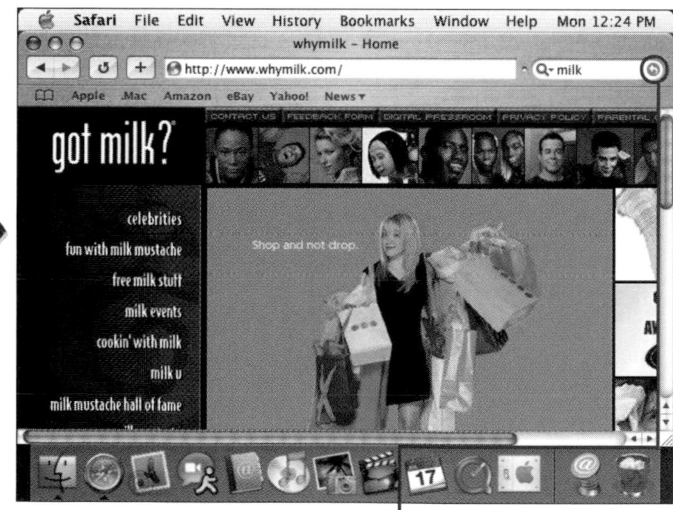

■ The Web page you selected appears.

■ You can click ⟲ in this area to return to the list of Web pages and select another Web page.

REPEAT A PREVIOUS SEARCH

1 To quickly repeat a search you previously performed, click Q▾ in this area to display a list of your previous search terms.

2 Click the search term for the search you want to repeat.

Stocks

Movies

Flights

eBay

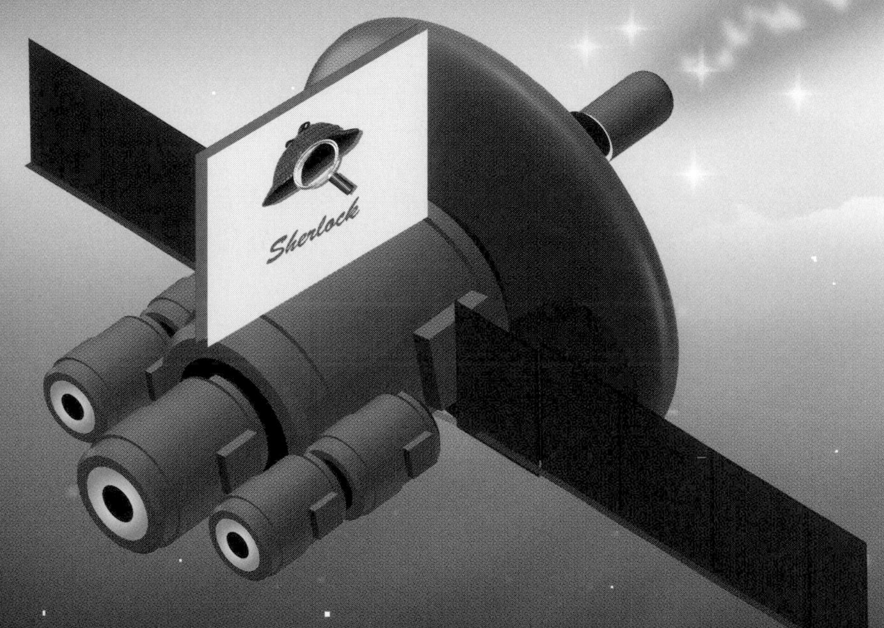
Sherlock

Phone Book

Picture

CHAPTER 12

Search the Internet Using Sherlock

Read this chapter to find out how to use Sherlock to search the Internet for information of interest, such as stock information, driving directions to a local business or movies playing in your area.

START SHERLOCK

You can start Sherlock to search the Internet for information of interest, such as pictures, flight information or movie schedules.

You need to be connected to the Internet to use Sherlock. To connect to the Internet, see page 236.

START SHERLOCK

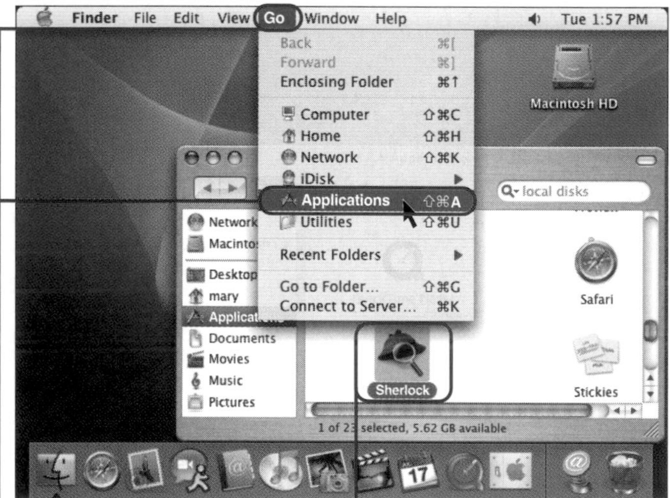

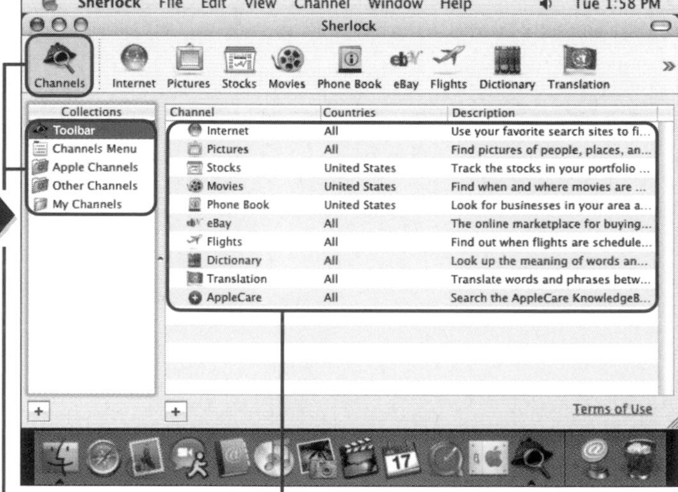

1 Click **Go**.

Note: If Go is not available, click a blank area on your desktop to display the Finder menu bar.

2 Click **Applications** to view the applications available on your computer.

■ The Applications window appears.

3 Double-click **Sherlock** to start Sherlock.

■ The Sherlock window appears.

4 Click **Channels**.

■ This area displays the available collections of channels. You can click a collection of interest to view the channels in the collection.

■ This area displays information about the channels available in the selected collection.

■ You can double-click a channel in this area to display the channel.

Note: The available collections and channels may change at any time. The channels displayed above may be different than the channels displayed on your screen.

What collections of channels does Sherlock provide?

Sherlock includes several collections of channels you can use to search for information.

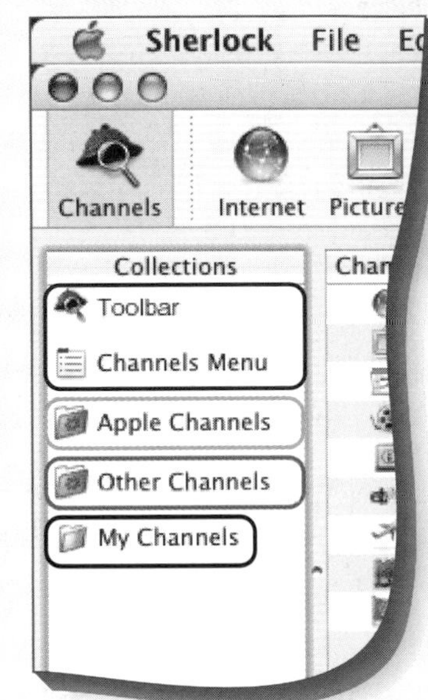

Toolbar and Channels Menu
The Toolbar and Channels Menu collections contain the most commonly used channels. Each channel in the Toolbar collection appears on the Sherlock toolbar. Each channel in the Channels Menu collection appears in the Channel menu.

Apple Channels
The Apple Channels collection contains many of the same channels as the Toolbar and Channels Menu collections, but also includes some specialized channels, such as a Japanese news channel.

Other Channels
The Other Channels collection contains a wide variety of channels from around the world.

Note: The first time you view the Other Channels collection, a dialog sheet appears. Click ***Proceed*** *to continue.*

My Channels
The My Channels collection allows you to create a personalized list of the channels you use most often. You can drag a channel of interest from any collection to the My Channels collection to add the channel to the collection.

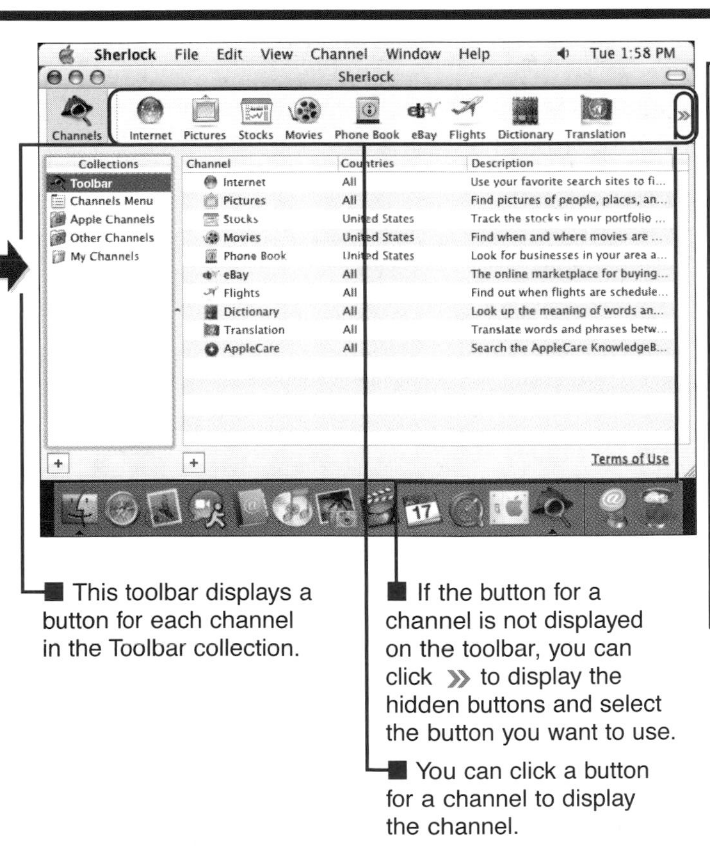

■ This toolbar displays a button for each channel in the Toolbar collection.

■ If the button for a channel is not displayed on the toolbar, you can click » to display the hidden buttons and select the button you want to use.

■ You can click a button for a channel to display the channel.

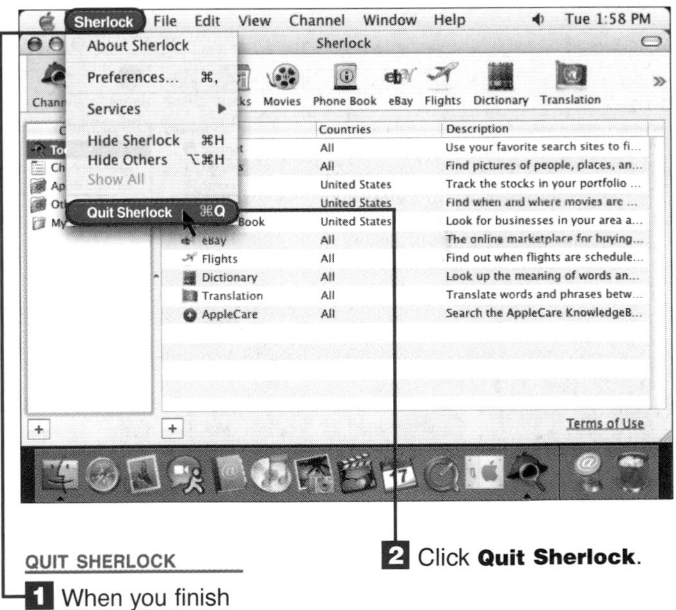

QUIT SHERLOCK

1 When you finish using Sherlock, click **Sherlock**.

2 Click **Quit Sherlock**.

SEARCH FOR WEB SITES

You can use the Internet channel to search for Web sites that discuss topics of interest to you.

SEARCH FOR WEB SITES

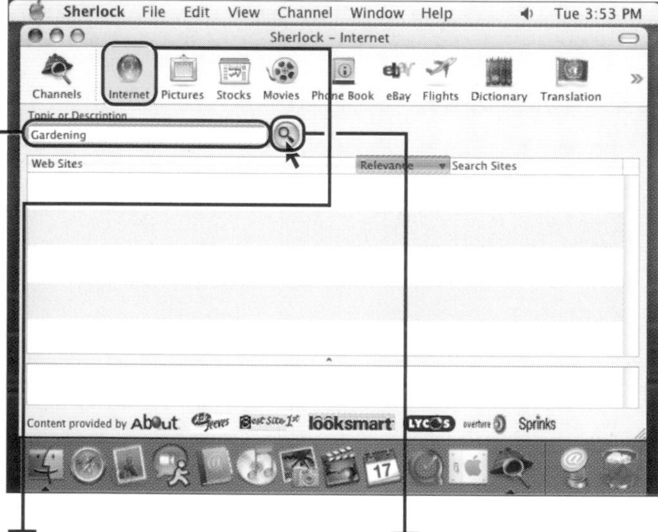

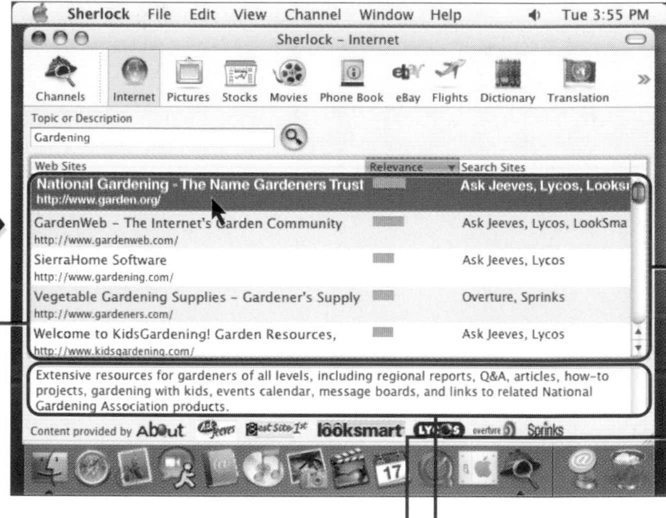

1 Click **Internet** to search for Web sites of interest.

2 Click this area and type the word or phrase you want to search for.

3 Click 🔍 to start the search.

■ This area lists the Web sites that contain the word or phrase you specified and the search site Sherlock used to find each Web site. A bar beside each Web site indicates the relevance of the Web site to the word or phrase you specified.

4 Click a Web site of interest.

■ This area displays a description of the Web site.

■ To display a Web site in your Web browser, double-click the Web site.

SEARCH FOR PICTURES

The Pictures channel allows you to search the Internet for pictures of people, places and things.

SEARCH FOR PICTURES

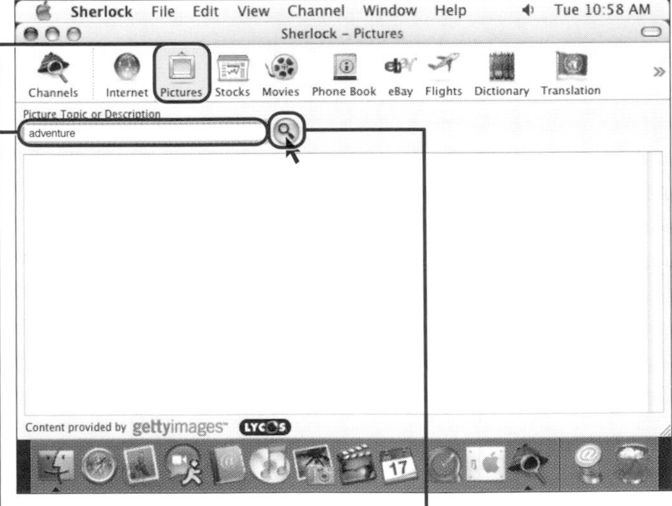

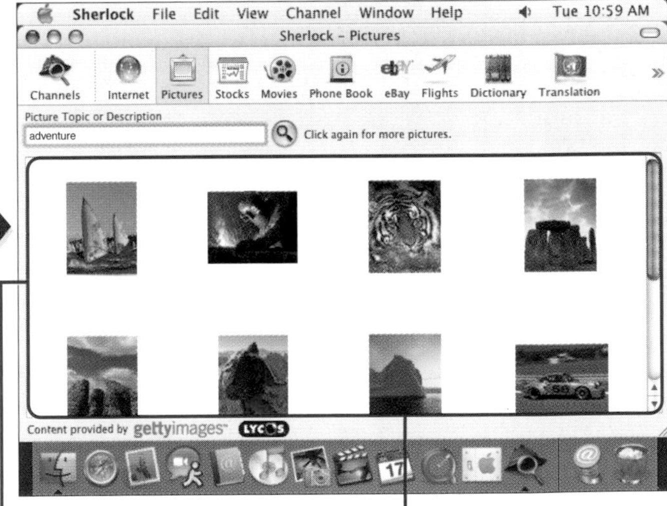

1 Click **Pictures** to search the Internet for pictures.

2 Click this area and type a word or phrase that describes the subject of the pictures you want to search for.

3 Click 🔍 to start the search.

■ This area displays the pictures that match the word or phrase you specified.

Note: You may be able to click 🔍 again to display additional pictures that match the word or phrase you specified.

■ You can double-click a picture to display the Web page that contains the picture in your Web browser.

Note: To save a picture displayed on a Web page so you can use the picture on your computer, see page 242.

SEARCH FOR STOCK INFORMATION

The Stocks channel allows you to search for information on stocks you want to monitor.

The stock quotes Sherlock displays are delayed by 15 minutes.

Sherlock automatically adds Apple Computer, Inc. to your list of stocks.

SEARCH FOR STOCK INFORMATION

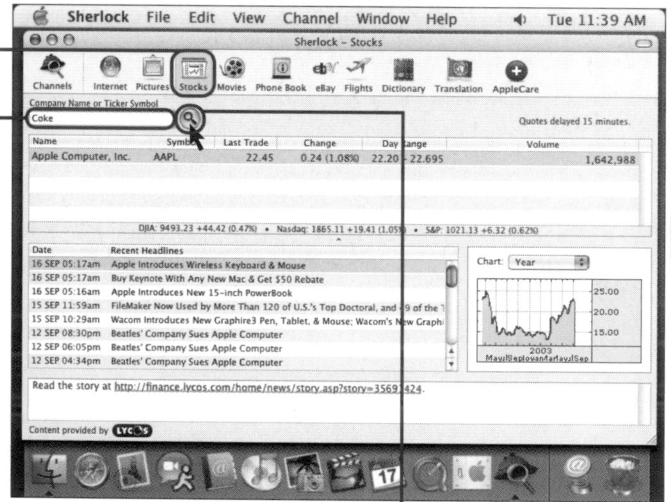

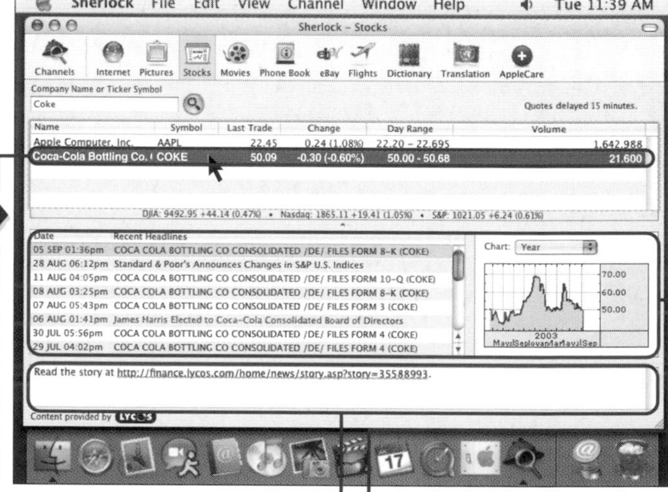

1 Click **Stocks** to search for stock information.

2 Click this area and type the company name or stock symbol for the stock you want to search for.

3 Click 🔍 to start the search.

*Note: If you specify a company name that matches more than one stock, a dialog sheet will appear. To display information for a stock that appears in the dialog sheet, click the stock and then click **Add**.*

■ This area displays the name of the stock and information about the stock.

4 To display headlines and a graph for a stock, click the stock.

■ This area displays recent headlines about the stock and a graph of the stock's performance.

■ This area displays the story or a link to the story for the currently selected headline.

Note: To delete a stock you added to your list of stocks, click the stock and then press the delete *key.*

SEARCH FOR BUSINESSES

You can use the Phone Book channel to find out where a business in your area is located.

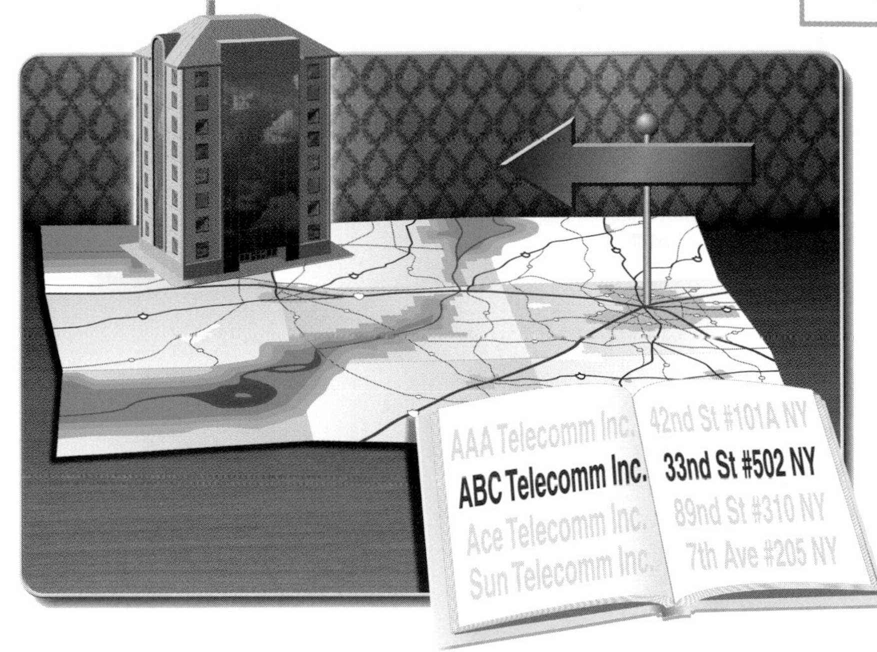

Sherlock uses your current location to find businesses in your area. Your current location is the address that was specified when Mac OS was installed on your computer.

SEARCH FOR BUSINESSES

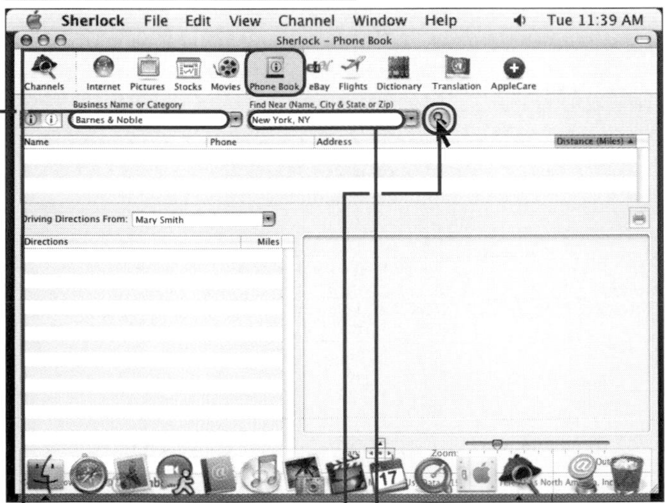

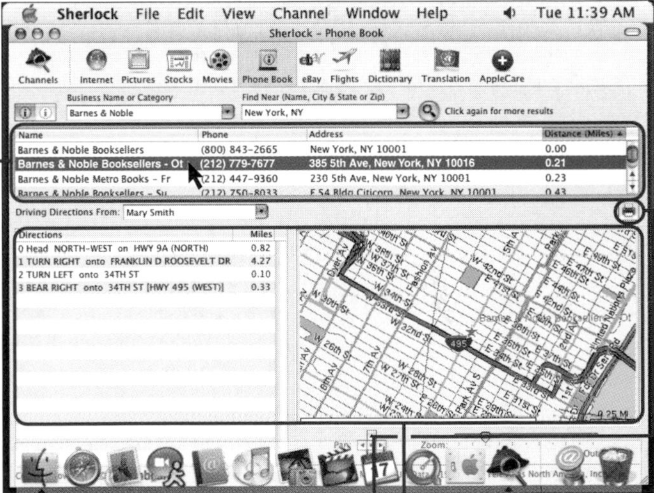

1 Click **Phone Book** to search for a business in your area.

2 Click this area and type all or part of the name of the business you want to search for.

■ To change the area where you want to search, drag the mouse I over the text in this area and type the city and state or zip code for the area where you want to search.

3 Click 🔍 to start the search.

■ This area lists the businesses that match the information you specified.

4 To display driving directions and a map for a business, click the business.

■ This area displays driving directions to the business and a map showing the location of the business.

■ To print the driving directions and map, click 🖶.

SEARCH FOR MOVIES

The Movies channel allows you to search for movies playing in your area.

SEARCH FOR MOVIES

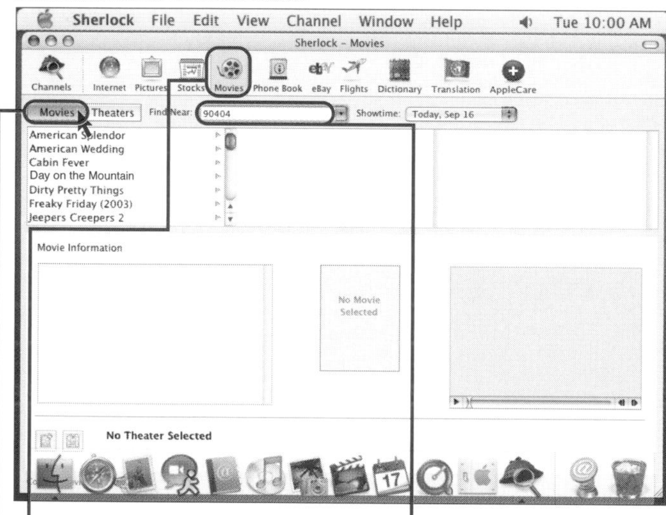

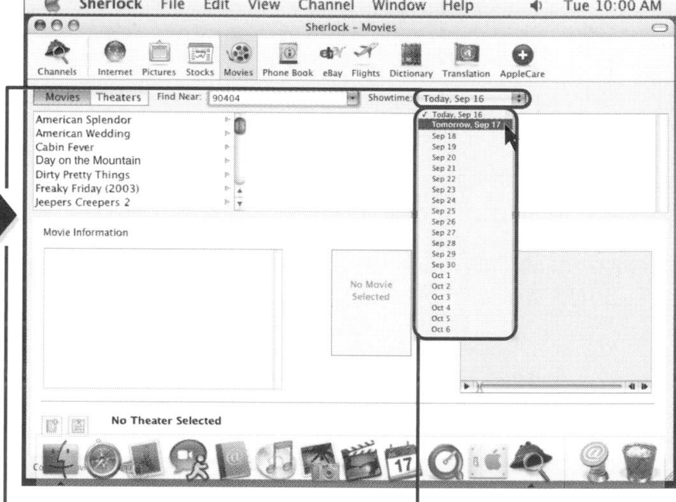

1 Click **Movies** to search for movies playing in your area.

Note: A dialog sheet may appear, asking you to specify a neighborhood in your area. Click the neighborhood and then click ***OK****.*

2 Click **Movies** to search by movie name.

■ To change the area where you want to search for movies, drag the mouse ⌶ over the text in this area and type the city and state or the zip code for the area where you want to search.

3 To specify the date the movies you want to find are playing, click this area.

4 Click the date of interest.

■ Sherlock automatically starts the search.

Can I search for movies playing at a particular theater?

Yes. Searching by theater is useful when you want to go to a particular theater to see a movie. Perform steps **1** to **4** below, except click **Theaters** in step **2**. In the list of theaters that appears, click a theater of interest to display the movies playing at the theater. Then click a movie of interest to display information about the movie.

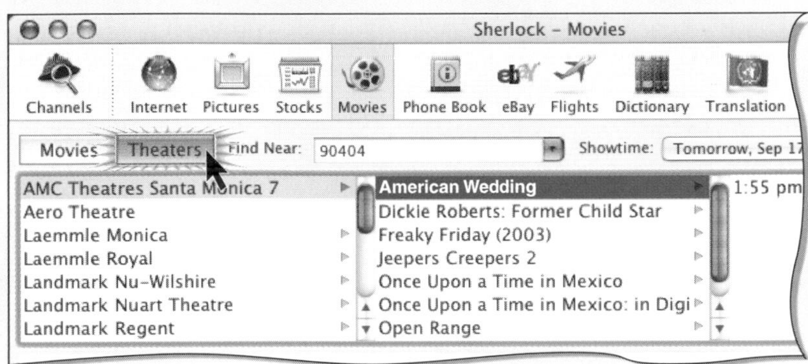

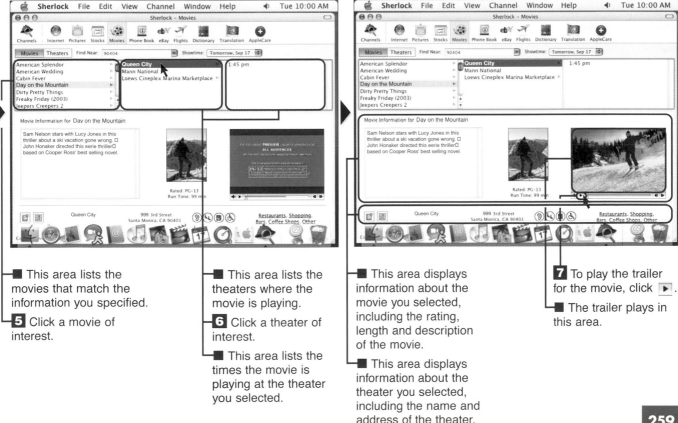

■ This area lists the movies that match the information you specified.

5 Click a movie of interest.

■ This area lists the theaters where the movie is playing.

6 Click a theater of interest.

■ This area lists the times the movie is playing at the theater you selected.

■ This area displays information about the movie you selected, including the rating, length and description of the movie.

■ This area displays information about the theater you selected, including the name and address of the theater.

7 To play the trailer for the movie, click ▶.

■ The trailer plays in this area.

SEARCH FOR GOODS AND SERVICES

You can use the eBay channel to search for goods and services you want to purchase on the Internet.

SEARCH FOR GOODS AND SERVICES

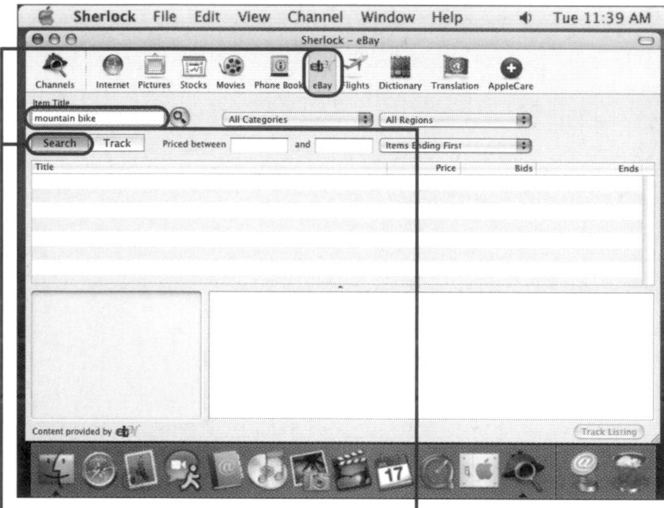

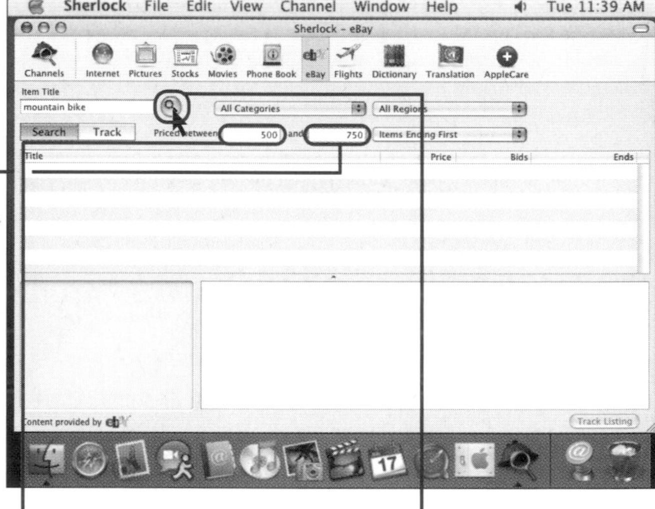

1 Click **eBay** to search for goods and services.

2 Click **Search** to search for an item you want to purchase.

3 Click this area and type a word or phrase that describes the item you want to purchase.

4 To specify the minimum price you want to pay, click this area and type a price.

5 To specify the maximum price you want to pay, click this area and type a price.

6 Click 🔍 to start the search.

Can I sort the items Sherlock found?

Yes. You can sort the items by title, price, number of bids or when the bidding will end. To sort the items, click the heading for the column you want to use to sort the items. To sort the items in the reverse order, you can click the heading again.

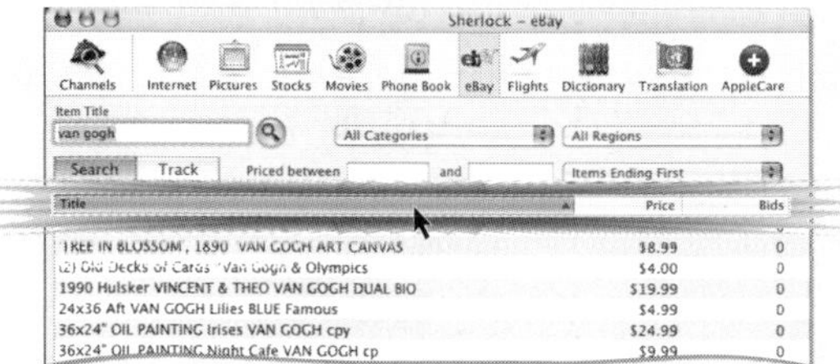

How can I view the auctions I selected to track?

To view the auctions you selected to track, click **Track**. A list of the auctions you selected to track appears. To remove an auction you no longer want to track from the list, click the auction and then press the delete key.

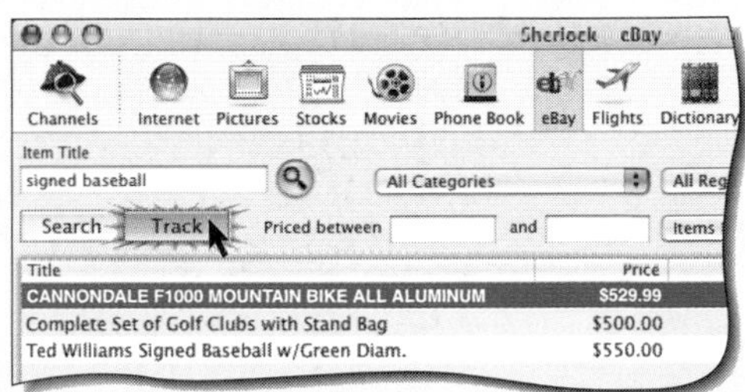

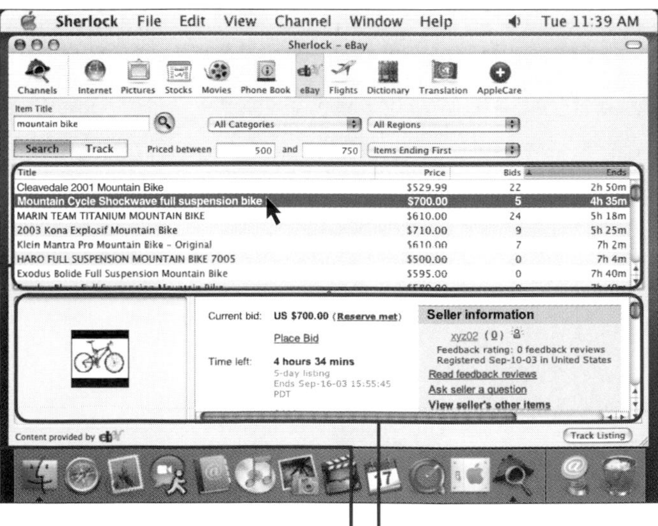

■ This area lists the items that match the information you specified and information about each item.

7 Click an item of interest.

■ This area displays a picture, if available, and details for the item you selected. You can use the scroller to view all the information.

■ To display the eBay Web page for the item, double-click the item.

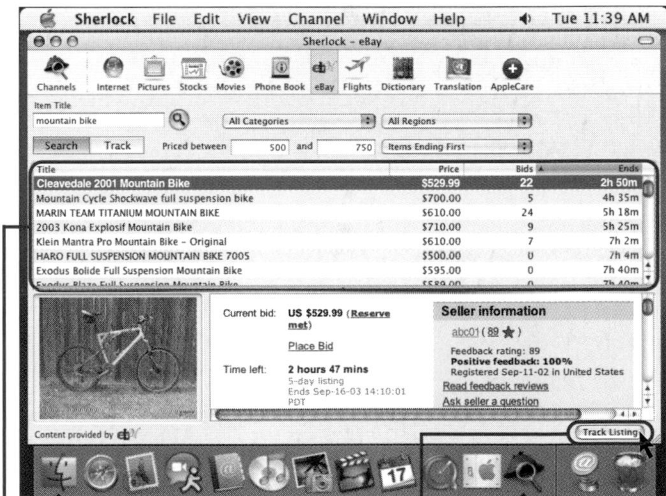

TRACK AN AUCTION

1 To track the auction for an item, click the item.

Note: Tracking an auction allows you to see the current status of the auction at any time. Sherlock will also notify you when an auction you are tracking is about to end.

2 Click **Track Listing**.

■ Sherlock adds the auction to the list of auctions you want to track.

Note: To view the auctions you selected to track, see the top of this page.

SEARCH FOR FLIGHT INFORMATION

The Flights channel allows you to search for information about a flight of interest.

You can find detailed information about a flight, including the departure and arrival times, the flight status and the amount of time before the flight lands.

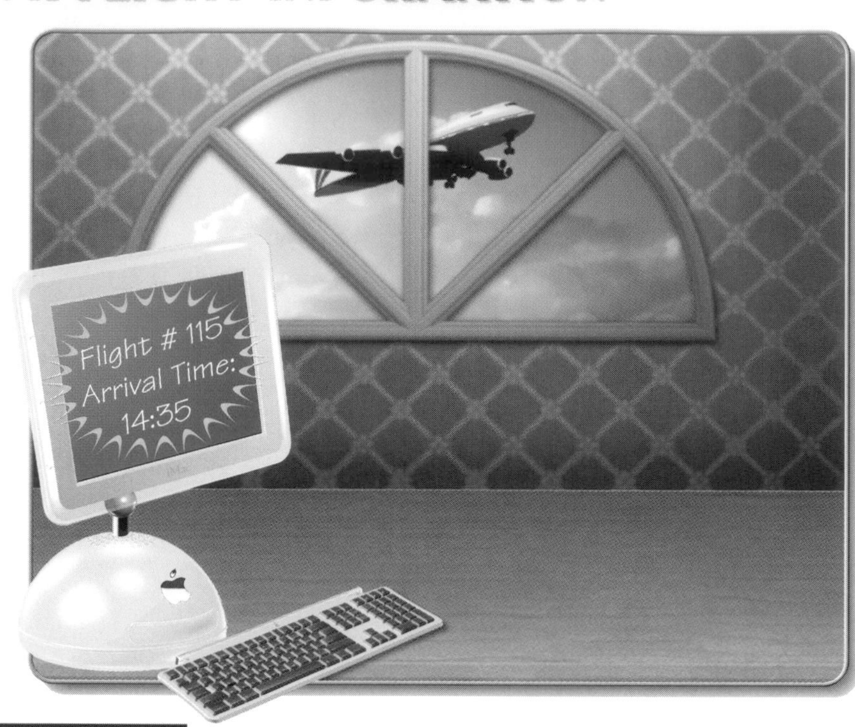

SEARCH FOR FLIGHT INFORMATION

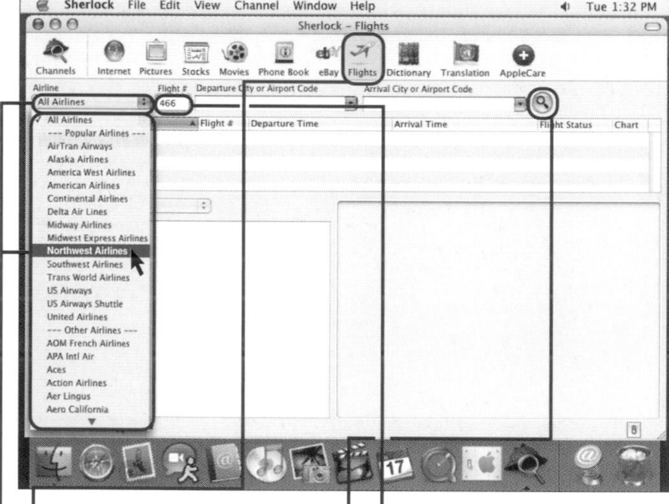

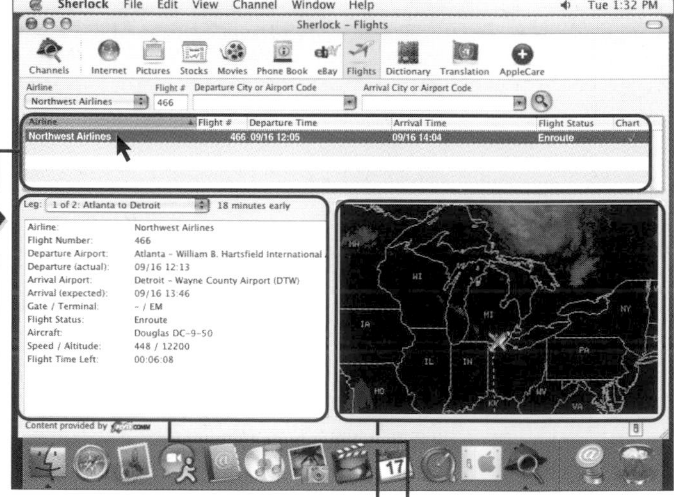

1 Click **Flights** to search for flight information.

2 Click this area to display a list of airlines.

3 Click the name of the airline you want to search for.

4 Click this area and type the flight number of the flight you want to search for.

5 Click 🔍 to start the search.

■ This area lists information about the flights that match the airline and flight number you specified.

6 To display details for a flight, click the flight.

■ This area displays details for the flight.

■ If a chart is available, this area displays a chart showing the location of the airplane and the route of the flight.

SEARCH FOR APPLECARE DOCUMENTS

You can use the AppleCare channel to search the AppleCare Knowledge Base for documents about Apple products.

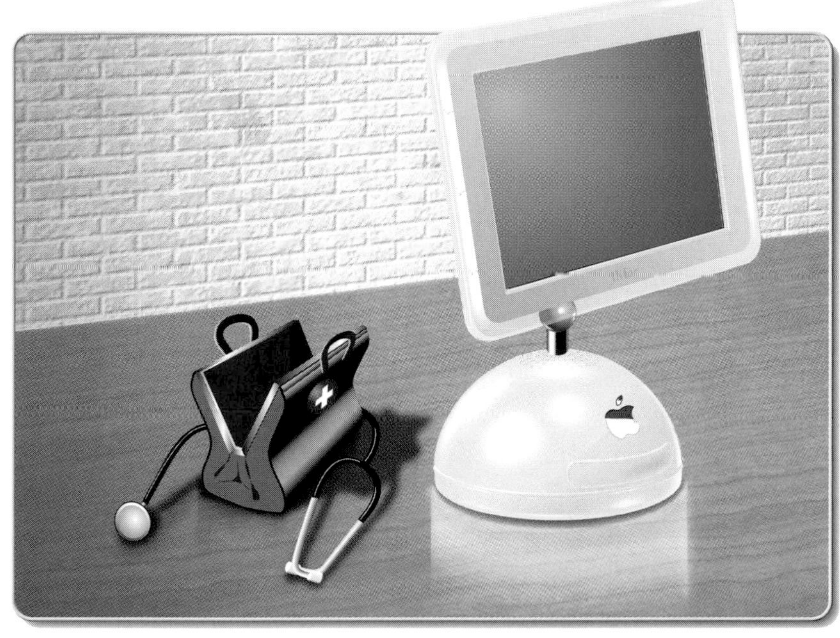

The AppleCare Knowledge Base contains thousands of documents that can help you troubleshoot the applications and hardware on your computer.

SEARCH FOR APPLECARE DOCUMENTS

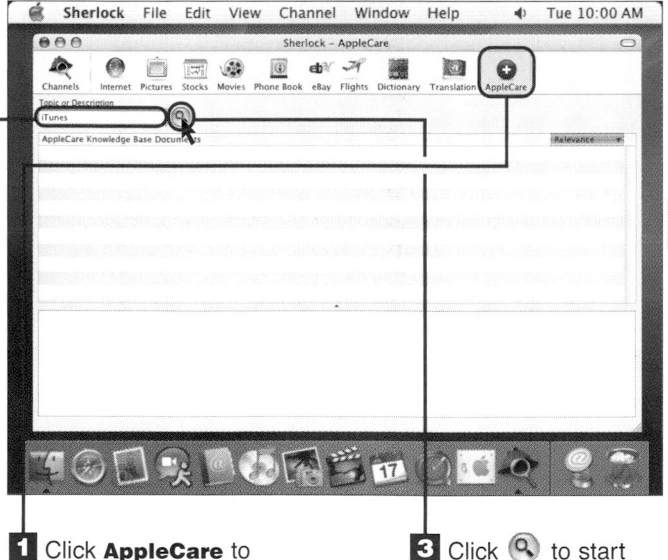

1 Click **AppleCare** to search for AppleCare documents.

2 Click this area and type the information you want to search for.

3 Click the search icon to start the search.

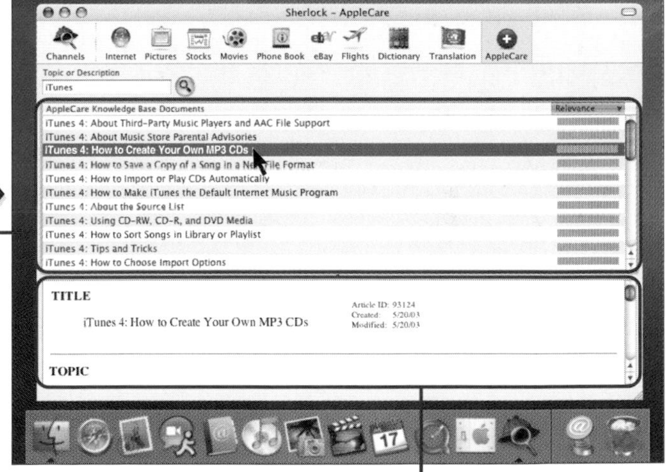

■ This area lists the documents in the AppleCare Knowledge Base that contain the information you specified. A bar beside each document indicates the relevance of the document to the information you specified.

4 Click a document of interest.

■ This area displays the contents of the document you selected.

SEARCH FOR A DEFINITION

You can use the Dictionary channel to look up the definition of a word.

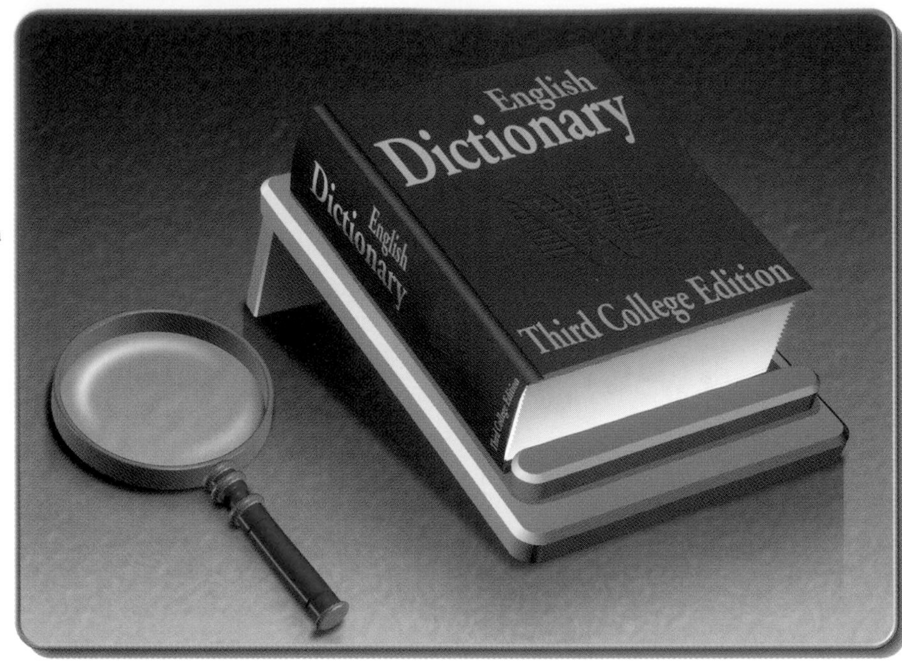

The Dictionary channel also allows you to search for the names of important people and places.

SEARCH FOR A DEFINITION

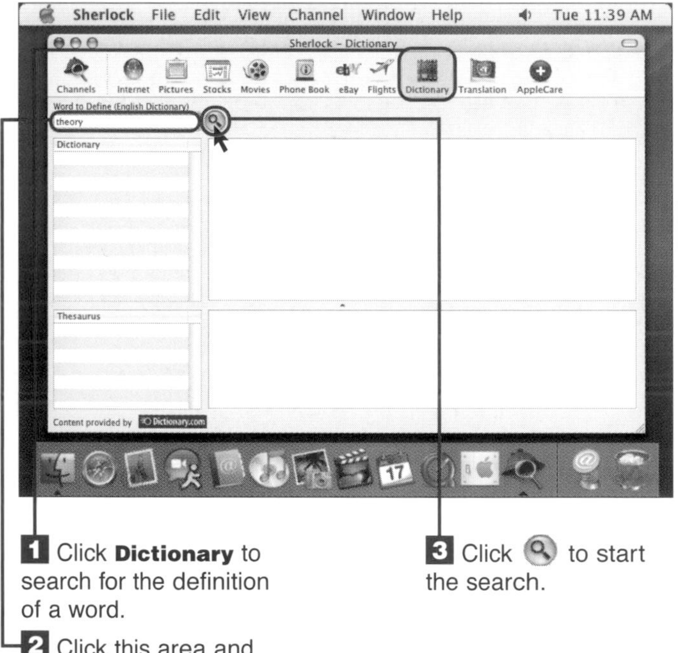

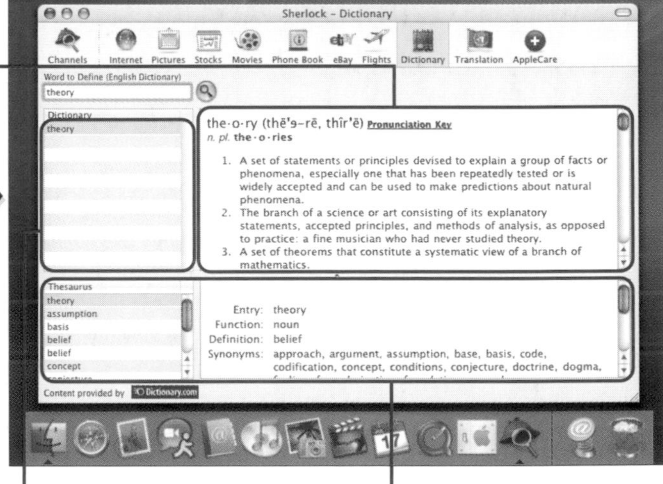

1 Click **Dictionary** to search for the definition of a word.

2 Click this area and type the word you want to look up.

3 Click 🔍 to start the search.

■ This area displays the word you specified.

■ This area displays definitions of the word you specified. You can use the scroller to view all the information.

■ This area displays words related to the word you specified and information about the currently selected word.

Note: To display information about a related word, click the word.

TRANSLATE TEXT

You can use the Translation channel to translate words and phrases from one language to another.

When translating text, keep in mind that the translation is performed by an application and may not always be accurate. If you need to translate important information, you may want to have a professional translator perform the translation.

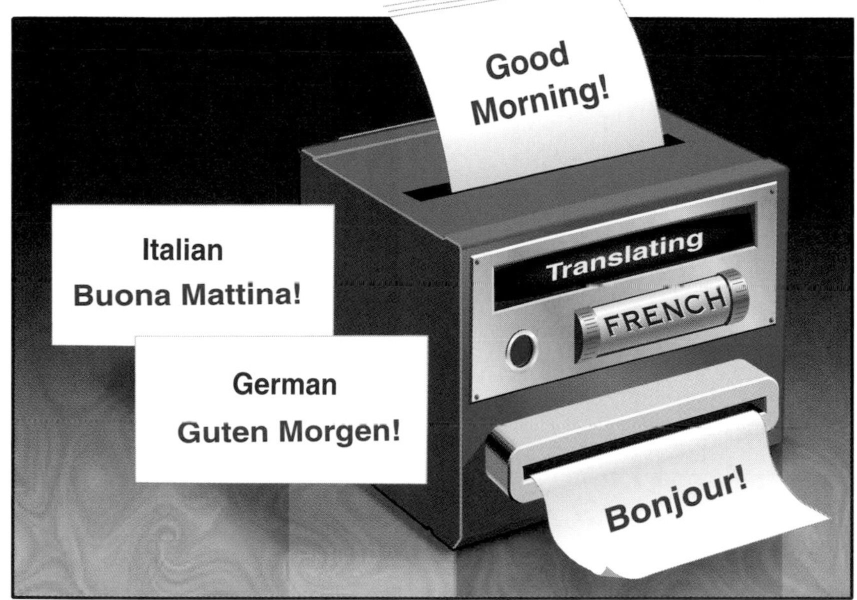

TRANSLATE TEXT

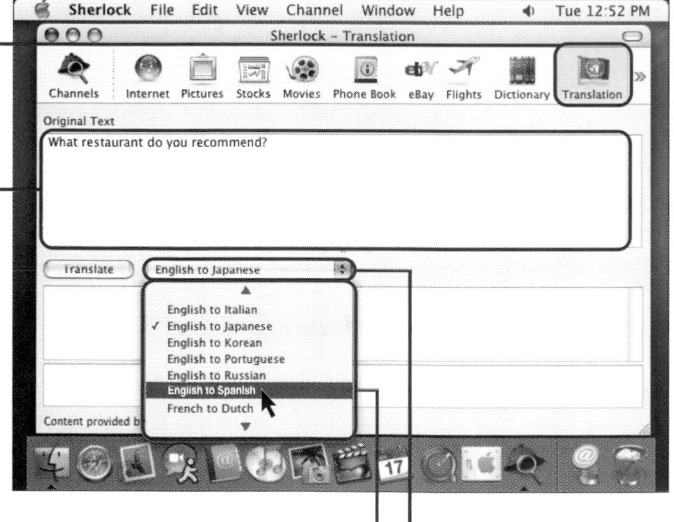

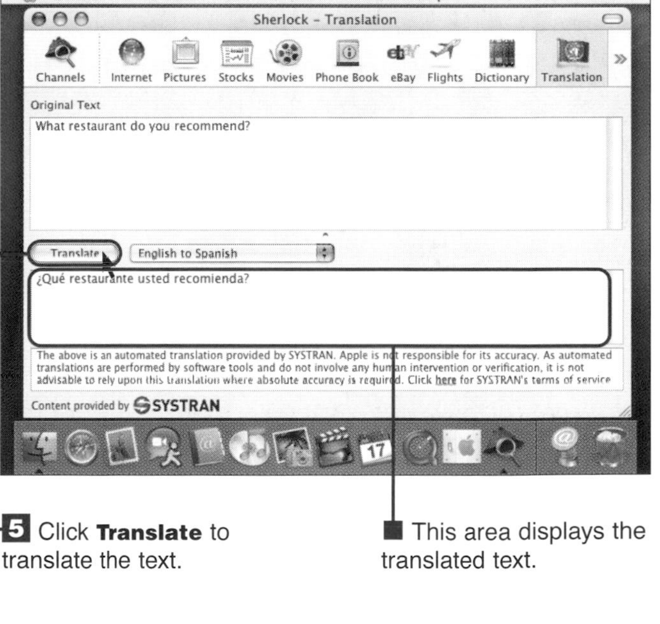

1 Click **Translation** to translate text.

2 Click this area and type the text you want to translate.

3 To specify the languages you want to use in the translation, click this area.

4 Click the option that specifies the language of the text you typed and the language you want to translate the text to.

5 Click **Translate** to translate the text.

■ This area displays the translated text.

CHAPTER 13

Exchange E-mail Using Mail

Mail allows you to exchange e-mail messages with people around the world. In this chapter, you will learn how to read, send and work with e-mail messages.

READ MESSAGES

You can use Mail to read the contents of your e-mail messages.

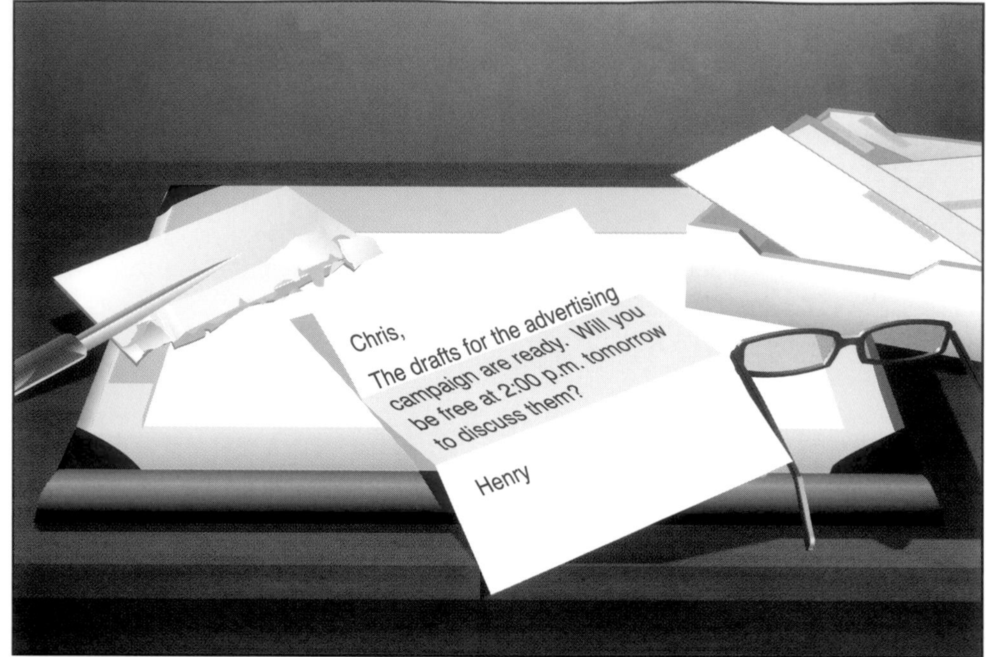

Chris,
The drafts for the advertising campaign are ready. Will you be free at 2:00 p.m. tomorrow to discuss them?
Henry

READ MESSAGES

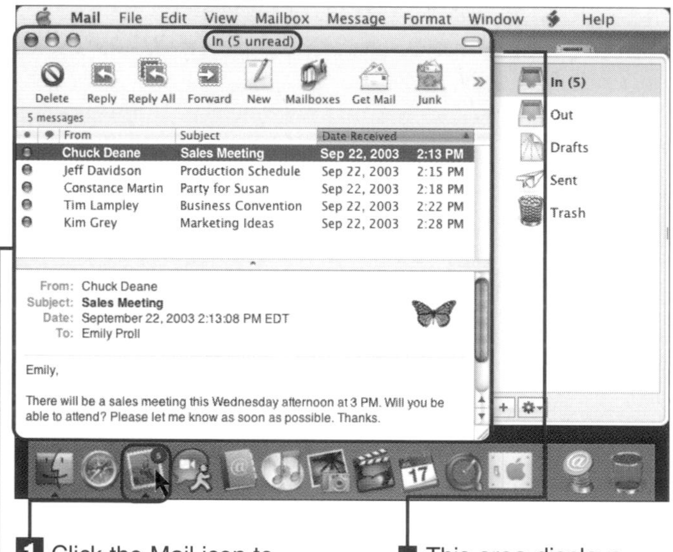

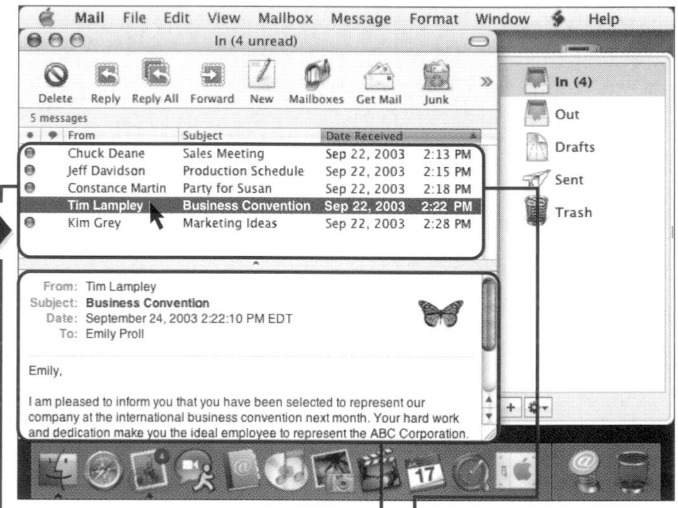

1 Click the Mail icon to start Mail.

■ A window appears, displaying the messages in the current mailbox.

■ This area displays the name of the current mailbox. If the mailbox contains unread messages, the number of unread messages in the mailbox appears in brackets beside the mailbox name.

■ This area displays the messages in the current mailbox. Unread messages display a dot (●).

Note: Messages considered to be junk mail appear brown in color. For more information on junk mail, see page 282.

2 Click the message you want to read.

■ This area displays the contents of the message you selected.

■ To display the contents of another message, repeat step **2**.

What mailboxes does Mail use to store my messages?

	In	Stores messages sent to you.
	Out	Temporarily stores messages that have not yet been sent.
	Drafts	Stores messages you have not yet completed.
	Sent	Stores copies of messages you have sent.
	Trash	Stores messages you have deleted.

Note: Mail creates the Trash mailbox the first time you delete a message.

Can I sort my messages?

Yes. You can sort your messages by name, subject or date received. To sort your messages, click the heading for the column you want to use to sort the messages. To sort the messages in the reverse order, you can click the heading again.

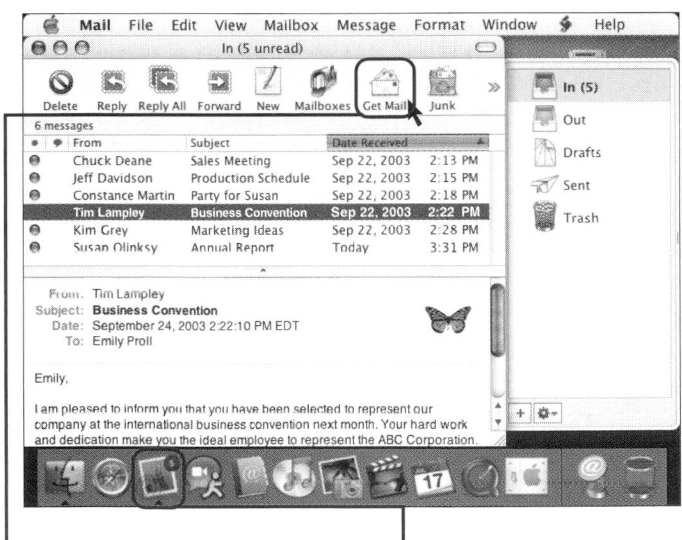

GET NEW MESSAGES

1 Click **Get Mail** to immediately check for new messages.

Note: When you are connected to the Internet, Mail automatically checks for new messages every five minutes.

■ When you have new messages, the Mail icon indicates the total number of new messages.

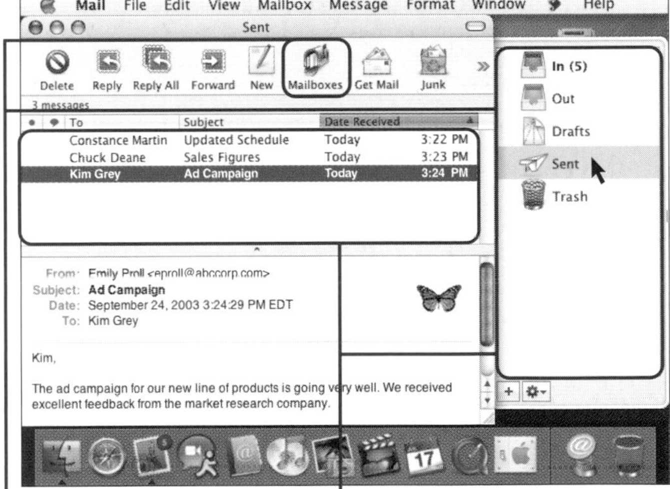

SWITCH BETWEEN MAILBOXES

■ The Mailbox drawer displays a list of mailboxes.

■ To hide or display the Mailbox drawer at any time, click **Mailboxes**.

Note: If you cannot see the Mailbox drawer, reduce the size of the window. To resize a window, see page 13.

1 Click the mailbox that contains the messages you want to view.

■ The messages in the mailbox you selected appear.

SEND A MESSAGE

You can send a message to express an idea or request information.

To practice sending a message, you can send a message to yourself.

SEND A MESSAGE

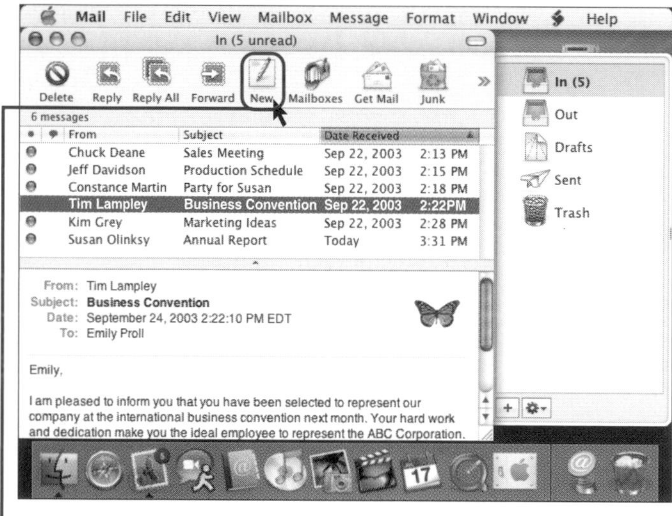

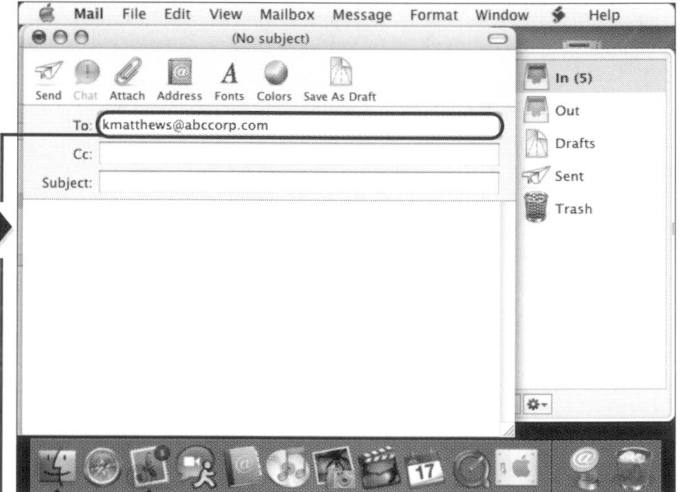

1 Click **New** to create a new message.

■ The New Message window appears.

2 Type the e-mail address of the person you want to receive the message.

Note: If you start typing the name or e-mail address of a person in Address Book, Mail will automatically complete the person's e-mail address for you. Press the return *key to accept Mail's suggestion. To add a person to Address Book, see page 116.*

How can I express emotions in my e-mail messages?

You can use special characters, called emoticons, to express emotions in e-mail messages. These characters resemble human faces if you turn them sideways. Emoticons are also called smileys.

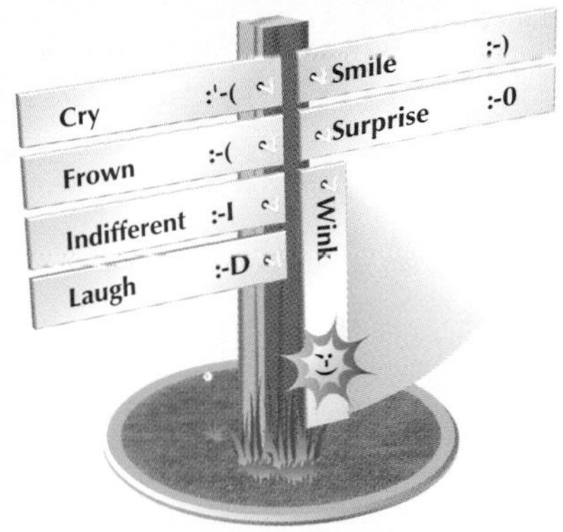

Can Mail help me correct a spelling error in a message?

Yes. To get help correcting a spelling error in a message, press and hold down the control key as you click the misspelled word. A menu appears, displaying suggestions to correct the spelling error. Click the suggestion you want to use to correct the spelling error.

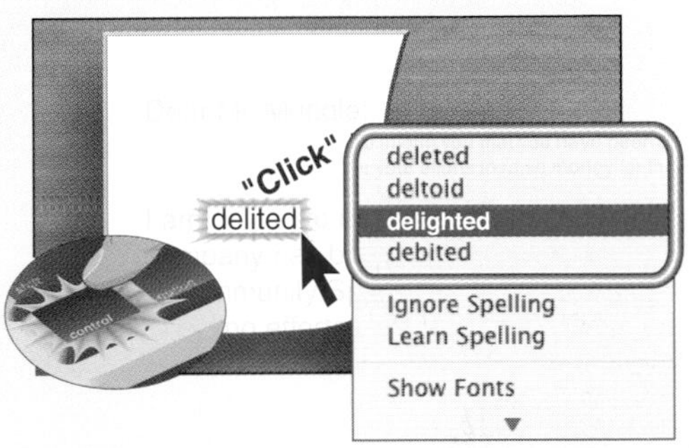

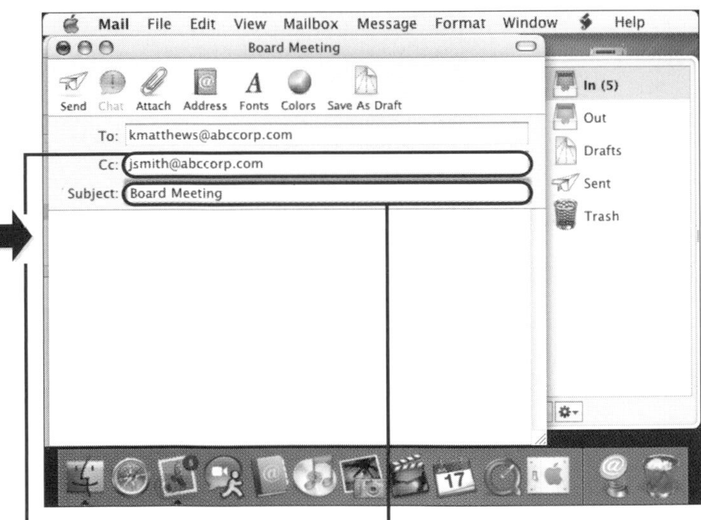

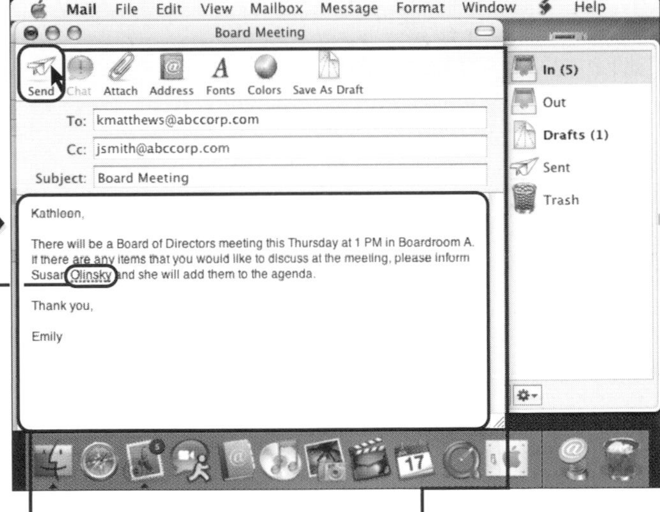

3 To send a copy of the message to a person who is not directly involved but would be interested in the message, click this area and then type the person's e-mail address.

Note: To send the message to more than one person in step **2** *or* **3**, *separate each e-mail address with a comma (,).*

4 Click this area and then type the subject of the message.

5 Click this area and then type the message.

■ Mail checks your spelling as you type and displays a dotted red underline under potential spelling errors. The person who receives the message will not see the dotted red underlines.

6 Click **Send** to send the message.

■ Mail sends the message and stores a copy of the message in the Sent mailbox.

SELECT A NAME FROM ADDRESS BOOK

When sending a message, you can select the name of the person you want to receive the message from Address Book.

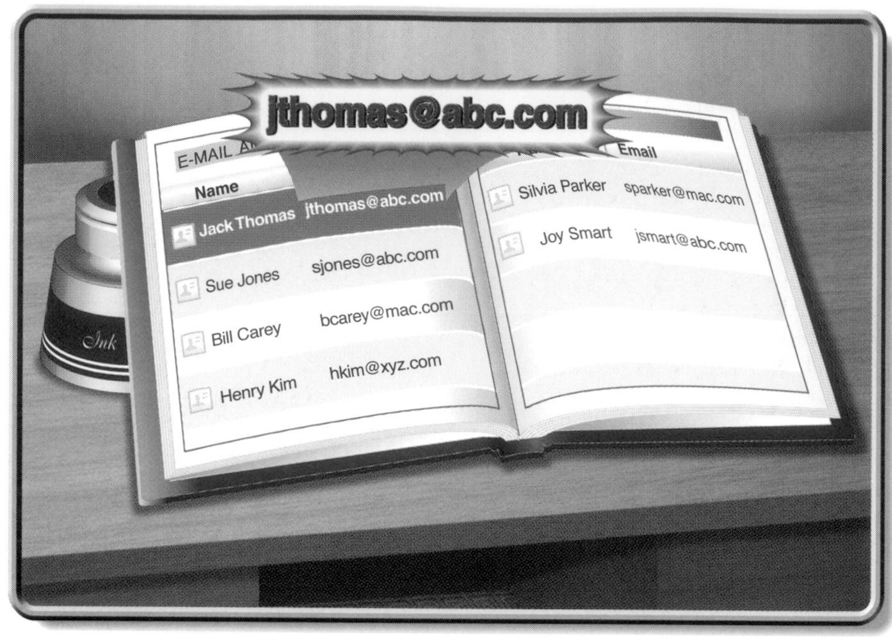

Address Book allows you to store information about people you frequently contact. To send a message to a person in Address Book, you must have entered an e-mail address for the person in Address Book. To add a person to Address Book, see page 116.

SELECT A NAME FROM ADDRESS BOOK

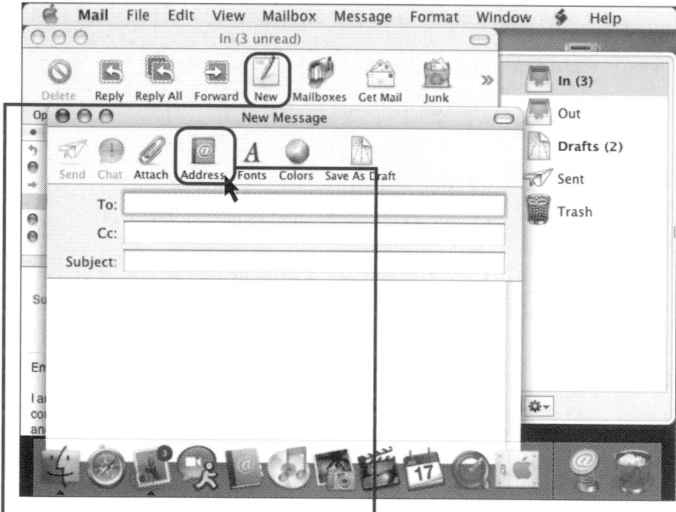

1 Click **New** to create a new message.

■ The New Message window appears.

2 Click **Address** to select a name from Address Book.

■ The Addresses window appears.

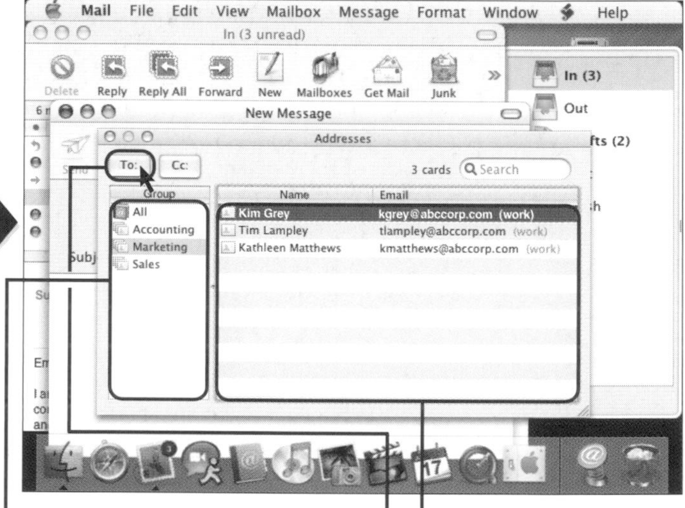

3 Click the group that contains the person you want to receive the message.

■ To send the message to every person in a group, click the group and then skip to step **5**.

Note: The All group contains all the people you have added to Address Book.

4 Click the name of the person you want to receive the message.

5 Click **To:**.

■ You can repeat steps **4** and **5** for each person you want to receive the message.

I accidentally selected a name from Address Book. How can I remove the name from the message?

To remove the name of a person you accidentally selected from Address Book, you must first select the name. If the person's name and e-mail address appear, drag the mouse I over the information until the information is highlighted. If the person's name appears in a blue oval, click the oval to select the oval. Press the delete key to remove the information you selected.

The person I want to select does not appear in Address Book. How can I quickly add the person to Address Book?

You can quickly add the name and e-mail address of a person who sent you an e-mail message to Address Book. Click a message you received from the person you want to add to Address Book and then press and hold down the ⌘ key as you press the Y key. The person's name and e-mail address will now appear in Address Book.

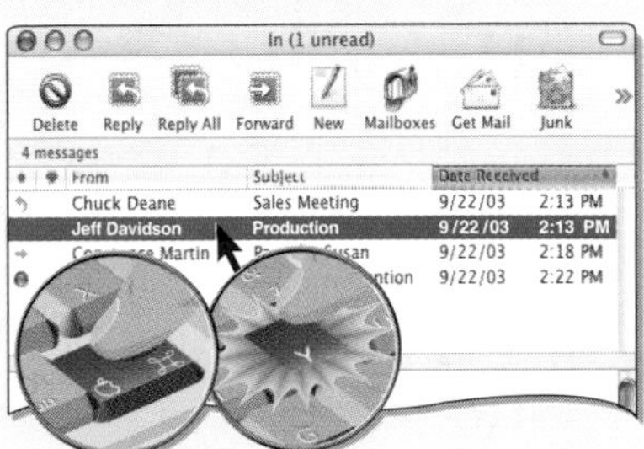

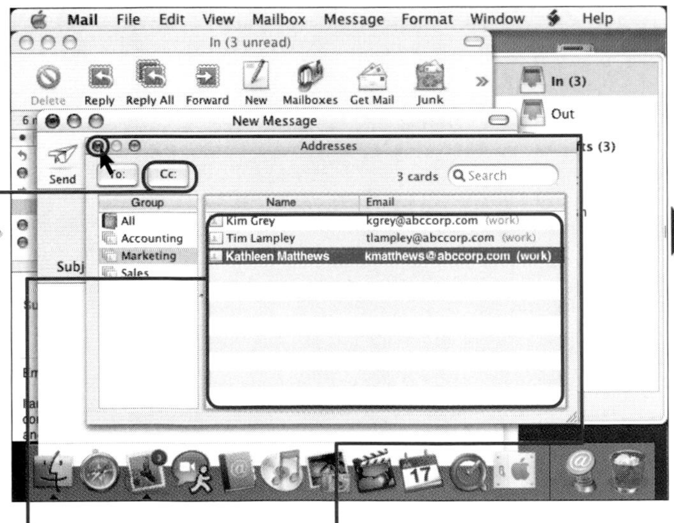

6 To send a copy of the message to a person who is not directly involved but would be interested in the message, click the name of the person.

7 Click **Cc:**.

■ You can repeat steps **6** and **7** for each person you want to receive a copy of the message.

8 When you finish selecting names from Address Book, click ● to close the Addresses window.

■ This area displays the name of each person you selected from Address Book. The name may appear in a blue oval or may include the person's e-mail address.

■ You can now finish composing the message.

*Note: To finish composing a message, perform steps **4** to **6** on page 271.*

SAVE A DRAFT OF A MESSAGE

If you are not ready to send a message, you can save a draft of the message so you can finish the message at a later time.

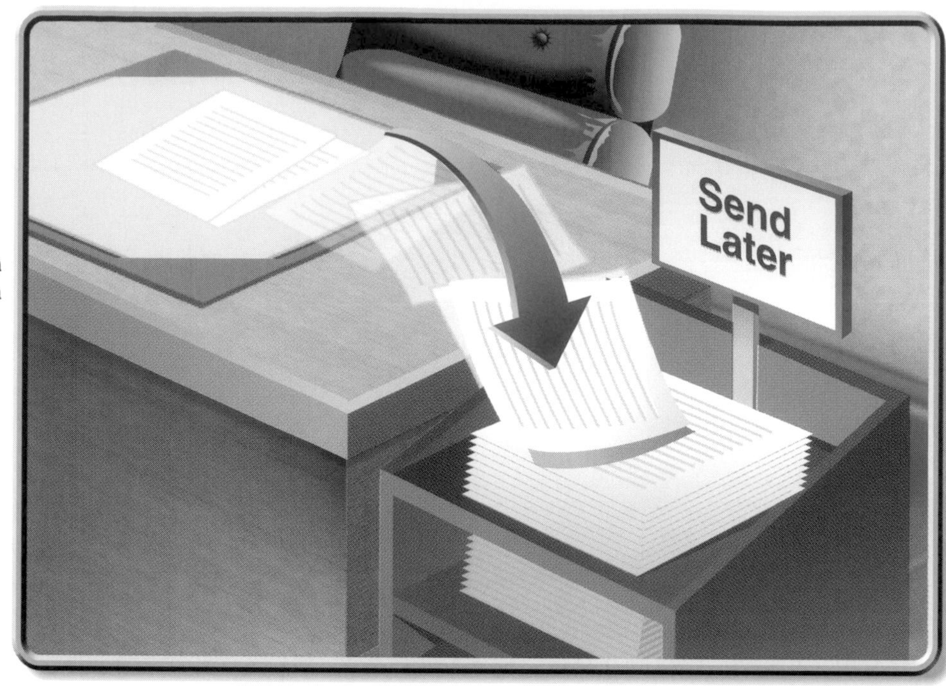

Saving a draft of a message allows you to later review and make changes to the message.

SAVE A DRAFT OF A MESSAGE

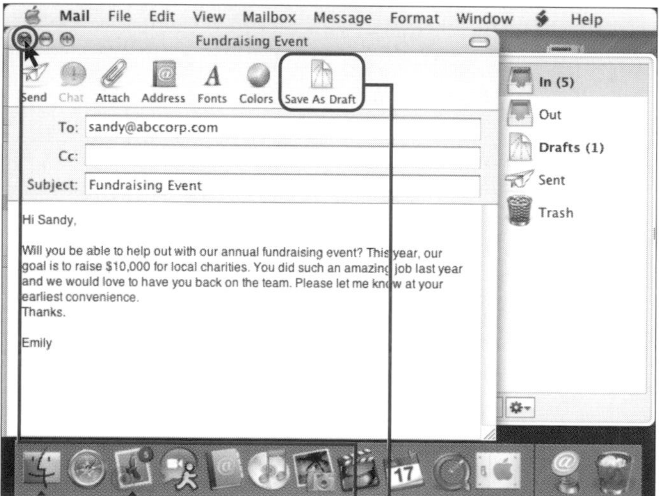

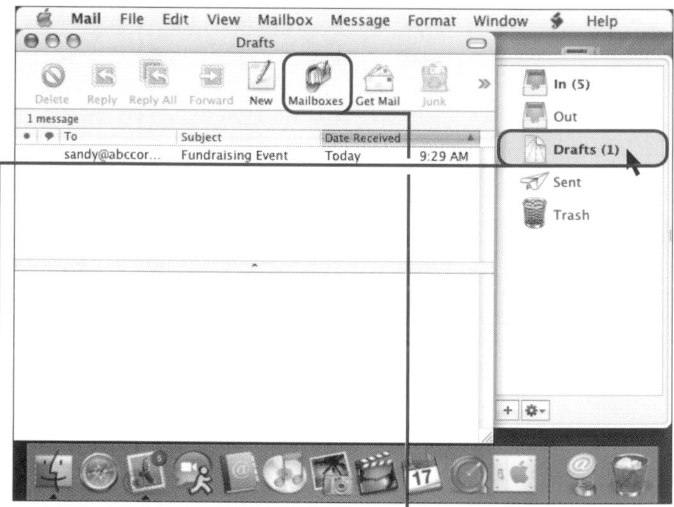

1 To create a message, perform steps **1** to **5** starting on page 270.

2 Click **Save As Draft** to save the message as a draft so you can send the message at a later time.

3 Click ● to close the message window.

SEND A DRAFT MESSAGE

■ When you save a draft of a message, Mail stores the message in the Drafts mailbox until you are ready to send the message.

1 Click **Drafts** to display the messages in the Drafts mailbox.

■ If the list of mailboxes is not displayed, click **Mailboxes** to display the list.

Note: You may also need to reduce the size of the window to display the list of mailboxes.

How can I save time when typing a message?

You can use abbreviations for words and phrases to save time when typing messages. Here are some commonly used abbreviations.

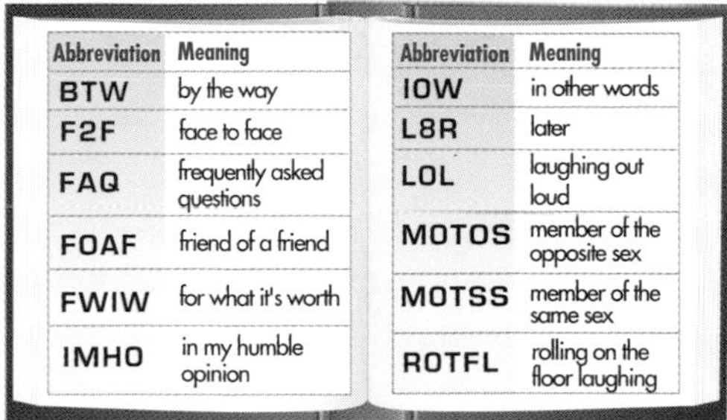

Abbreviation	Meaning
BTW	by the way
F2F	face to face
FAQ	frequently asked questions
FOAF	friend of a friend
FWIW	for what it's worth
IMHO	in my humble opinion

Abbreviation	Meaning
IOW	in other words
L8R	later
LOL	laughing out loud
MOTOS	member of the opposite sex
MOTSS	member of the same sex
ROTFL	rolling on the floor laughing

I no longer want to send a message I saved as a draft. How can I delete the message?

If you no longer want to send a message you saved as a draft, you can delete the message from the Drafts mailbox. To delete the message, click the message and then press the delete key.

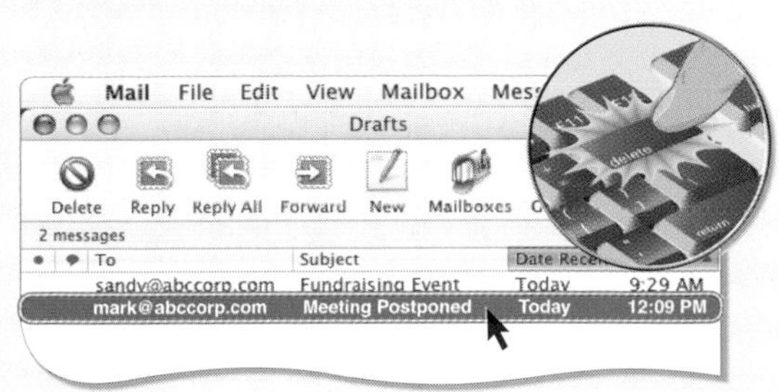

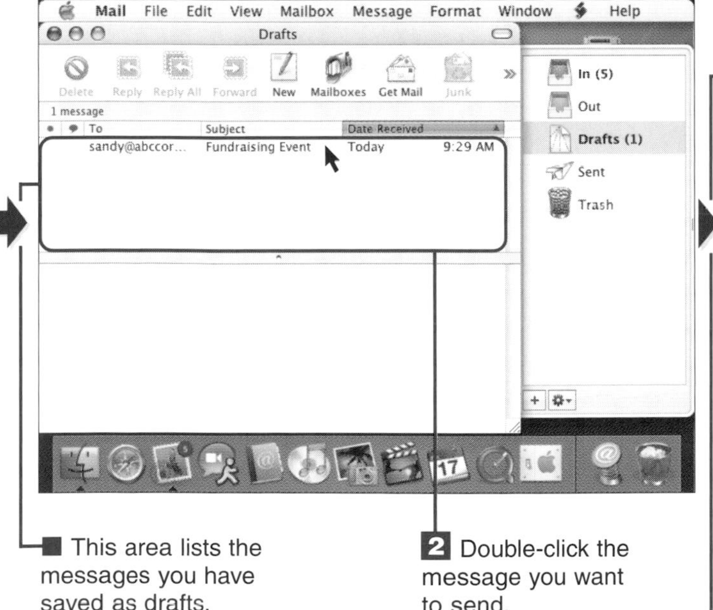

■ This area lists the messages you have saved as drafts.

2 Double-click the message you want to send.

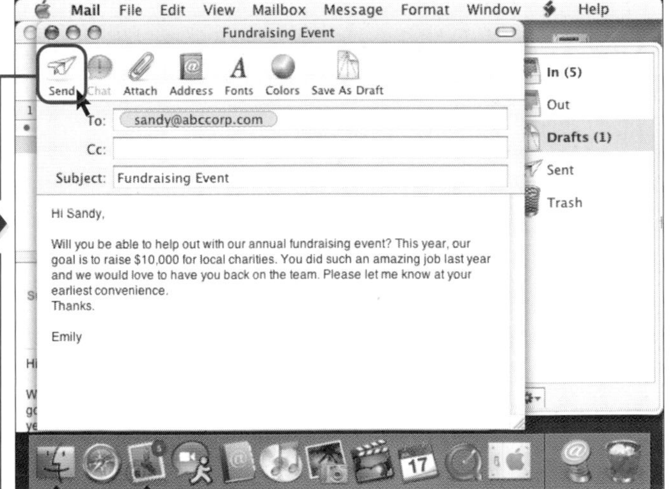

■ A window appears, displaying the contents of the message. You can review and make changes to the message.

3 To send the message, click **Send**.

■ After sending the message, Mail removes the message from the Drafts mailbox and places a copy of the message in the Sent mailbox.

REPLY TO A MESSAGE

You can reply to a message to answer a question, express an opinion or supply additional information.

When you reply to a message, Mail includes a copy of the original message to help the reader identify which message you are replying to. The original message appears in blue.

After you reply to a message, a curved arrow (↩) appears beside the message.

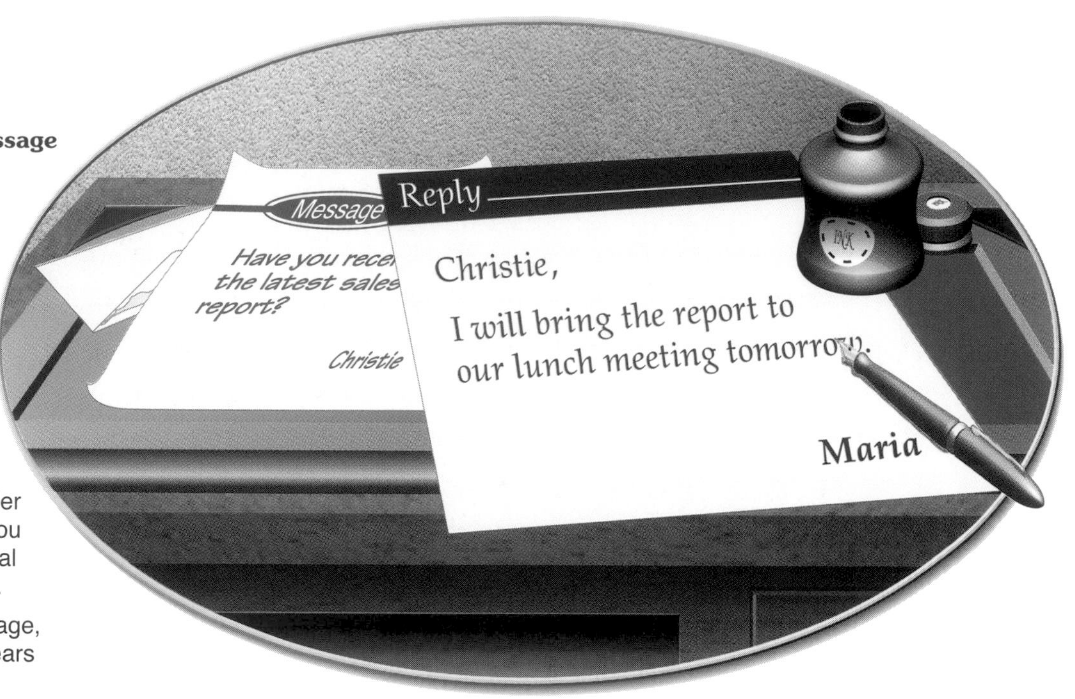

REPLY TO A MESSAGE

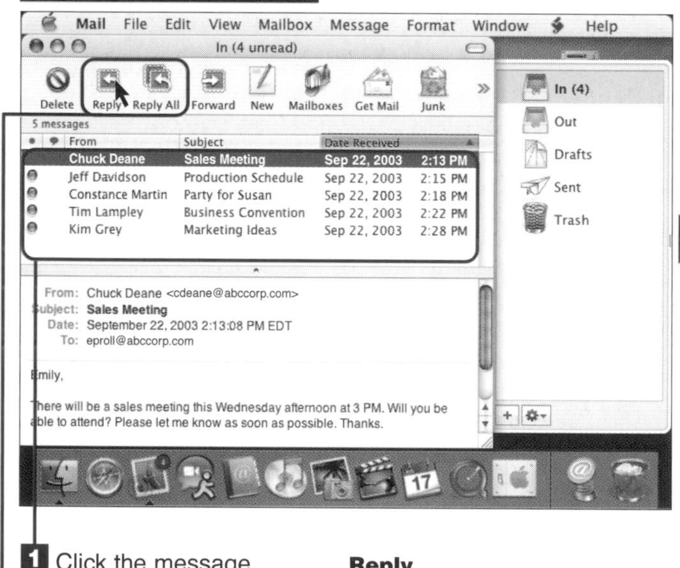

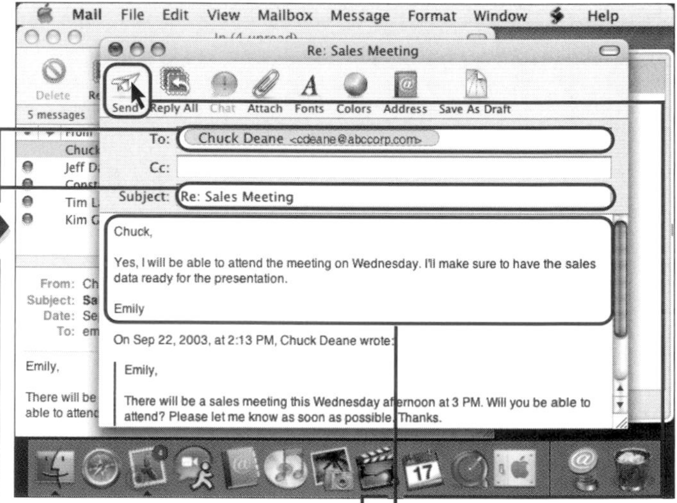

1 Click the message you want to reply to.

2 Click the reply option you want to use.

Reply
Sends a reply to only the author.

Reply All
Sends a reply to the author and everyone who received the original message.

■ A window appears for you to compose your reply.

■ Mail fills in the e-mail address(es) for you.

■ Mail also fills in the subject, starting the subject with **Re:**.

3 Click this area and then type your reply.

4 Click **Send** to send the reply.

■ Mail stores a copy of the message in the Sent mailbox.

FORWARD A MESSAGE

After reading a message, you can add comments and then forward the message to another person who would be interested in the message.

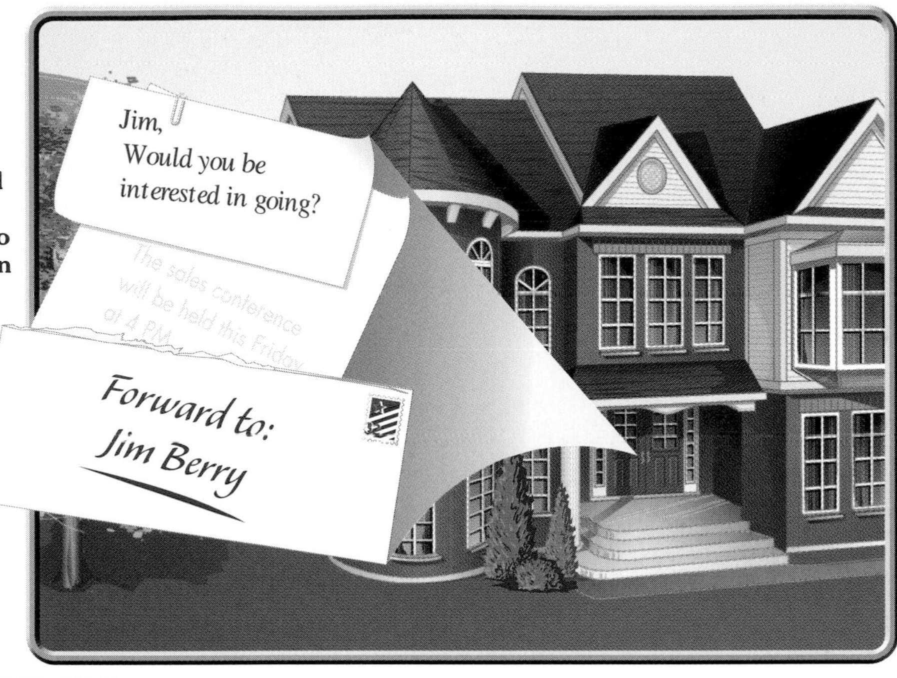

Jim,
Would you be interested in going?
The sales conference will be held this Friday at 4 PM.
Forward to:
Jim Berry

After you forward a message, an arrow (➡) appears beside the message.

FORWARD A MESSAGE

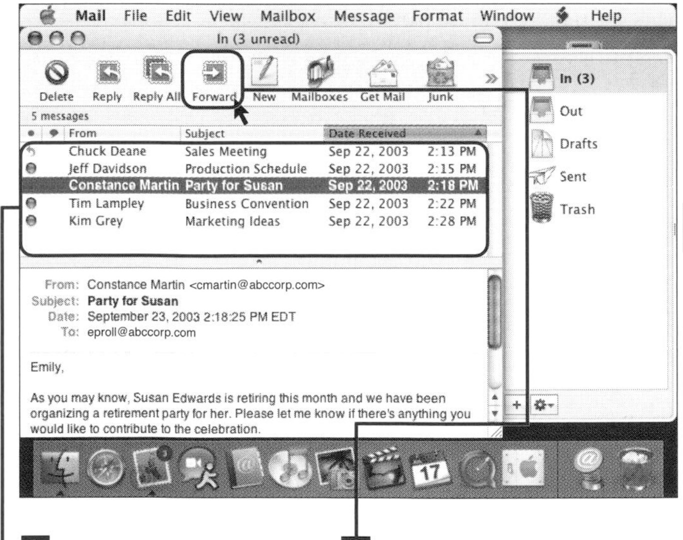

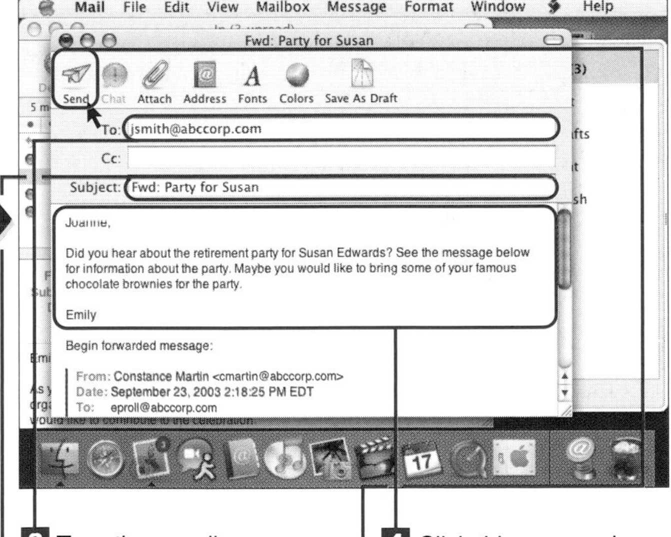

1 Click the message you want to forward.

2 Click **Forward**.

■ A window appears, displaying the contents of the message you are forwarding.

3 Type the e-mail address of the person you want to receive the message.

■ Mail fills in the subject for you, starting the subject with **Fwd:**.

4 Click this area and then type any comments about the message you are forwarding.

5 Click **Send** to forward the message.

PRINT A MESSAGE

You can produce a paper copy of a message.

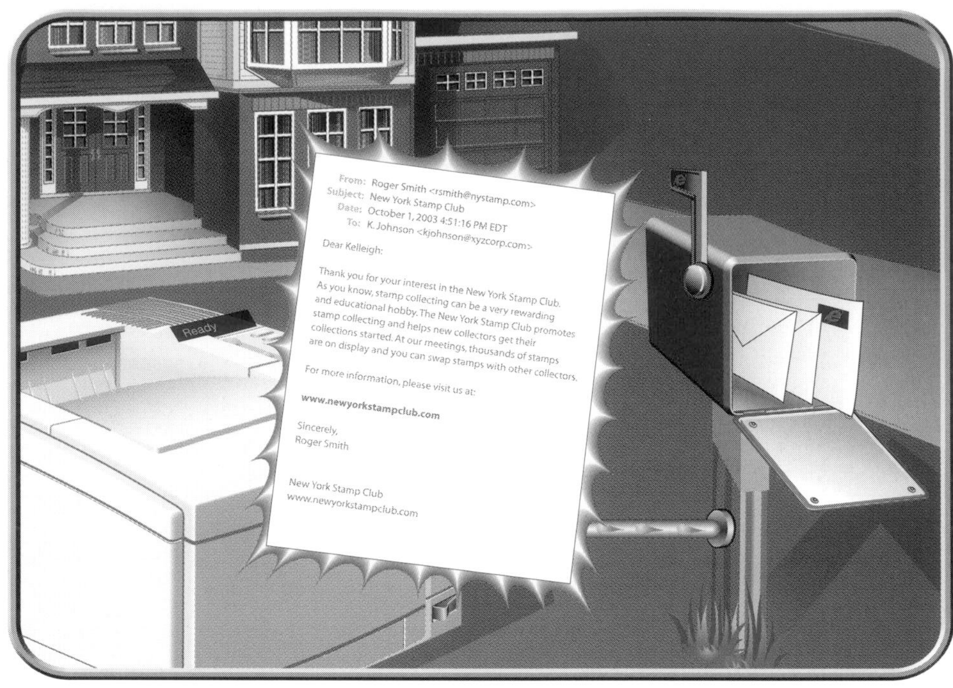

Before printing, make sure your printer is turned on and contains paper.

PRINT A MESSAGE

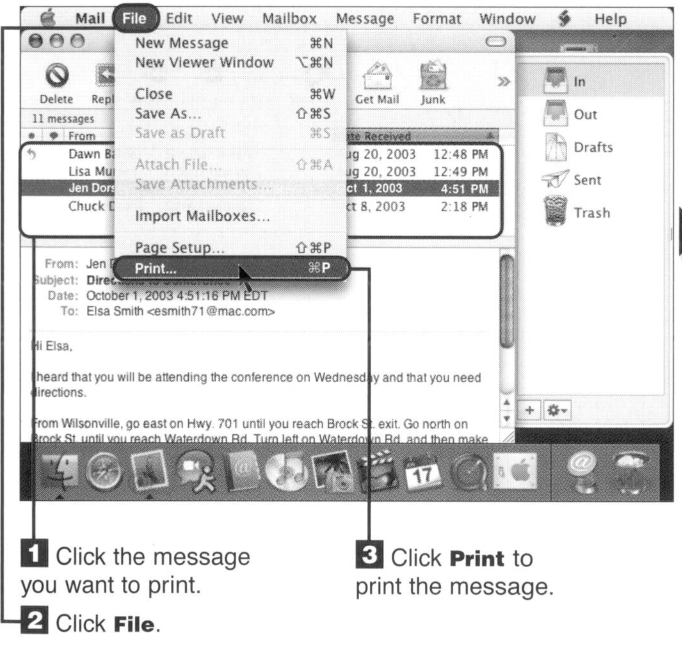

1 Click the message you want to print.

2 Click **File**.

3 Click **Print** to print the message.

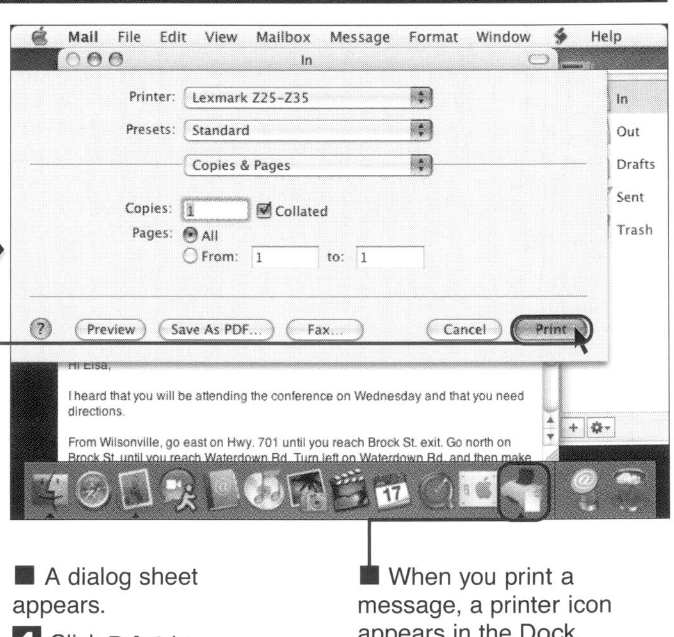

■ A dialog sheet appears.

4 Click **Print** to print the message.

■ When you print a message, a printer icon appears in the Dock. The icon disappears when the message has finished printing.

DELETE A MESSAGE

You can delete a message you no longer need. Deleting messages frees up storage space on your computer and helps prevent your mailboxes from becoming cluttered.

Chris,
The drafts for the advertising campaign are ready. Will you be free at 2:00 p.m. tomorrow to discuss them?
Henry
Messages

DELETE A MESSAGE

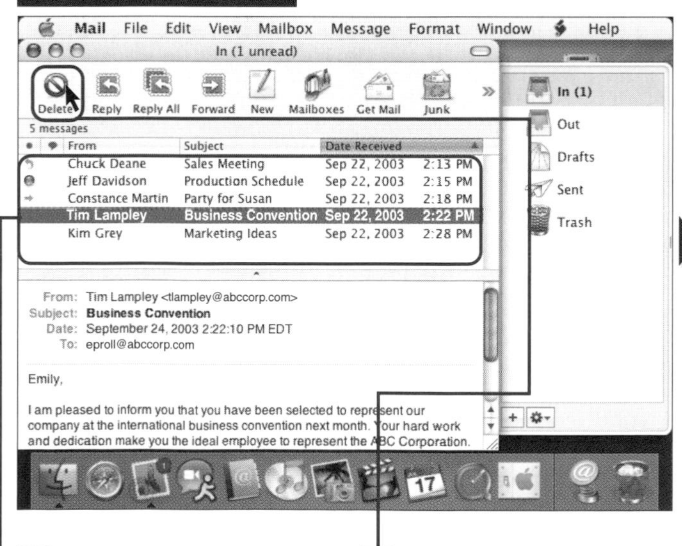

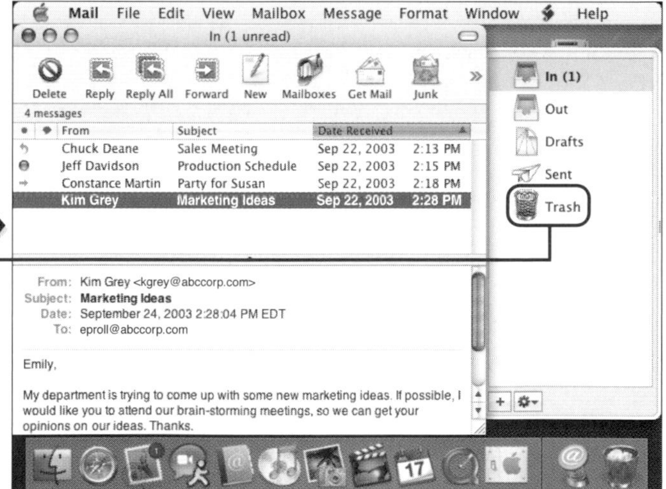

1 Click the message you want to delete.

2 Click **Delete** to delete the message.

■ Mail removes the message from the current mailbox and places the message in the Trash mailbox.

Note: Deleting a message from the Trash mailbox will permanently remove the message from your computer. To view the contents of the Trash mailbox, see page 269.

ATTACH A FILE TO A MESSAGE

You can attach a file to a message you are sending. Attaching a file to a message is useful when you want to include additional information with the message.

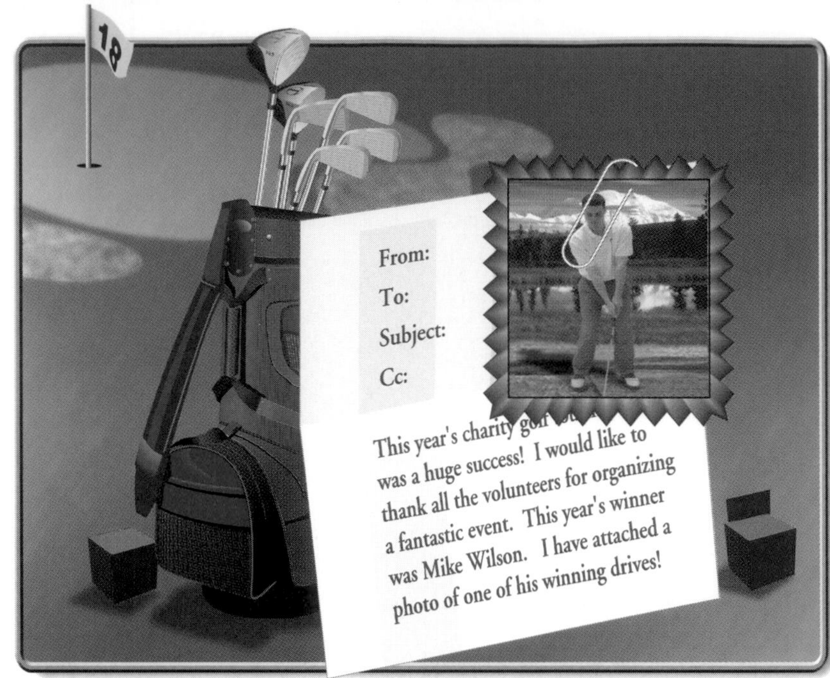

From:
To:
Subject:
Cc:
This year's charity golf ... was a huge success! I would like to thank all the volunteers for organizing a fantastic event. This year's winner was Mike Wilson. I have attached a photo of one of his winning drives!

You can attach many types of files to a message, including documents, pictures, videos and sounds. The computer receiving the message must have the necessary software installed to display or play the file you attach.

ATTACH A FILE TO A MESSAGE

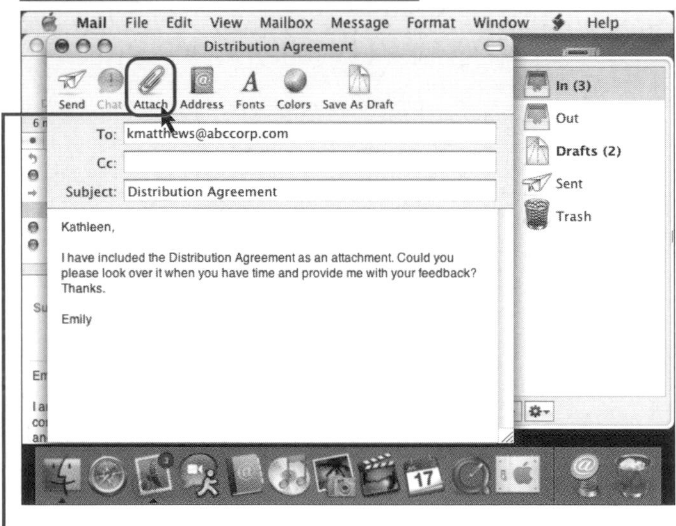

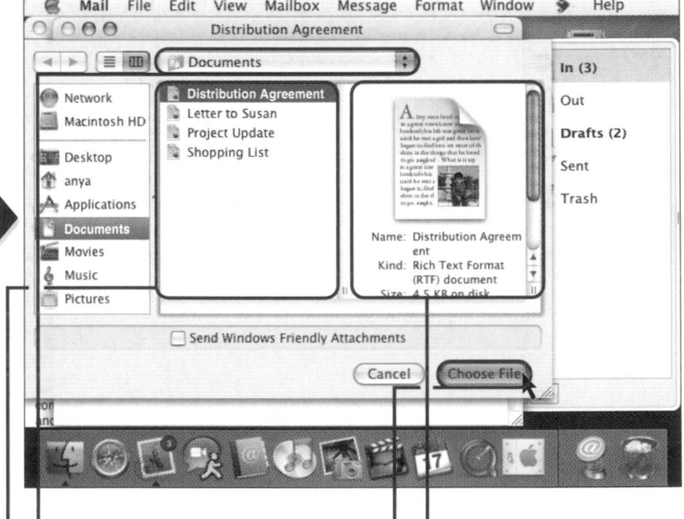

1 To create a message, perform steps **1** to **5** starting on page 270.

2 Click **Attach** to attach a file to the message.

■ A dialog sheet appears.

■ This area shows the location for the displayed files. You can click this area to change the location.

3 Click the name of the file you want to attach to the message.

■ This area displays information about the file you selected.

4 Click **Choose File** to attach the file to the message.

Can I attach a large file to a message?

The company that provides your e-mail account may limit the size of the messages that you can send and receive over the Internet. Most companies do not allow you to send or receive messages larger than 2 MB, which includes all attached files. Some companies provide premium services you can purchase that will allow you to send and receive messages larger than 2 MB.

How can I remove a file I accidentally attached to a message?

To remove a file you accidentally attached to a message, click the icon for the file you want to remove and then press the delete key. The file disappears from the message.

Note: To remove a picture, click the picture in the message and then press the delete key.

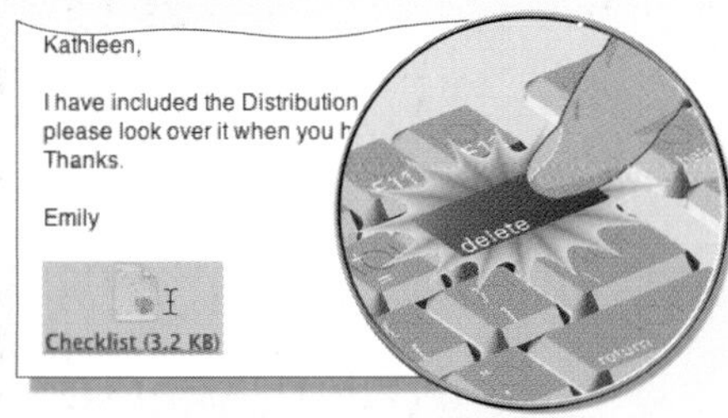

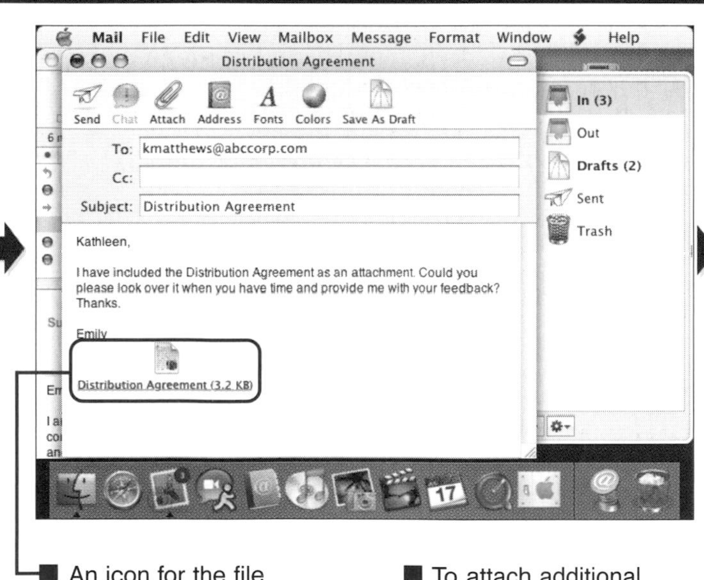

■ An icon for the file appears in the message.

Note: If you attached a picture to the message, the picture appears in the message.

■ To attach additional files to the message, perform steps **2** to **4** for each file you want to attach.

5 Click **Send** to send the message.

■ Mail sends the message and the attached files(s) to the e-mail address(es) you specified. Mail also stores a copy of the message in the Sent mailbox.

SORT JUNK MAIL

Mail can examine messages you receive to determine if the messages are junk mail.

By default, Mail changes the color of potential junk e-mail messages to brown so you can easily recognize junk mail when reading your messages.

You can mark messages as junk mail to help Mail learn how to identify junk e-mail. You can also have Mail automatically move new junk mail you receive to the Junk mailbox.

SORT JUNK MAIL

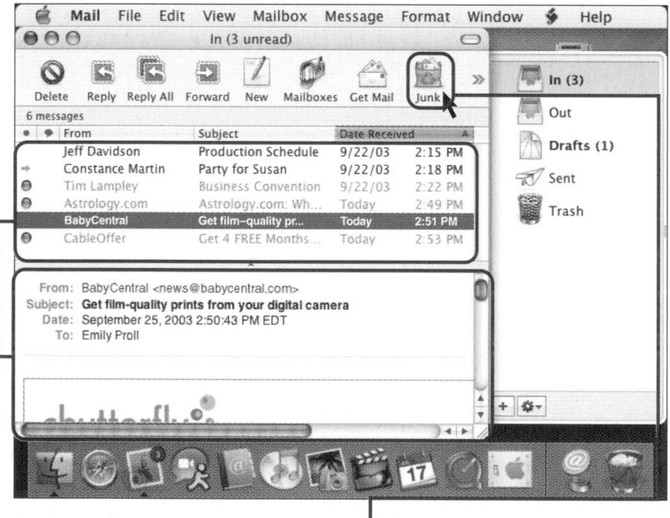

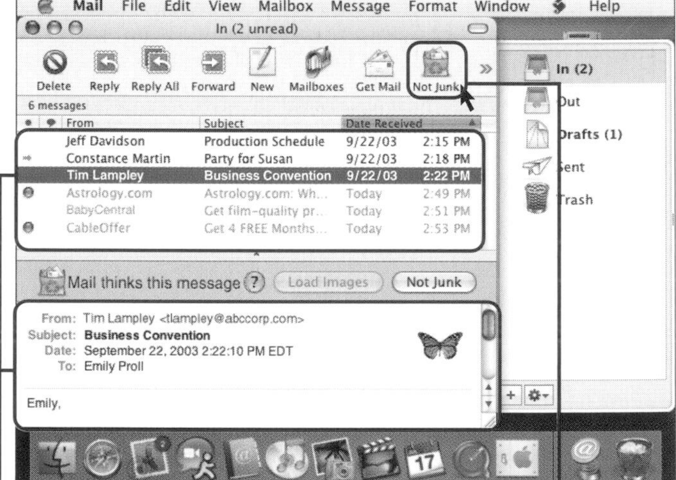

MARK A MESSAGE AS JUNK MAIL

1 Click the message you want to mark as junk mail.

■ This area displays the contents of the message.

2 Click **Junk**.

■ The message will appear brown in color.

*Note: The first time you mark a message as junk mail, a dialog box appears, providing information about junk mail. To close the dialog box, click **OK**.*

MARK A MESSAGE AS NOT JUNK MAIL

1 Click the message that Mail incorrectly identified as junk mail.

■ This area displays the contents of the message.

Note: A bar appears at the top of the message, indicating that Mail thinks the message is junk mail.

2 Click **Not Junk**.

■ The message will no longer appear brown in color.

Can I stop Mail from identifying and sorting junk mail?

Yes. You can turn off the junk mail feature to stop Mail from automatically identifying and sorting junk mail. To turn off the junk mail feature, perform steps **1** to **3** on page 283 to access your Mail preferences. Click **Enable Junk Mail filtering** to turn off the junk mail feature (☑ changes to ☐).

Can I permanently erase the contents of the Junk mailbox?

Yes. You can erase the contents of the Junk mailbox to delete all the junk e-mail messages it contains from your computer. Click the **Mailbox** menu and then click **Erase Junk Mail**. In the confirmation dialog box that appears, click **Yes** to erase all the junk mail in your Junk mailbox.

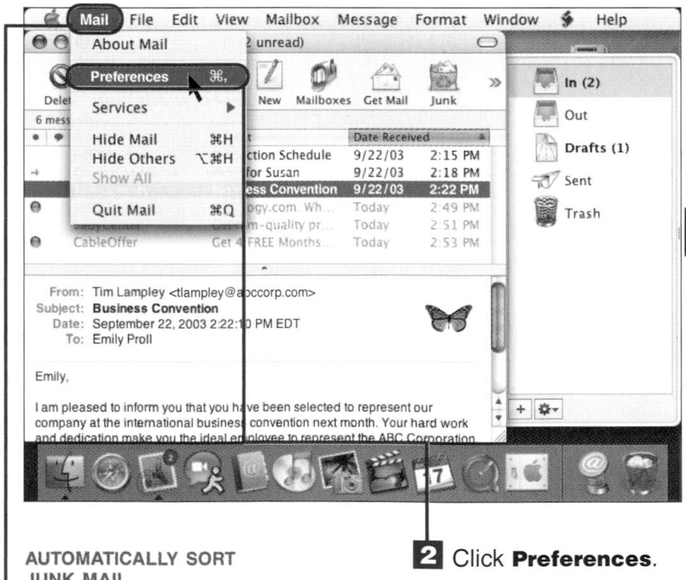

AUTOMATICALLY SORT JUNK MAIL

1 To have Mail create a Junk mailbox and automatically move junk mail to the Junk mailbox, click **Mail**.

2 Click **Preferences**.

■ A window appears, allowing you to change your Mail preferences.

3 Click **Junk Mail** to change your junk mail preferences.

4 Click this option to have Mail automatically move junk mail to the Junk mailbox (○ changes to ◉).

5 A dialog box appears, asking if you want to move all junk e-mail messages to the Junk mailbox now. Click **Yes** or **No** to continue.

6 Click ● to close the window.

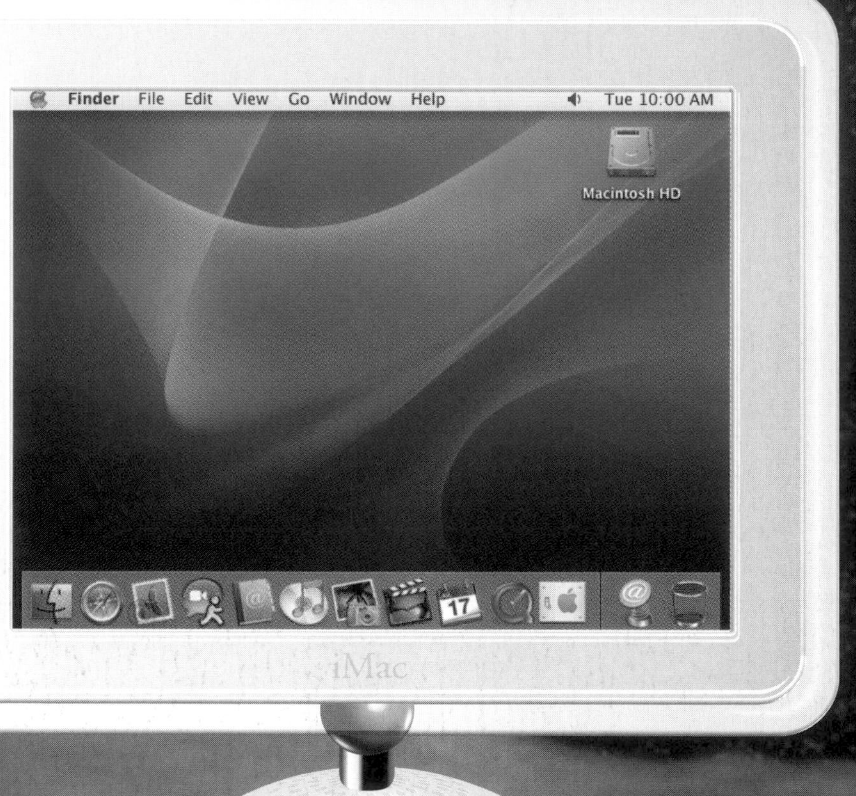
Finder File Edit View Go Window Help
Tue 10:00 AM
Macintosh HD
iMac

Buddy List
Lindsay Sandman
Available
Emily Johnson
Elsa Smith
Doug Gibson
Jack Smith
Tom Harris

CHAPTER 14

Exchange Instant Messages Using iChat

You can use iChat to exchange instant messages with your friends and family. This chapter shows you how to add a person to your Buddy List, send an instant message and send a file.

iChat

START iCHAT

You can use iChat to see when your friends are available and exchange instant messages and files with them.

START iCHAT

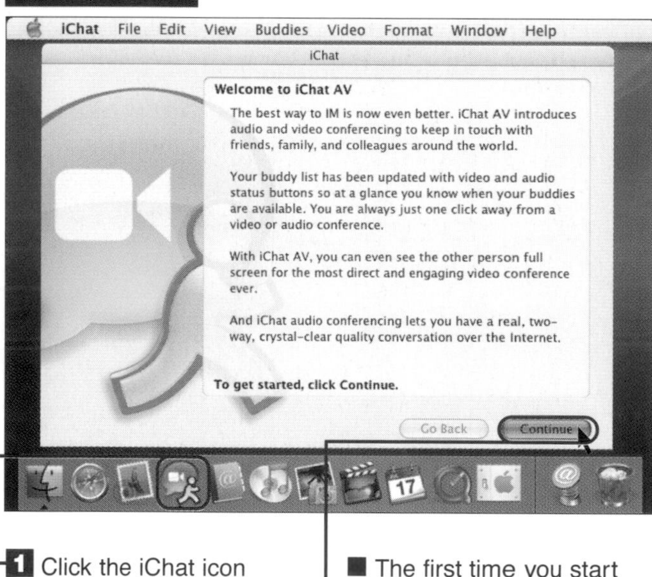

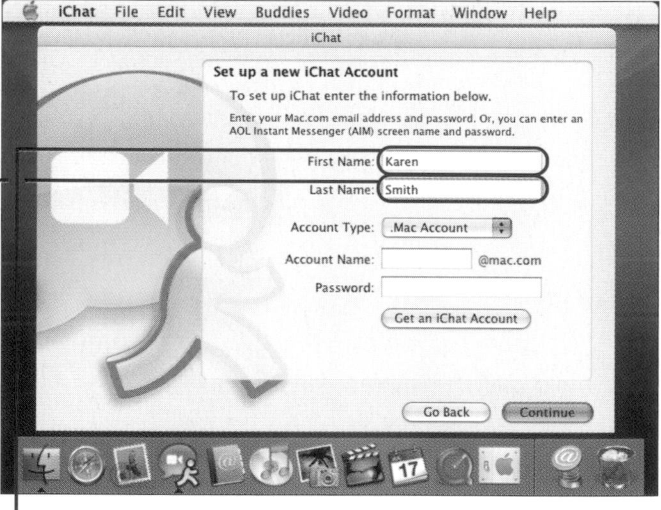

1 Click the iChat icon to start iChat.

■ The first time you start iChat, the iChat dialog box appears, allowing you to set up iChat.

2 Click **Continue**.

3 Click this area and type your first name.

4 Click this area and type your last name.

Note: Some or all of the information in the dialog box may already be filled in for you. To change existing information, drag the mouse ⌶ over the information until the information is highlighted. Then type the new information.

How do I obtain an account that I can use with iChat?

.Mac Account

You can use a .Mac account with iChat. If you do not have a .Mac account, click **Get an iChat Account** in the iChat dialog box. Your Web browser opens, displaying a Web page that allows you to obtain a .Mac account.

AIM Account

If you use the AIM (AOL Instant Messenger) application, you can use the screen name and password for your AIM account with iChat. If you use AOL (America Online) to access the Internet, you can use the screen name and password for your AOL account with iChat.

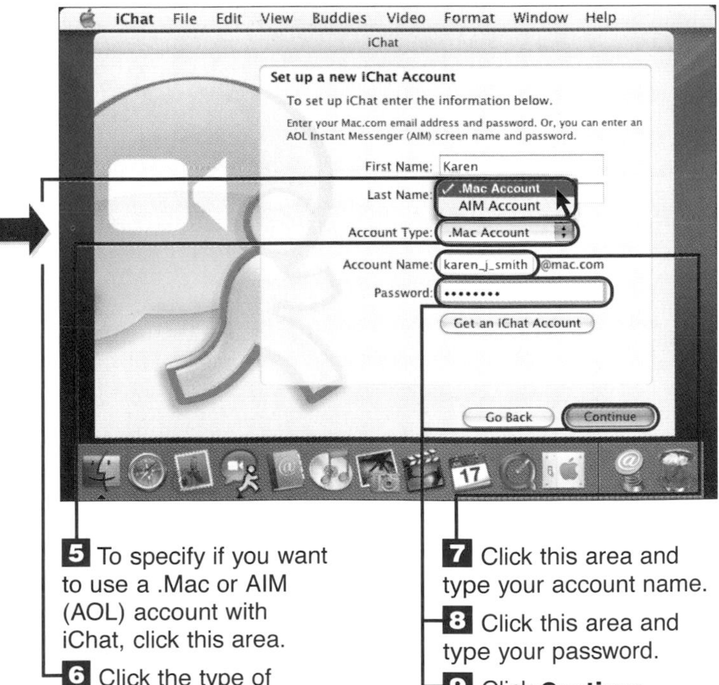

5 To specify if you want to use a .Mac or AIM (AOL) account with iChat, click this area.

6 Click the type of account you want to use.

7 Click this area and type your account name.

8 Click this area and type your password.

9 Click **Continue**.

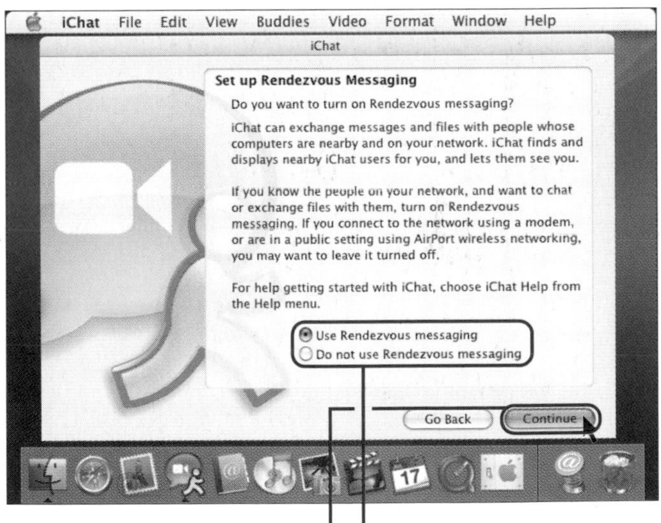

■ iChat asks if you want to turn on Rendezvous messaging. If you are connected to a network, Rendezvous messaging allows you to exchange messages with other people using iChat on the network.

10 Click an option to specify if you want to turn on Rendezvous messaging (○ changes to ◉).

11 Click **Continue**.

CONTINUED

START iCHAT

You can use iChat to talk to another person over the Internet. You can also view live video of the other person during a conversation.

Using iChat to talk to other people over the Internet allows you to avoid long-distance telephone charges.

START iCHAT (CONTINUED)

■ If your video camera is attached to the computer and turned on, this area displays the video area another person will see on their screen during a video chat.

*Note: If your computer does not support video chat, skip to step **13**.*

12 Position your camera until this area displays the video area you want other people to see.

13 Click **Continue**.

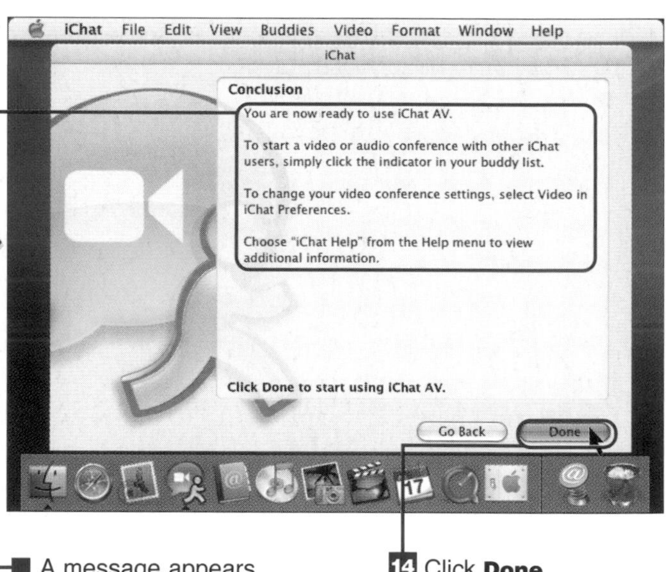

■ A message appears, stating that you are now ready to use iChat.

14 Click **Done**.

What hardware and software do I need to set up iChat for video chat?

To participate in a video chat with another person, your computer and the other person's computer must both be Macintosh G4 computers or G3 computers with at least a 600 MHz processor. Both your computer and the other person's computer must also have a video camera connected using a FireWire connection.

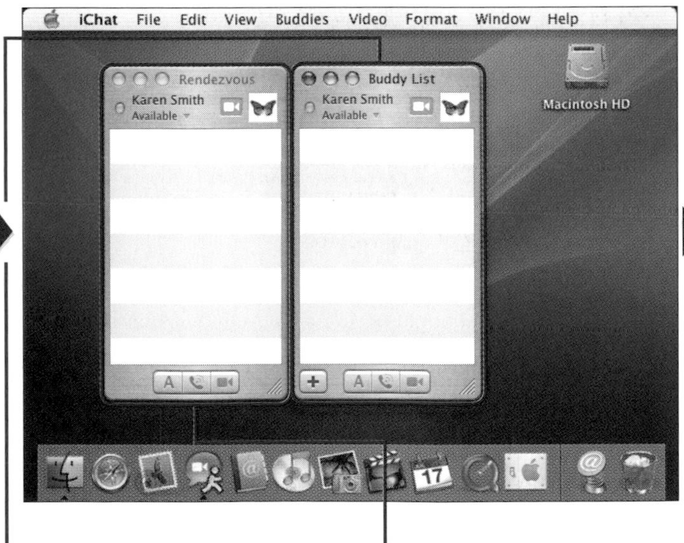

■ The Buddy List window appears. You can add people to your Buddy List so you can quickly send them instant messages.

Note: To add a person to your Buddy List, see page 290.

■ If you chose to turn on Rendezvous messaging in step **10**, the Rendezvous window also appears, displaying each person currently using iChat on your network.

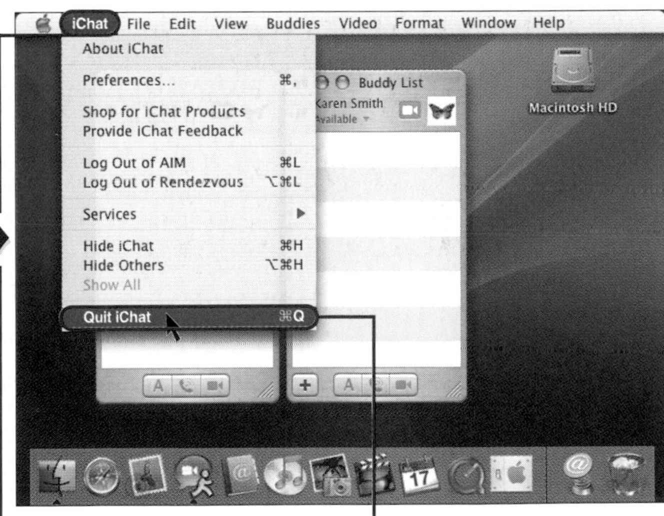

15 When you finish using iChat, click **iChat**.

16 Click **Quit iChat**.

ADD A PERSON TO YOUR BUDDY LIST

You can add a person to your Buddy List so you can see when the person is available to exchange instant messages.

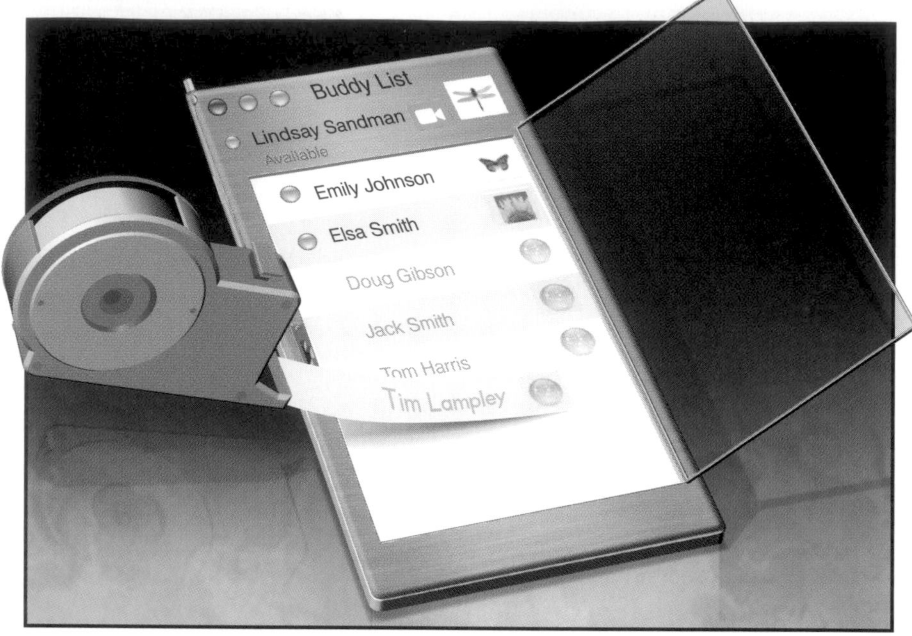

ADD A PERSON TO YOUR BUDDY LIST

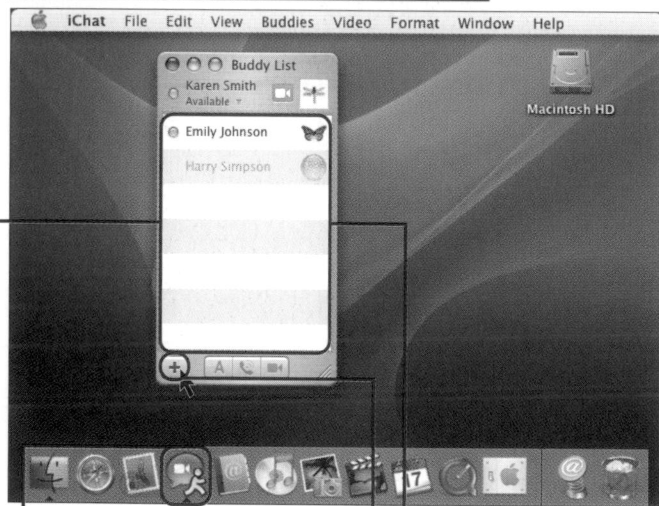

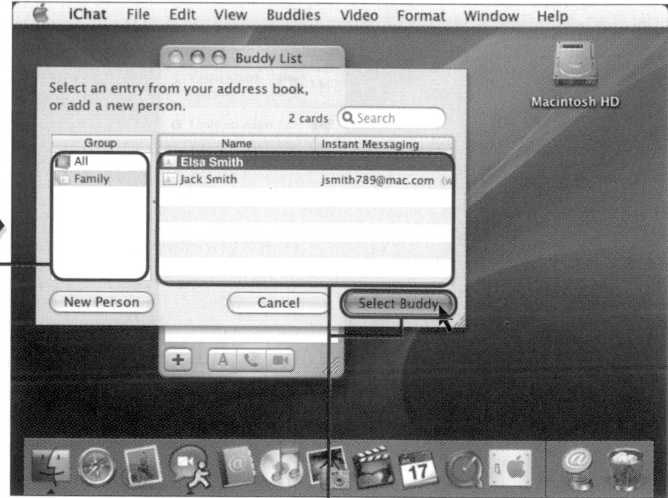

1 Click the iChat icon to start iChat.

■ The Buddy List window appears, displaying each person you have added to your Buddy List.

■ Each person who is available displays a green dot ( ). Each person who is not available appears dim or displays a red dot ( ).

2 Click + to add a person to your Buddy List.

■ A dialog sheet appears, listing the people in Address Book.

Note: For information on Address Book, see page 116.

3 Click the group that contains the person you want to add to your Buddy List.

Note: The All group contains all the people in Address Book.

4 Click the person you want to add to your Buddy List.

Note: If the person you want to add is not listed, see the top of page 291.

5 Click **Select Buddy**.

Can I add a person who is not listed in Address Book to my Buddy List?

Yes. Click + in the Buddy List window. In the dialog sheet that appears, click **New Person** and then perform steps **6** to **8** below. You can also enter the person's first name, last name and e-mail address to provide additional information for Address Book. Click **Add** to add the person to your Buddy List and to Address Book.

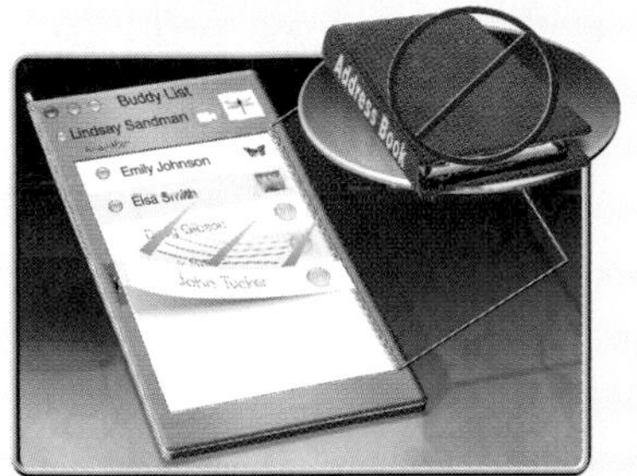

How do I remove a person from my Buddy List?

In the Buddy List window, click the name of the person you want to remove and then press the delete key. In the confirmation dialog sheet that appears, click **OK** to delete the person from your Buddy List.

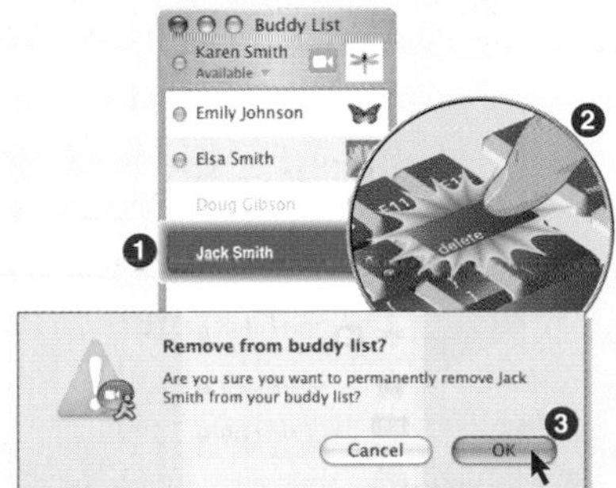

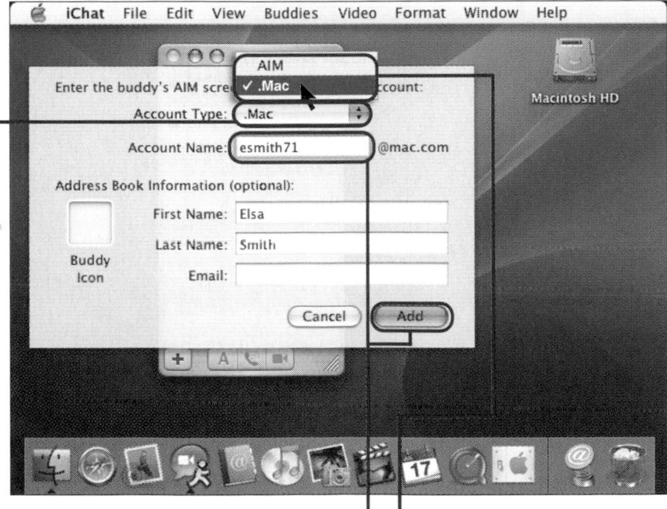

■ If Address Book does not contain an instant message account for the person, a dialog sheet appears, asking you to enter the person's account name.

6 Click this area to select the type of account the person uses.

7 Click an option to specify if the person uses a .Mac account or an AIM (AOL) account.

8 Click this area and type the person's account name.

9 Click **Add** to add the person to your Buddy List.

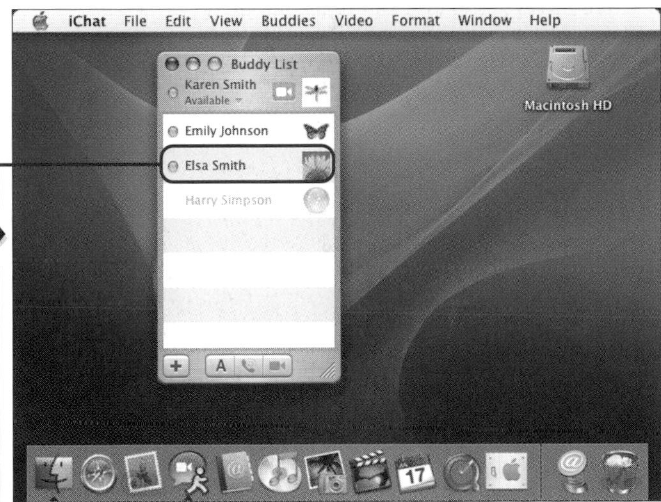

■ The person appears in your Buddy List.

SEND AN INSTANT MESSAGE

You can send an instant message to a person in your Buddy List.

When sending instant messages, never give out your password or credit card information.

SEND AN INSTANT MESSAGE

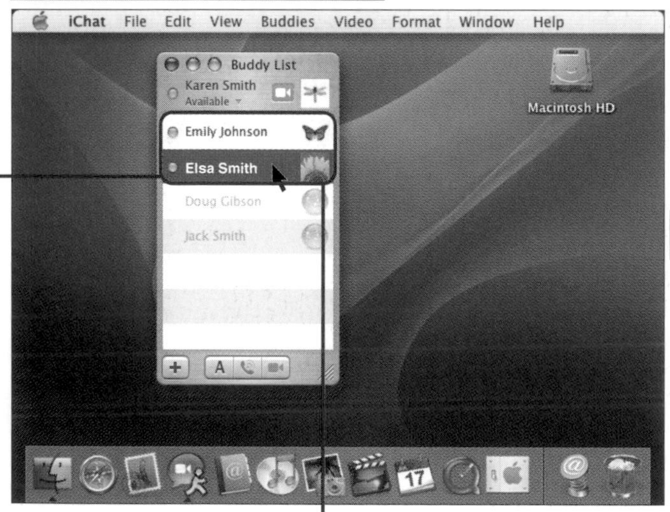

■ You can send an instant message to a person in your Buddy List who is available. A green dot (●) appears beside the name of each person who is available.

Note: To add a person to your Buddy List, see page 290.

1 Double-click the name of a person you want to send an instant message to.

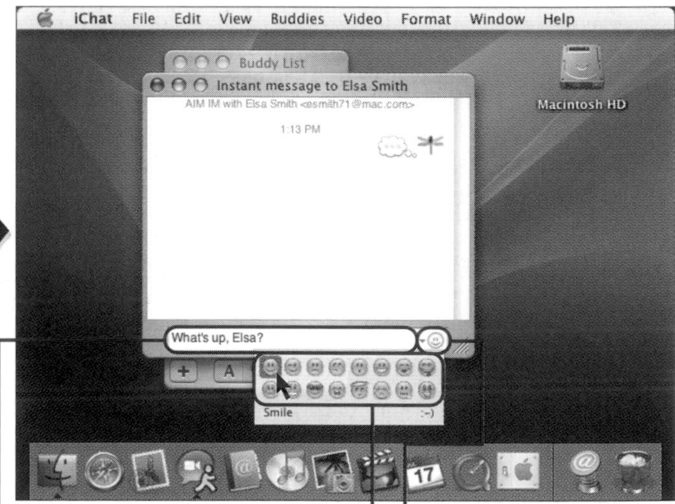

■ A chat window appears.

2 Click this area and type your message.

Note: To start a new paragraph while typing a message, press and hold down the option *key as you press the* return *key.*

3 To express an emotion in your message, click ☺.

4 Click the emoticon you want to include in your message.

5 To send the message, press the return key.

How can I start a video chat with another person in my Buddy List?

Both computers must support video and audio conferencing in iChat to start a video chat.

1 Click the name of the person you want to video chat with.

2 Click the video button to start a video chat.

■ A preview window appears, displaying what the other person will view on their screen.

Note: When the other person accepts your invitation to video chat, the other person's image appears on your screen.

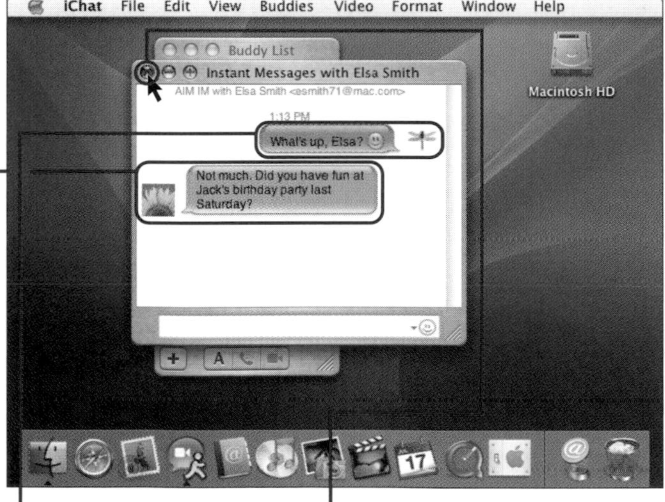

■ This area displays the message you sent.

■ The other person's response appears below the message you sent.

Note: While you or the other person type a message, a new icon with an empty balloon appears in the chat window.

6 When you finish exchanging instant messages, click the close button to close the chat window.

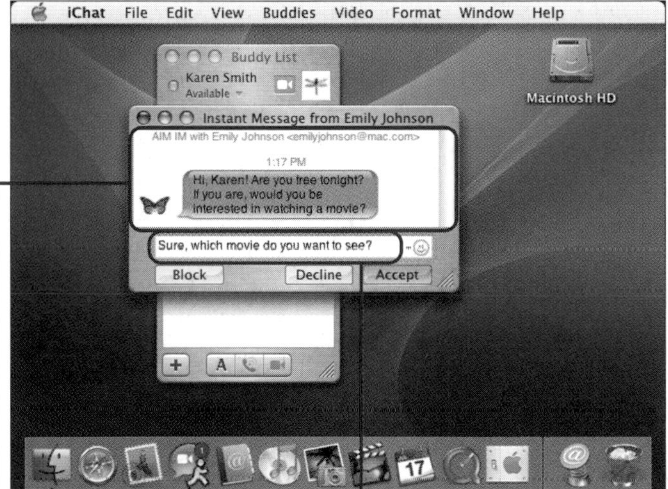

RECEIVE AN INSTANT MESSAGE

■ When you receive an instant message that is not part of an ongoing conversation, a window appears, displaying the message.

1 To respond to the message, click anywhere in the window.

■ An area appears, allowing you to type a reply.

2 Click this area and type your reply. Then press the return key.

SEND A FILE

While exchanging instant messages with another person, you can send the person a file.

You can send many types of files, including documents, pictures, videos and sounds. The computer receiving the file must have the necessary software installed to display or play the file.

There is no limit on the size of files you can send in your instant messages, but larger files will take longer to transfer.

SEND A FILE

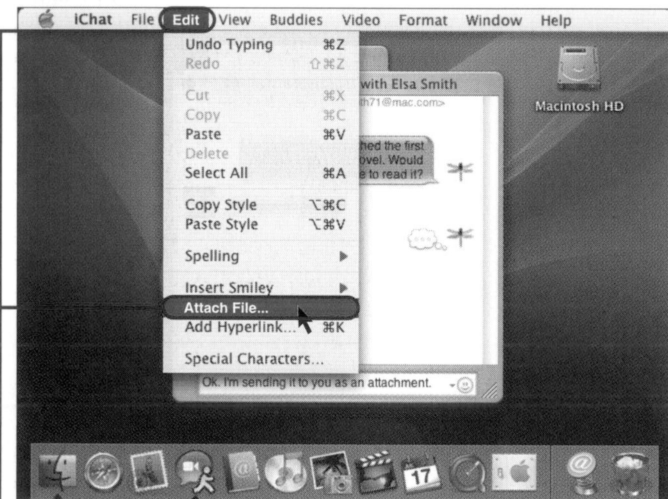

1 While exchanging instant messages with another person, click **Edit**.

2 Click **Attach File** to send a file.

Note: For information on sending instant messages, see page 292.

■ A dialog sheet appears.

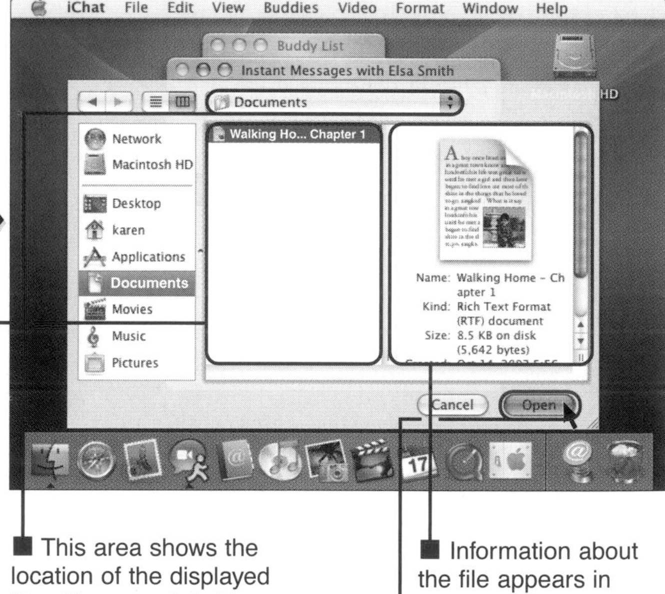

■ This area shows the location of the displayed files. You can click this area to change the location.

3 Click the name of the file you want to send.

■ Information about the file appears in this area.

4 Click **Open** to select the file.

How do I accept a file I receive?

To accept a file you receive, click the name of the file in the chat window. After Mac OS transfers the file to your computer, the Desktop window appears, displaying an icon for the file. You can double-click the icon to open the file. An icon for the file also appears on your desktop.

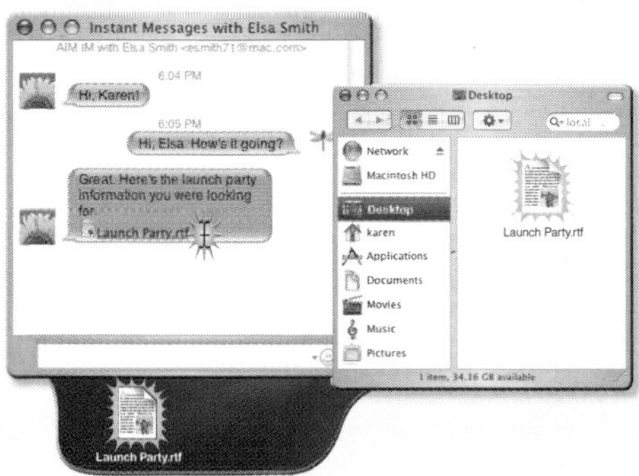

Is there another way to send a file?

Yes. To quickly send a file, click the area where you type your instant messages. Position the mouse over the file you want to send and then drag the file into the area. An icon for the file appears in the area. To send the file, press the return key.

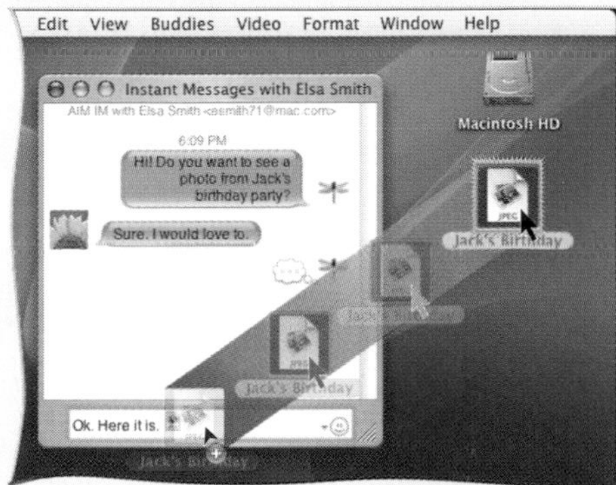

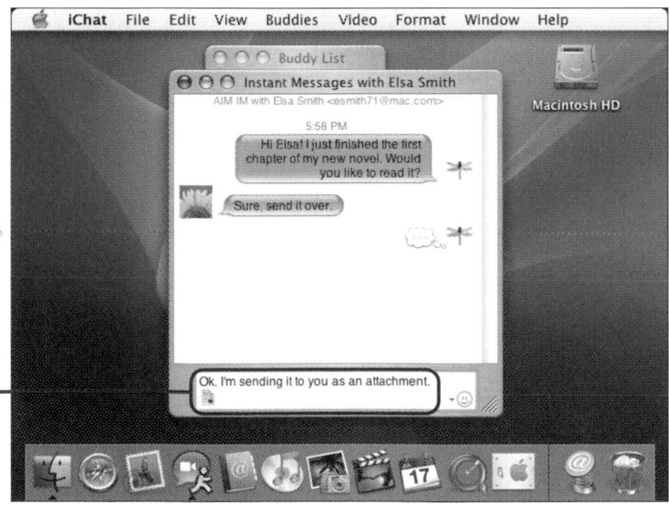

■ An icon for the file appears in this area.

5 To send the file, press the return key.

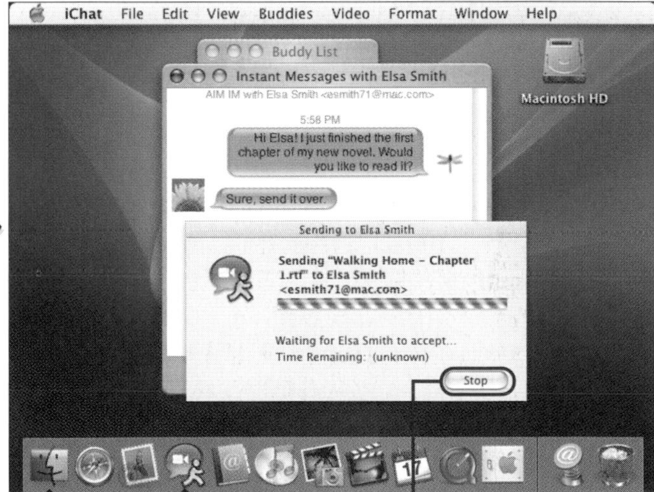

■ A dialog box appears on your screen until the other person accepts the file.

■ To cancel the file transfer at any time, click **Stop**.

Note: If you send a picture, the picture may automatically appear in the chat window without displaying a dialog box.

INDEX

D

INDEX

G

H

I

N

O

P

Q

R

S

W

Z

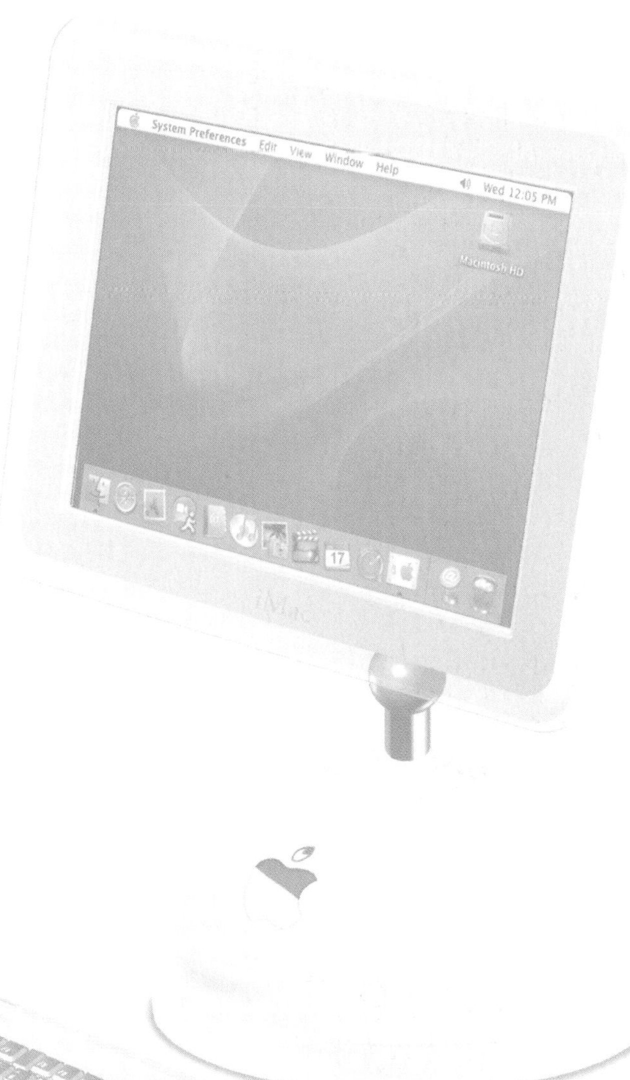
System Preferences
Edit
View
Window
Help
Wed 12:05 PM
Macintosh HD
iMac

Introducing Our New Consumer Books...

Our new Teach Yourself VISUALLY Consumer books are an excellent resource for people who want to learn more about general interest topics. We have launched this new groundbreaking series with three exciting titles: ***Teach Yourself VISUALLY Weight Training***, ***Teach Yourself VISUALLY Yoga*** and ***Teach Yourself VISUALLY Guitar***. These books maintain the same design and structure of our computer books—graphical, two-page lessons that are jam-packed with useful, easy-to-understand information.

Each full-color book includes over **500** photographs, accompanied by step-by-step instructions to guide you through the fundamentals of each topic. "Teach Yourself" sidebars also provide practical tips and tricks to further fine tune your skills and introduce more advanced techniques.

By using top experts in their respective fields to consult on our books, we offer our readers an extraordinary opportunity to access first-class, superior knowledge in conjunction with our award winning communication process. Teach Yourself VISUALLY Consumer is simply the best way to learn!

Teach Yourself VISUALLY **WEIGHT TRAINING**

ISBN: 0-7645-2582-4
Price: $24.99 US; $36.99 CDN; £14.99 UK
Page count: 320

Teach Yourself VISUALLY **YOGA**

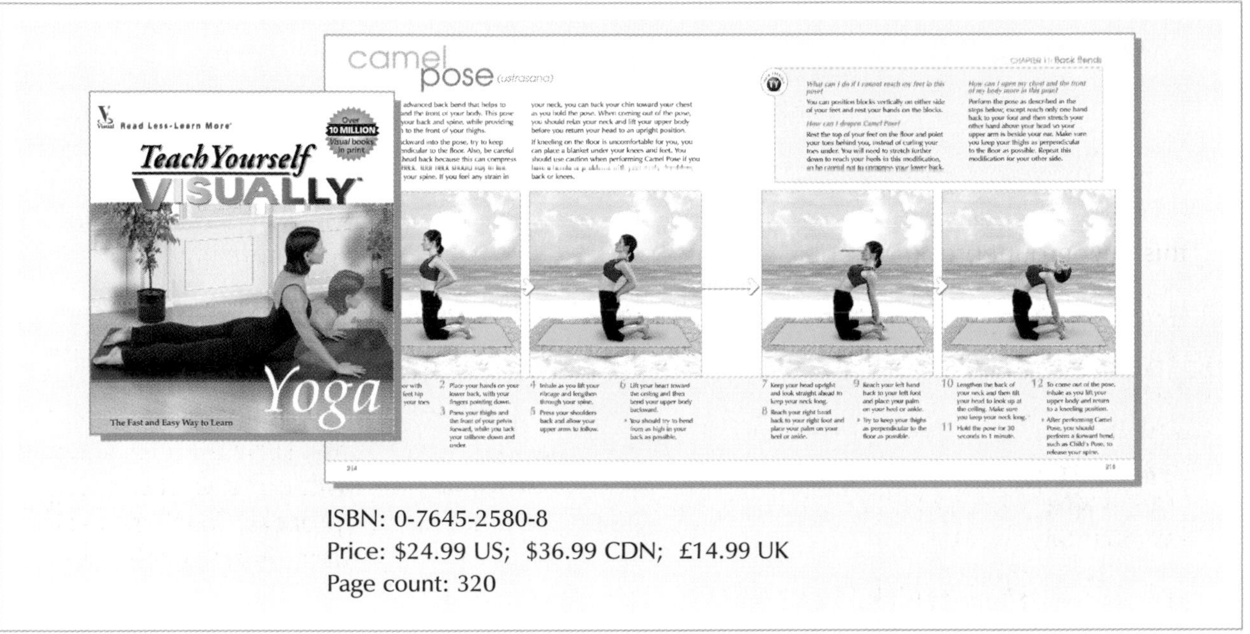

ISBN: 0-7645-2580-8
Price: $24.99 US; $36.99 CDN; £14.99 UK
Page count: 320

Teach Yourself VISUALLY **GUITAR**

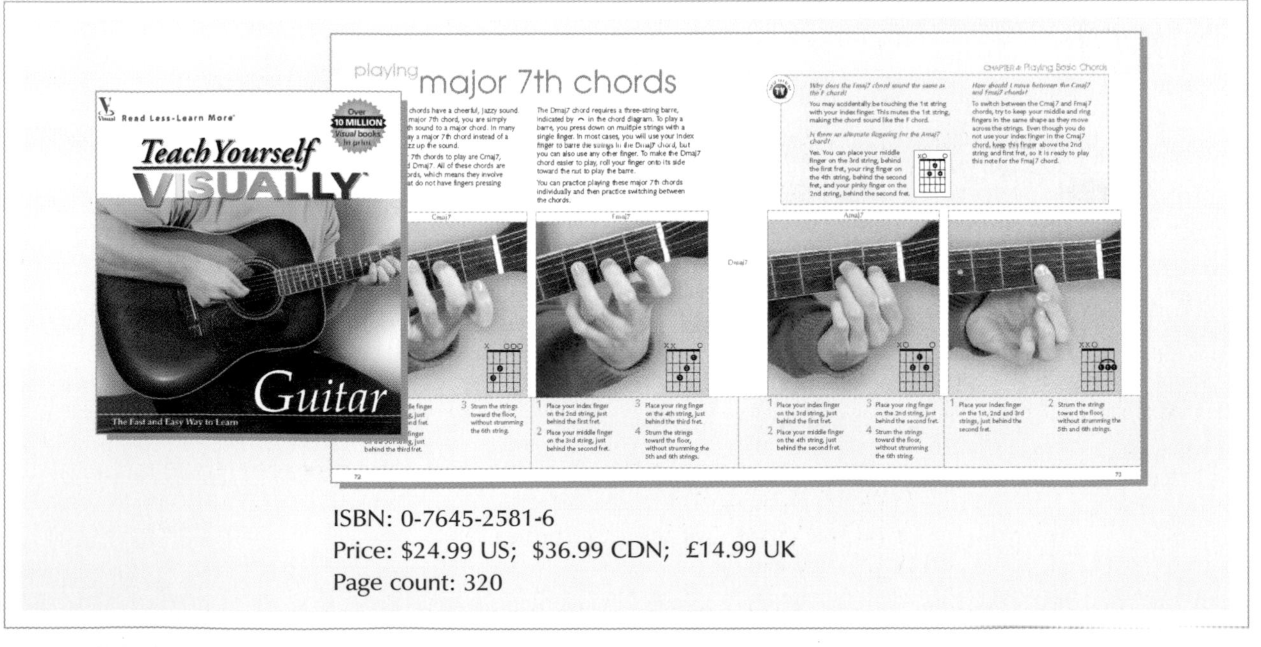

ISBN: 0-7645-2581-6
Price: $24.99 US; $36.99 CDN; £14.99 UK
Page count: 320

with these full-color Visual™ guides

The Fast and Easy Way to Learn

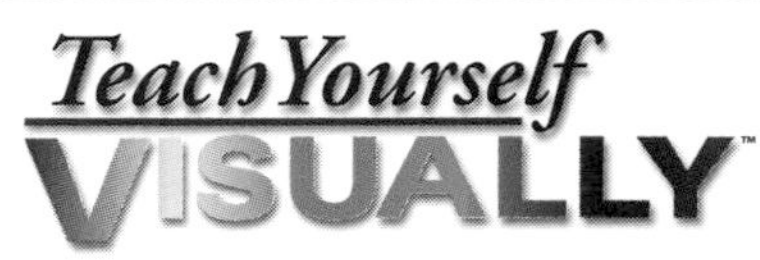

Title	ISBN	U.S. Price
Teach Yourself FrontPage 2000 VISUALLY	0-7645-3451-3	$29.99
Teach Yourself HTML VISUALLY	0-7645-3423-8	$29.99
Teach Yourself the Internet and World Wide Web VISUALLY, 2nd Ed.	0-7645-3410-6	$29.99
Teach Yourself Microsoft Access 2000 VISUALLY	0-7645-6059-X	$29.99
Teach Yourself Microsoft Excel 2000 VISUALLY	0-7645-6056-5	$29.99
Teach Yourself Microsoft Office 2000 VISUALLY	0-7645-6051-4	$29.99
Teach Yourself Microsoft Word 2000 VISUALLY	0-7645-6055-7	$29.99
Teach Yourself VISUALLY Access 2002	0-7645-3591-9	$29.99
Teach Yourself VISUALLY Adobe Acrobat 5 PDF	0-7645-3667-2	$29.99
Teach Yourself VISUALLY Adobe Premiere 6	0-7645-3664-8	$29.99
Teach Yourself VISUALLY Computers, 3rd Ed.	0-7645-3525-0	$29.99
Teach Yourself VISUALLY Digital Photography	0-7645-3565-X	$29.99
Teach Yourself VISUALLY Digital Video	0-7645-3688-5	$29.99
Teach Yourself VISUALLY Dreamweaver 3	0-7645-3470-X	$29.99
Teach Yourself VISUALLY Dreamweaver MX	0-7645-3697-4	$29.99
Teach Yourself VISUALLY E-commerce with FrontPage	0-7645-3579-X	$29.99
Teach Yourself VISUALLY Excel 2003	0-7645-3996-5	$29.99
Teach Yourself VISUALLY Excel 2002	0-7645-3594-3	$29.99
Teach Yourself VISUALLY Fireworks 4	0-7645-3566-8	$29.99
Teach Yourself VISUALLY Flash 5	0-7645-3540-4	$29.99
Teach Yourself VISUALLY Flash MX	0-7645-3661-3	$29.99
Teach Yourself VISUALLY FrontPage 2002	0-7645 3590-0	$29.99
Teach Yourself VISUALLY Illustrator 10	0-7645-3654-0	$29.99
Teach Yourself VISUALLY iMac	0-7645-3453-X	$29.99
Teach Yourself VISUALLY Investing Online	0-7645-3459-9	$29.99
Teach Yourself VISUALLY Mac OS X Panther	0-7645-4393-8	$29.99
Teach Yourself VISUALLY Mac OS X Jaguar	0-7645-1802-X	$29.99
Teach Yourself VISUALLY Macromedia Web Collection	0-7645-3648-6	$29.99
Teach Yourself VISUALLY Networking, 2nd Ed.	0-7645-3534-X	$29.99
Teach Yourself VISUALLY Office 2003	0-7645-3980-9	$29.99
Teach Yourself VISUALLY Office XP	0-7645-0854-7	$29.99
Teach Yourself VISUALLY Photoshop 6	0-7645-3513-7	$29.99
Teach Yourself VISUALLY Photoshop 7	0-7645-3682-6	$29.99
Teach Yourself VISUALLY Photoshop Elements 2.0	0-7645-2515-8	$29.99
Teach Yourself VISUALLY PowerPoint 2002	0-7645-3660-5	$29.99
Teach Yourself VISUALLY Quicken 2001	0-7645-3526-9	$29.99
Teach Yourself VISUALLY Restoration & Retouching with Photoshop Elements	0-7645-2601-4	$29.99
Teach Yourself VISUALLY Windows 2000 Server	0-7645-3428-9	$29.99
Teach Yourself VISUALLY Windows Me Millennium Edition	0-7645-3495-5	$29.99
Teach Yourself VISUALLY Windows XP	0-7645-3619-2	$29.99
Teach Yourself VISUALLY MORE Windows XP	0-7645-3698-2	$29.99
Teach Yourself VISUALLY Word 2002	0-7645-3587-0	$29.99
Teach Yourself Windows 95 VISUALLY	0-7645-6001-8	$29.99
Teach Yourself Windows 98 VISUALLY	0-7645-6025-5	$29.99
Teach Yourself Windows 2000 Professional VISUALLY	0-7645-6040-9	$29.99

For visual learners who want to guide themselves through the basics of any technology topic. ***Teach Yourself VISUALLY*** **offers more expanded coverage than our best-selling** ***Simplified*** **series.**

The Visual™ series is available wherever books are sold, or call

1-800-762-2974.

Outside the US, call

317-572-3993.